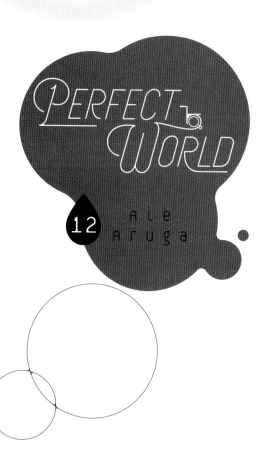

PERFECT WORLD

12 Rie Aruga

Research Help /
Kazuo Abe (Abe Kensetsu Inc.)
Certified NPO Florence

contents

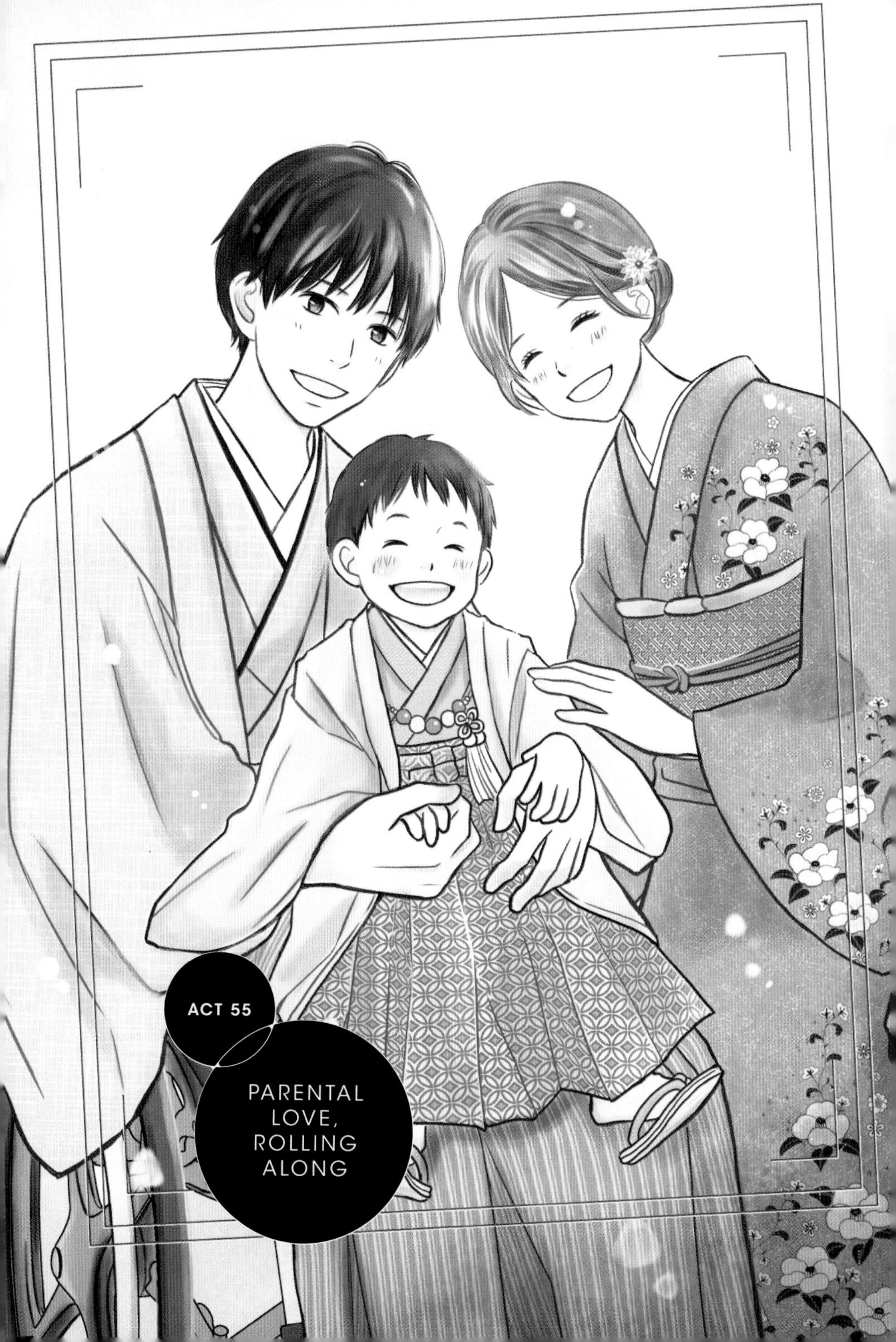
ACT 55
PARENTAL LOVE, ROLLING ALONG

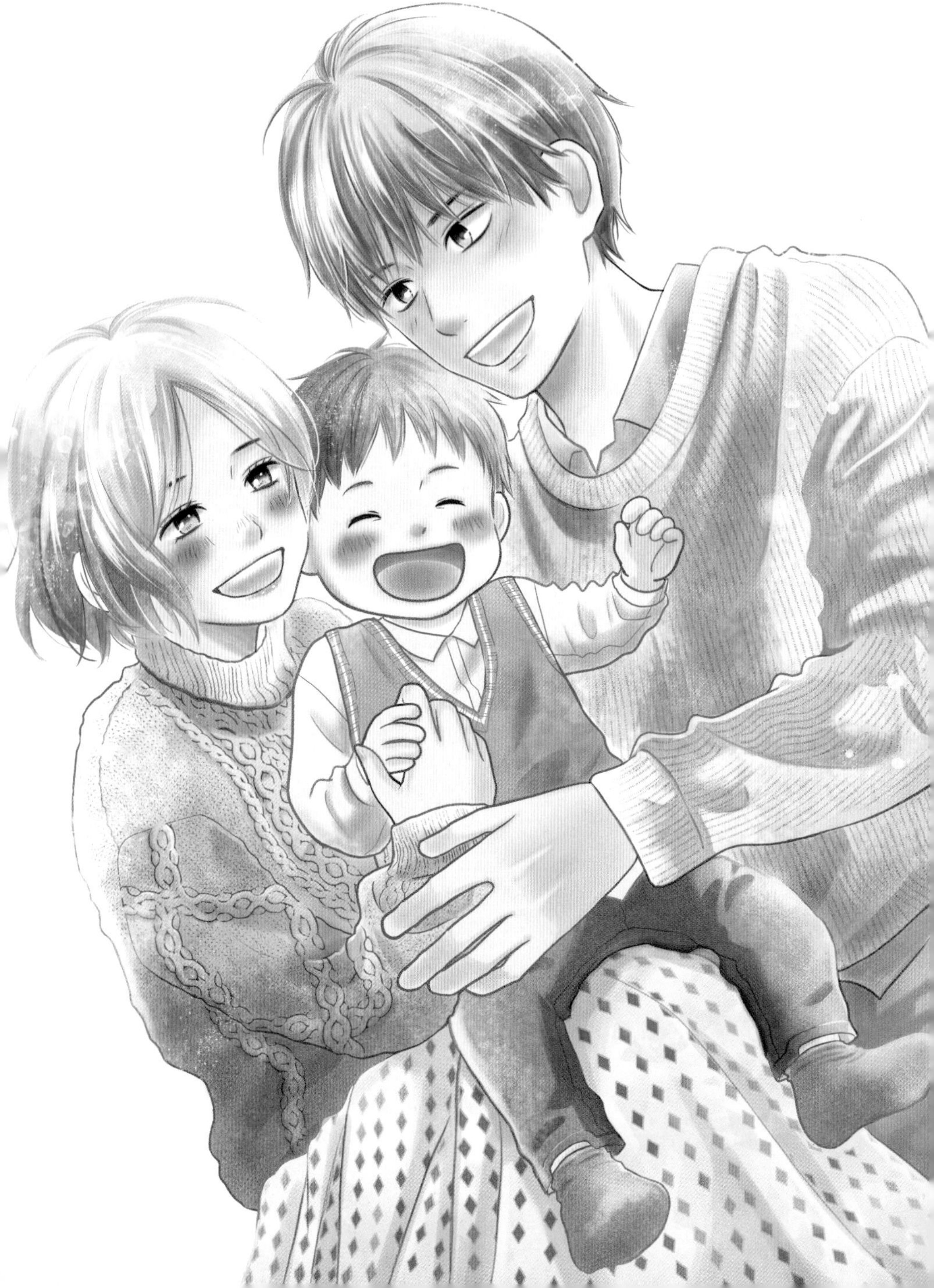

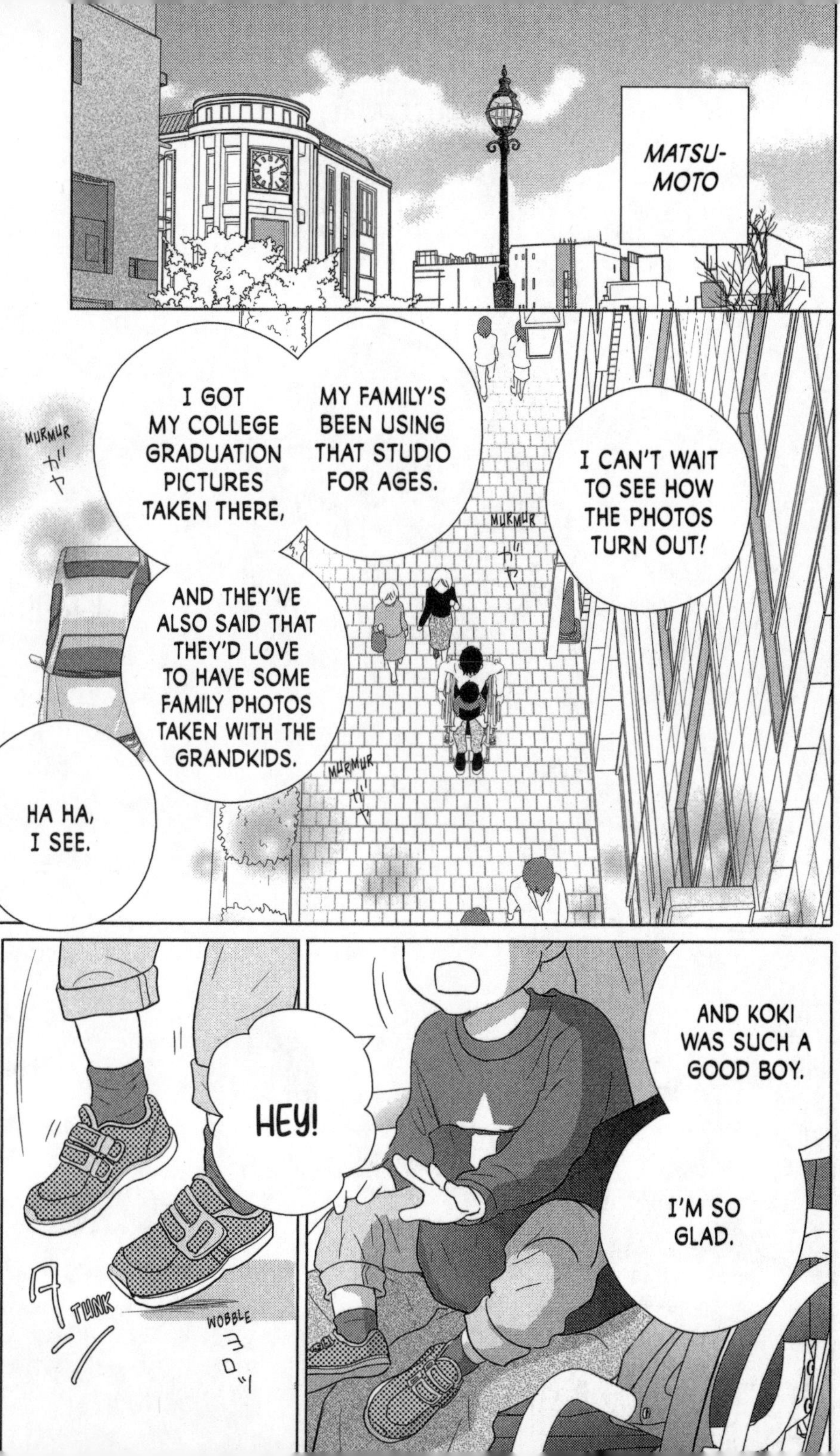
MATSU-MOTO
I CAN'T WAIT TO SEE HOW THE PHOTOS TURN OUT!
MURMUR
MY FAMILY'S BEEN USING THAT STUDIO FOR AGES.
I GOT MY COLLEGE GRADUATION PICTURES TAKEN THERE,
MURMUR
AND THEY'VE ALSO SAID THAT THEY'D LOVE TO HAVE SOME FAMILY PHOTOS TAKEN WITH THE GRANDKIDS.
MURMUR
HA HA, I SEE.
AND KOKI WAS SUCH A GOOD BOY.
I'M SO GLAD.
WOBBLE
HEY!
TUNK

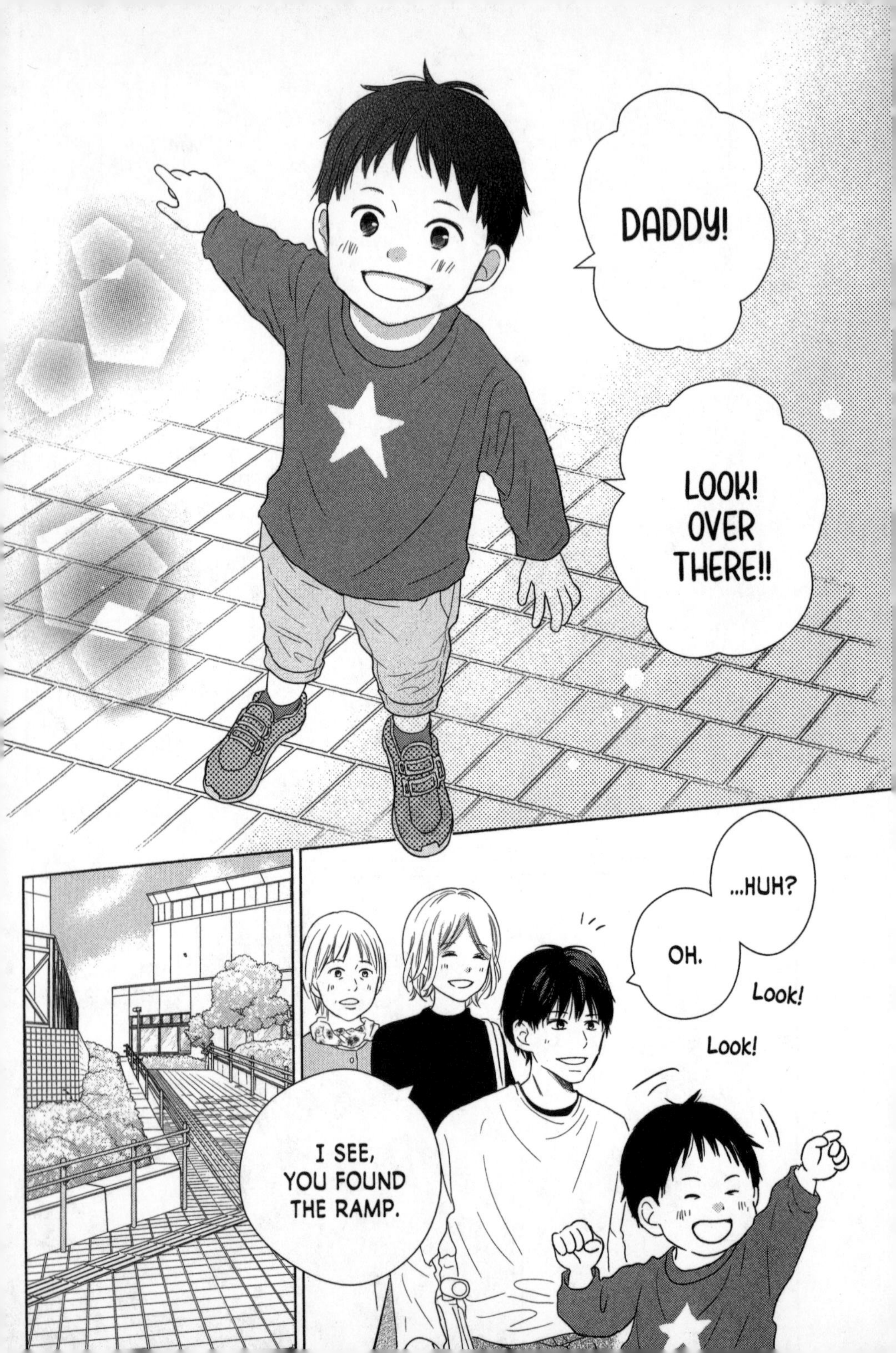
DADDY!
LOOK! OVER THERE!!
...HUH?
OH.
Look!
Look!
I SEE, YOU FOUND THE RAMP.

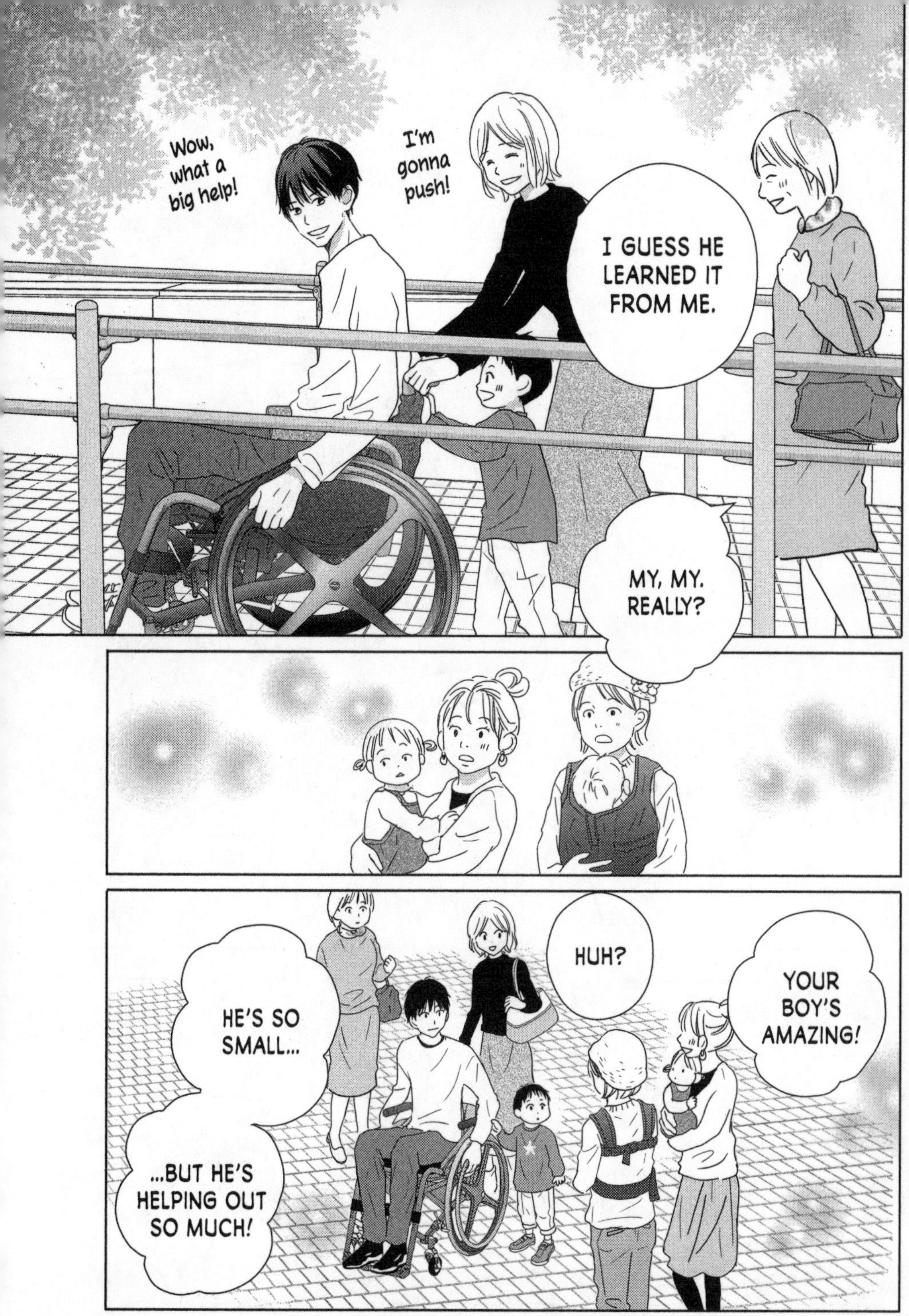
I'm gonna push!
Wow, what a big help!
I GUESS HE LEARNED IT FROM ME.
MY, MY. REALLY?
YOUR BOY'S AMAZING!
HUH?
HE'S SO SMALL...
...BUT HE'S HELPING OUT SO MUCH!

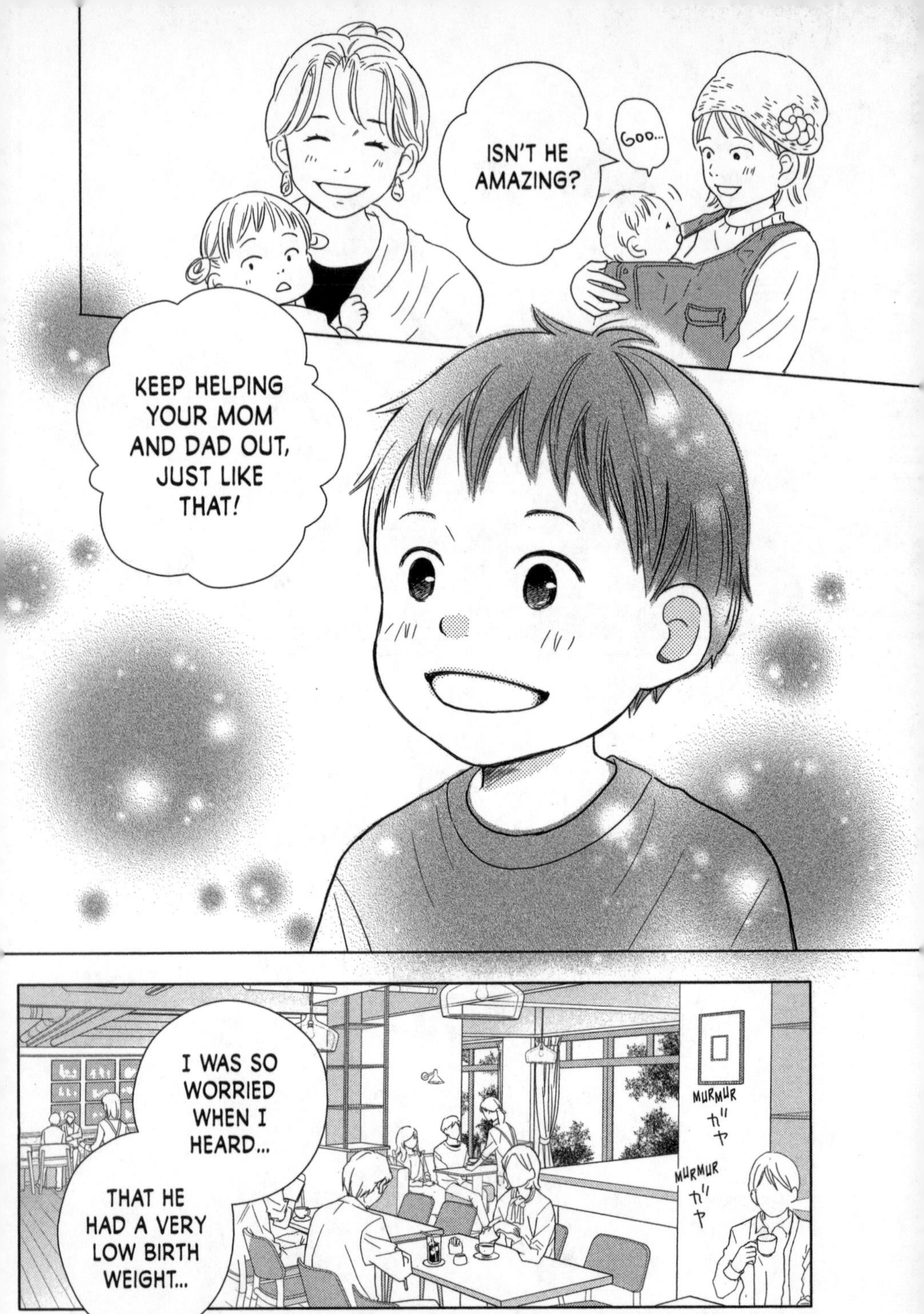
Goo...
ISN'T HE AMAZING?
KEEP HELPING YOUR MOM AND DAD OUT, JUST LIKE THAT!
MURMUR ガヤ
MURMUR ガヤ
I WAS SO WORRIED WHEN I HEARD...
THAT HE HAD A VERY LOW BIRTH WEIGHT...

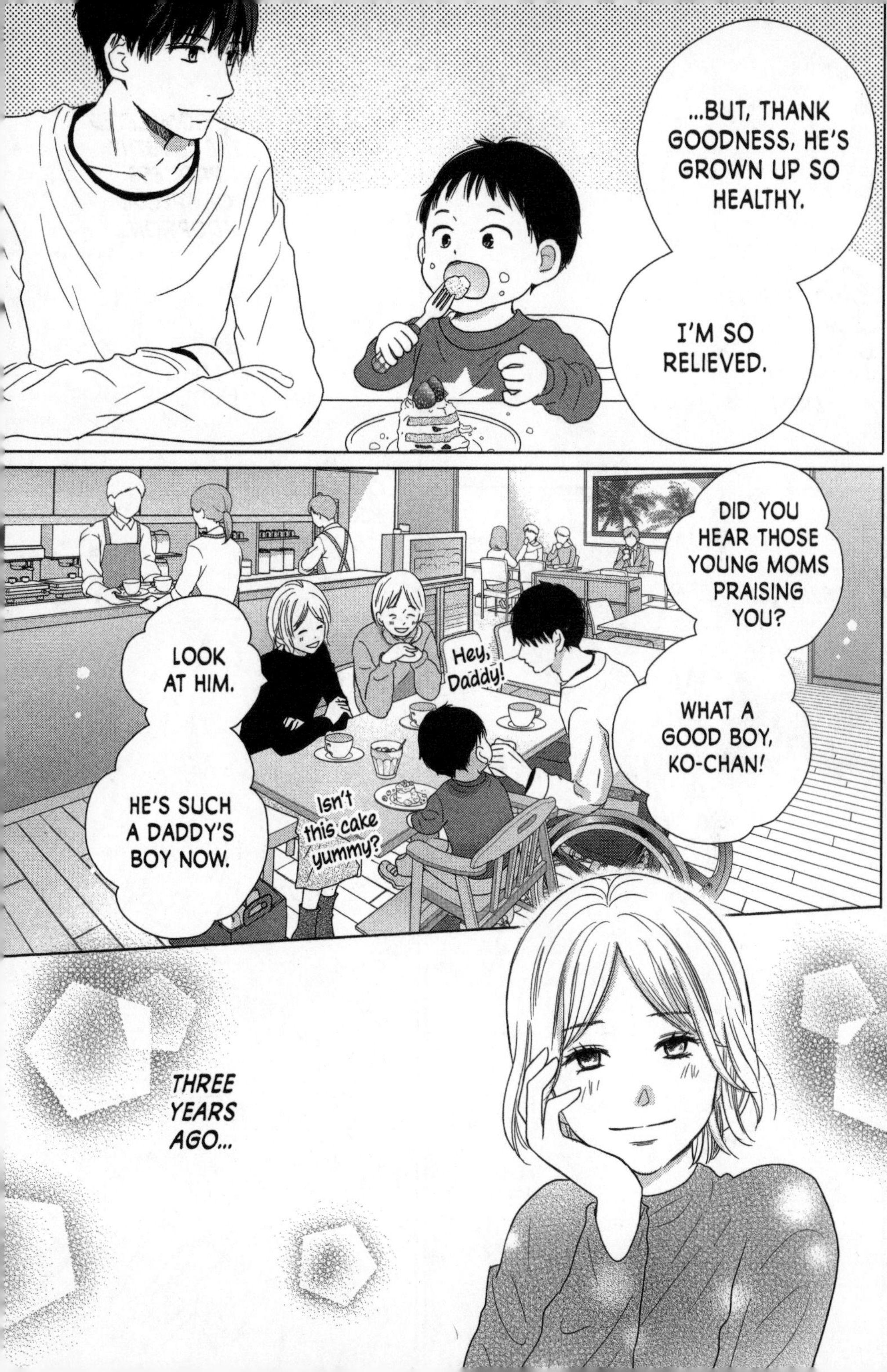
...BUT, THANK GOODNESS, HE'S GROWN UP SO HEALTHY.
I'M SO RELIEVED.
DID YOU HEAR THOSE YOUNG MOMS PRAISING YOU?
WHAT A GOOD BOY, KO-CHAN!
Hey, Daddy!
LOOK AT HIM.
Isn't this cake yummy?
HE'S SUCH A DADDY'S BOY NOW.
THREE YEARS AGO...

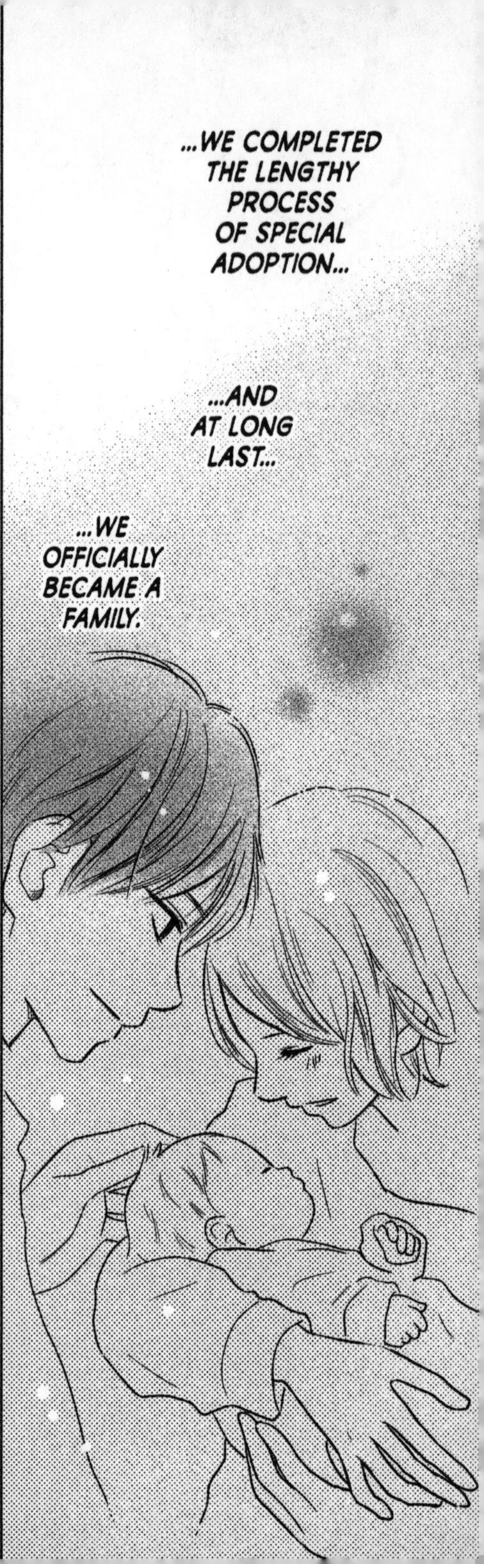
...WE COMPLETED THE LENGTHY PROCESS OF SPECIAL ADOPTION...
...AND AT LONG LAST...
...WE OFFICIALLY BECAME A FAMILY.

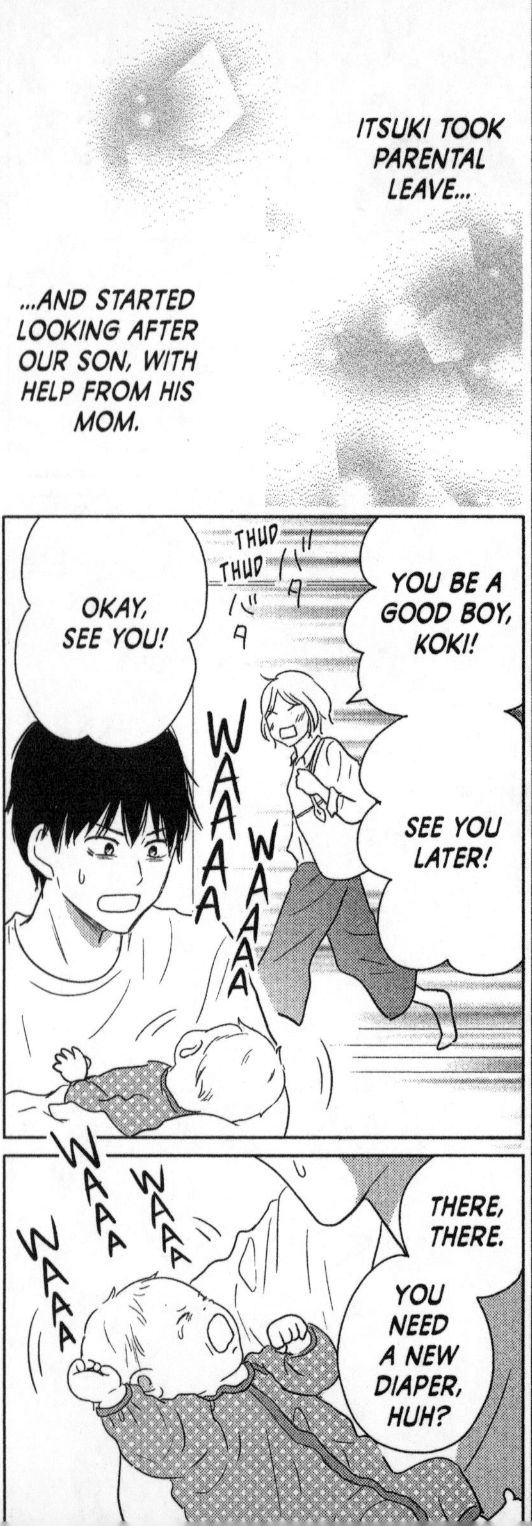
ITSUKI TOOK PARENTAL LEAVE...
...AND STARTED LOOKING AFTER OUR SON, WITH HELP FROM HIS MOM.
YOU BE A GOOD BOY, KOKI!
SEE YOU LATER!
THUD THUD
バタバタ
OKAY, SEE YOU!
WAAAA
WAAAAAA
THERE, THERE.
YOU NEED A NEW DIAPER, HUH?
WAAAA
WAAAA
WAAAA

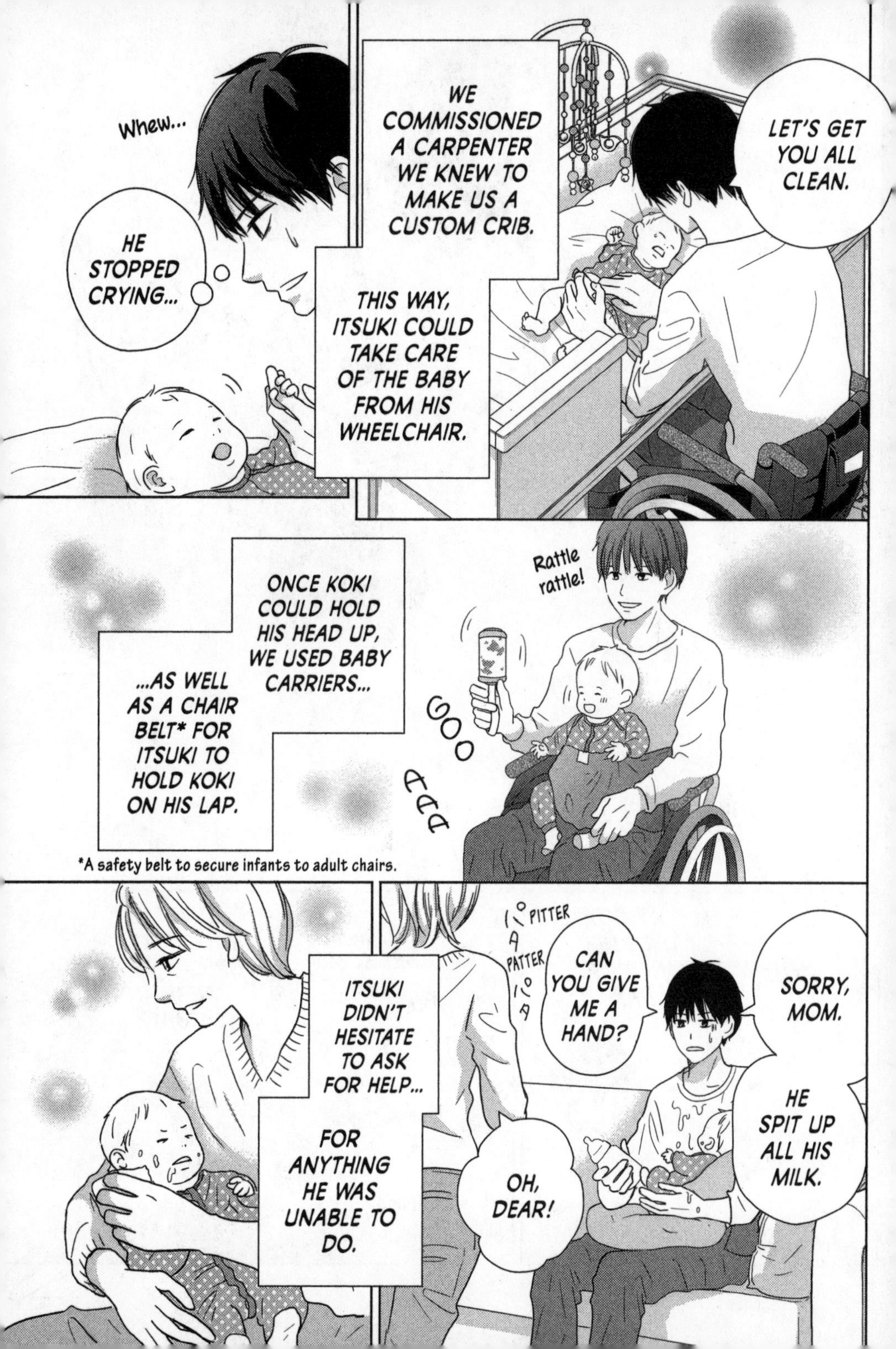
WE COMMISSIONED A CARPENTER WE KNEW TO MAKE US A CUSTOM CRIB.
LET'S GET YOU ALL CLEAN.
THIS WAY, ITSUKI COULD TAKE CARE OF THE BABY FROM HIS WHEELCHAIR.
Whew...
HE STOPPED CRYING...
Rattle rattle!
GOO AAA
ONCE KOKI COULD HOLD HIS HEAD UP, WE USED BABY CARRIERS...
...AS WELL AS A CHAIR BELT* FOR ITSUKI TO HOLD KOKI ON HIS LAP.
*A safety belt to secure infants to adult chairs.
SORRY, MOM.
HE SPIT UP ALL HIS MILK.
CAN YOU GIVE ME A HAND?
PITTER A PATTER
ITSUKI DIDN'T HESITATE TO ASK FOR HELP...
OH, DEAR!
FOR ANYTHING HE WAS UNABLE TO DO.

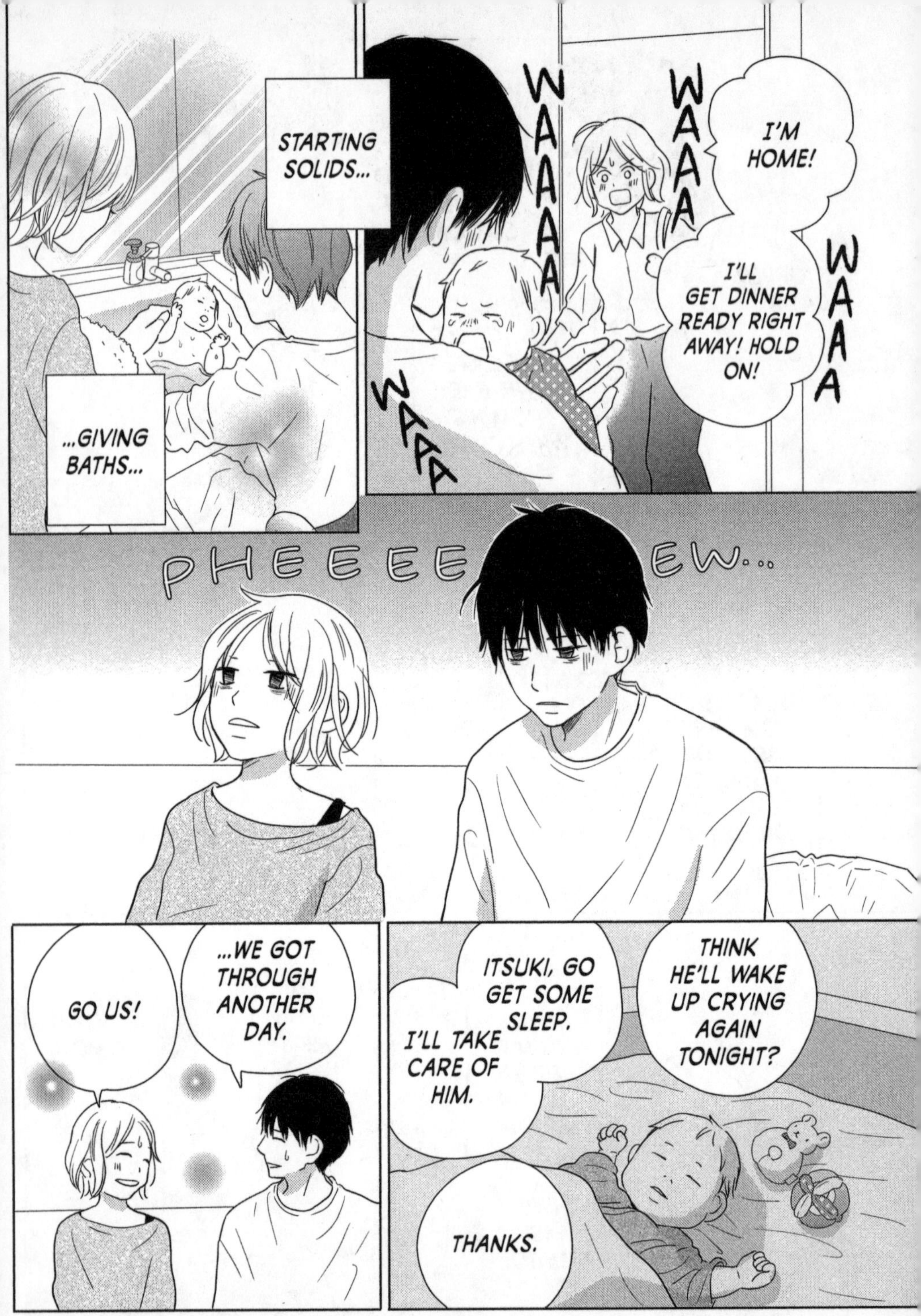
WAAAAA
WAAAA
I'M HOME!
I'LL GET DINNER READY RIGHT AWAY! HOLD ON!
WAAAA
WAAA
STARTING SOLIDS...
...GIVING BATHS...
PHEEEEEW...
THINK HE'LL WAKE UP CRYING AGAIN TONIGHT?
ITSUKI, GO GET SOME SLEEP.
I'LL TAKE CARE OF HIM.
THANKS.
...WE GOT THROUGH ANOTHER DAY.
GO US!

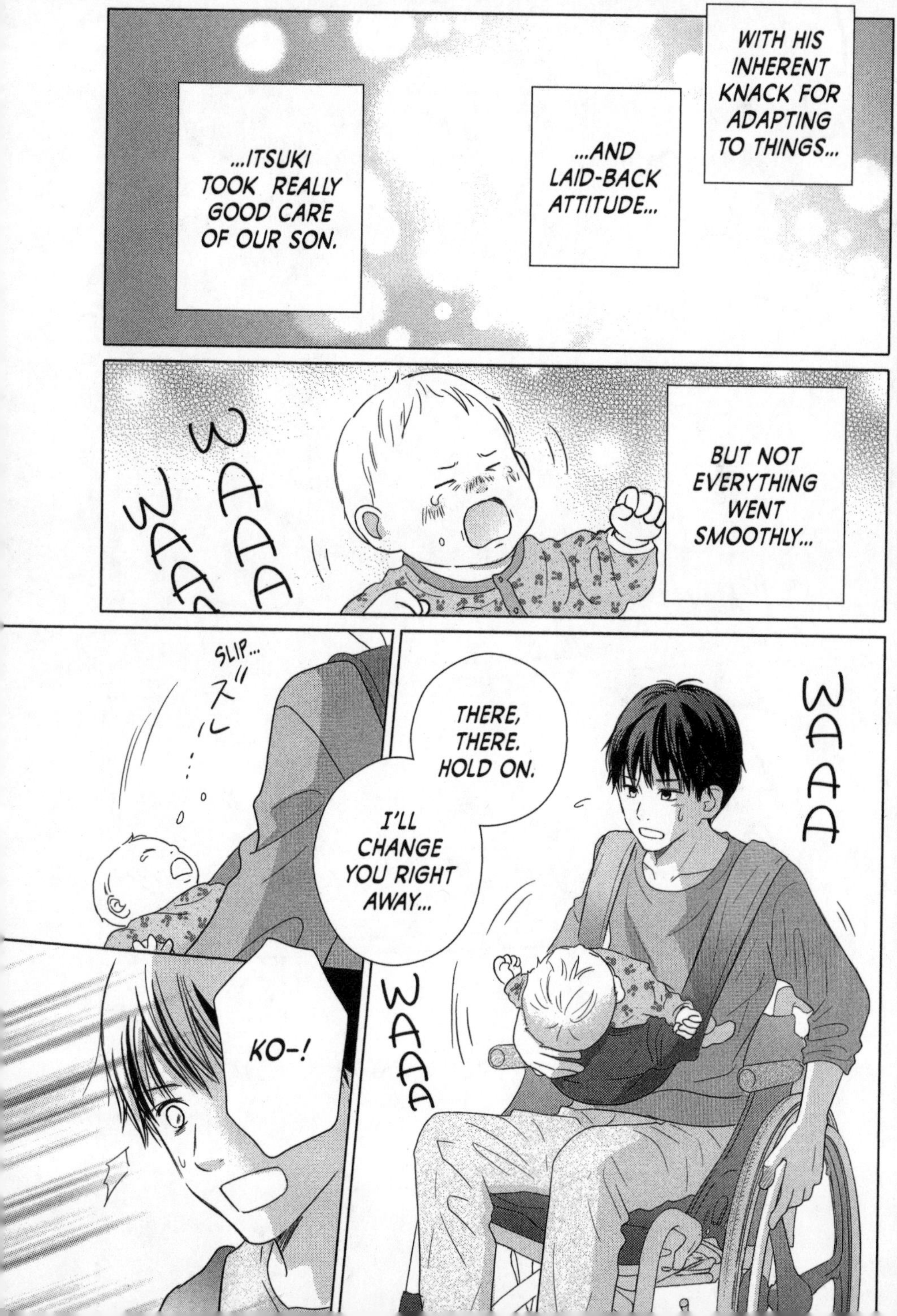
WITH HIS INHERENT KNACK FOR ADAPTING TO THINGS...
...AND LAID-BACK ATTITUDE...
...ITSUKI TOOK REALLY GOOD CARE OF OUR SON.
BUT NOT EVERYTHING WENT SMOOTHLY...
WAAAA
WAAAA
WAAA
THERE, THERE. HOLD ON.
I'LL CHANGE YOU RIGHT AWAY...
WAAA
SLIP...
ズル...
KO-!

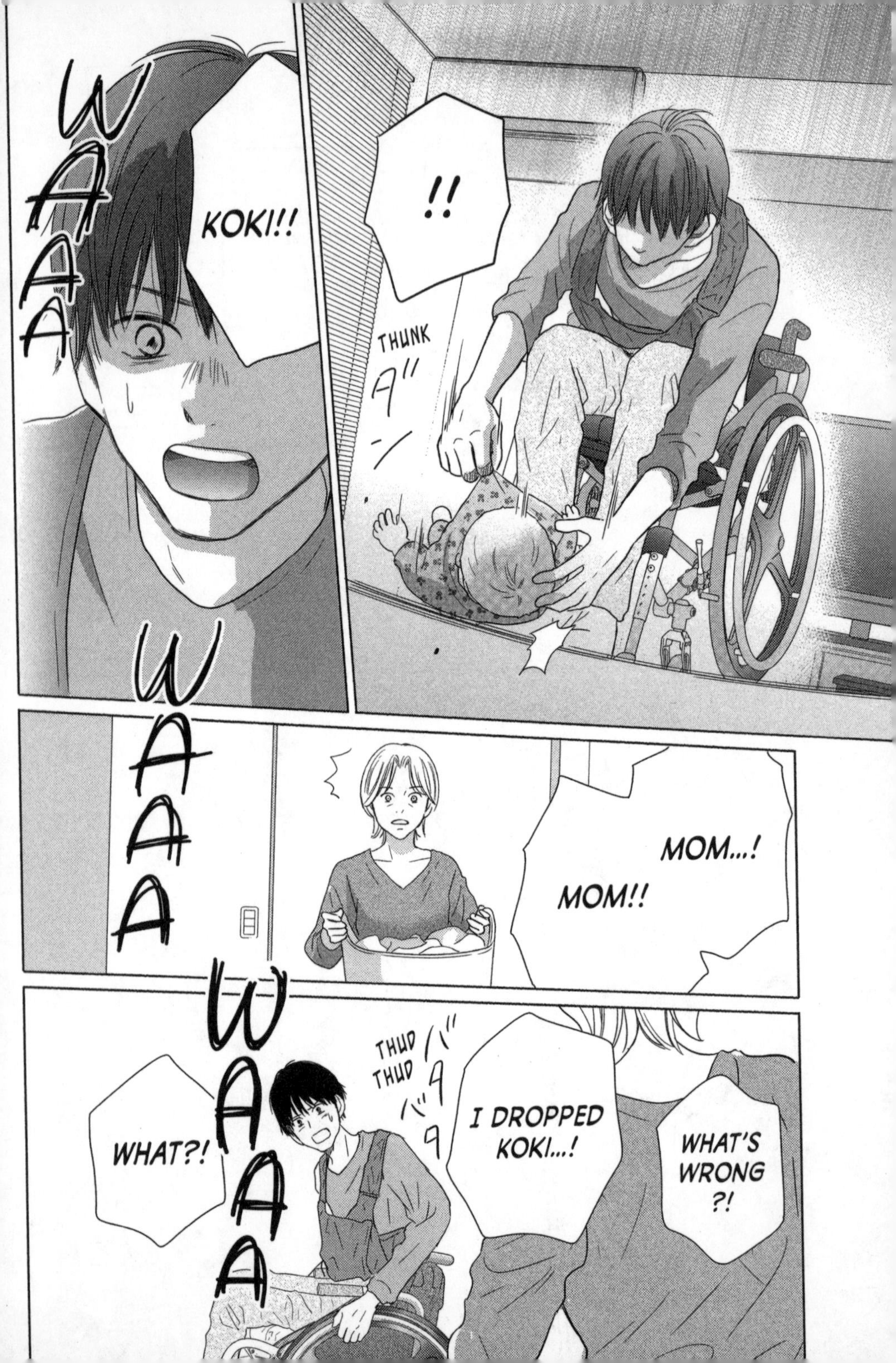
!!
THUNK
ダン
KOKI!!
WAAAA
MOM...!
MOM!!
WAAAA
WHAT'S WRONG?!
I DROPPED KOKI...!
THUD THUD
バタバタ
WHAT?!
WAAAA

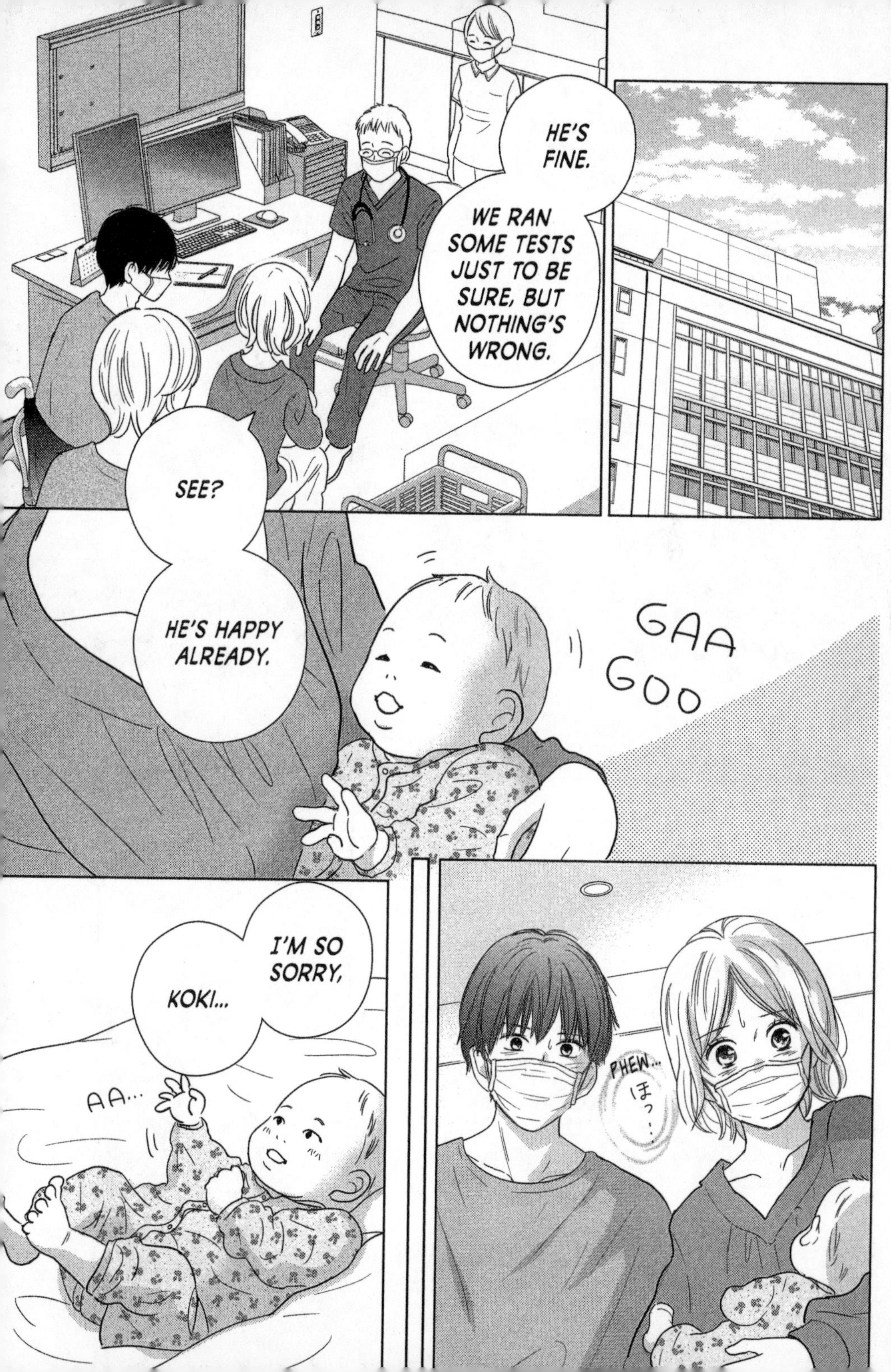
HE'S FINE.
WE RAN SOME TESTS JUST TO BE SURE, BUT NOTHING'S WRONG.
SEE?
HE'S HAPPY ALREADY.
GAA GOO
PHEW...
ほっ…
I'M SO SORRY, KOKI...
AA...

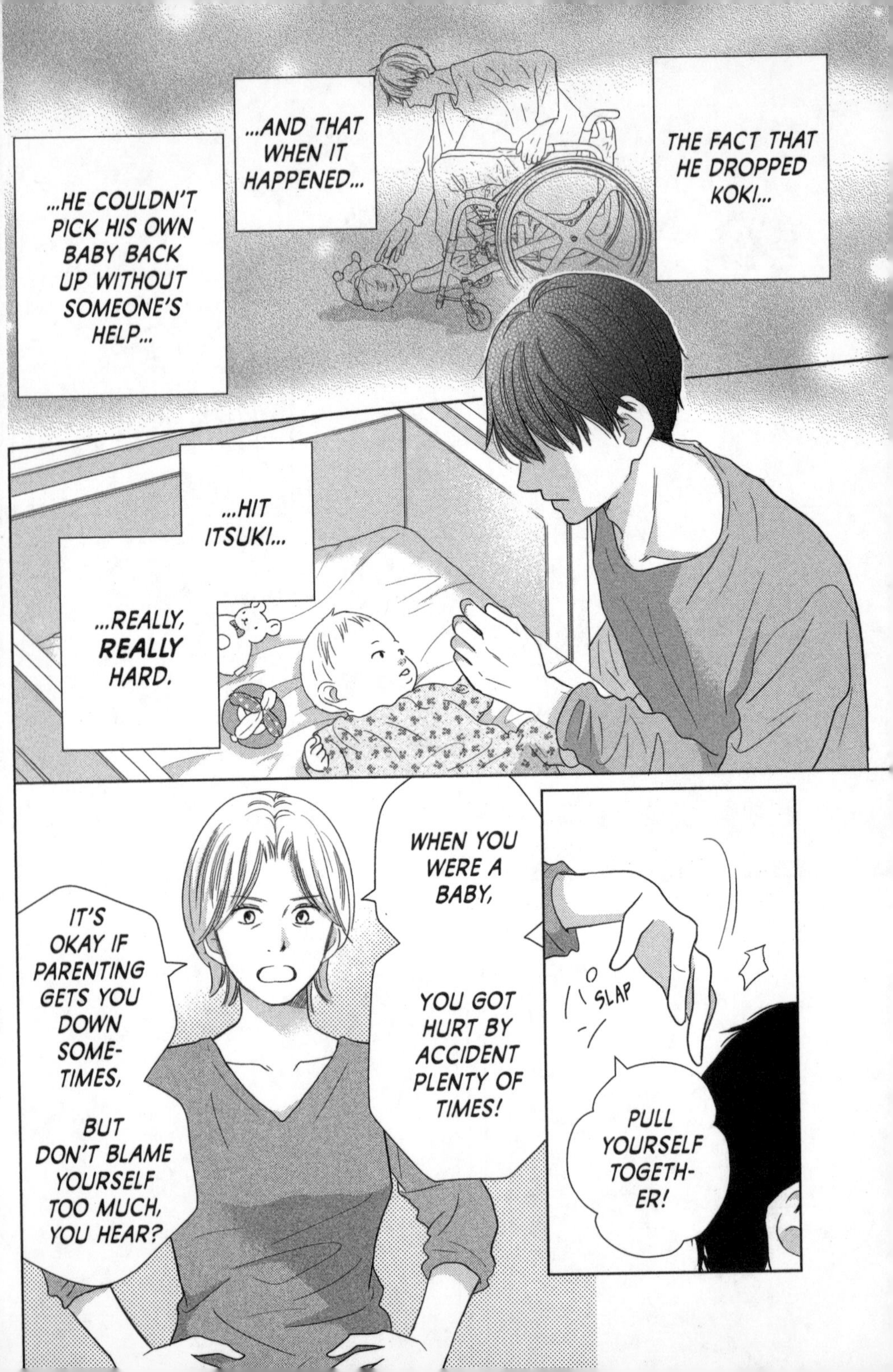
THE FACT THAT HE DROPPED KOKI...
...AND THAT WHEN IT HAPPENED...
...HE COULDN'T PICK HIS OWN BABY BACK UP WITHOUT SOMEONE'S HELP...
...HIT ITSUKI...
...REALLY, **REALLY** HARD.
SLAP
PULL YOURSELF TOGETH-ER!
WHEN YOU WERE A BABY,
YOU GOT HURT BY ACCIDENT PLENTY OF TIMES!
IT'S OKAY IF PARENTING GETS YOU DOWN SOME-TIMES,
BUT DON'T BLAME YOURSELF TOO MUCH, YOU HEAR?

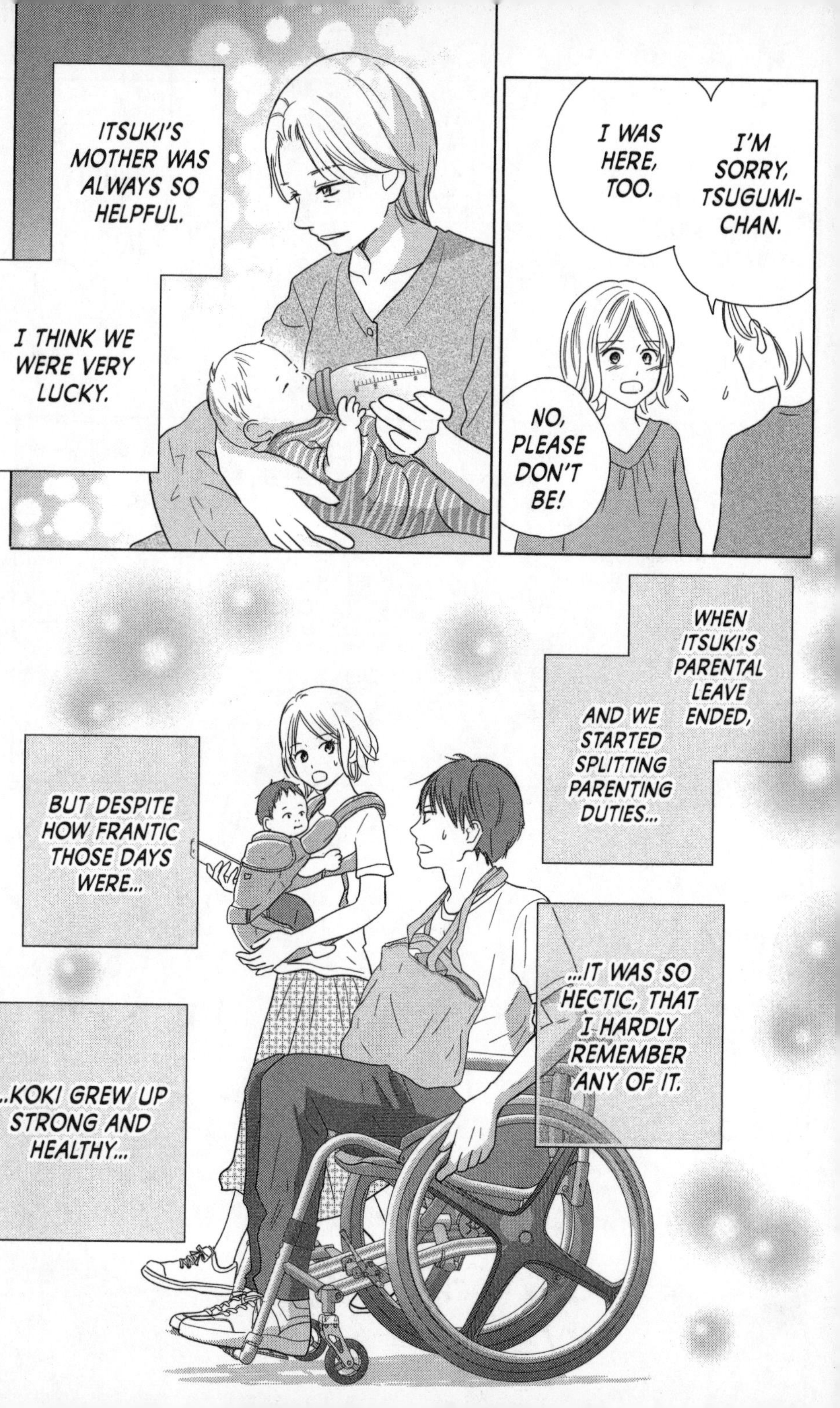
I'M SORRY, TSUGUMI-CHAN.
I WAS HERE, TOO.
NO, PLEASE DON'T BE!
ITSUKI'S MOTHER WAS ALWAYS SO HELPFUL.
I THINK WE WERE VERY LUCKY.
WHEN ITSUKI'S PARENTAL LEAVE ENDED,
AND WE STARTED SPLITTING PARENTING DUTIES...
...IT WAS SO HECTIC, THAT I HARDLY REMEMBER ANY OF IT.
BUT DESPITE HOW FRANTIC THOSE DAYS WERE...
...KOKI GREW UP STRONG AND HEALTHY...

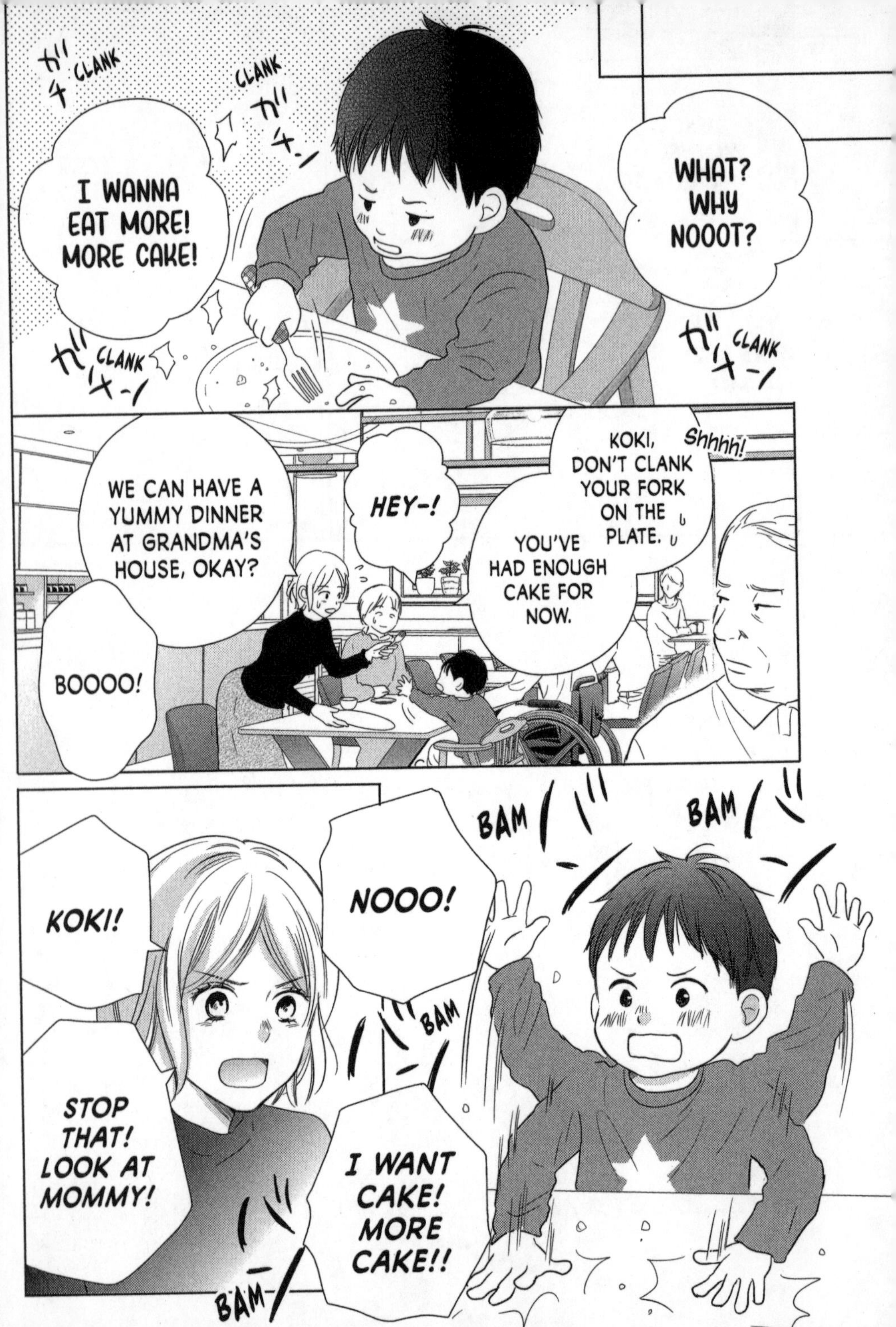
CLANK
WHAT? WHY NOOOT?
CLANK
CLANK
I WANNA EAT MORE! MORE CAKE!
CLANK
Shhhh!
KOKI, DON'T CLANK YOUR FORK ON THE PLATE.
YOU'VE HAD ENOUGH CAKE FOR NOW.
HEY-!
WE CAN HAVE A YUMMY DINNER AT GRANDMA'S HOUSE, OKAY?
BOOOO!
BAM
BAM
NOOO!
KOKI!
BAM
I WANT CAKE! MORE CAKE!!
STOP THAT! LOOK AT MOMMY!
BAM

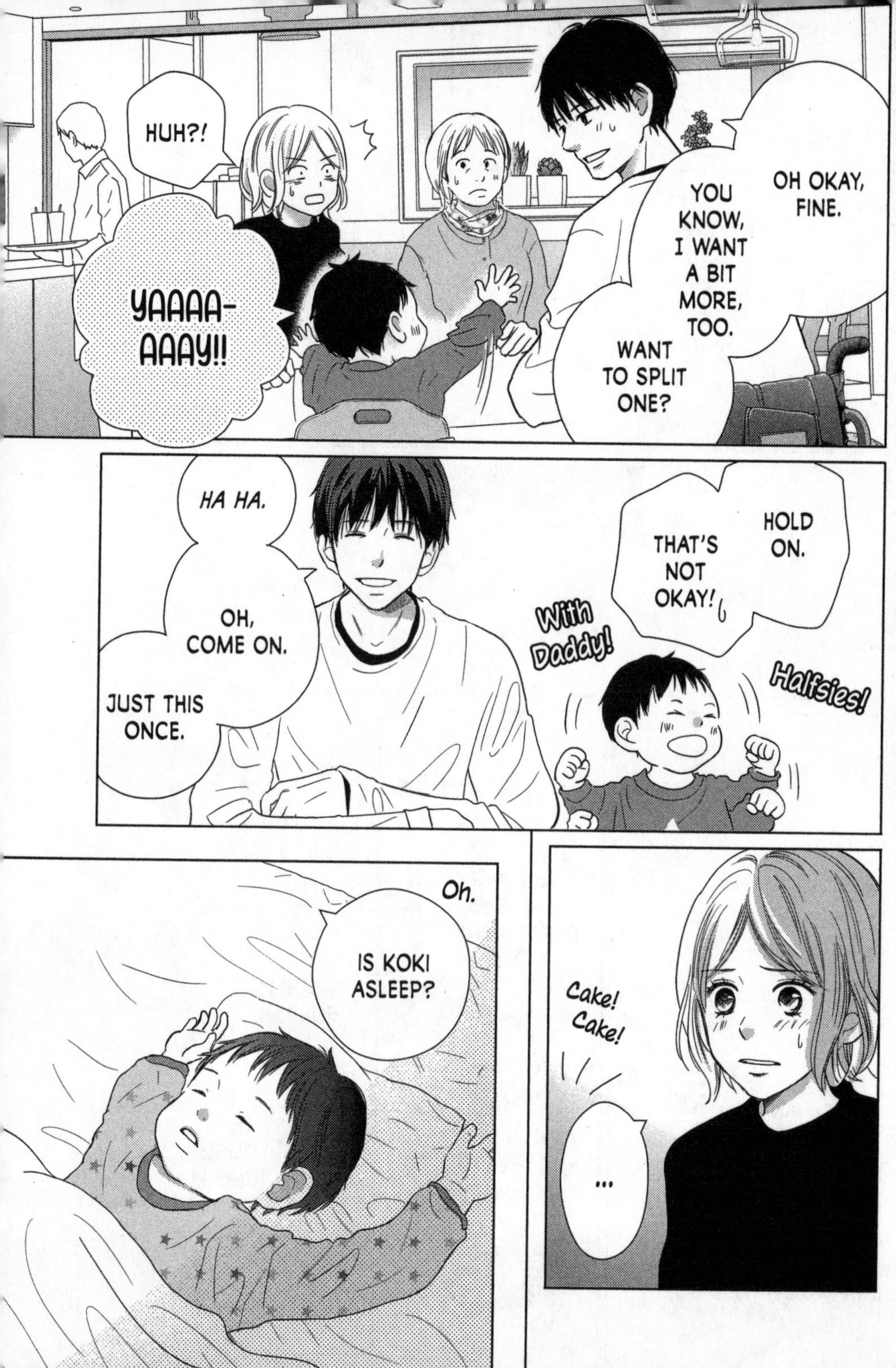
OH OKAY, FINE.
YOU KNOW, I WANT A BIT MORE, TOO.
WANT TO SPLIT ONE?
HUH?!
YAAAA-AAAY!!
HOLD ON.
THAT'S NOT OKAY!
Halfsies!
With Daddy!
HA HA.
OH, COME ON.
JUST THIS ONCE.
Cake! Cake!
...
Oh.
IS KOKI ASLEEP?

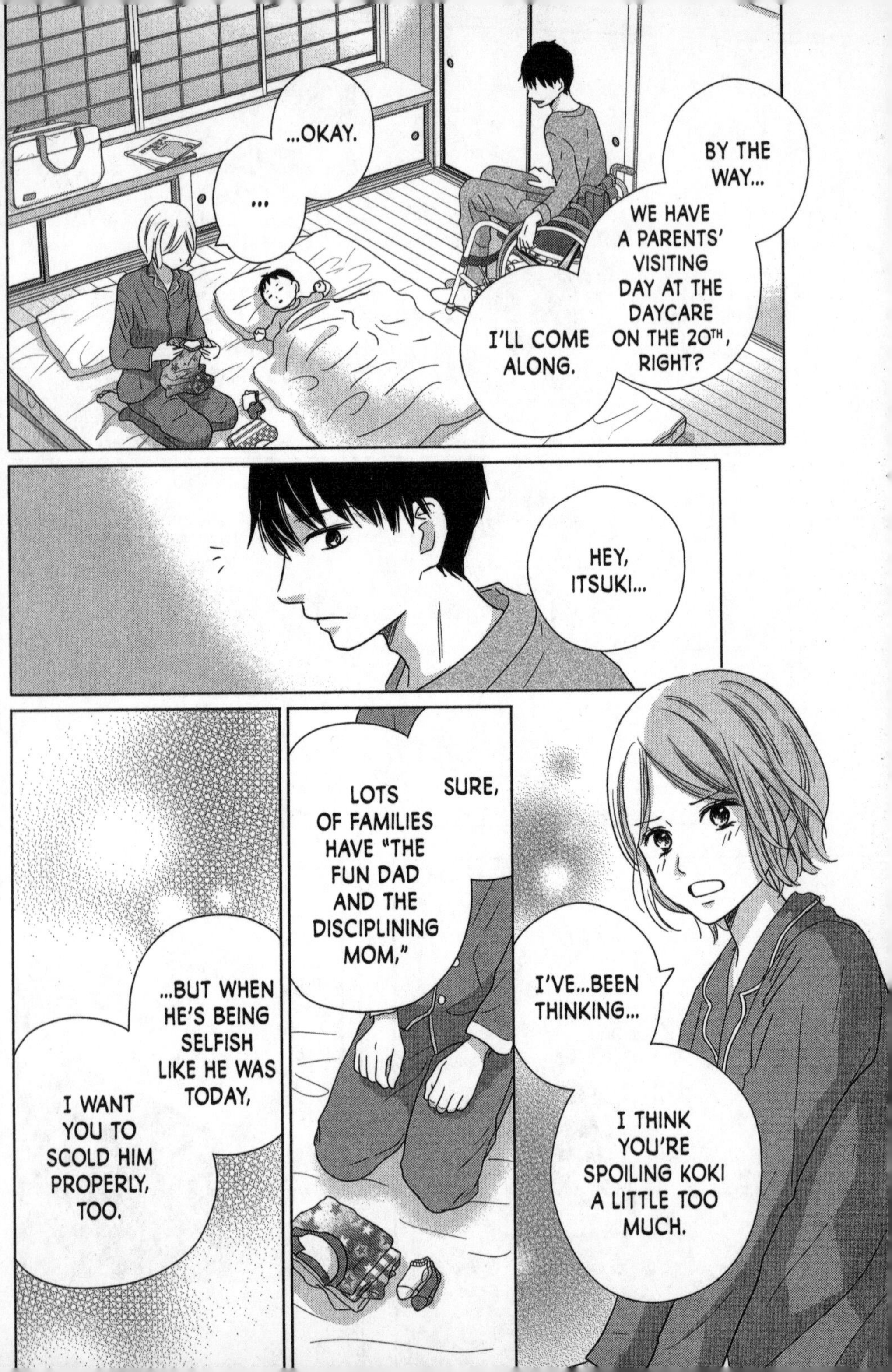
BY THE WAY... WE HAVE A PARENTS' VISITING DAY AT THE DAYCARE ON THE 20TH, RIGHT?
I'LL COME ALONG.
...OKAY.
...
HEY, ITSUKI...
I'VE...BEEN THINKING...
I THINK YOU'RE SPOILING KOKI A LITTLE TOO MUCH.
SURE, LOTS OF FAMILIES HAVE "THE FUN DAD AND THE DISCIPLINING MOM,"
...BUT WHEN HE'S BEING SELFISH LIKE HE WAS TODAY,
I WANT YOU TO SCOLD HIM PROPERLY, TOO.

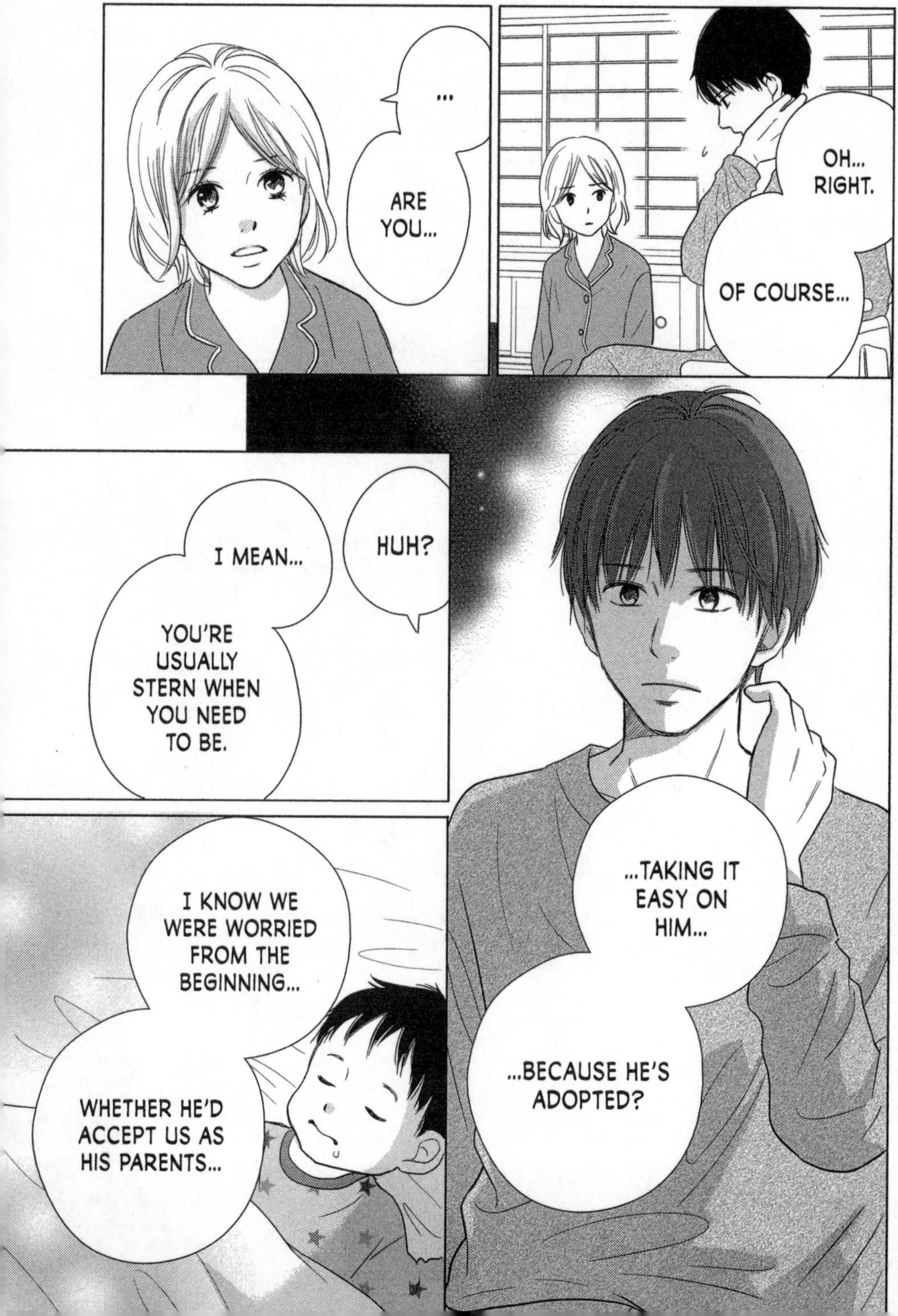
OH... RIGHT.
OF COURSE...
...
ARE YOU...
...TAKING IT EASY ON HIM...
...BECAUSE HE'S ADOPTED?
HUH?
I MEAN...
YOU'RE USUALLY STERN WHEN YOU NEED TO BE.
I KNOW WE WERE WORRIED FROM THE BEGINNING...
WHETHER HE'D ACCEPT US AS HIS PARENTS...

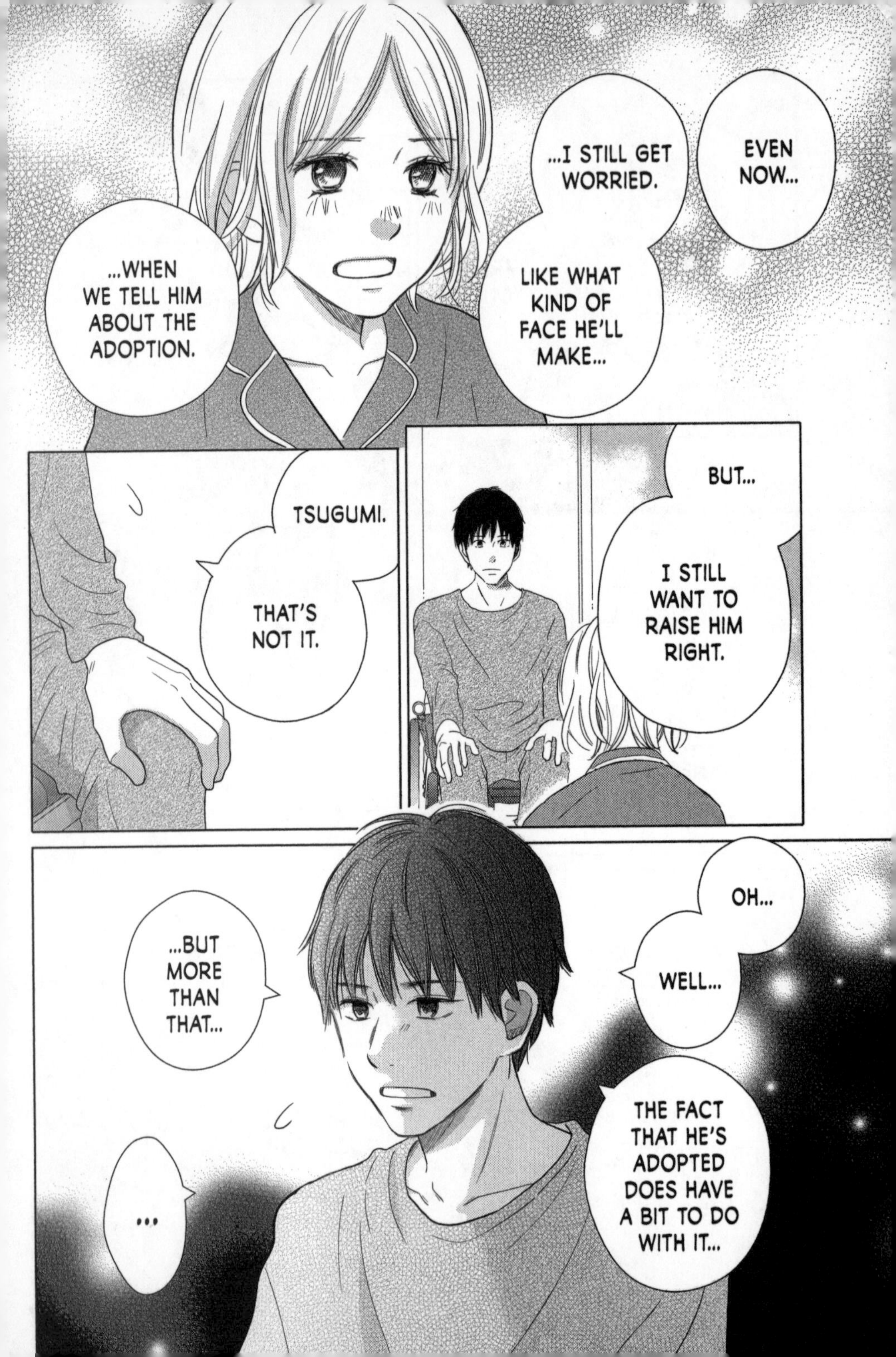
EVEN NOW...
...I STILL GET WORRIED.
LIKE WHAT KIND OF FACE HE'LL MAKE...
...WHEN WE TELL HIM ABOUT THE ADOPTION.
BUT...
I STILL WANT TO RAISE HIM RIGHT.
TSUGUMI.
THAT'S NOT IT.
OH...
WELL...
THE FACT THAT HE'S ADOPTED DOES HAVE A BIT TO DO WITH IT...
...BUT MORE THAN THAT...
...

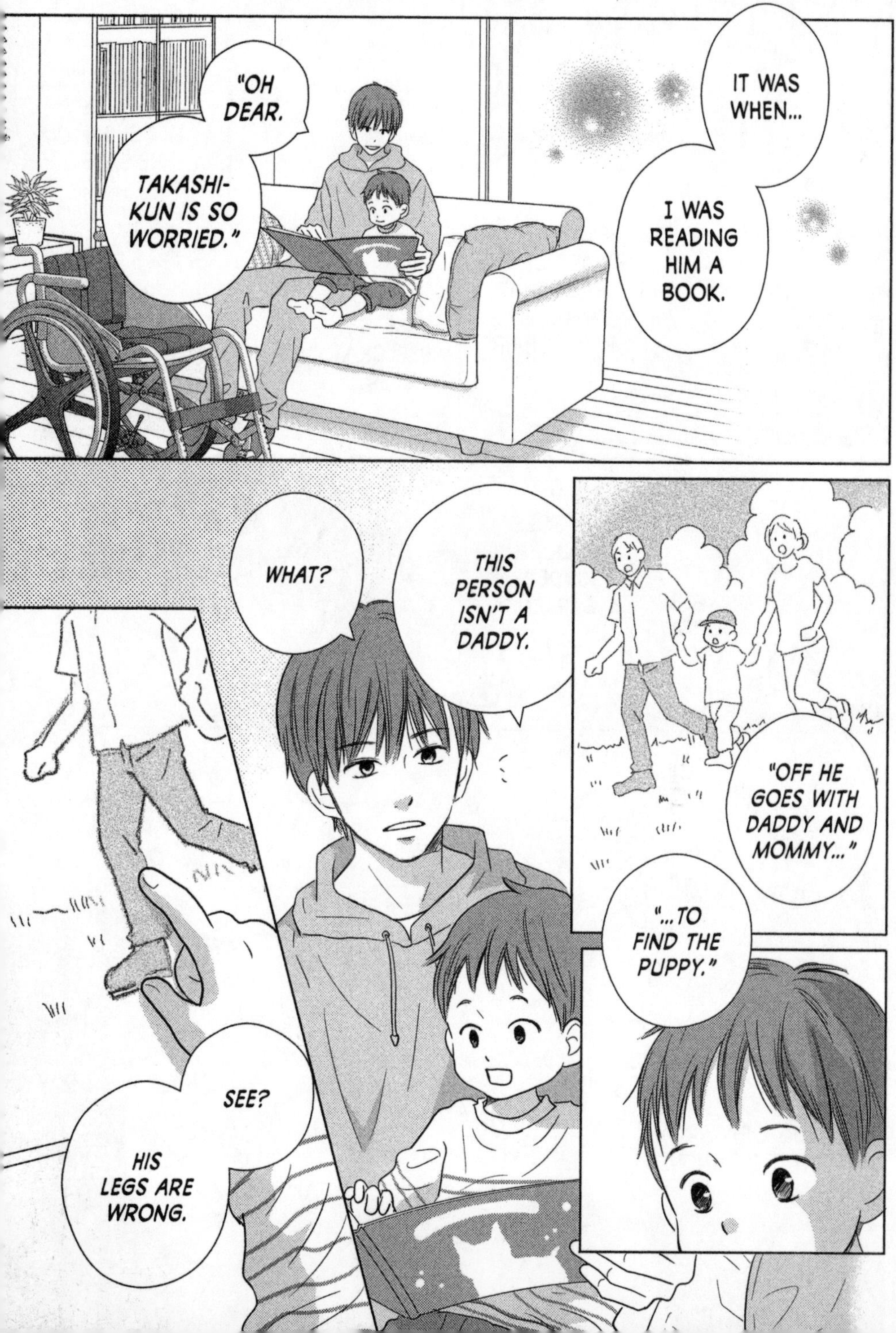
IT WAS WHEN...
I WAS READING HIM A BOOK.
"OH DEAR.
TAKASHI-KUN IS SO WORRIED."
"OFF HE GOES WITH DADDY AND MOMMY..."
"...TO FIND THE PUPPY."
THIS PERSON ISN'T A DADDY.
WHAT?
SEE?
HIS LEGS ARE WRONG.

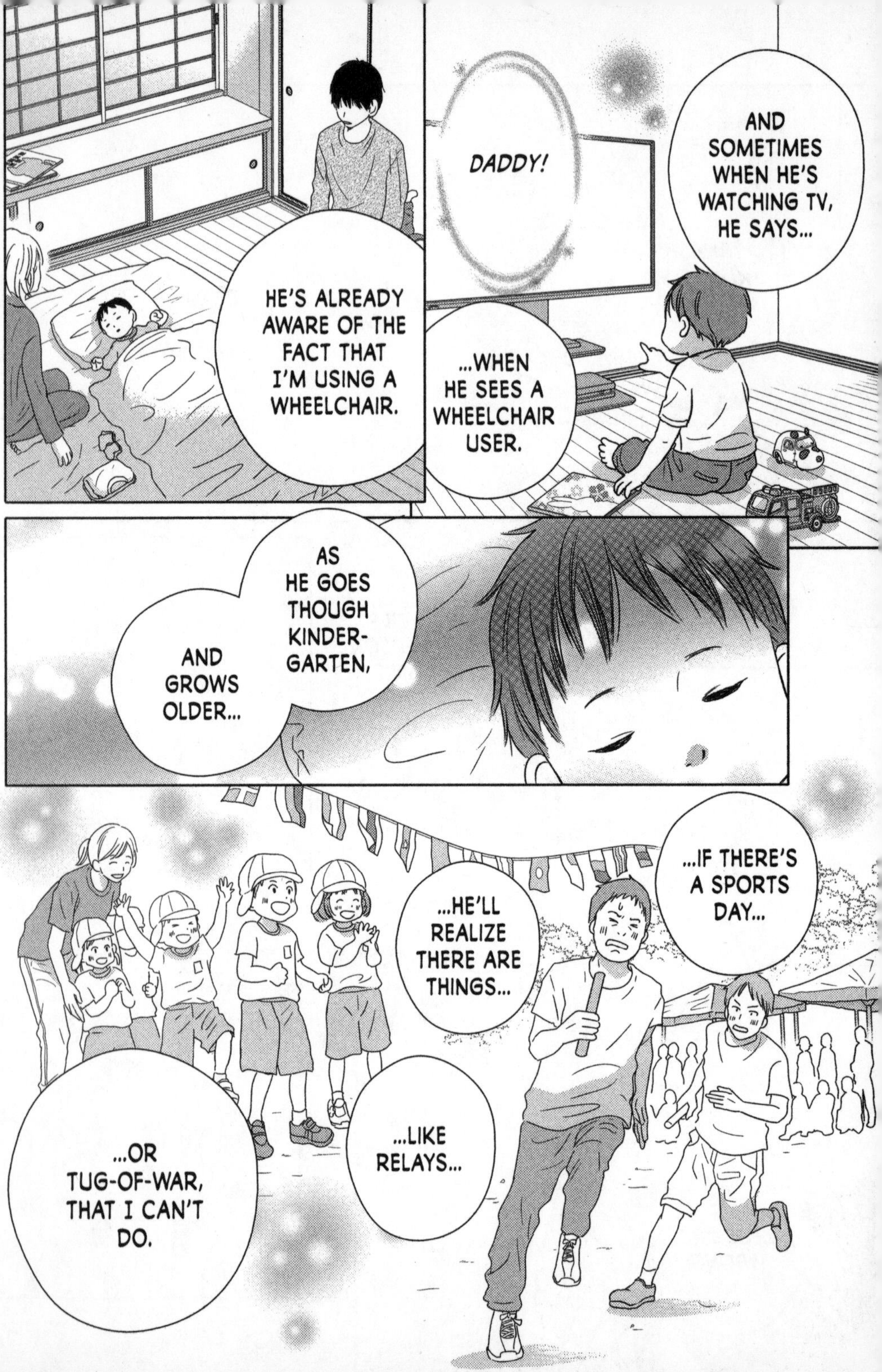
AND SOMETIMES WHEN HE'S WATCHING TV, HE SAYS...
DADDY!
...WHEN HE SEES A WHEELCHAIR USER.
HE'S ALREADY AWARE OF THE FACT THAT I'M USING A WHEELCHAIR.
AS HE GOES THOUGH KINDER-GARTEN,
AND GROWS OLDER...
...IF THERE'S A SPORTS DAY...
...HE'LL REALIZE THERE ARE THINGS...
...LIKE RELAYS...
...OR TUG-OF-WAR, THAT I CAN'T DO.

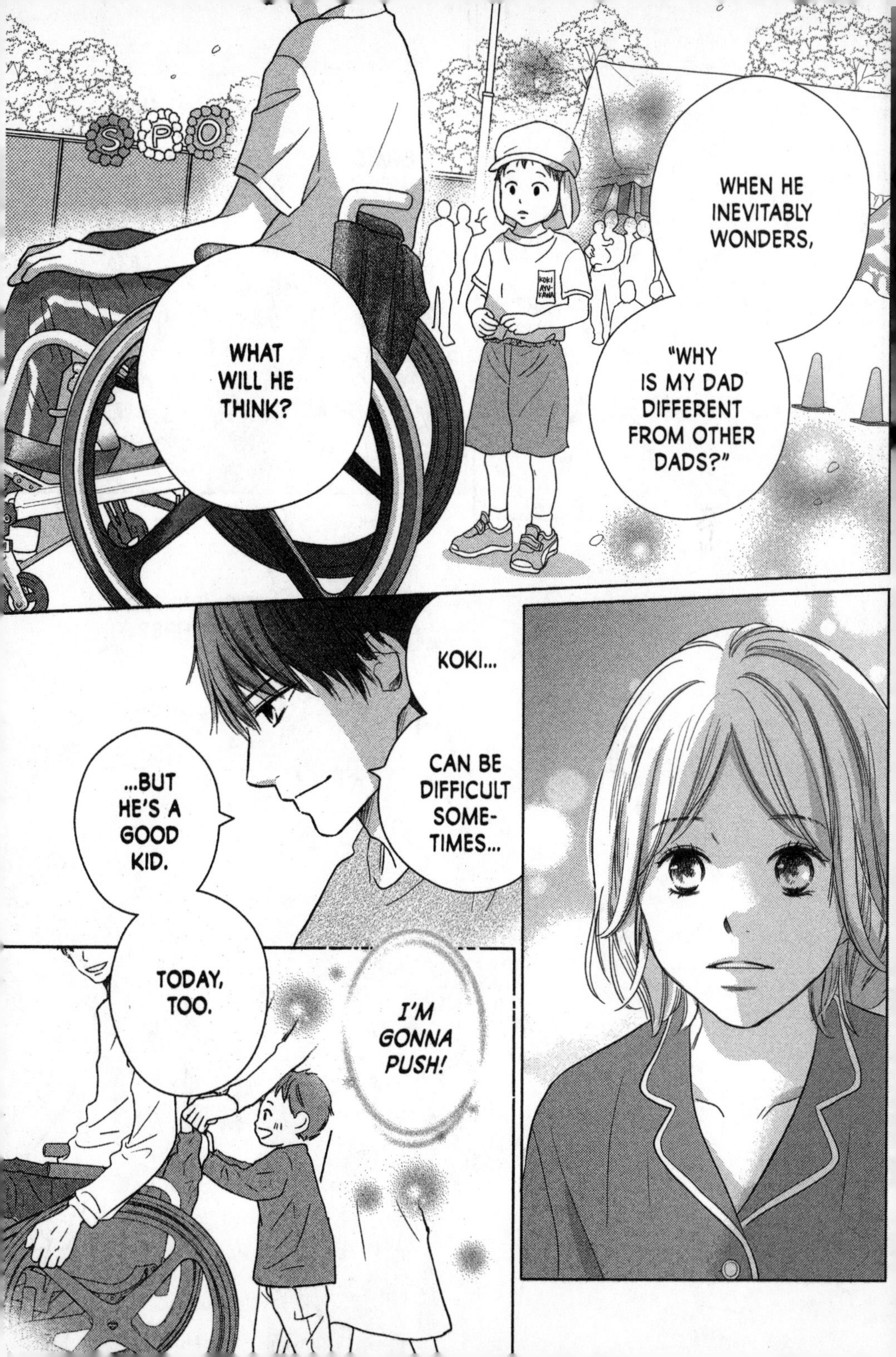
WHEN HE INEVITABLY WONDERS,
"WHY IS MY DAD DIFFERENT FROM OTHER DADS?"
WHAT WILL HE THINK?
SPO
KOKI...
CAN BE DIFFICULT SOME-TIMES...
...BUT HE'S A GOOD KID.
TODAY, TOO.
I'M GONNA PUSH!

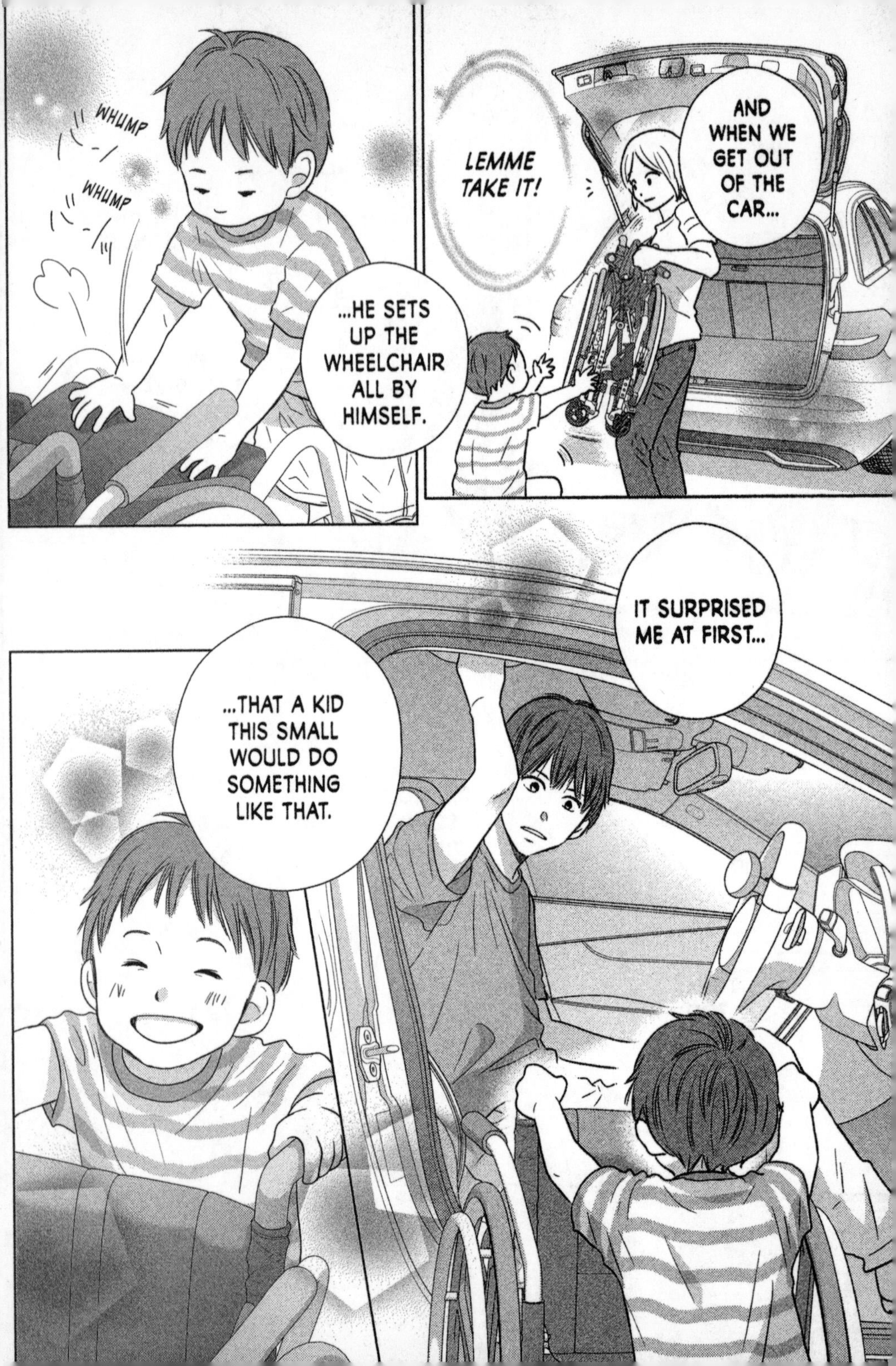
AND WHEN WE GET OUT OF THE CAR...
LEMME TAKE IT!
...HE SETS UP THE WHEELCHAIR ALL BY HIMSELF.
WHUMP
WHUMP
IT SURPRISED ME AT FIRST...
...THAT A KID THIS SMALL WOULD DO SOMETHING LIKE THAT.

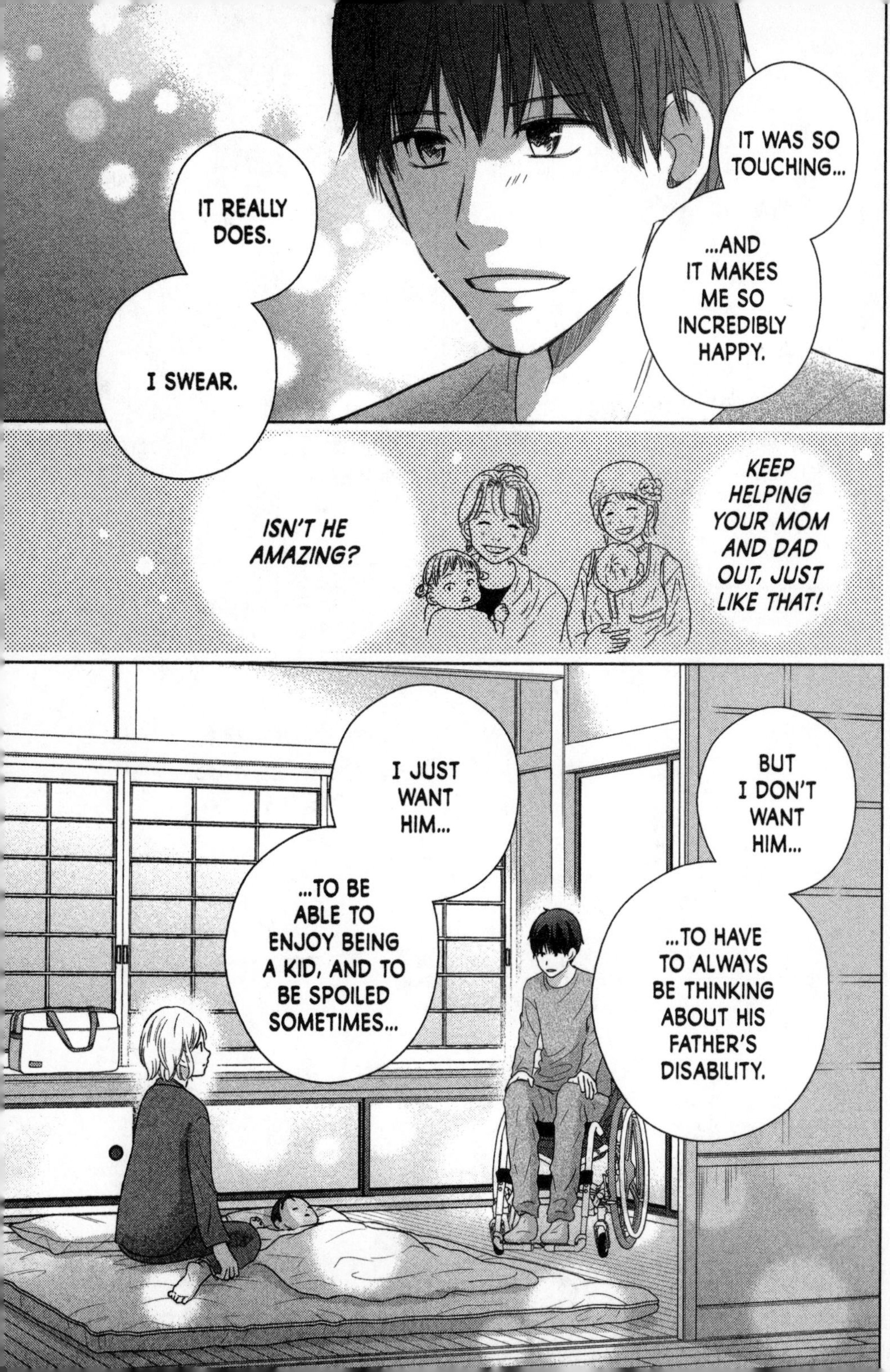
IT WAS SO TOUCHING...
...AND IT MAKES ME SO INCREDIBLY HAPPY.
IT REALLY DOES.
I SWEAR.
KEEP HELPING YOUR MOM AND DAD OUT, JUST LIKE THAT!
ISN'T HE AMAZING?
BUT I DON'T WANT HIM...
...TO HAVE TO ALWAYS BE THINKING ABOUT HIS FATHER'S DISABILITY.
I JUST WANT HIM...
...TO BE ABLE TO ENJOY BEING A KID, AND TO BE SPOILED SOMETIMES...

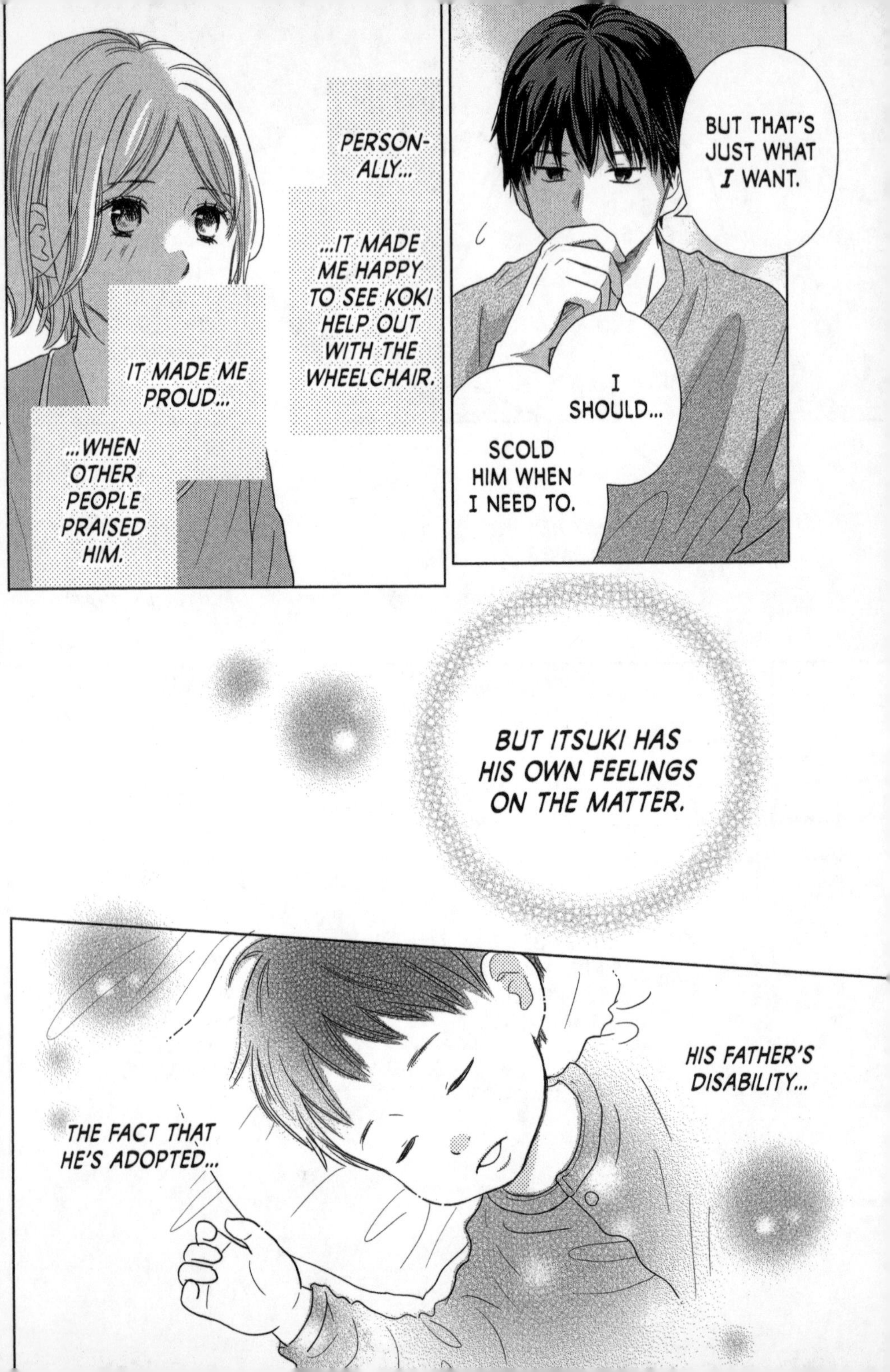
BUT THAT'S JUST WHAT *I* WANT.
I SHOULD...
SCOLD HIM WHEN I NEED TO.
PERSONALLY...
...IT MADE ME HAPPY TO SEE KOKI HELP OUT WITH THE WHEELCHAIR.
IT MADE ME PROUD...
...WHEN OTHER PEOPLE PRAISED HIM.
BUT ITSUKI HAS HIS OWN FEELINGS ON THE MATTER.
HIS FATHER'S DISABILITY...
THE FACT THAT HE'S ADOPTED...

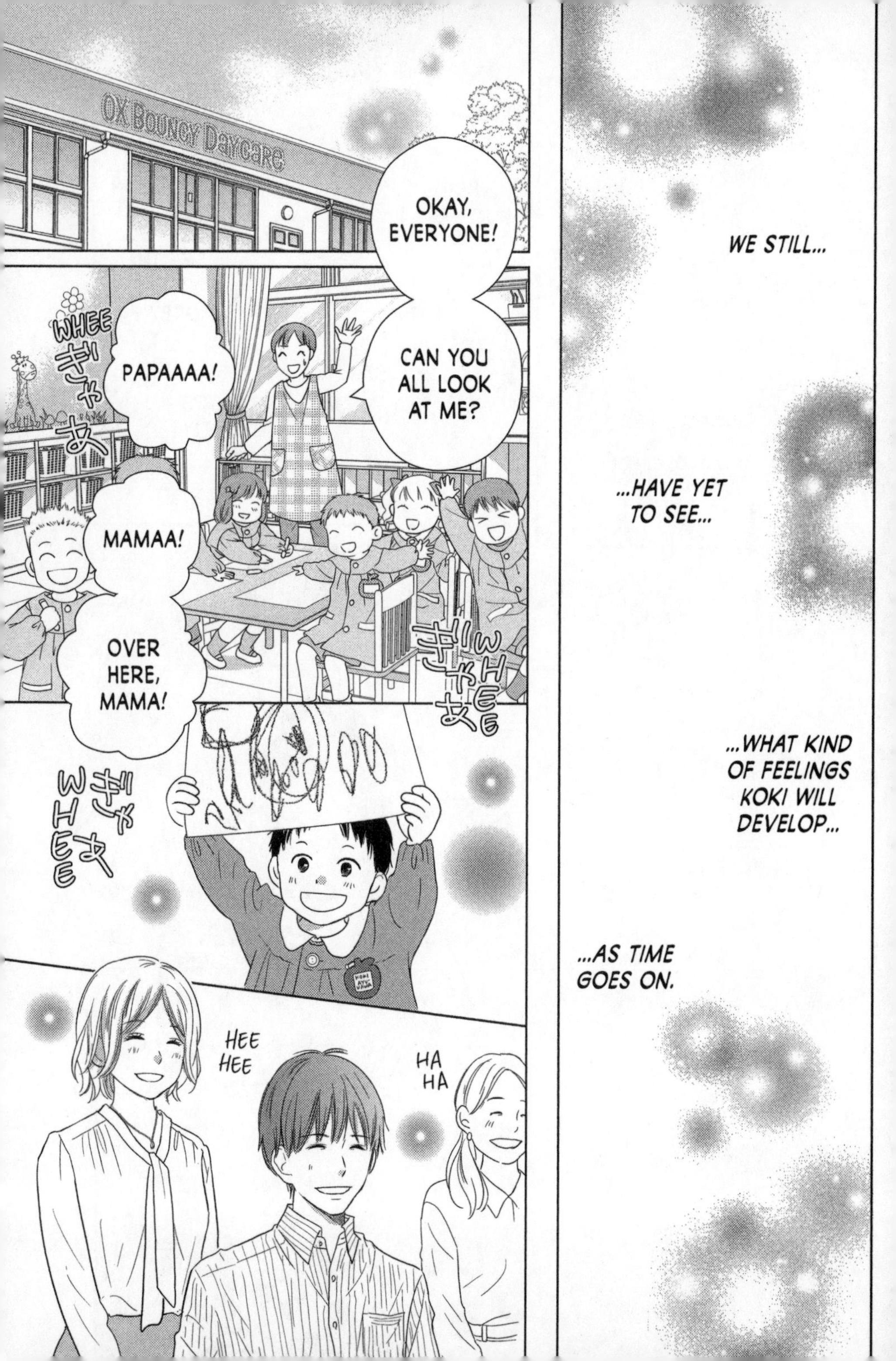
WE STILL...
...HAVE YET TO SEE...
...WHAT KIND OF FEELINGS KOKI WILL DEVELOP...
...AS TIME GOES ON.
OX Bouncy Daycare
OKAY, EVERYONE!
CAN YOU ALL LOOK AT ME?
WHEE ぎゃあ
PAPAAAA!
MAMAA!
OVER HERE, MAMA!
WHEE ぎゃあ
WHEE ぎゃあ
HEE HEE
HA HA

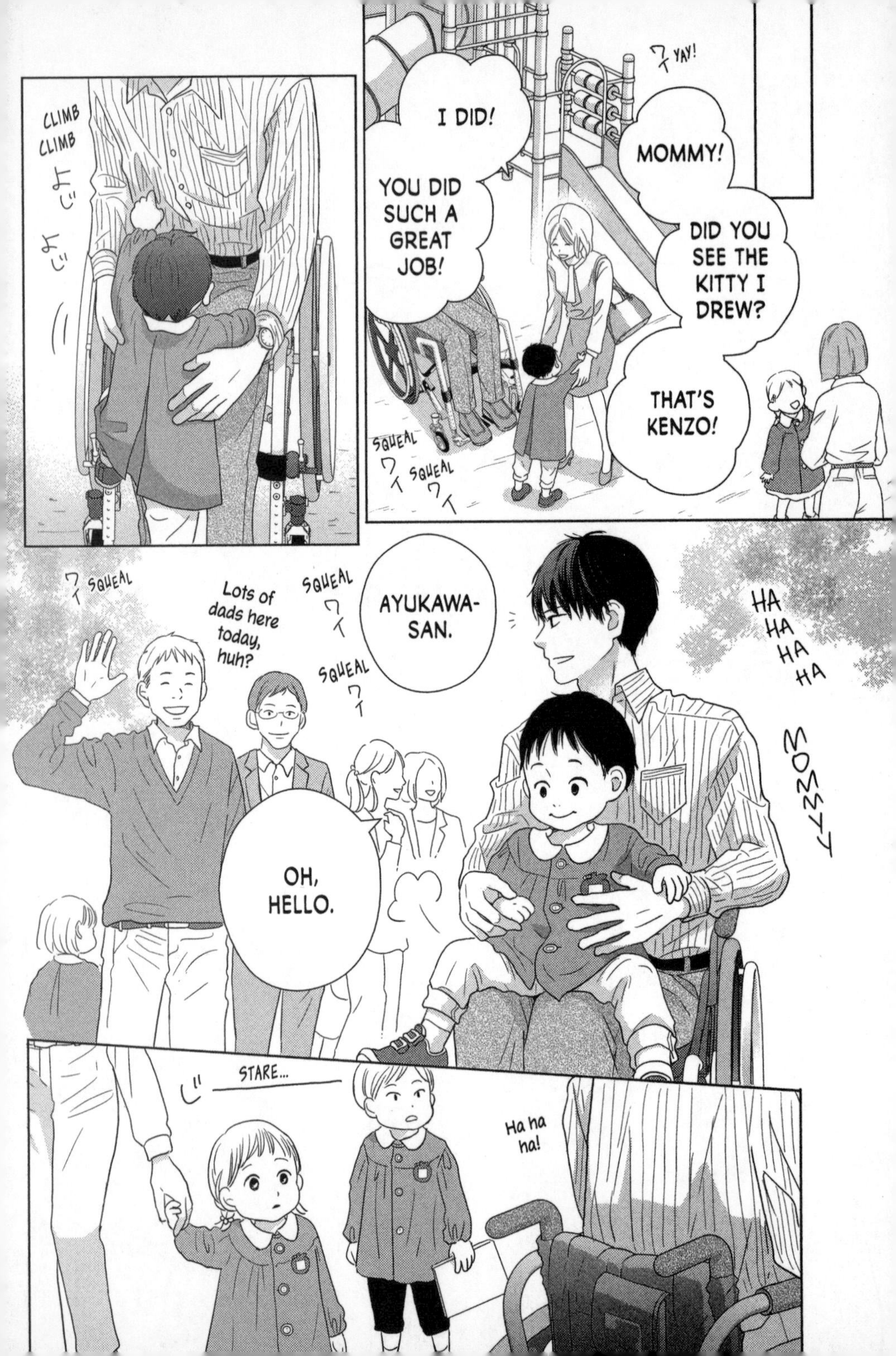
ワイ YAY!
MOMMY!
I DID!
YOU DID SUCH A GREAT JOB!
DID YOU SEE THE KITTY I DREW?
THAT'S KENZO!
ワイ SQUEAL
ワイ SQUEAL
CLIMB CLIMB
よじ よじ
HA HA HA HA
MOMMY
AYUKAWA-SAN.
SQUEAL ワイ
SQUEAL ワイ
Lots of dads here today, huh?
ワイ SQUEAL
OH, HELLO.
Ha ha ha!
じ STARE...

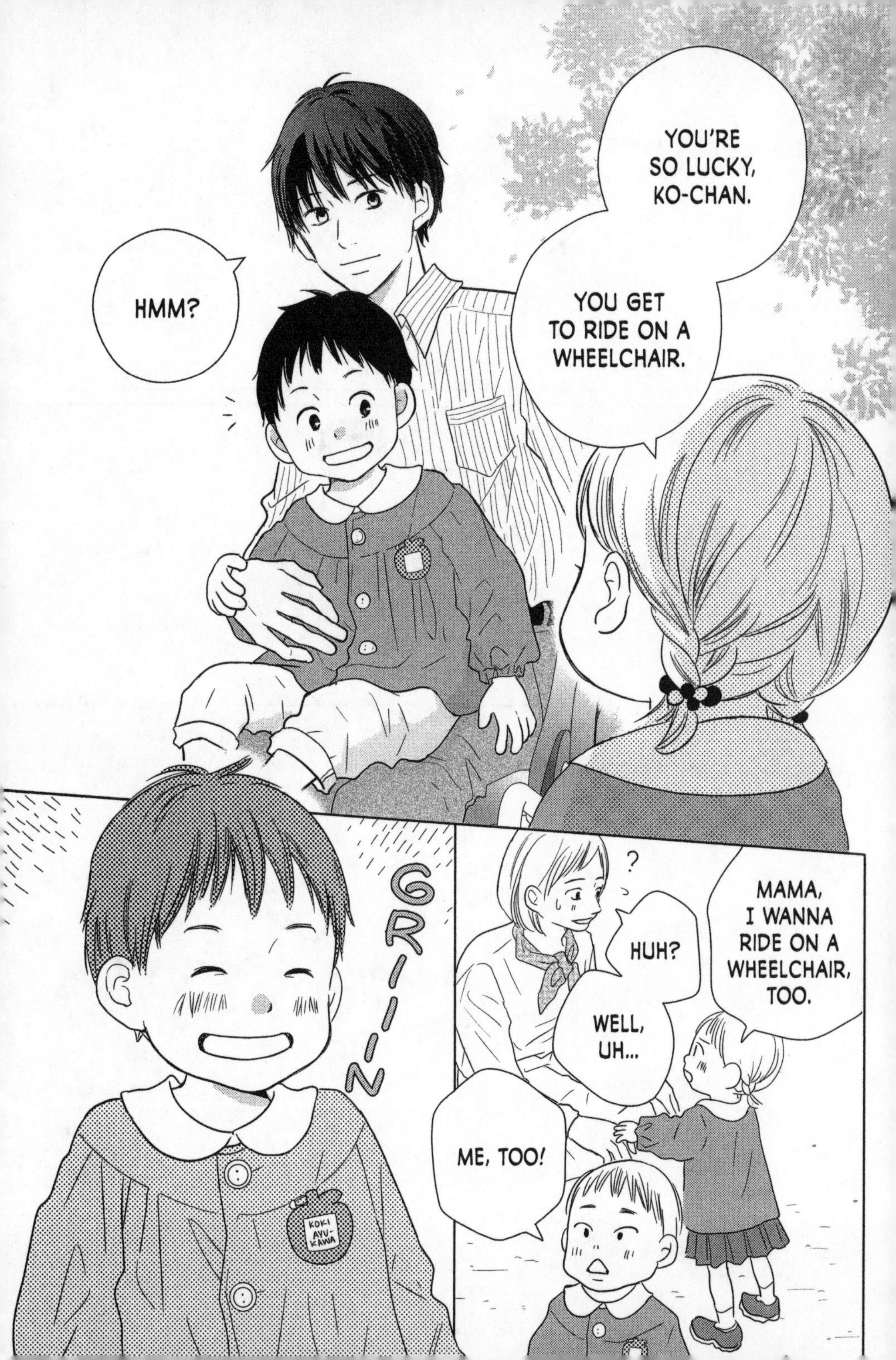
YOU'RE SO LUCKY, KO-CHAN.
YOU GET TO RIDE ON A WHEELCHAIR.
HMM?
MAMA, I WANNA RIDE ON A WHEELCHAIR, TOO.
?
HUH?
WELL, UH...
ME, TOO!
GRIIIN
KOKI AYU-KAWA

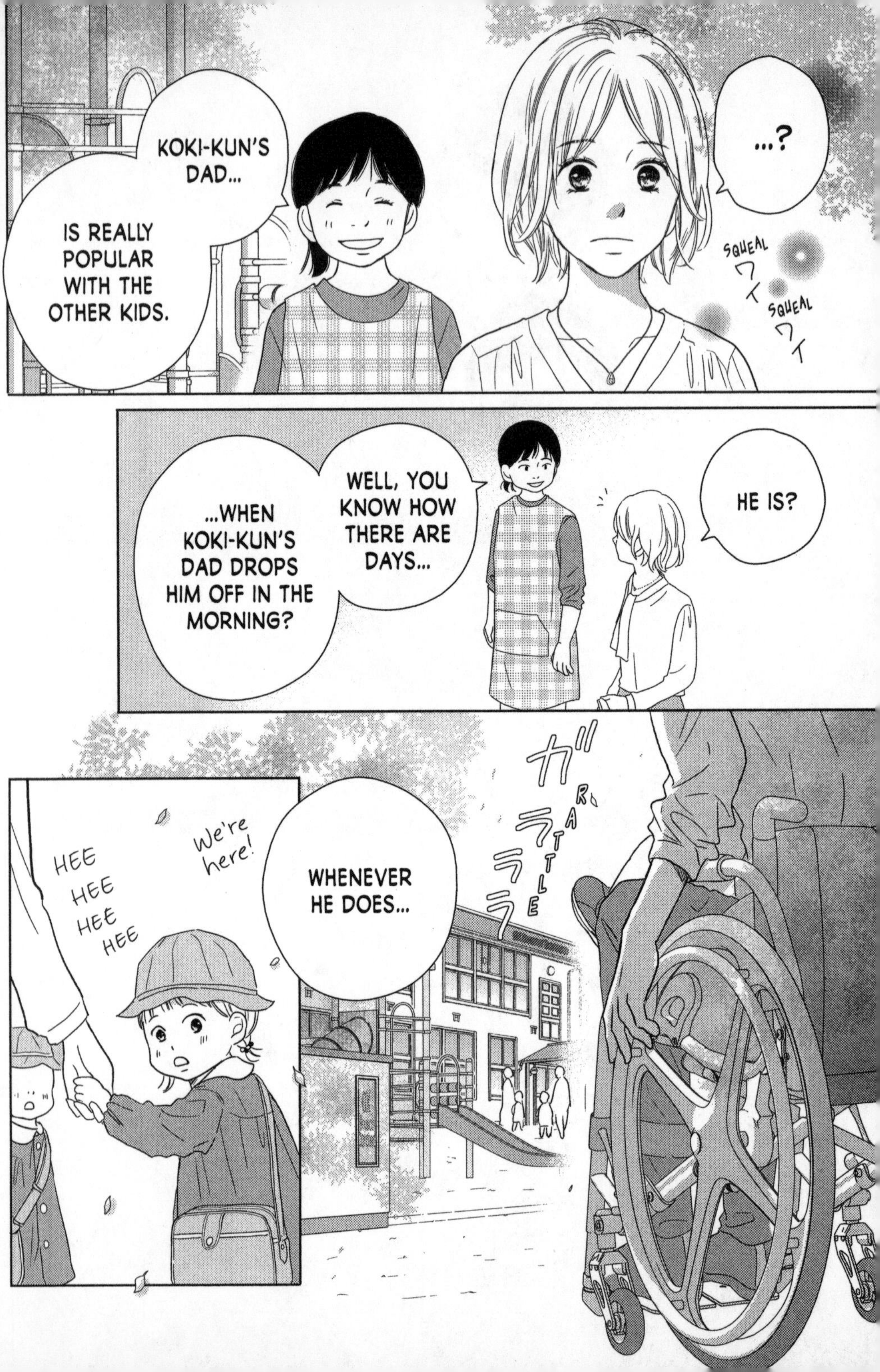
...?
SQUEAL
ワイ
SQUEAL
ワイ
KOKI-KUN'S DAD...
IS REALLY POPULAR WITH THE OTHER KIDS.
HE IS?
WELL, YOU KNOW HOW THERE ARE DAYS...
...WHEN KOKI-KUN'S DAD DROPS HIM OFF IN THE MORNING?
ガラララ
RATTLE
WHENEVER HE DOES...
We're here!
HEE HEE HEE HEE

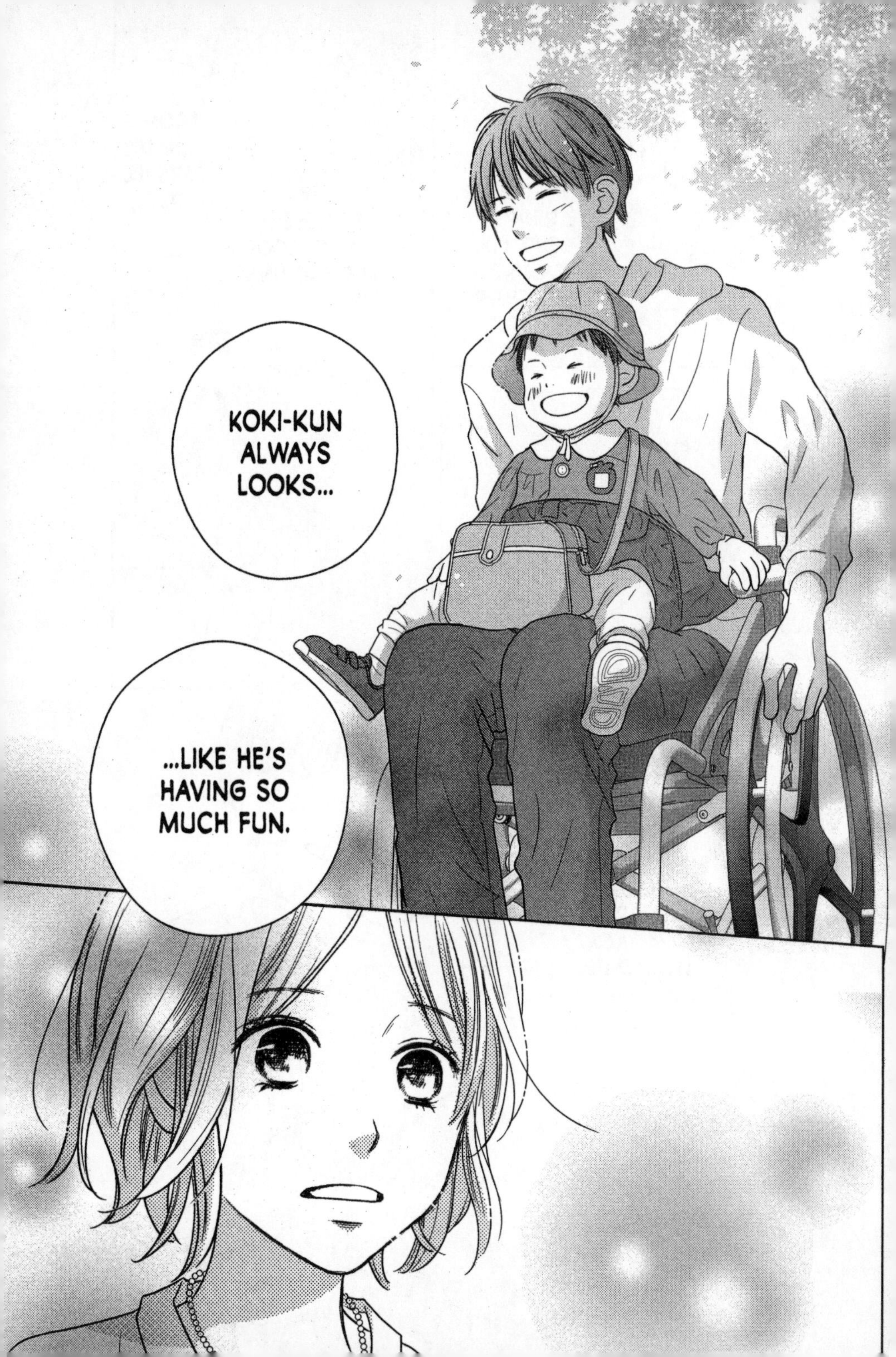
KOKI-KUN ALWAYS LOOKS...
...LIKE HE'S HAVING SO MUCH FUN.

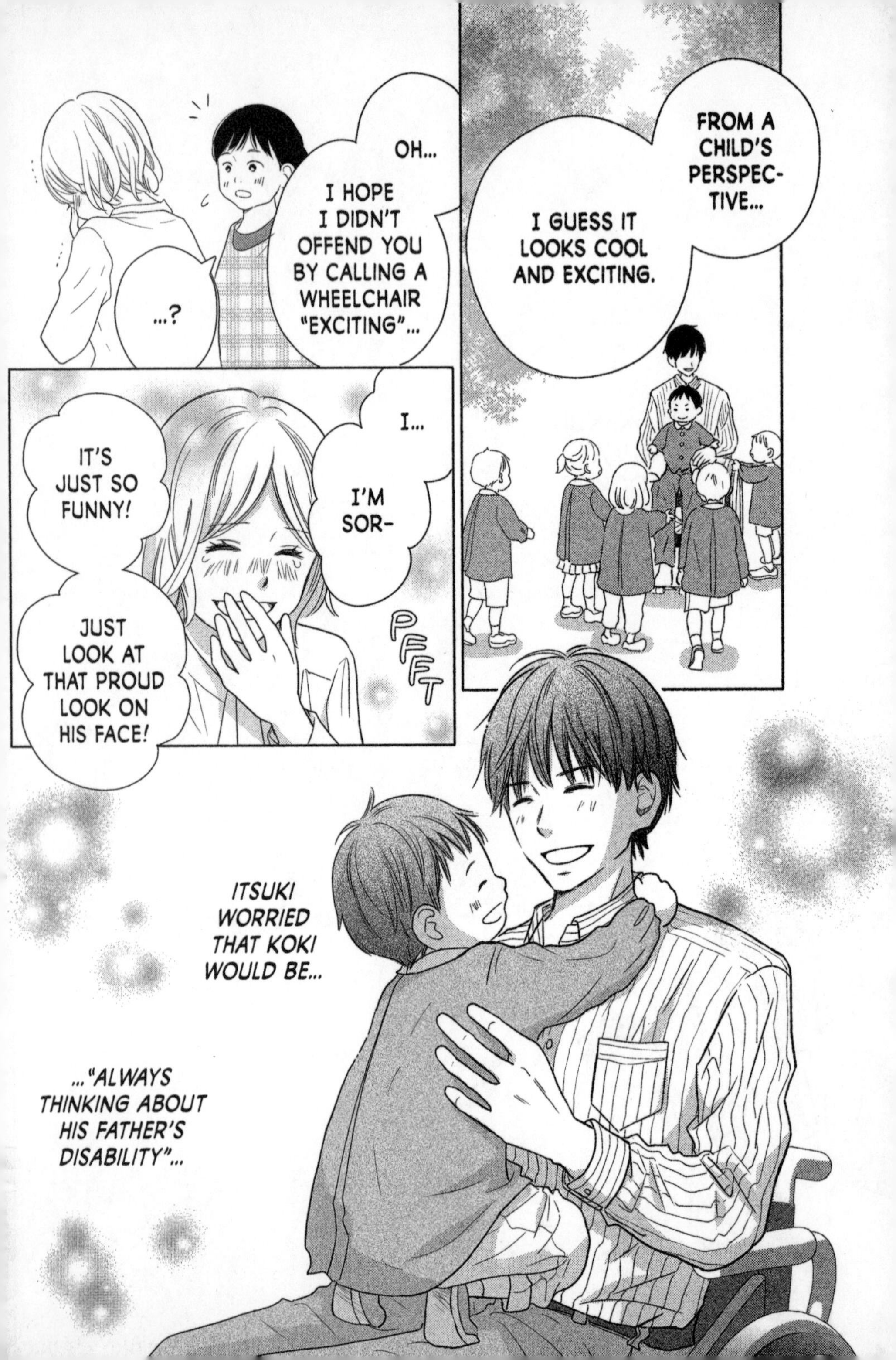
FROM A CHILD'S PERSPEC-TIVE...
I GUESS IT LOOKS COOL AND EXCITING.
OH...
I HOPE I DIDN'T OFFEND YOU BY CALLING A WHEELCHAIR "EXCITING"...
...?
I...
I'M SOR-
IT'S JUST SO FUNNY!
JUST LOOK AT THAT PROUD LOOK ON HIS FACE!
PFFT
ITSUKI WORRIED THAT KOKI WOULD BE...
..."ALWAYS THINKING ABOUT HIS FATHER'S DISABILITY"...

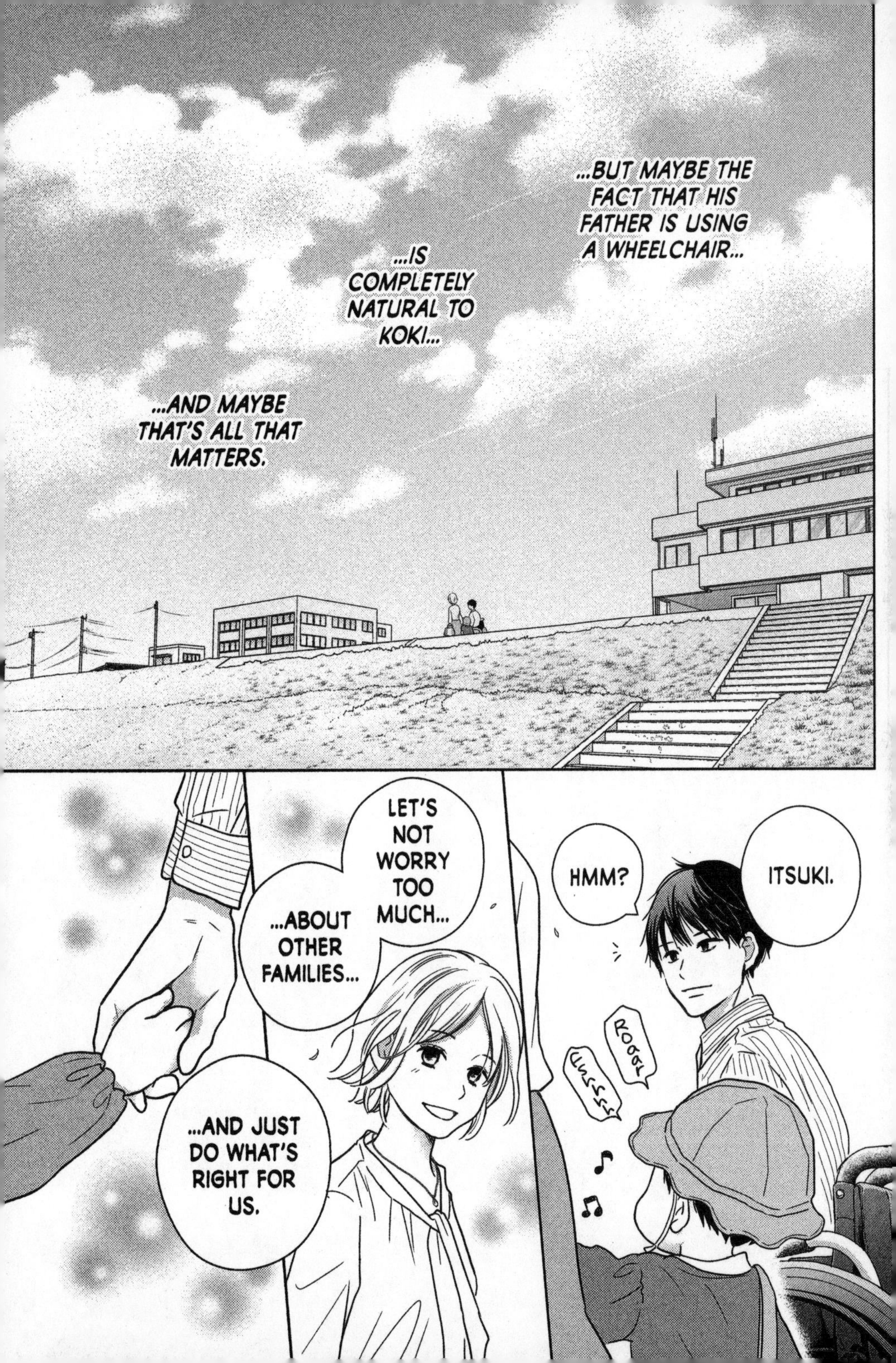
...BUT MAYBE THE FACT THAT HIS FATHER IS USING A WHEELCHAIR...
...IS COMPLETELY NATURAL TO KOKI...
...AND MAYBE THAT'S ALL THAT MATTERS.
ITSUKI.
HMM?
Rooar
LET'S NOT WORRY TOO MUCH...
...ABOUT OTHER FAMILIES...
...AND JUST DO WHAT'S RIGHT FOR US.

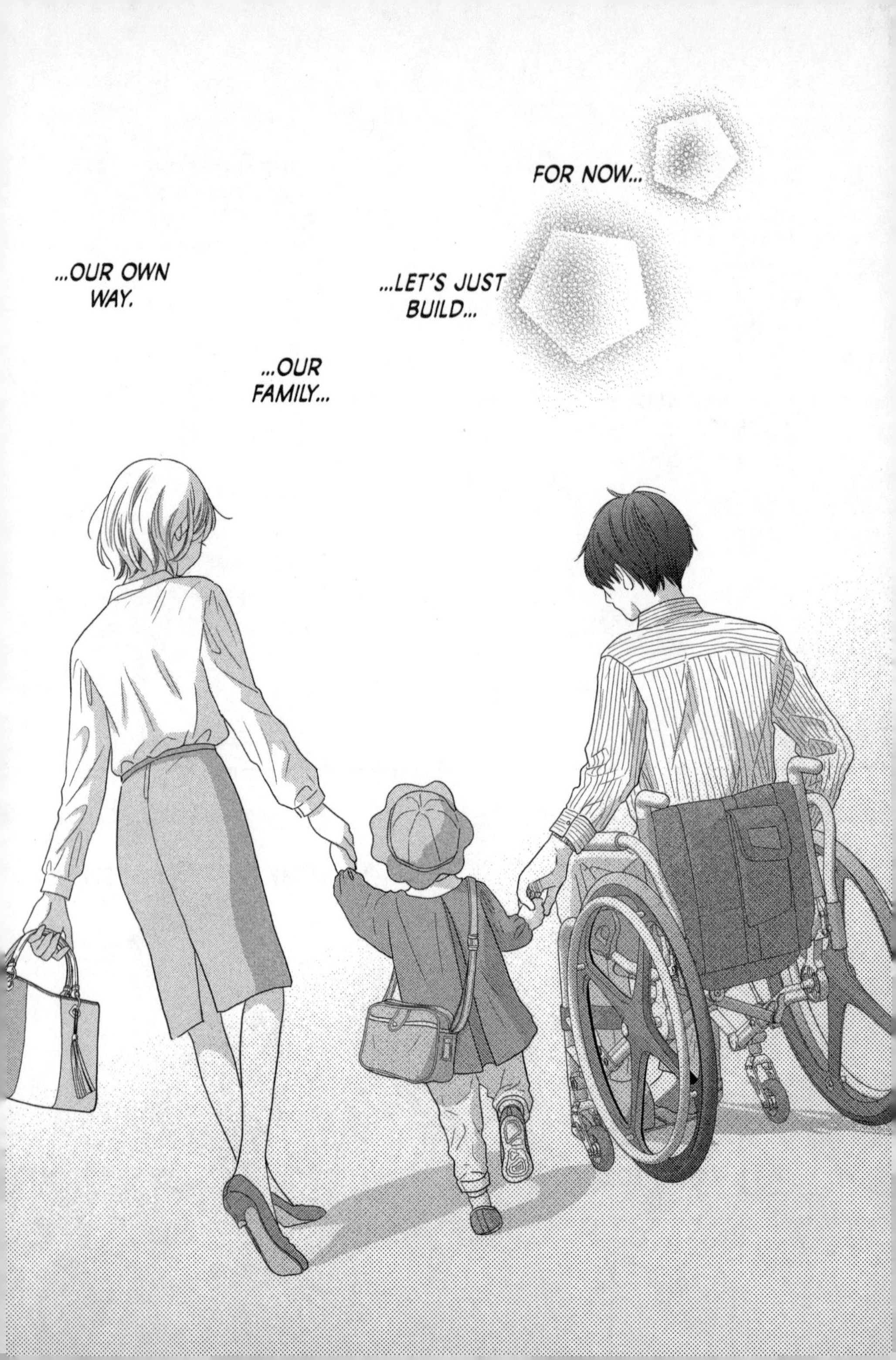
FOR NOW...
...LET'S JUST BUILD...
...OUR FAMILY...
...OUR OWN WAY.

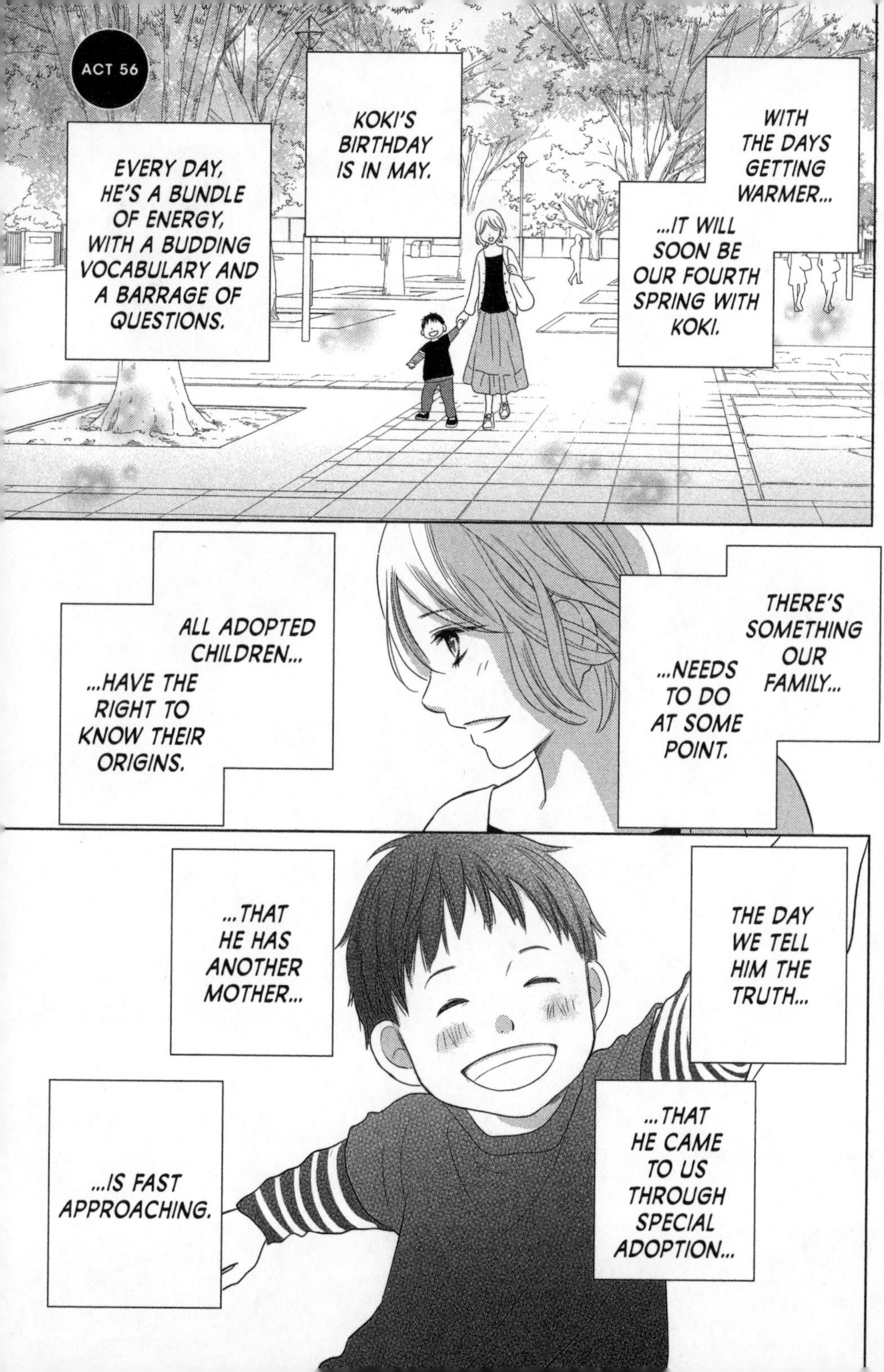
ACT 56
WITH THE DAYS GETTING WARMER...
...IT WILL SOON BE OUR FOURTH SPRING WITH KOKI.
KOKI'S BIRTHDAY IS IN MAY.
EVERY DAY, HE'S A BUNDLE OF ENERGY, WITH A BUDDING VOCABULARY AND A BARRAGE OF QUESTIONS.
THERE'S SOMETHING OUR FAMILY...
...NEEDS TO DO AT SOME POINT.
ALL ADOPTED CHILDREN...
...HAVE THE RIGHT TO KNOW THEIR ORIGINS.
THE DAY WE TELL HIM THE TRUTH...
...THAT HE HAS ANOTHER MOTHER...
...THAT HE CAME TO US THROUGH SPECIAL ADOPTION...
...IS FAST APPROACHING.

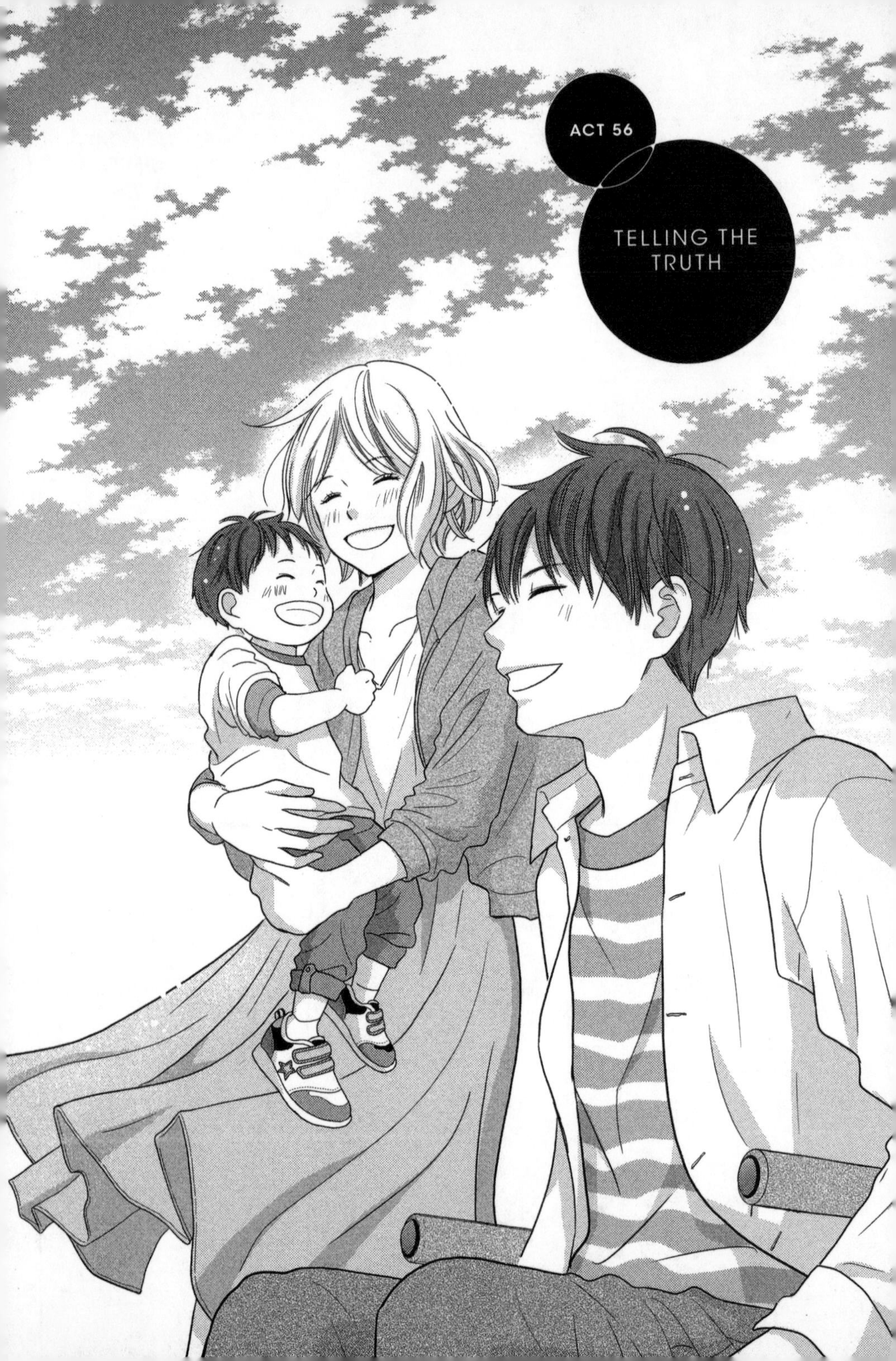
ACT 56
TELLING THE TRUTH

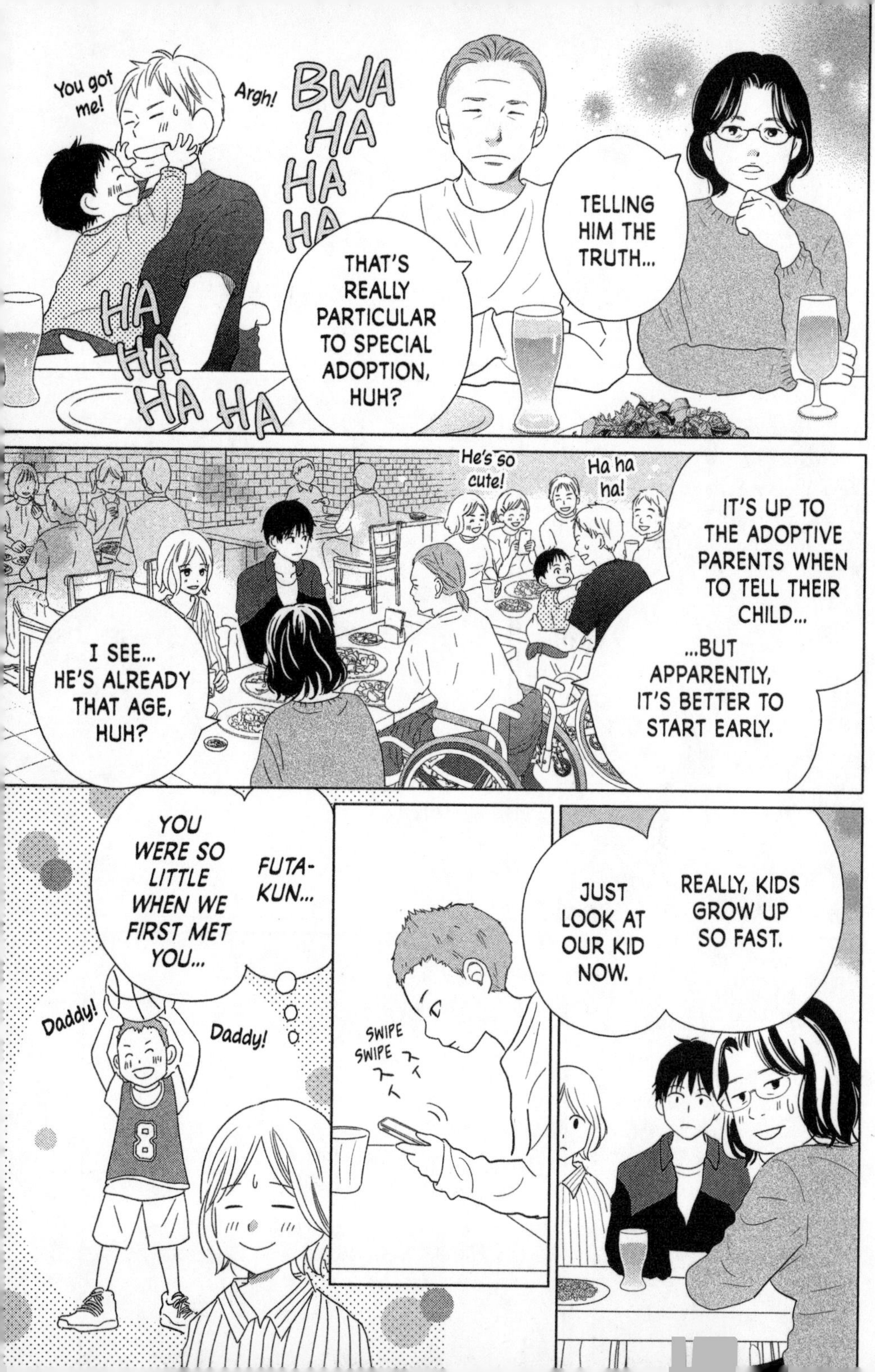
TELLING HIM THE TRUTH...
THAT'S REALLY PARTICULAR TO SPECIAL ADOPTION, HUH?
BWA HA HA HA
Argh!
You got me!
HA HA HA HA HA
IT'S UP TO THE ADOPTIVE PARENTS WHEN TO TELL THEIR CHILD...
...BUT APPARENTLY, IT'S BETTER TO START EARLY.
Ha ha ha!
He's so cute!
I SEE... HE'S ALREADY THAT AGE, HUH?
REALLY, KIDS GROW UP SO FAST.
JUST LOOK AT OUR KID NOW.
SWIPE SWIPE
スイ スイ
FUTA-KUN...
YOU WERE SO LITTLE WHEN WE FIRST MET YOU...
Daddy!
Daddy!

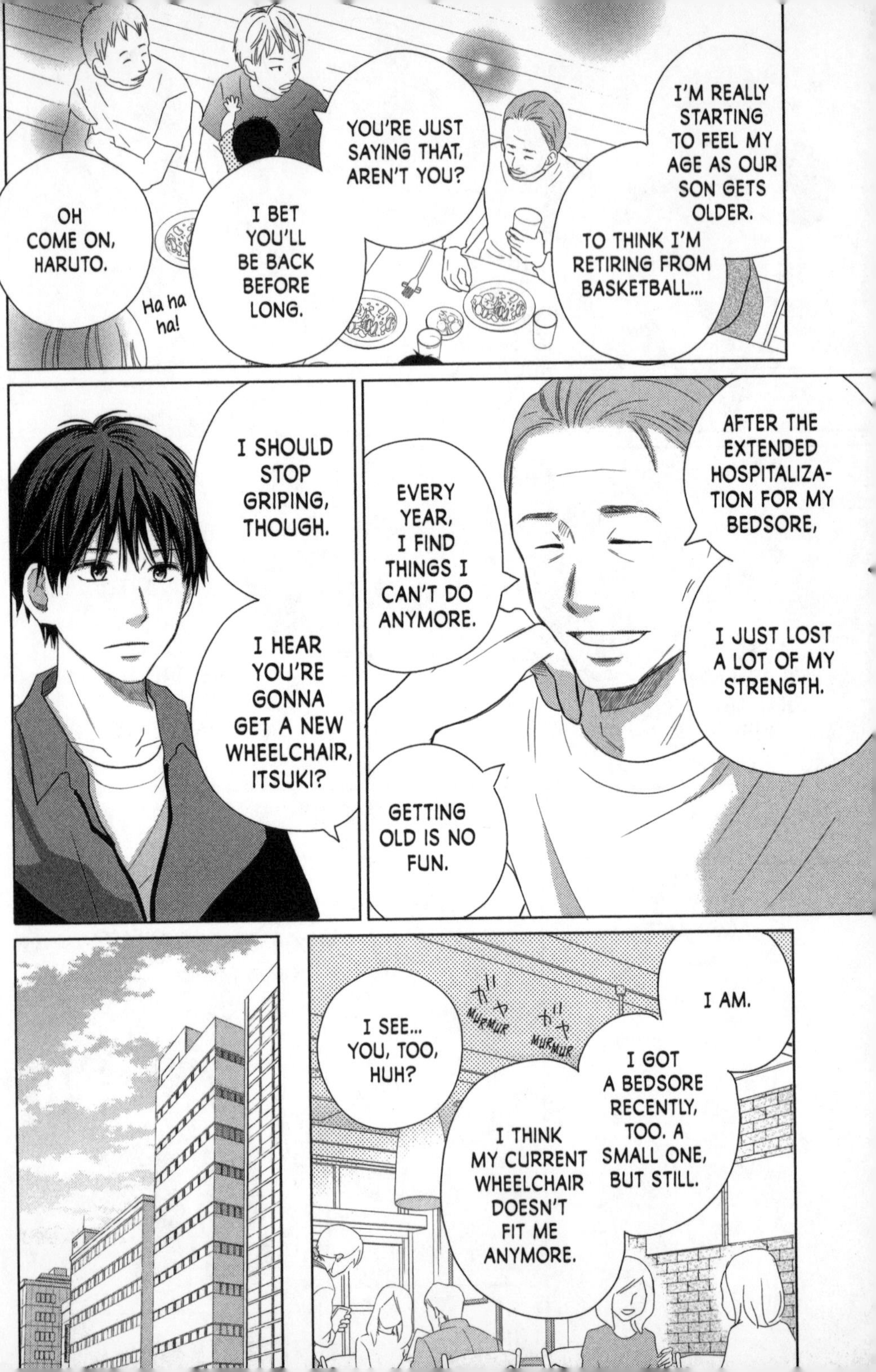
I'M REALLY STARTING TO FEEL MY AGE AS OUR SON GETS OLDER.
TO THINK I'M RETIRING FROM BASKETBALL...
YOU'RE JUST SAYING THAT, AREN'T YOU?
I BET YOU'LL BE BACK BEFORE LONG.
OH COME ON, HARUTO.
Ha ha ha!
AFTER THE EXTENDED HOSPITALIZATION FOR MY BEDSORE,
I JUST LOST A LOT OF MY STRENGTH.
EVERY YEAR, I FIND THINGS I CAN'T DO ANYMORE.
GETTING OLD IS NO FUN.
I SHOULD STOP GRIPING, THOUGH.
I HEAR YOU'RE GONNA GET A NEW WHEELCHAIR, ITSUKI?
I AM.
I GOT A BEDSORE RECENTLY, TOO. A SMALL ONE, BUT STILL.
I THINK MY CURRENT WHEELCHAIR DOESN'T FIT ME ANYMORE.
MURMUR
MURMUR
I SEE... YOU, TOO, HUH?

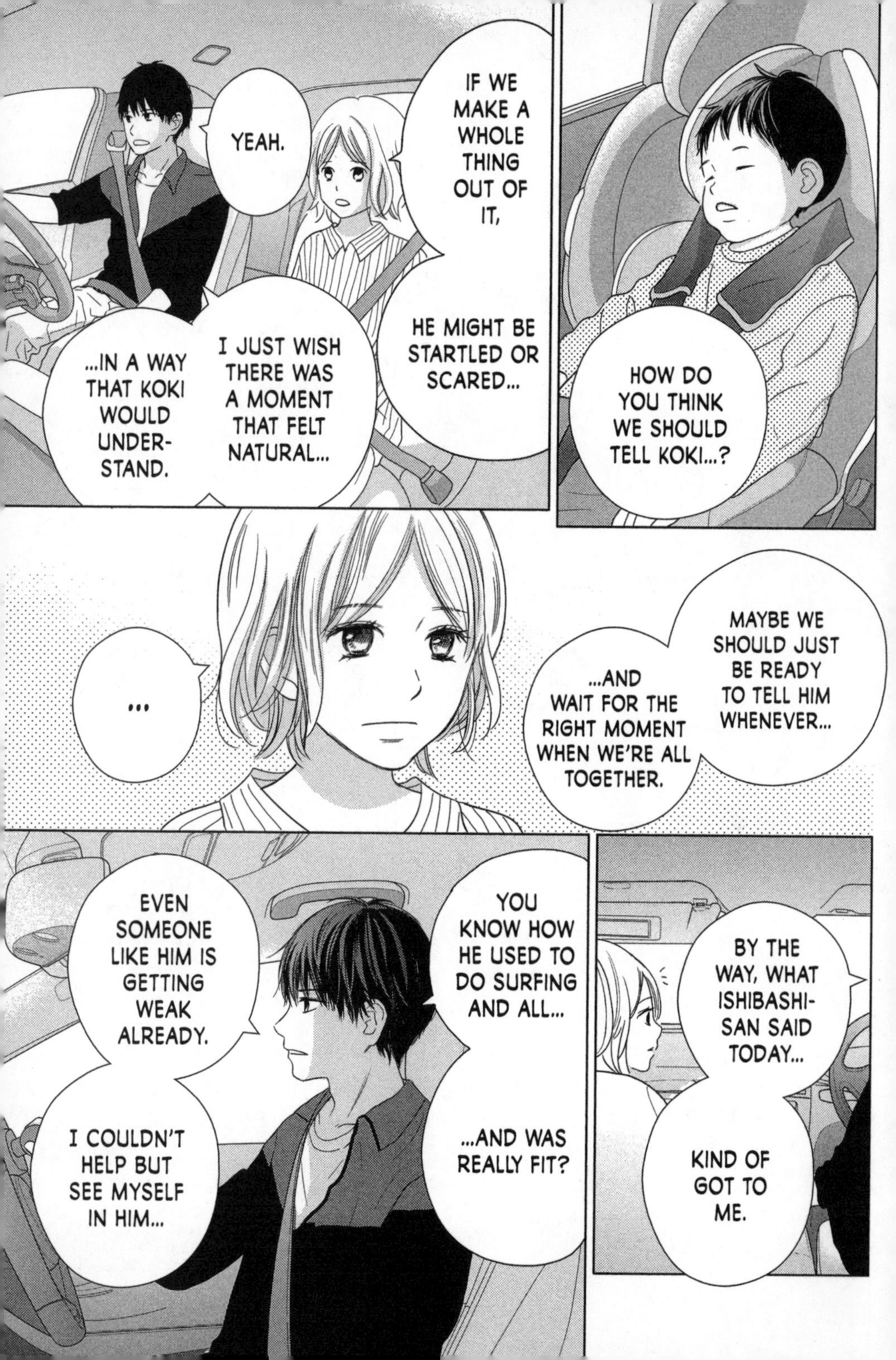
HOW DO YOU THINK WE SHOULD TELL KOKI...?
IF WE MAKE A WHOLE THING OUT OF IT,
HE MIGHT BE STARTLED OR SCARED...
YEAH.
I JUST WISH THERE WAS A MOMENT THAT FELT NATURAL...
...IN A WAY THAT KOKI WOULD UNDER-STAND.
MAYBE WE SHOULD JUST BE READY TO TELL HIM WHENEVER...
...AND WAIT FOR THE RIGHT MOMENT WHEN WE'RE ALL TOGETHER.
...
BY THE WAY, WHAT ISHIBASHI-SAN SAID TODAY...
KIND OF GOT TO ME.
YOU KNOW HOW HE USED TO DO SURFING AND ALL...
...AND WAS REALLY FIT?
EVEN SOMEONE LIKE HIM IS GETTING WEAK ALREADY.
I COULDN'T HELP BUT SEE MYSELF IN HIM...

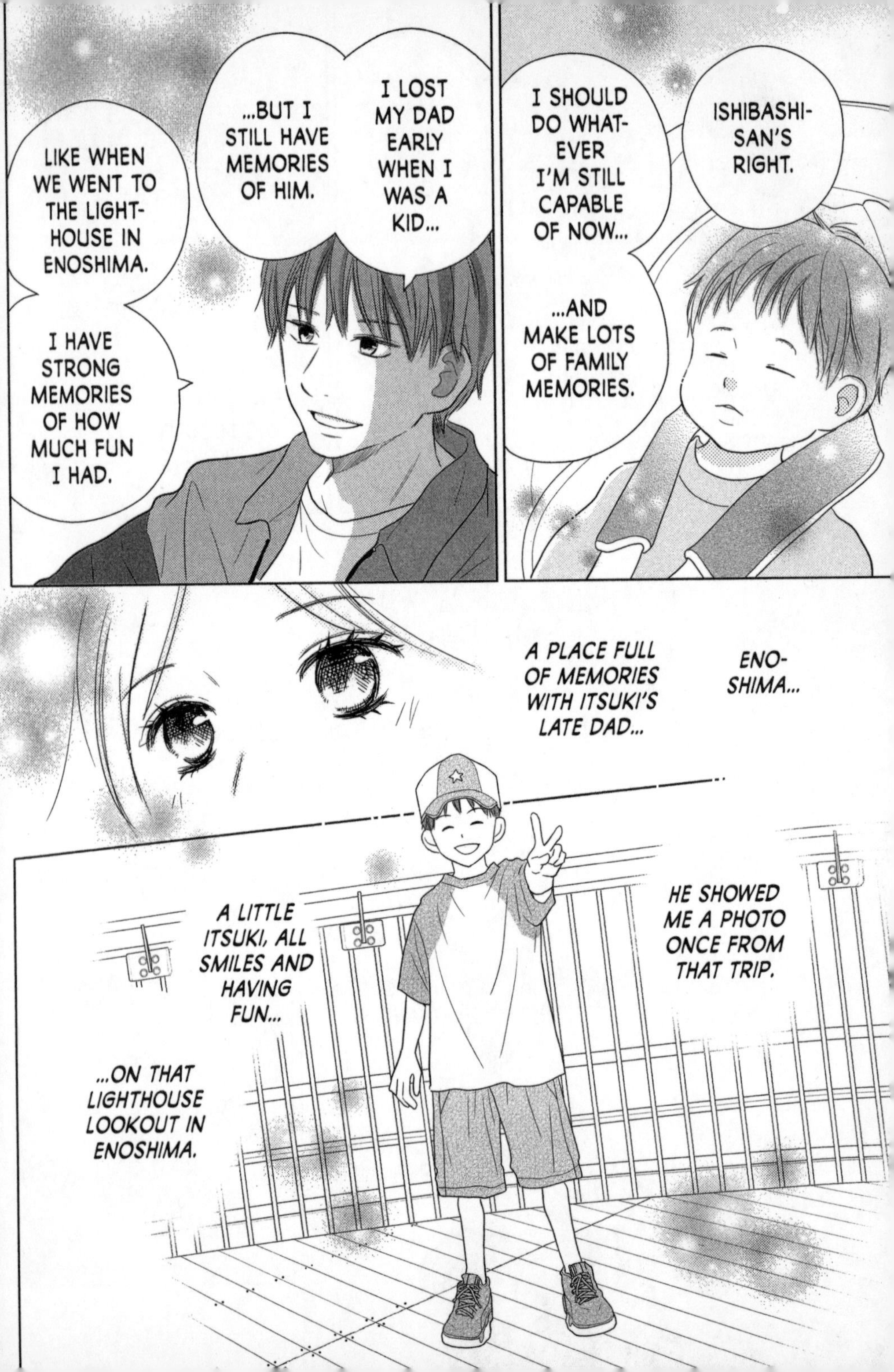
ISHIBASHI-SAN'S RIGHT.
I SHOULD DO WHATEVER I'M STILL CAPABLE OF NOW...
...AND MAKE LOTS OF FAMILY MEMORIES.
I LOST MY DAD EARLY WHEN I WAS A KID...
...BUT I STILL HAVE MEMORIES OF HIM.
LIKE WHEN WE WENT TO THE LIGHTHOUSE IN ENOSHIMA.
I HAVE STRONG MEMORIES OF HOW MUCH FUN I HAD.
ENOSHIMA...
A PLACE FULL OF MEMORIES WITH ITSUKI'S LATE DAD...
HE SHOWED ME A PHOTO ONCE FROM THAT TRIP.
A LITTLE ITSUKI, ALL SMILES AND HAVING FUN...
...ON THAT LIGHTHOUSE LOOKOUT IN ENOSHIMA.

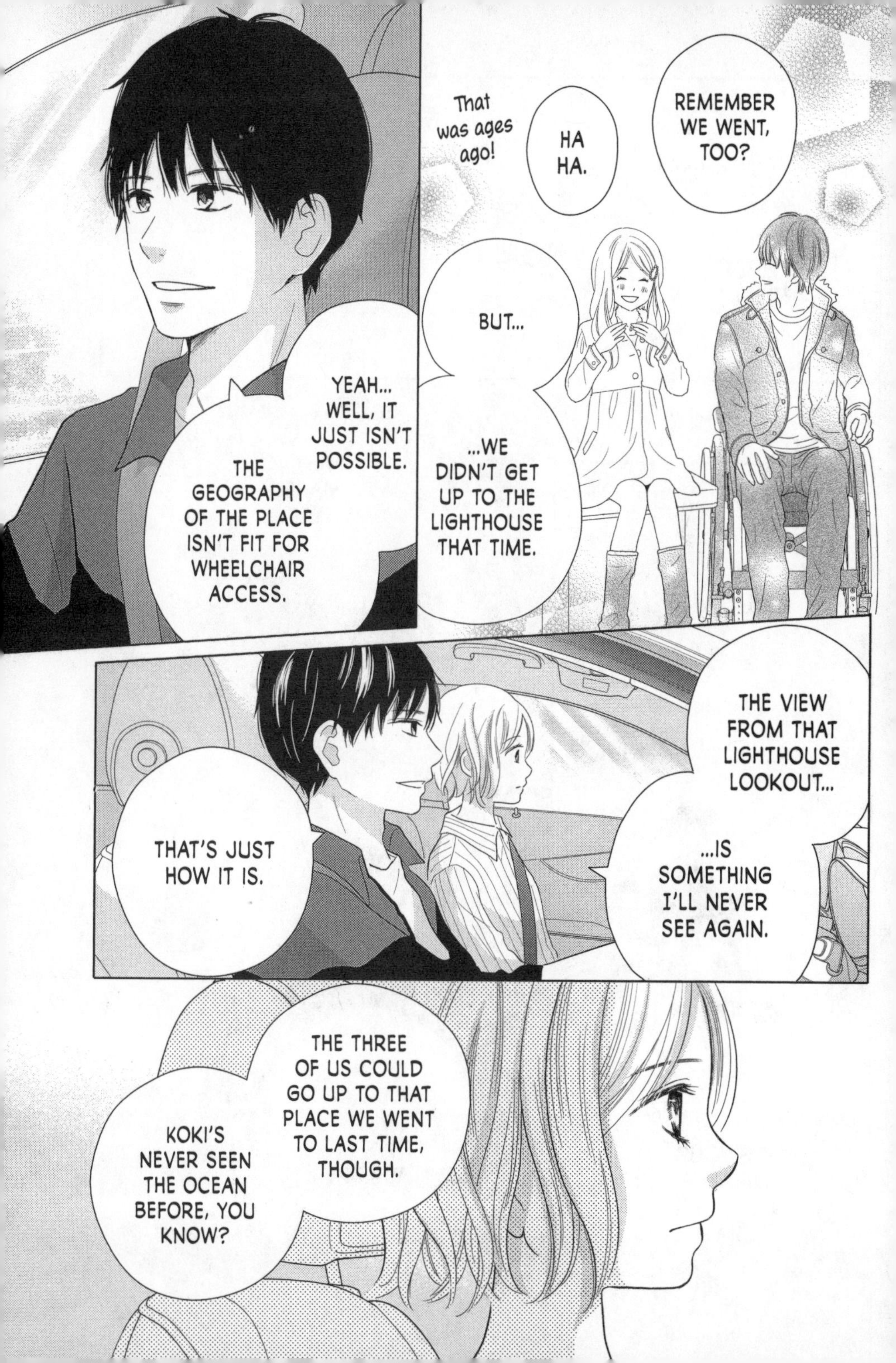
REMEMBER WE WENT, TOO?
HA HA.
That was ages ago!
BUT...
...WE DIDN'T GET UP TO THE LIGHTHOUSE THAT TIME.
YEAH... WELL, IT JUST ISN'T POSSIBLE.
THE GEOGRAPHY OF THE PLACE ISN'T FIT FOR WHEELCHAIR ACCESS.
THE VIEW FROM THAT LIGHTHOUSE LOOKOUT...
...IS SOMETHING I'LL NEVER SEE AGAIN.
THAT'S JUST HOW IT IS.
THE THREE OF US COULD GO UP TO THAT PLACE WE WENT TO LAST TIME, THOUGH.
KOKI'S NEVER SEEN THE OCEAN BEFORE, YOU KNOW?

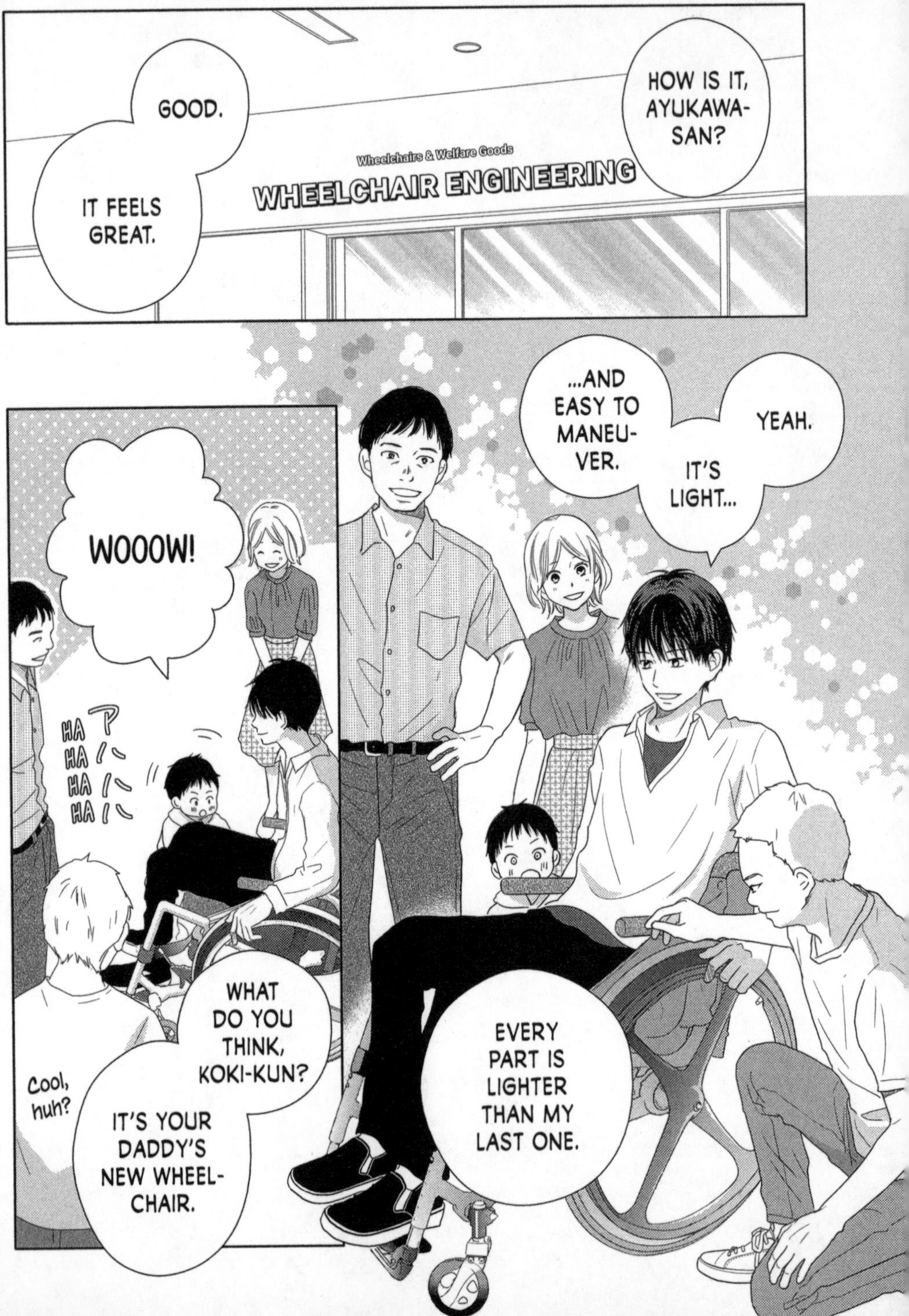
HOW IS IT, AYUKAWA-SAN?
GOOD.
IT FEELS GREAT.
Wheelchairs & Welfare Goods
WHEELCHAIR ENGINEERING
YEAH.
IT'S LIGHT...
...AND EASY TO MANEU-VER.
EVERY PART IS LIGHTER THAN MY LAST ONE.
WOOOW!
HA HA HA HA
WHAT DO YOU THINK, KOKI-KUN?
IT'S YOUR DADDY'S NEW WHEEL-CHAIR.
Cool, huh?

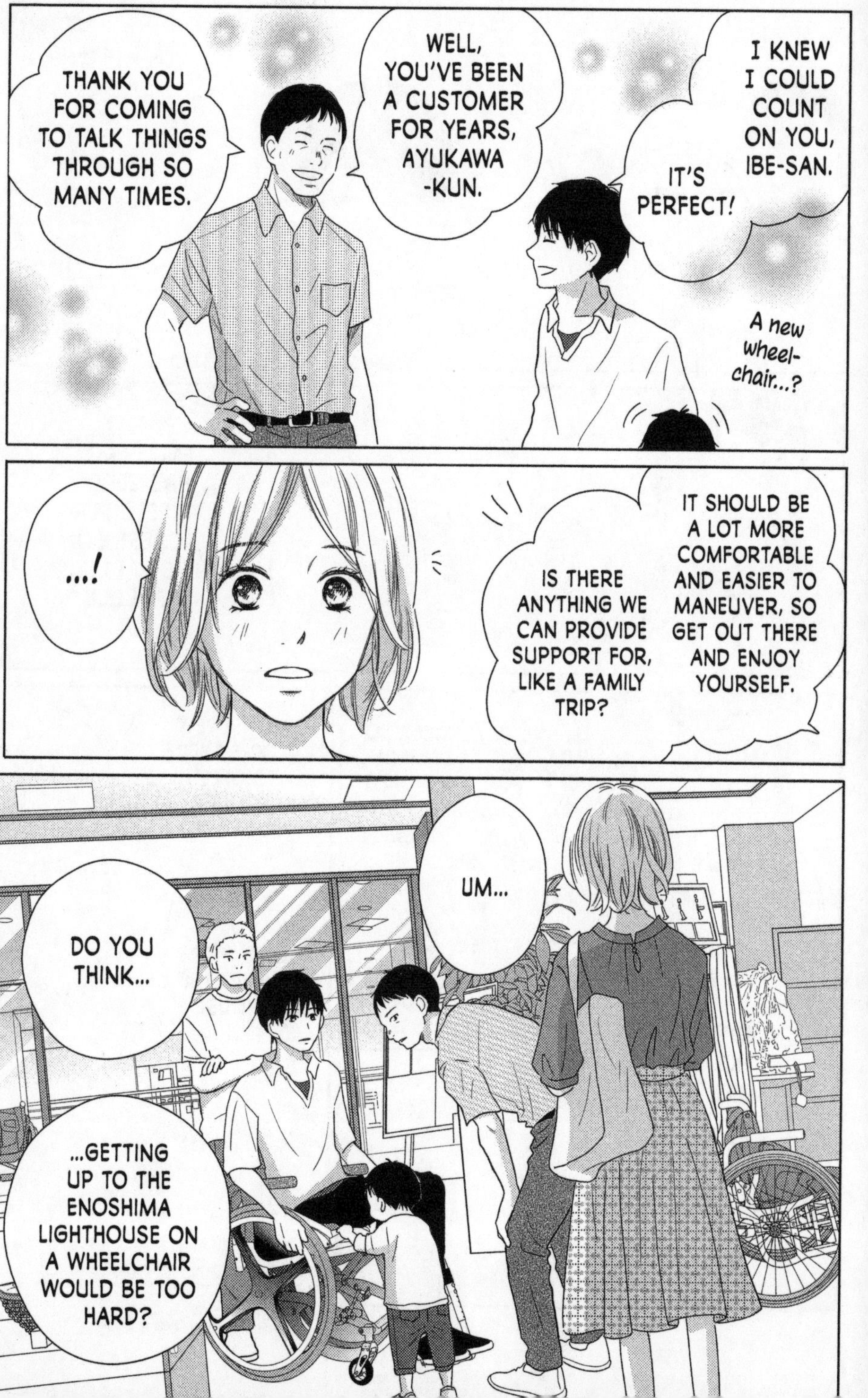
I KNEW I COULD COUNT ON YOU, IBE-SAN.
IT'S PERFECT!
A new wheel-chair...?
WELL, YOU'VE BEEN A CUSTOMER FOR YEARS, AYUKAWA-KUN.
THANK YOU FOR COMING TO TALK THINGS THROUGH SO MANY TIMES.
IT SHOULD BE A LOT MORE COMFORTABLE AND EASIER TO MANEUVER, SO GET OUT THERE AND ENJOY YOURSELF.
IS THERE ANYTHING WE CAN PROVIDE SUPPORT FOR, LIKE A FAMILY TRIP?
...!
UM...
DO YOU THINK...
...GETTING UP TO THE ENOSHIMA LIGHTHOUSE ON A WHEELCHAIR WOULD BE TOO HARD?

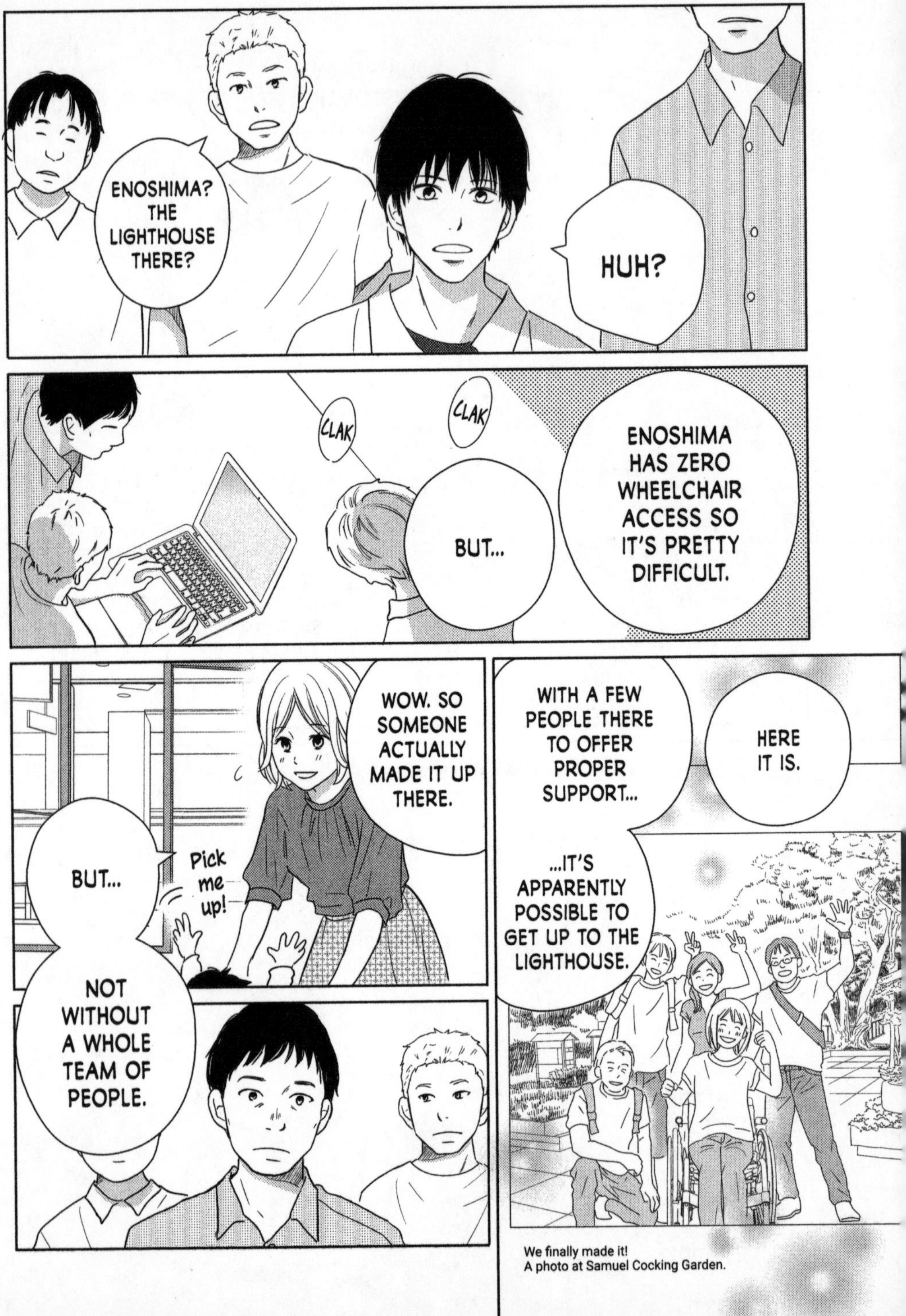
HUH?
ENOSHIMA? THE LIGHTHOUSE THERE?
CLAK
CLAK
ENOSHIMA HAS ZERO WHEELCHAIR ACCESS SO IT'S PRETTY DIFFICULT.
BUT...
HERE IT IS.
WITH A FEW PEOPLE THERE TO OFFER PROPER SUPPORT...
...IT'S APPARENTLY POSSIBLE TO GET UP TO THE LIGHTHOUSE.
WOW. SO SOMEONE ACTUALLY MADE IT UP THERE.
Pick me up!
BUT...
NOT WITHOUT A WHOLE TEAM OF PEOPLE.

We finally made it!
A photo at Samuel Cocking Garden.

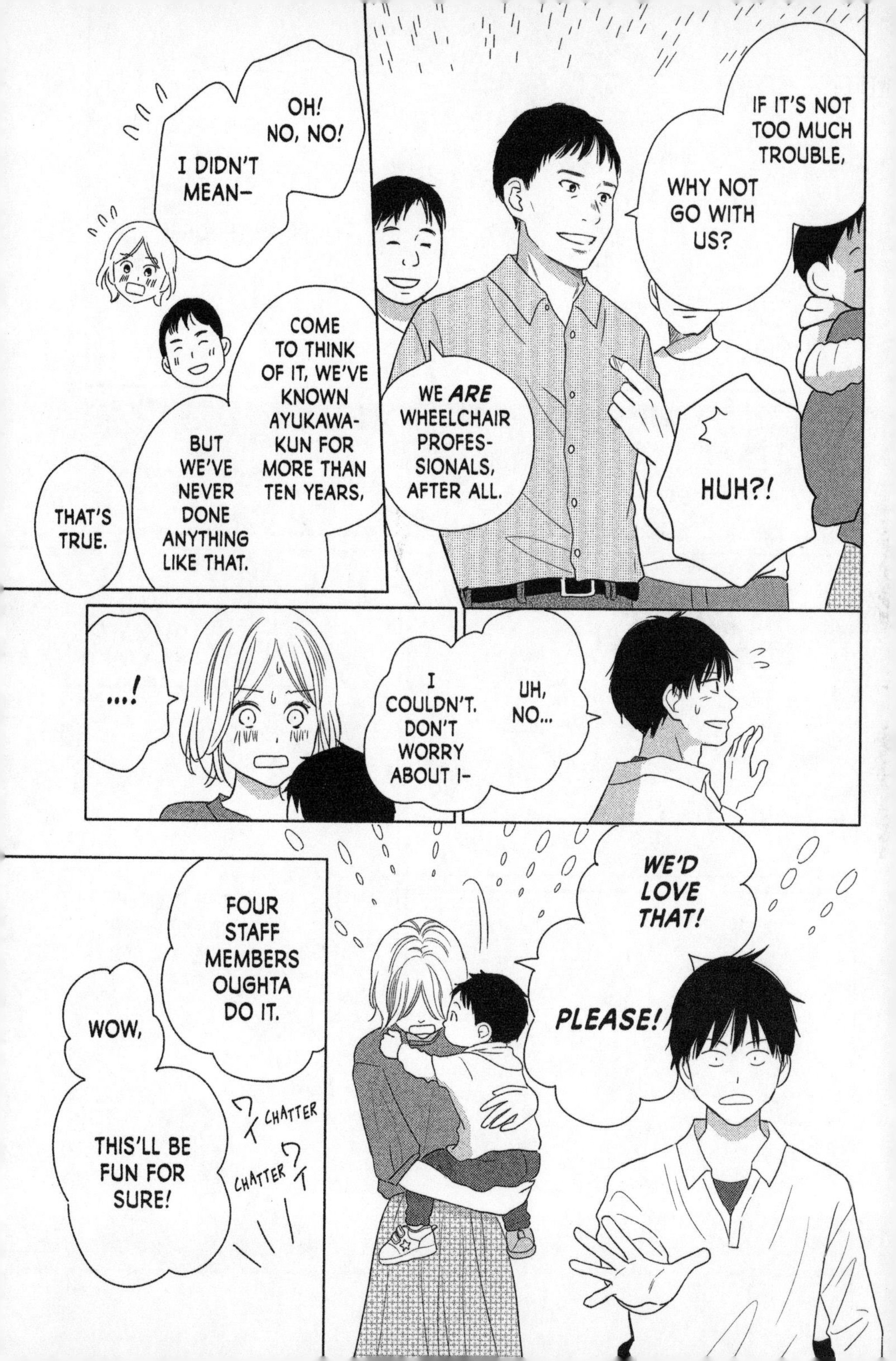
IF IT'S NOT TOO MUCH TROUBLE,
WHY NOT GO WITH US?
HUH?!
WE *ARE* WHEELCHAIR PROFES-SIONALS, AFTER ALL.
OH! NO, NO!
I DIDN'T MEAN—
COME TO THINK OF IT, WE'VE KNOWN AYUKAWA-KUN FOR MORE THAN TEN YEARS,
BUT WE'VE NEVER DONE ANYTHING LIKE THAT.
THAT'S TRUE.
UH, NO...
I COULDN'T. DON'T WORRY ABOUT I—
...!
WE'D LOVE THAT!
PLEASE!
FOUR STAFF MEMBERS OUGHTA DO IT.
WOW,
THIS'LL BE FUN FOR SURE!
CHATTER
CHATTER

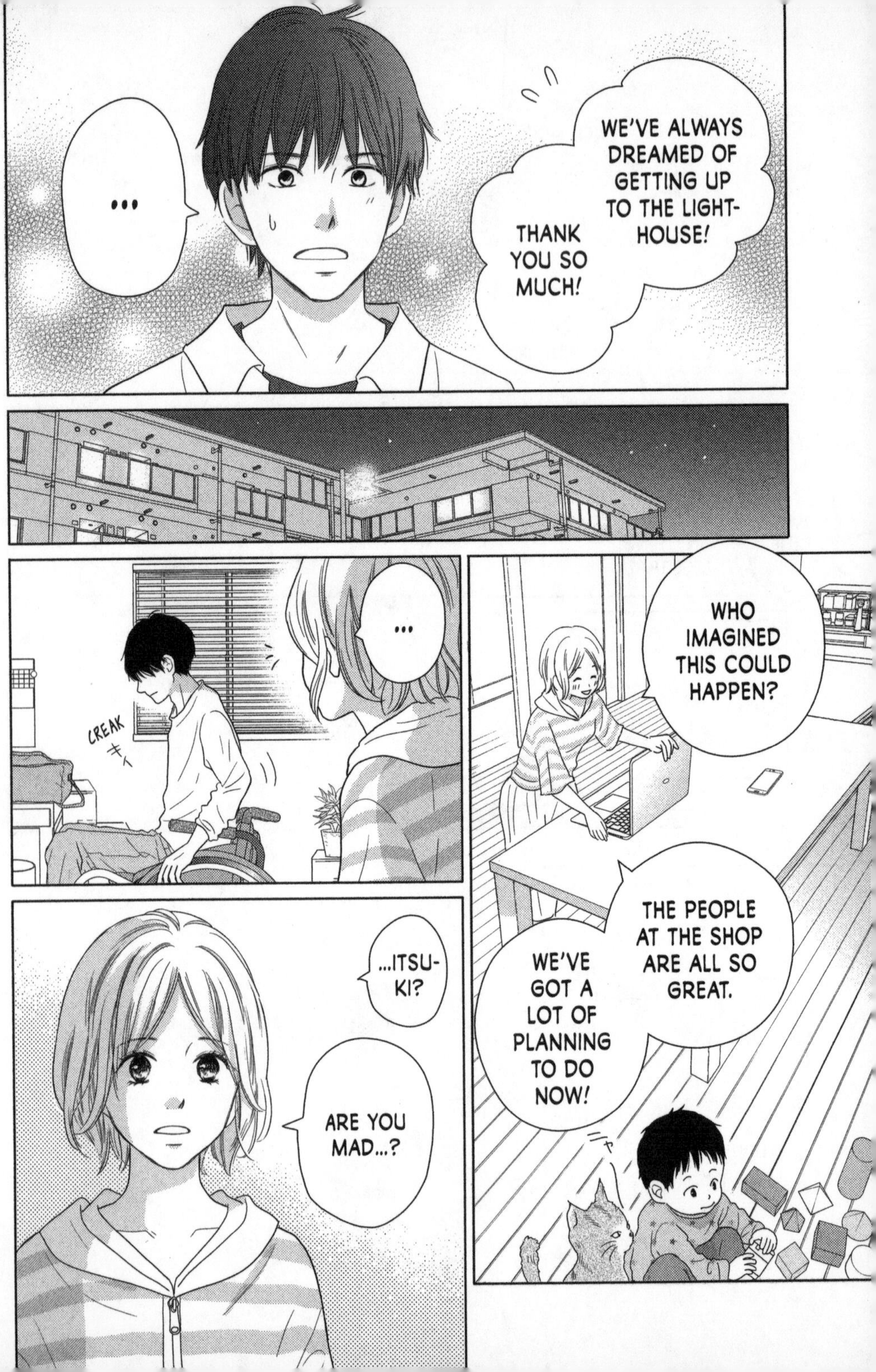
WE'VE ALWAYS DREAMED OF GETTING UP TO THE LIGHTHOUSE!
THANK YOU SO MUCH!
...
WHO IMAGINED THIS COULD HAPPEN?
THE PEOPLE AT THE SHOP ARE ALL SO GREAT.
WE'VE GOT A LOT OF PLANNING TO DO NOW!
ニャ
...
CREAK
キィ
...ITSUKI?
ARE YOU MAD...?

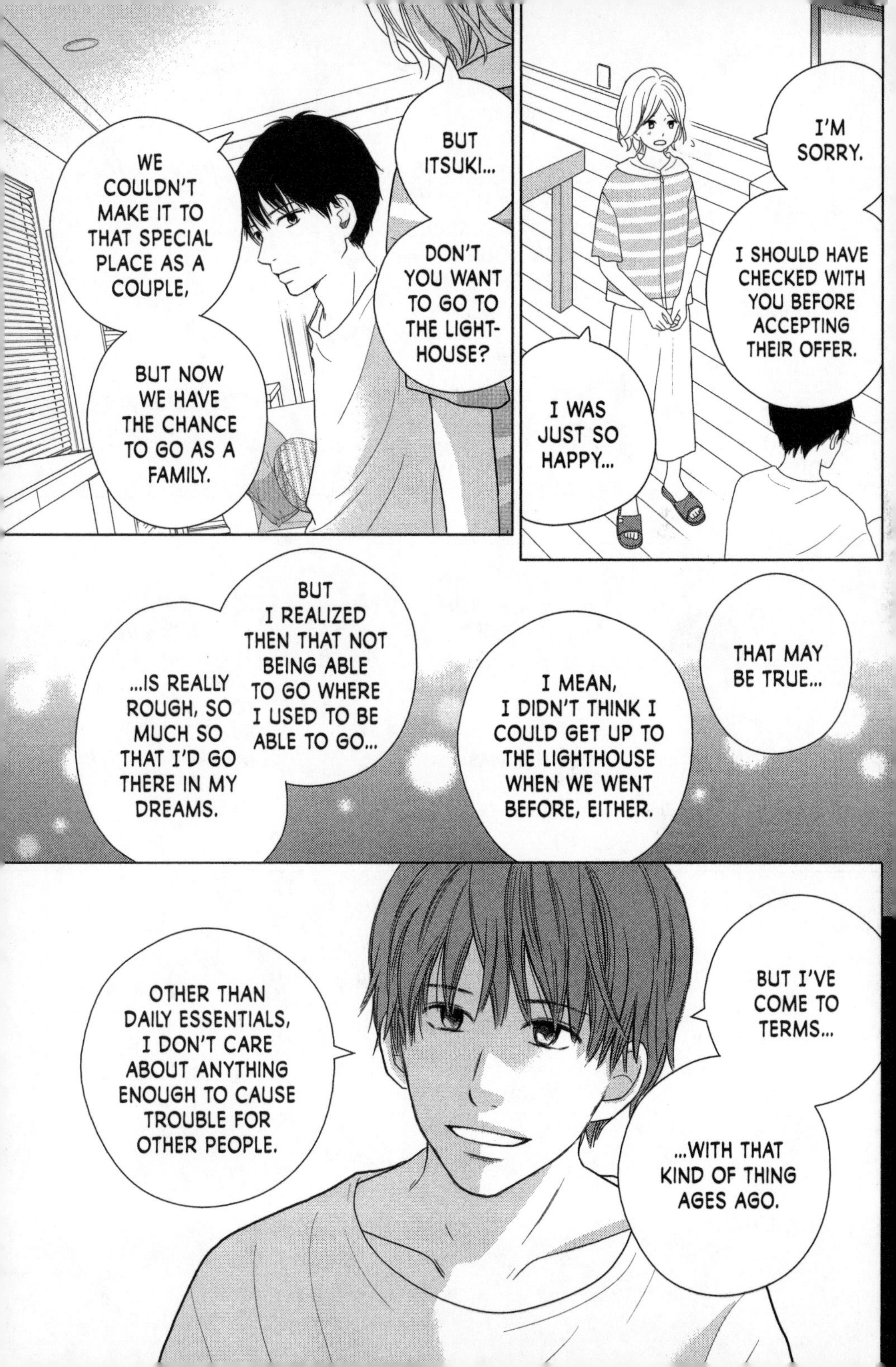
I'M SORRY.
I SHOULD HAVE CHECKED WITH YOU BEFORE ACCEPTING THEIR OFFER.
I WAS JUST SO HAPPY...
BUT ITSUKI...
DON'T YOU WANT TO GO TO THE LIGHT-HOUSE?
WE COULDN'T MAKE IT TO THAT SPECIAL PLACE AS A COUPLE,
BUT NOW WE HAVE THE CHANCE TO GO AS A FAMILY.
THAT MAY BE TRUE...
I MEAN, I DIDN'T THINK I COULD GET UP TO THE LIGHTHOUSE WHEN WE WENT BEFORE, EITHER.
BUT I REALIZED THEN THAT NOT BEING ABLE TO GO WHERE I USED TO BE ABLE TO GO...
...IS REALLY ROUGH, SO MUCH SO THAT I'D GO THERE IN MY DREAMS.
BUT I'VE COME TO TERMS...
...WITH THAT KIND OF THING AGES AGO.
OTHER THAN DAILY ESSENTIALS, I DON'T CARE ABOUT ANYTHING ENOUGH TO CAUSE TROUBLE FOR OTHER PEOPLE.

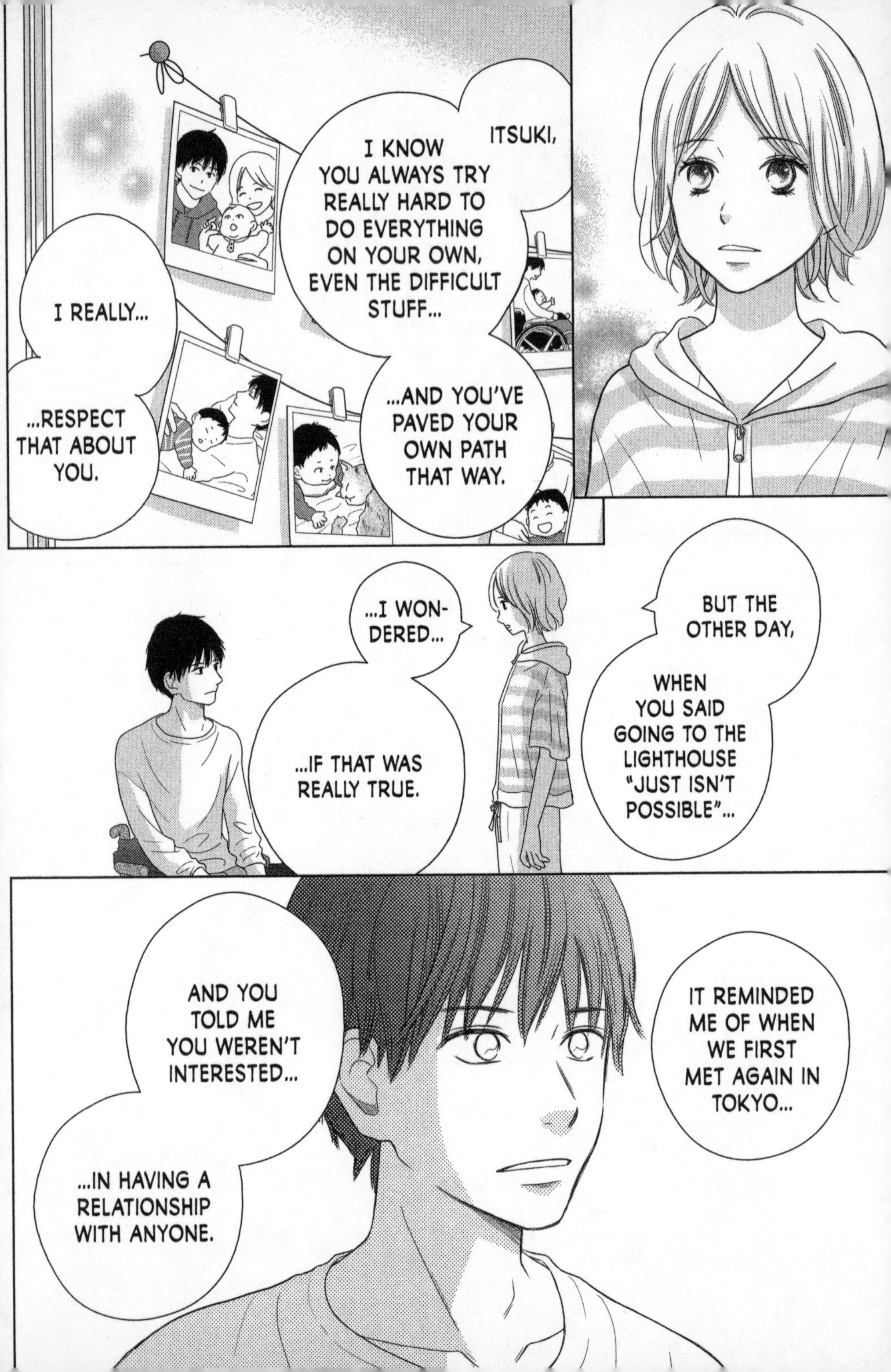
ITSUKI,
I KNOW YOU ALWAYS TRY REALLY HARD TO DO EVERYTHING ON YOUR OWN, EVEN THE DIFFICULT STUFF...
...AND YOU'VE PAVED YOUR OWN PATH THAT WAY.
I REALLY...
...RESPECT THAT ABOUT YOU.
BUT THE OTHER DAY,
WHEN YOU SAID GOING TO THE LIGHTHOUSE "JUST ISN'T POSSIBLE"...
...I WON-DERED...
...IF THAT WAS REALLY TRUE.
IT REMINDED ME OF WHEN WE FIRST MET AGAIN IN TOKYO...
AND YOU TOLD ME YOU WEREN'T INTERESTED...
...IN HAVING A RELATIONSHIP WITH ANYONE.

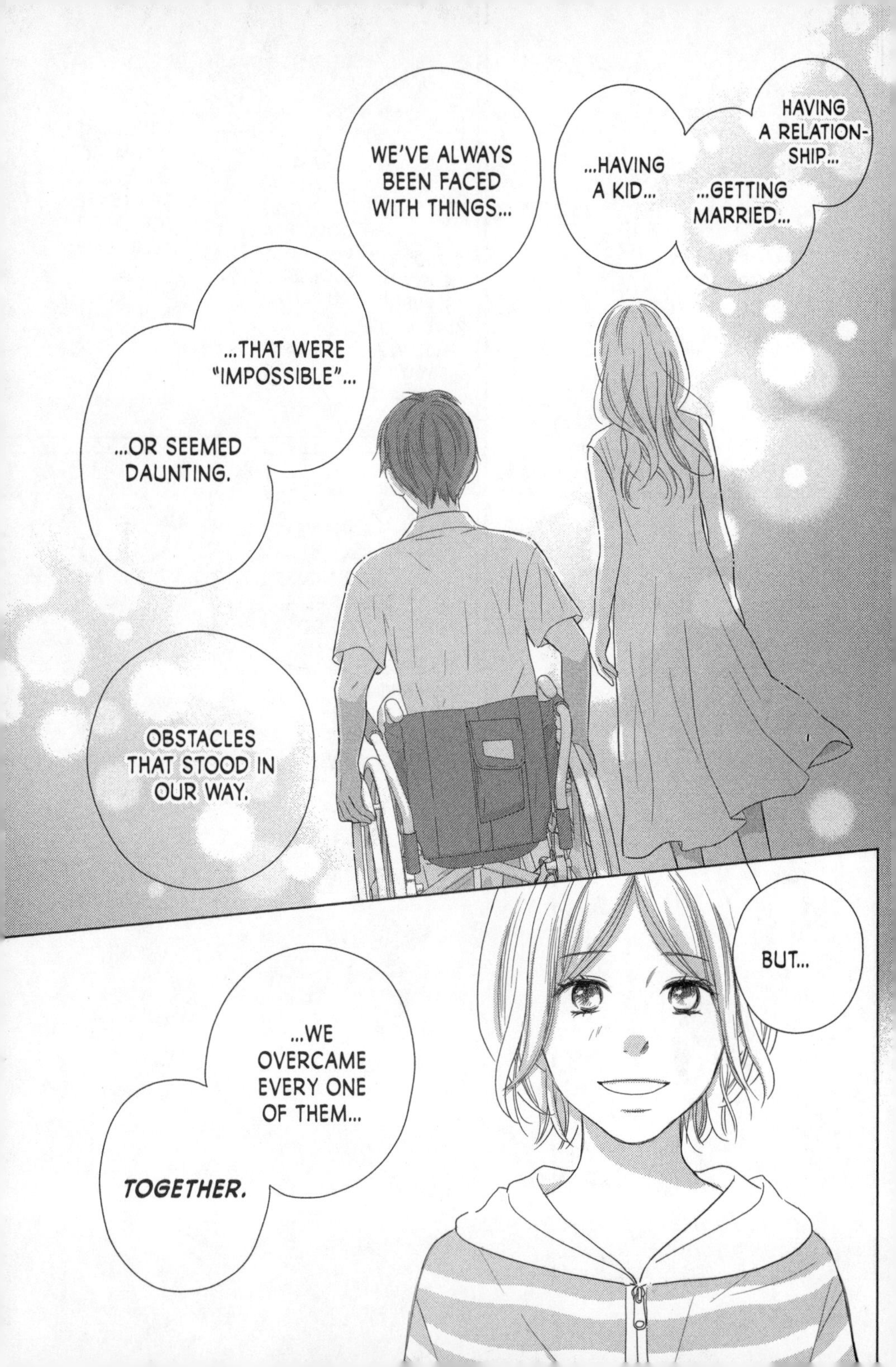
HAVING A RELATION-SHIP...
...GETTING MARRIED...
...HAVING A KID...
WE'VE ALWAYS BEEN FACED WITH THINGS...
...THAT WERE "IMPOSSIBLE"...
...OR SEEMED DAUNTING.
OBSTACLES THAT STOOD IN OUR WAY.
BUT...
...WE OVERCAME EVERY ONE OF THEM...
TOGETHER.

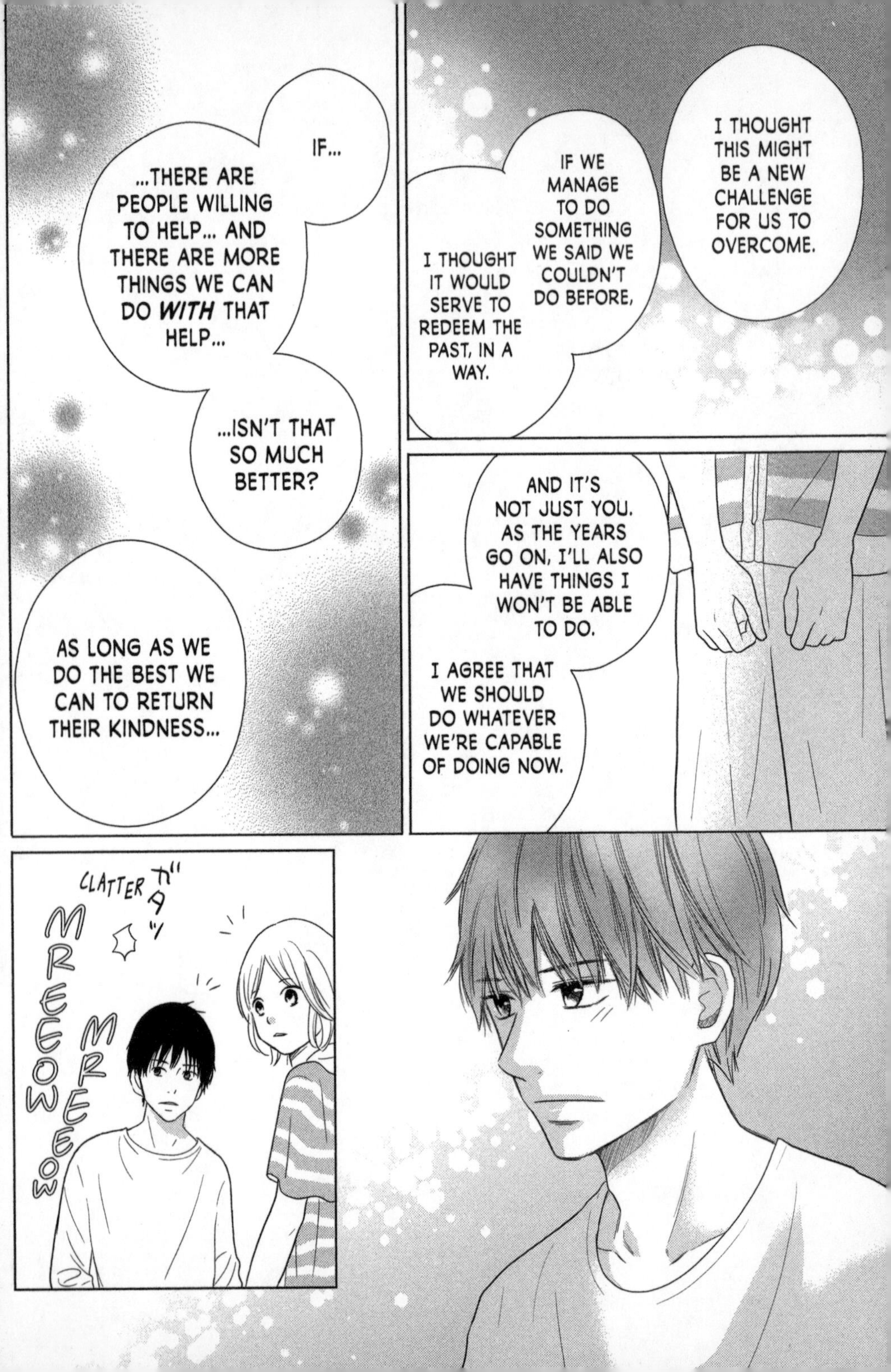
I THOUGHT THIS MIGHT BE A NEW CHALLENGE FOR US TO OVERCOME.
IF WE MANAGE TO DO SOMETHING WE SAID WE COULDN'T DO BEFORE,
I THOUGHT IT WOULD SERVE TO REDEEM THE PAST, IN A WAY.
AND IT'S NOT JUST YOU. AS THE YEARS GO ON, I'LL ALSO HAVE THINGS I WON'T BE ABLE TO DO.
I AGREE THAT WE SHOULD DO WHATEVER WE'RE CAPABLE OF DOING NOW.
IF...
...THERE ARE PEOPLE WILLING TO HELP... AND THERE ARE MORE THINGS WE CAN DO *WITH* THAT HELP...
...ISN'T THAT SO MUCH BETTER?
AS LONG AS WE DO THE BEST WE CAN TO RETURN THEIR KINDNESS...
CLATTER ガタッ
MREEOW
MREEOW

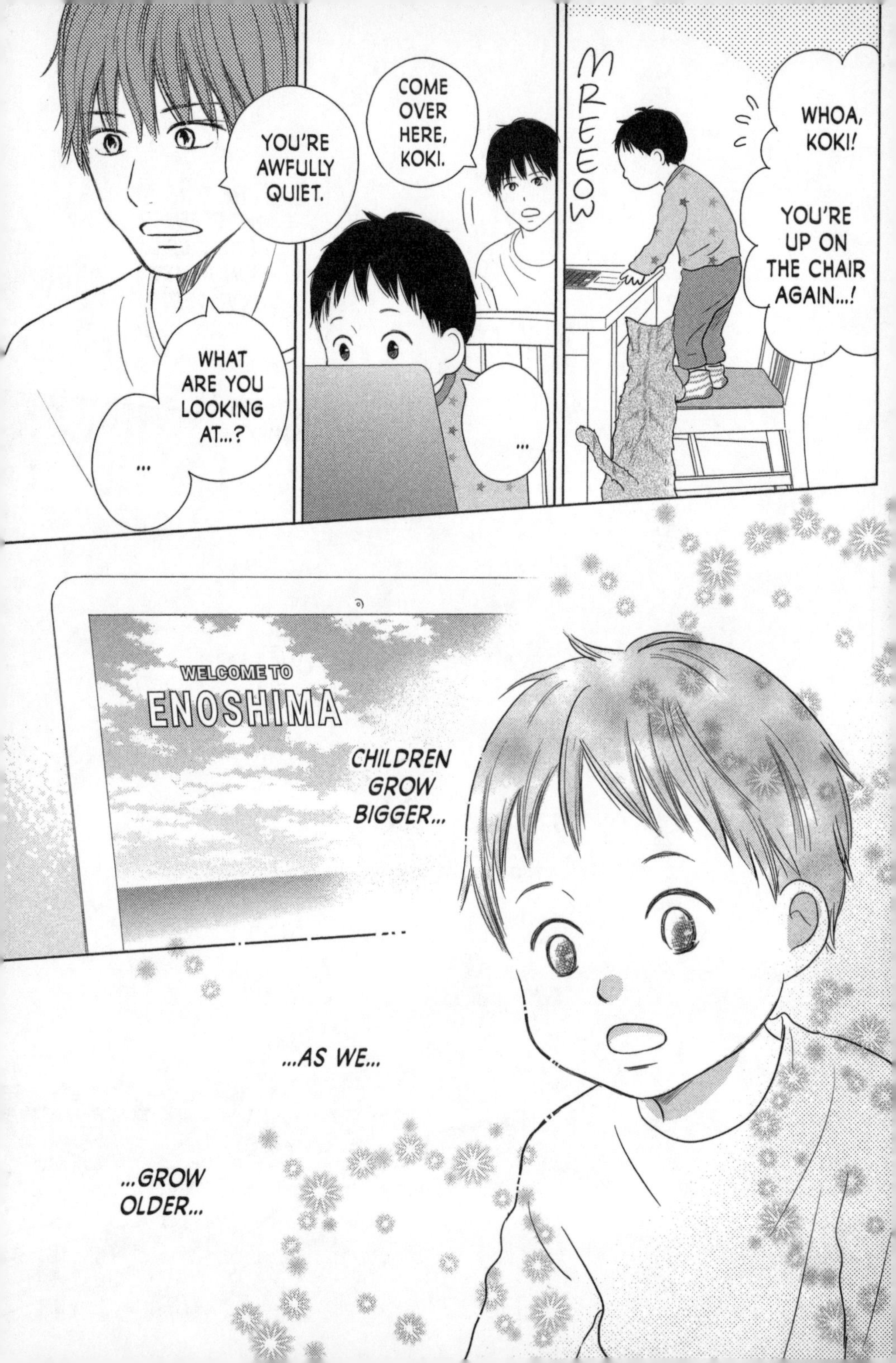
WHOA, KOKI!
YOU'RE UP ON THE CHAIR AGAIN...!
MREEOW
COME OVER HERE, KOKI.
...
YOU'RE AWFULLY QUIET.
WHAT ARE YOU LOOKING AT...?
...
WELCOME TO ENOSHIMA
CHILDREN GROW BIGGER...
...AS WE...
...GROW OLDER...

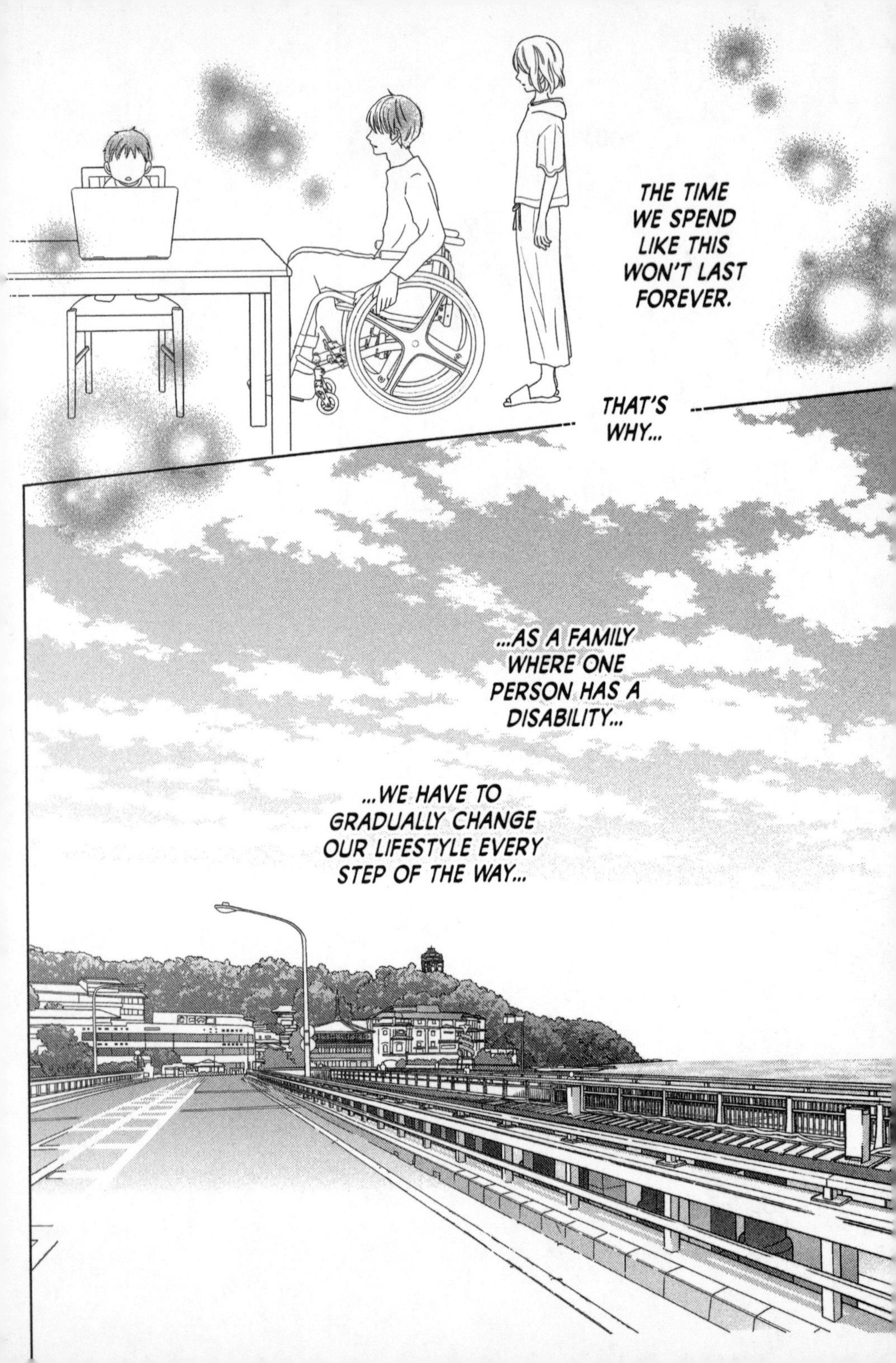
THE TIME WE SPEND LIKE THIS WON'T LAST FOREVER.
THAT'S WHY...
...AS A FAMILY WHERE ONE PERSON HAS A DISABILITY...
...WE HAVE TO GRADUALLY CHANGE OUR LIFESTYLE EVERY STEP OF THE WAY...

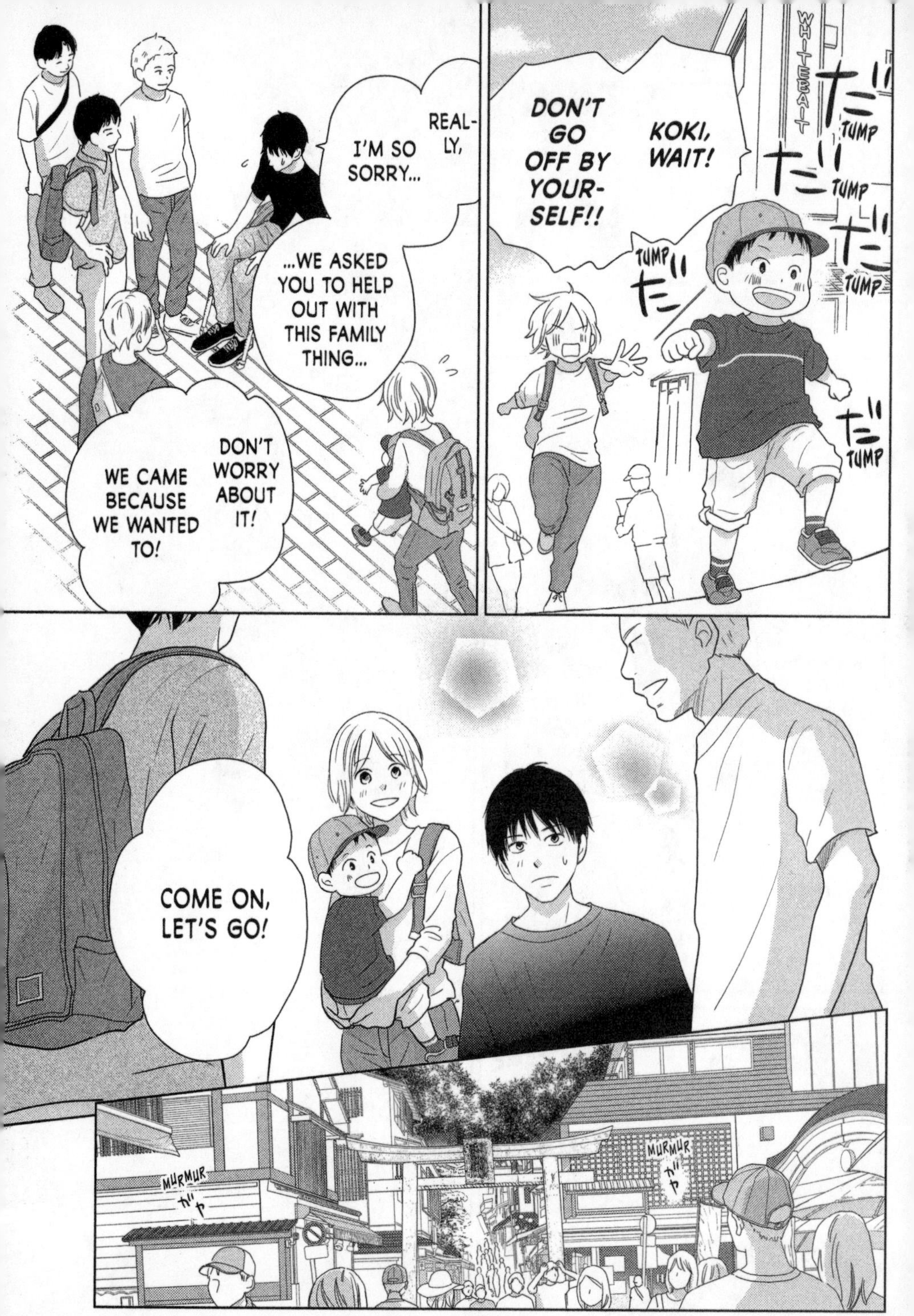
WHITEBAIT
TUMP
TUMP
TUMP
KOKI, WAIT!
DON'T GO OFF BY YOURSELF!!
TUMP
TUMP
REALLY, I'M SO SORRY...
...WE ASKED YOU TO HELP OUT WITH THIS FAMILY THING...
DON'T WORRY ABOUT IT!
WE CAME BECAUSE WE WANTED TO!
COME ON, LET'S GO!
MURMUR
MURMUR

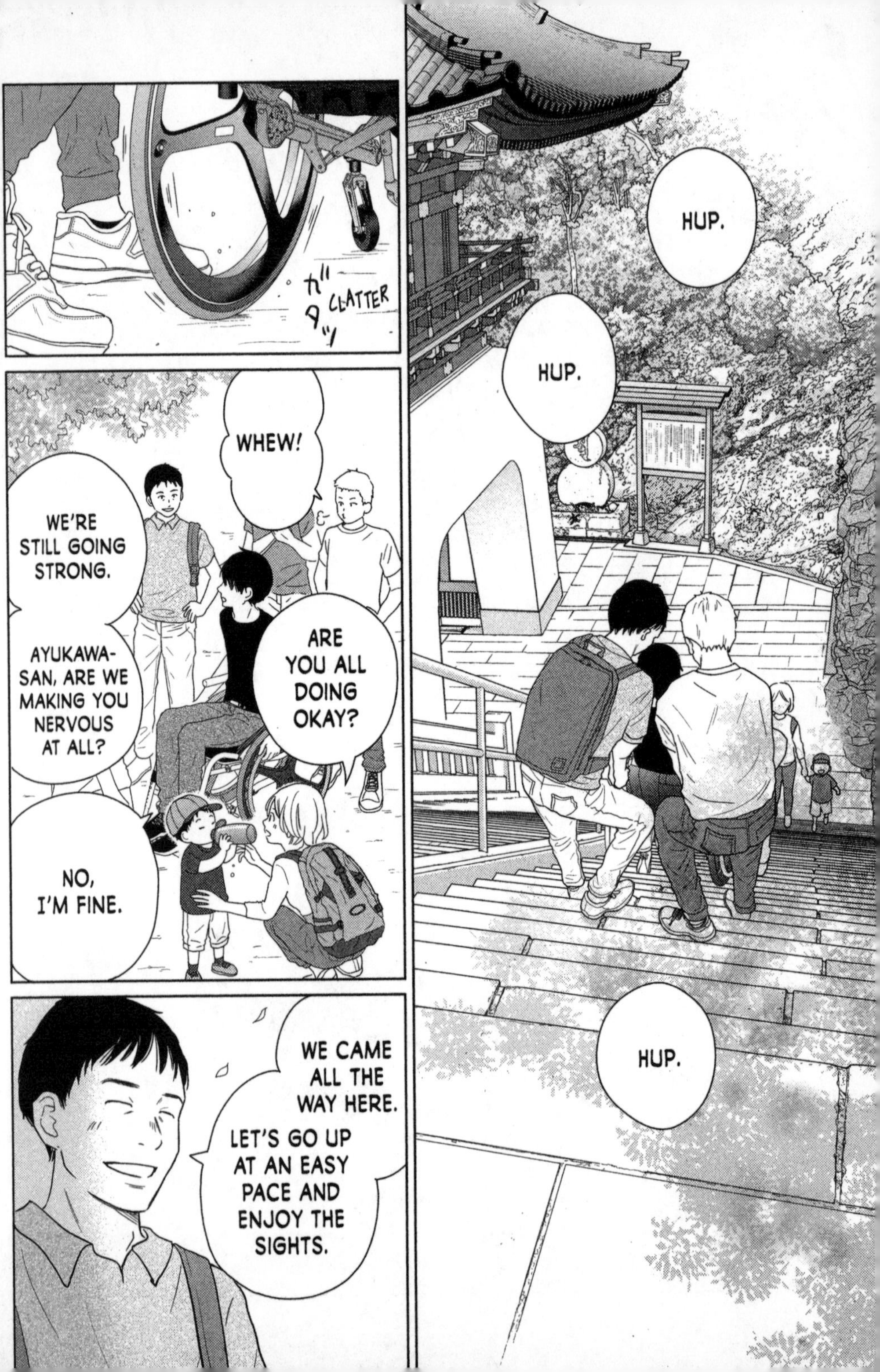
HUP.
HUP.
HUP.
ガタッ
CLATTER
WHEW!
WE'RE STILL GOING STRONG.
ARE YOU ALL DOING OKAY?
AYUKAWA-SAN, ARE WE MAKING YOU NERVOUS AT ALL?
NO, I'M FINE.
WE CAME ALL THE WAY HERE.
LET'S GO UP AT AN EASY PACE AND ENJOY THE SIGHTS.

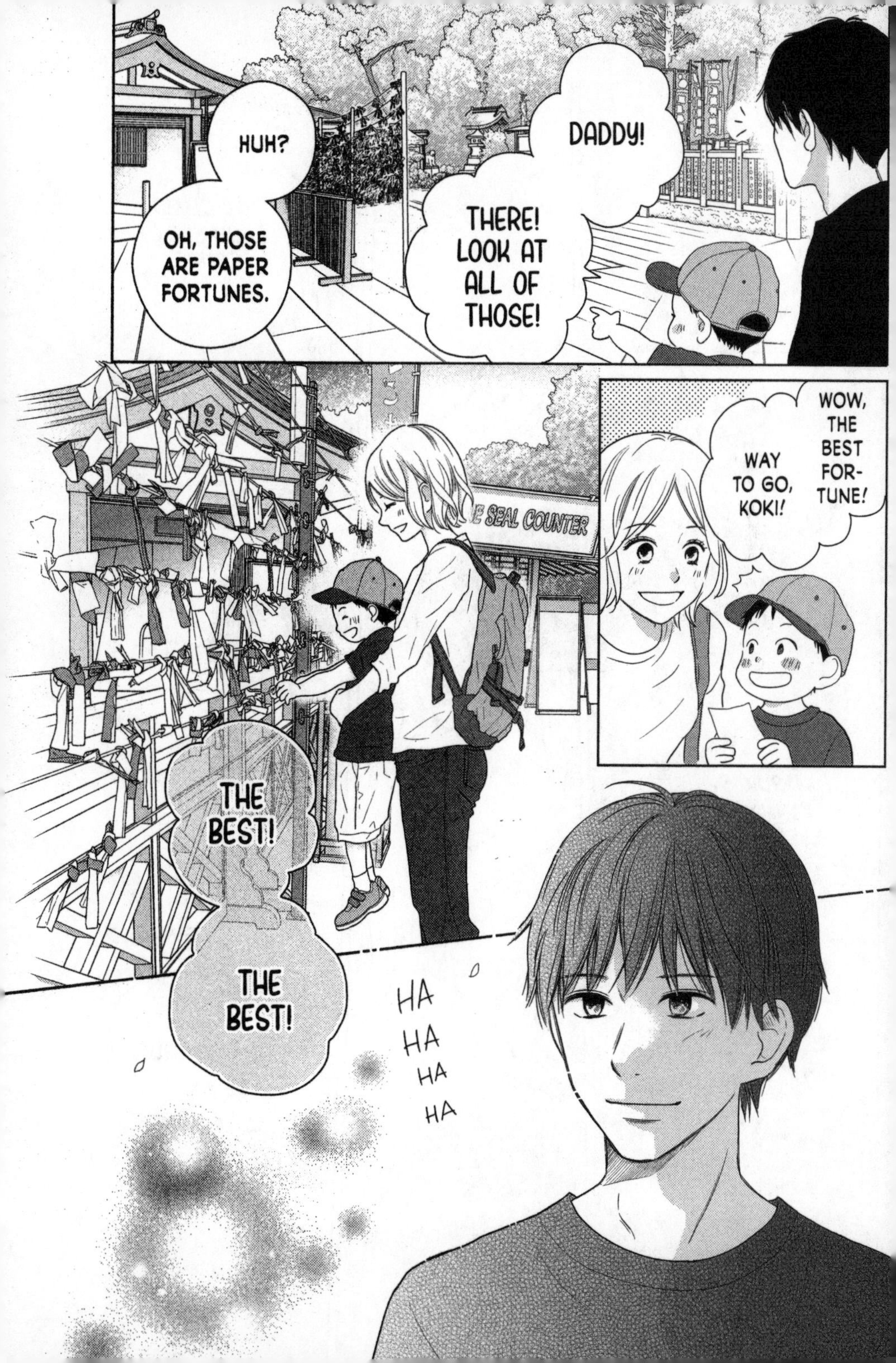
DADDY!
THERE! LOOK AT ALL OF THOSE!
HUH?
OH, THOSE ARE PAPER FORTUNES.
WOW, THE BEST FOR-TUNE!
WAY TO GO, KOKI!
SEAL COUNTER
THE BEST!
THE BEST!
HA HA HA HA

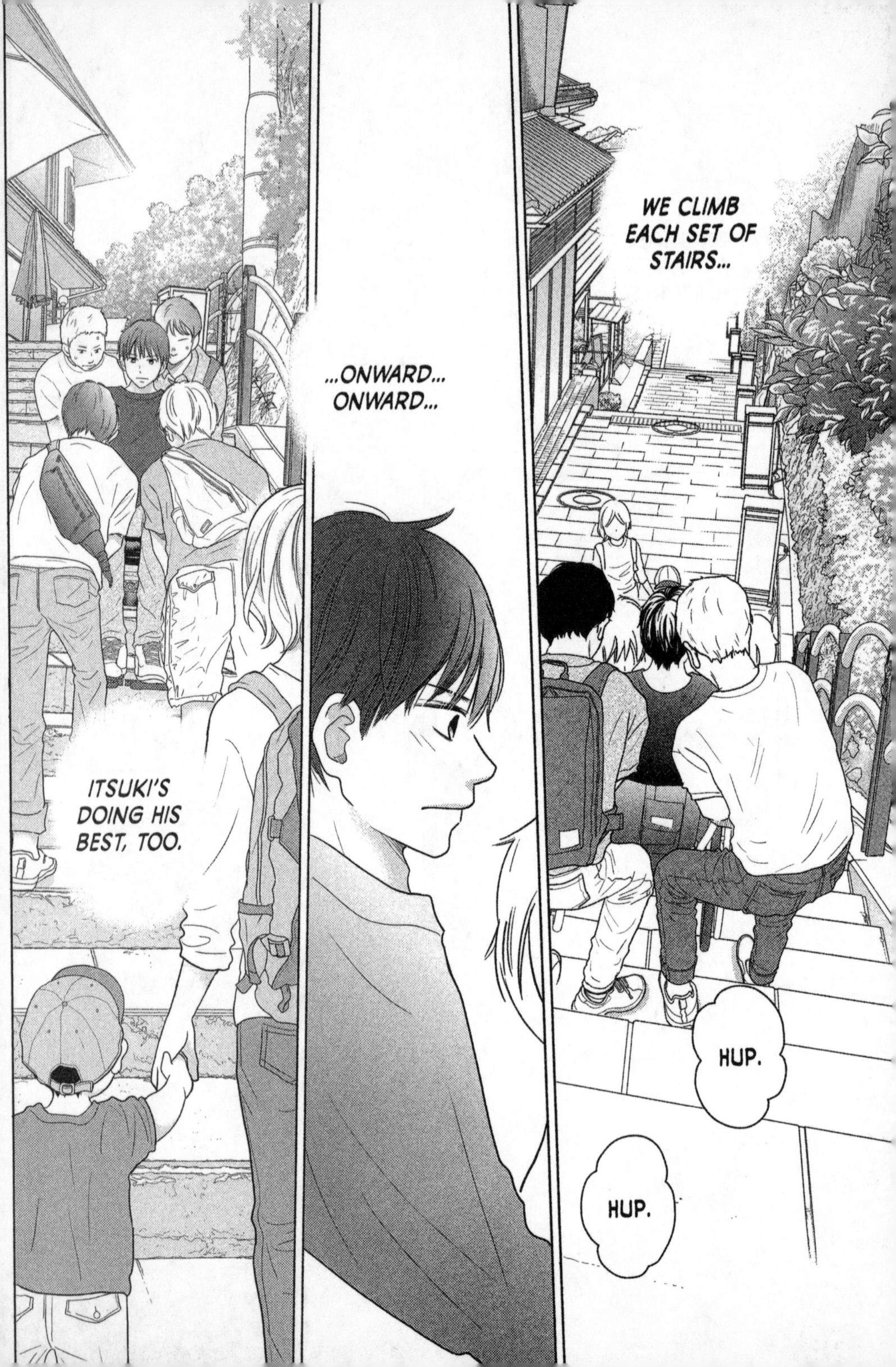
WE CLIMB EACH SET OF STAIRS...
HUP.
HUP.
...ONWARD... ONWARD...
ITSUKI'S DOING HIS BEST, TOO.

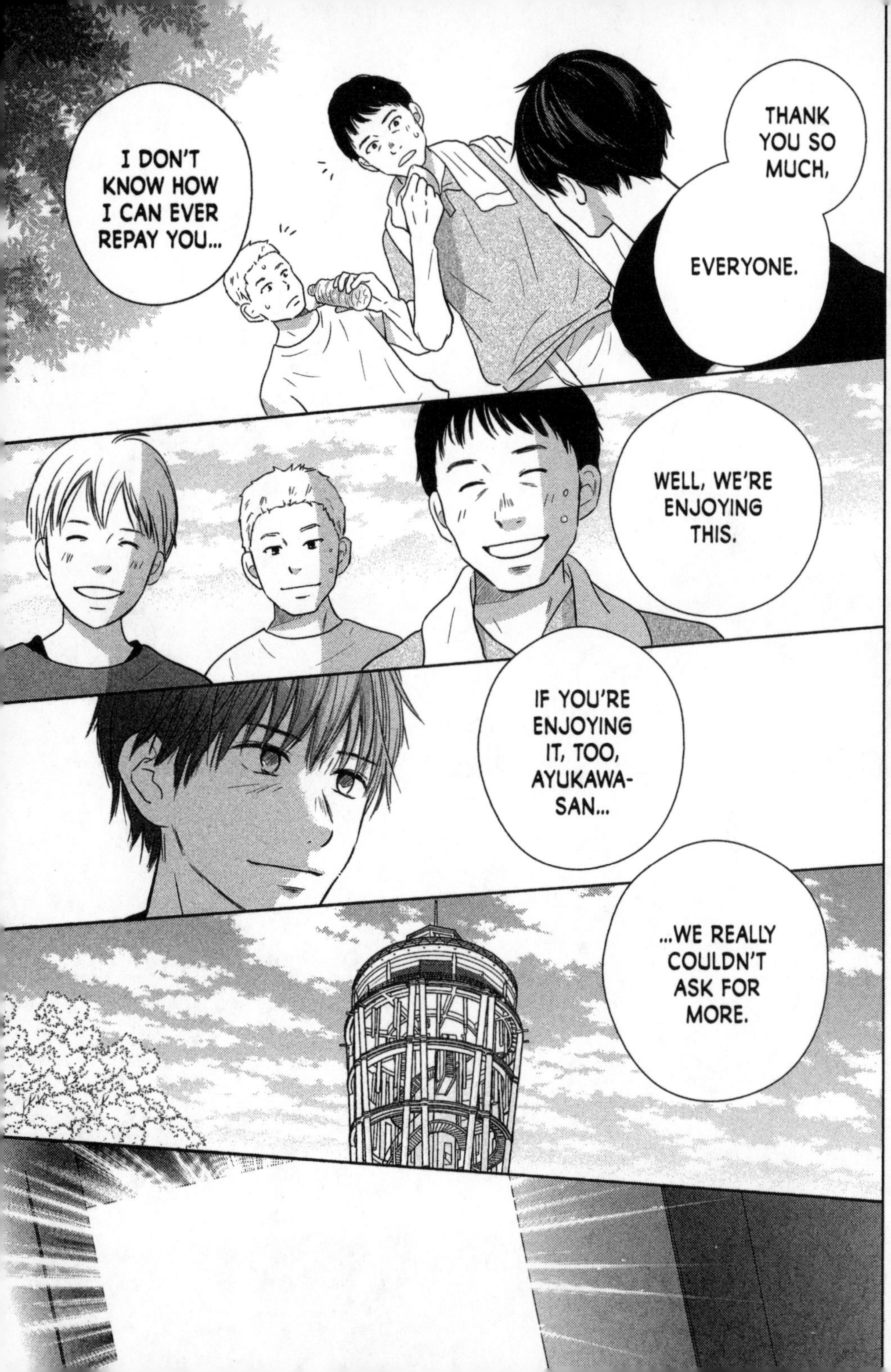
THANK YOU SO MUCH,
EVERYONE.
I DON'T KNOW HOW I CAN EVER REPAY YOU...
WELL, WE'RE ENJOYING THIS.
IF YOU'RE ENJOYING IT, TOO, AYUKAWA-SAN...
...WE REALLY COULDN'T ASK FOR MORE.

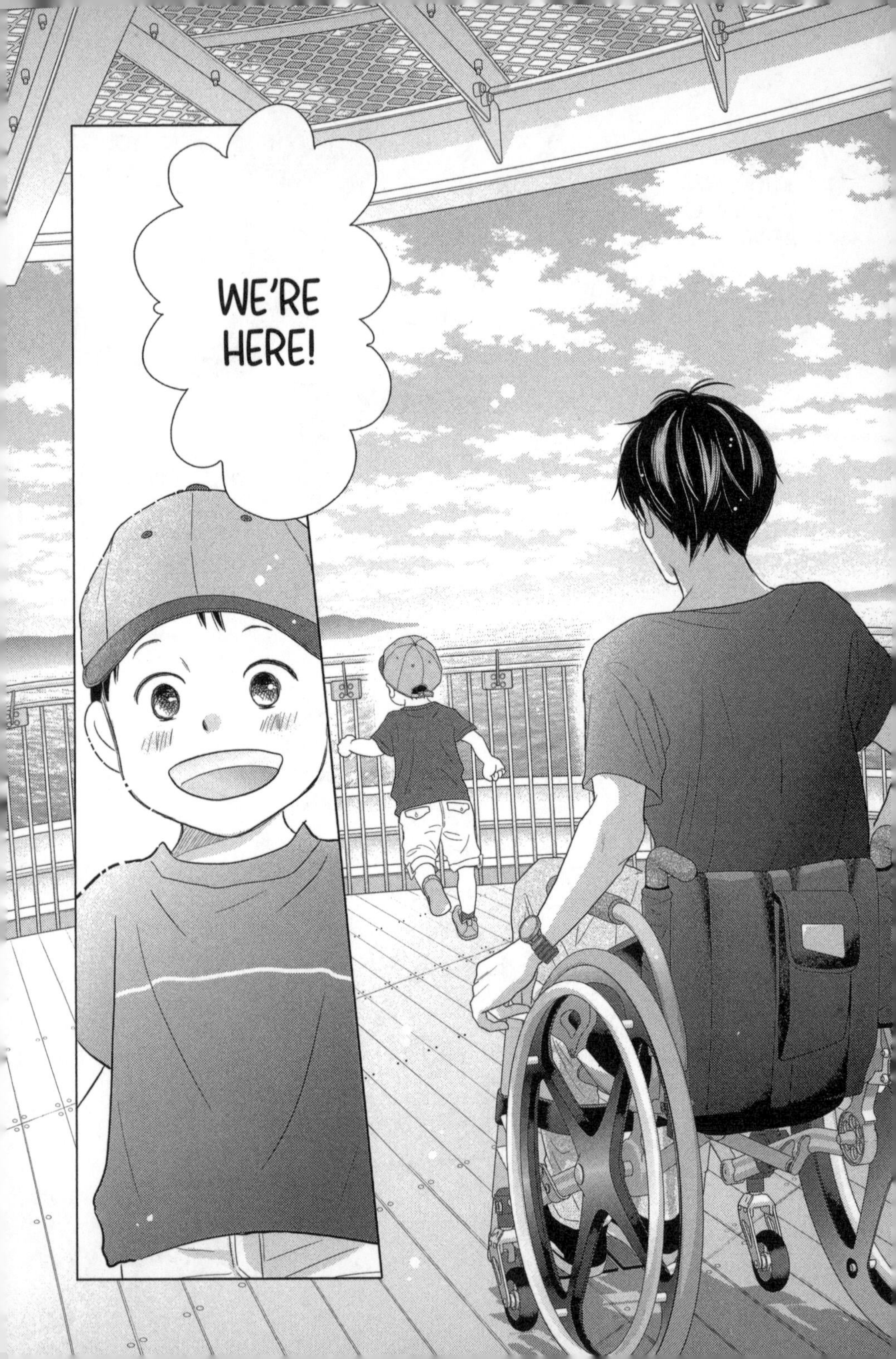
WE'RE HERE!

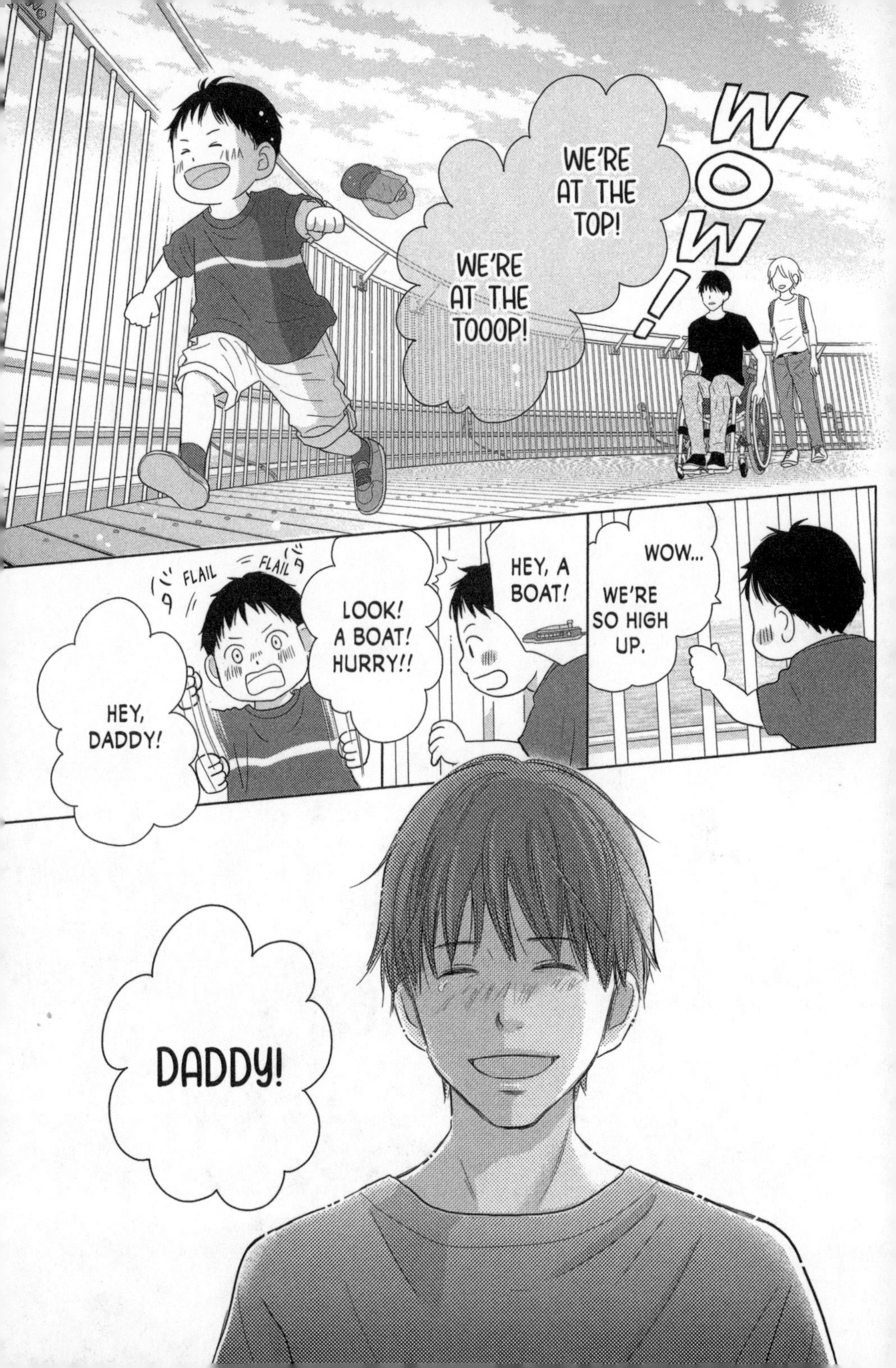
WOW!!
WE'RE AT THE TOP!
WE'RE AT THE TOOOP!
WOW... WE'RE SO HIGH UP.
HEY, A BOAT!
FLAIL FLAIL
LOOK! A BOAT! HURRY!!
HEY, DADDY!
DADDY!

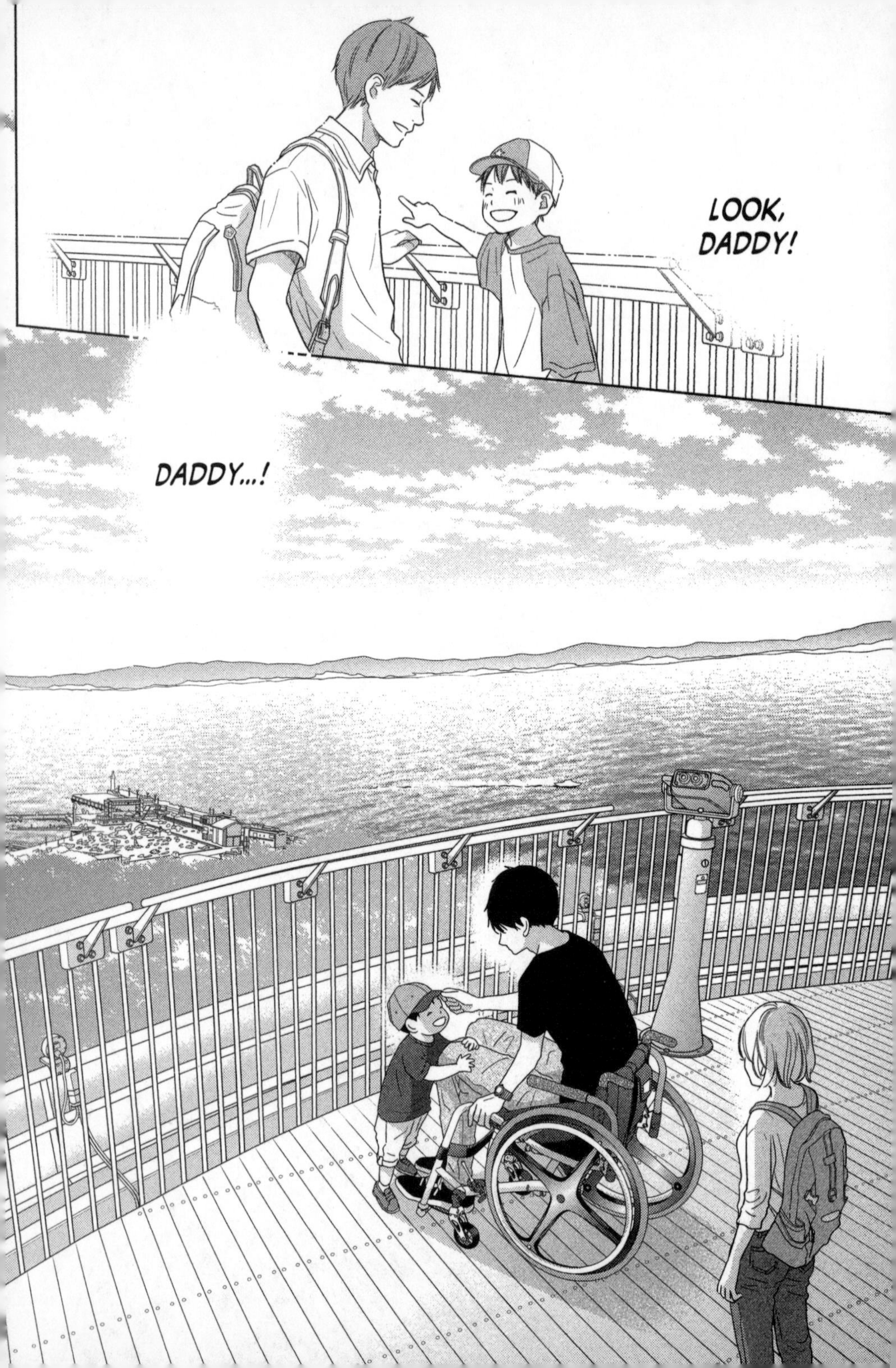
LOOK, DADDY!
DADDY...!

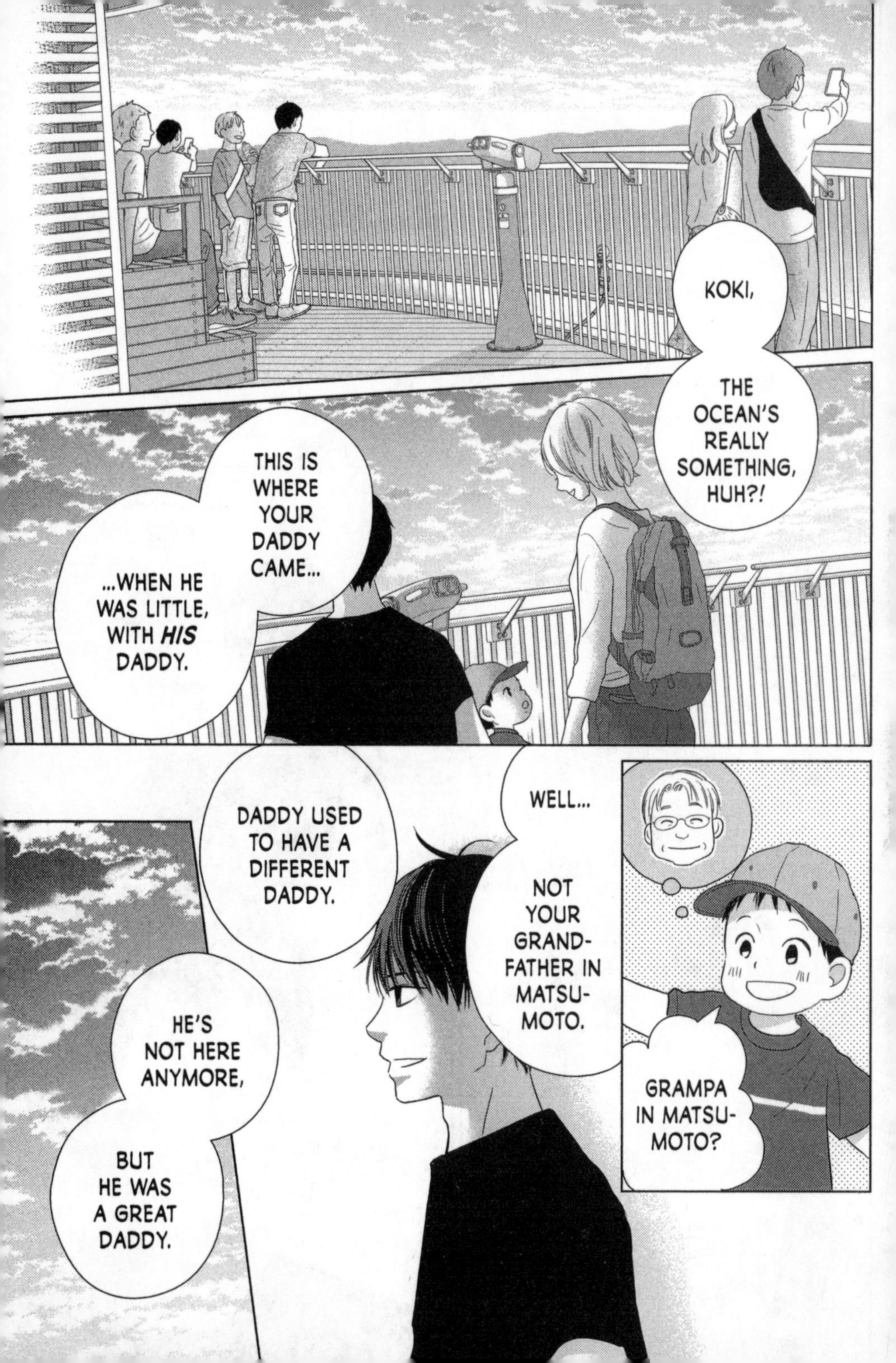
KOKI,
THE OCEAN'S REALLY SOMETHING, HUH?!
THIS IS WHERE YOUR DADDY CAME...
...WHEN HE WAS LITTLE, WITH *HIS* DADDY.
GRAMPA IN MATSU-MOTO?
WELL...
NOT YOUR GRAND-FATHER IN MATSU-MOTO.
DADDY USED TO HAVE A DIFFERENT DADDY.
HE'S NOT HERE ANYMORE,
BUT HE WAS A GREAT DADDY.

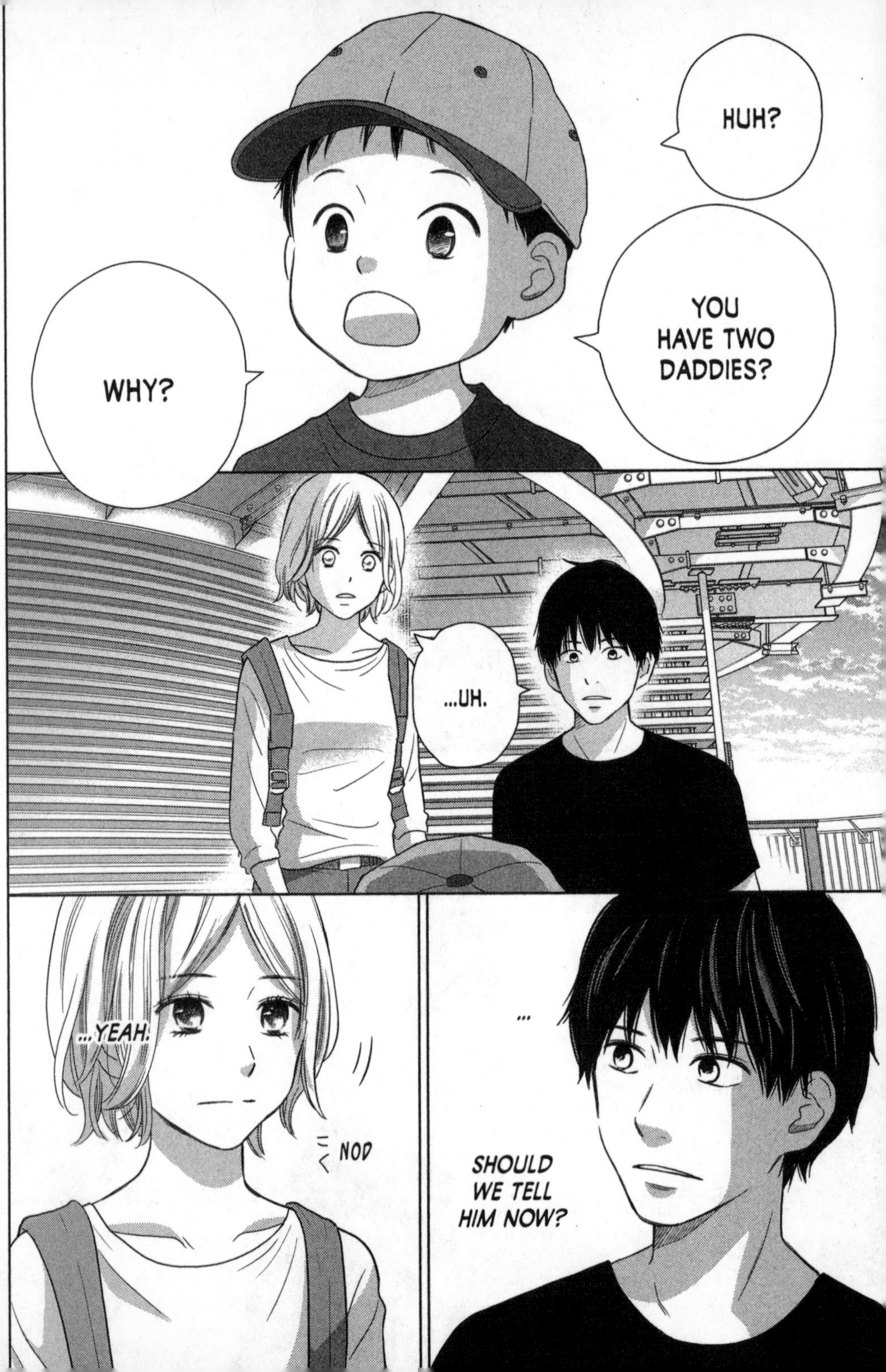
HUH?
YOU HAVE TWO DADDIES?
WHY?
...UH.
...
SHOULD WE TELL HIM NOW?
...YEAH.
NOD

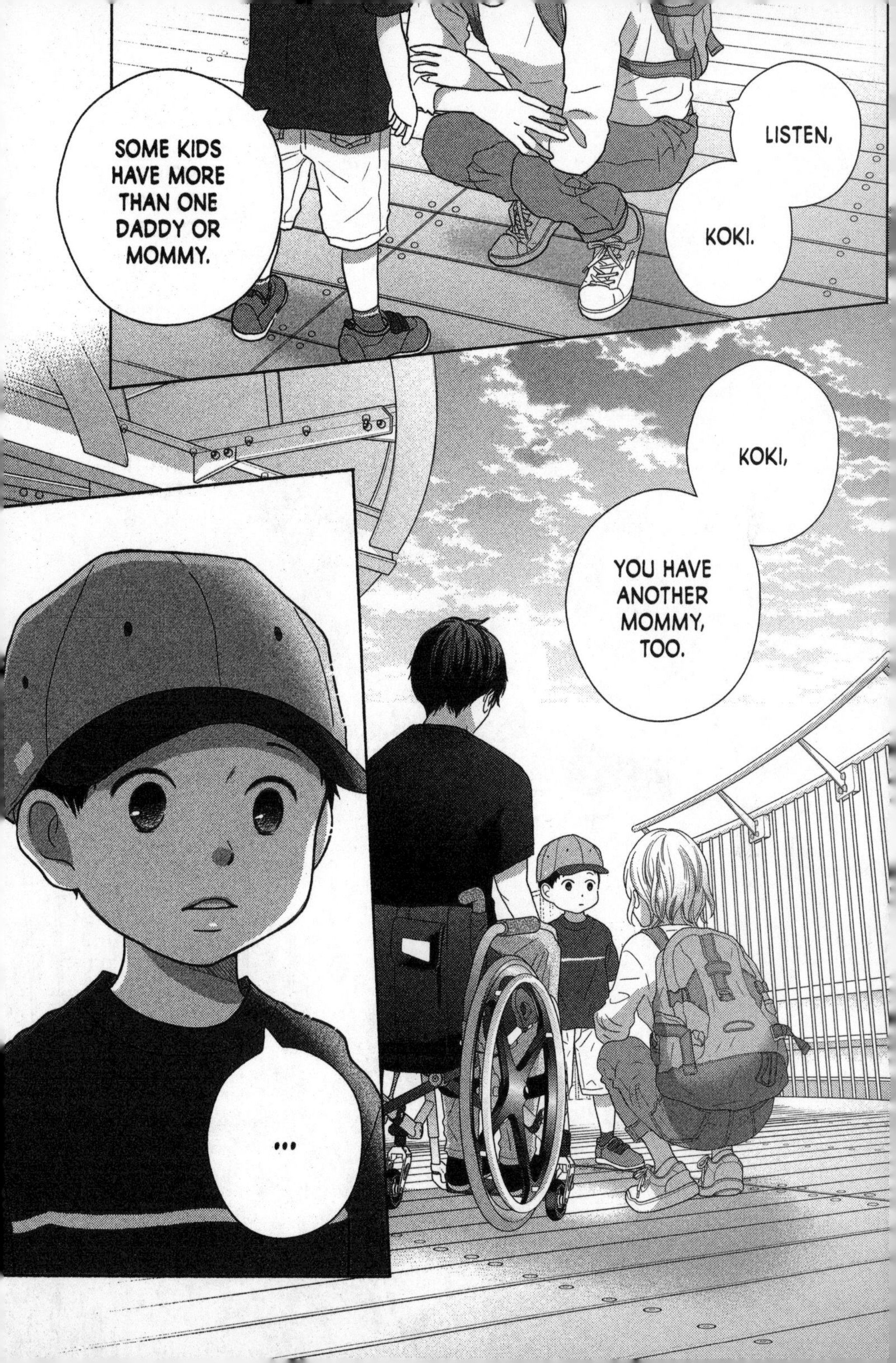
LISTEN,
KOKI.
SOME KIDS HAVE MORE THAN ONE DADDY OR MOMMY.
KOKI,
YOU HAVE ANOTHER MOMMY, TOO.
...

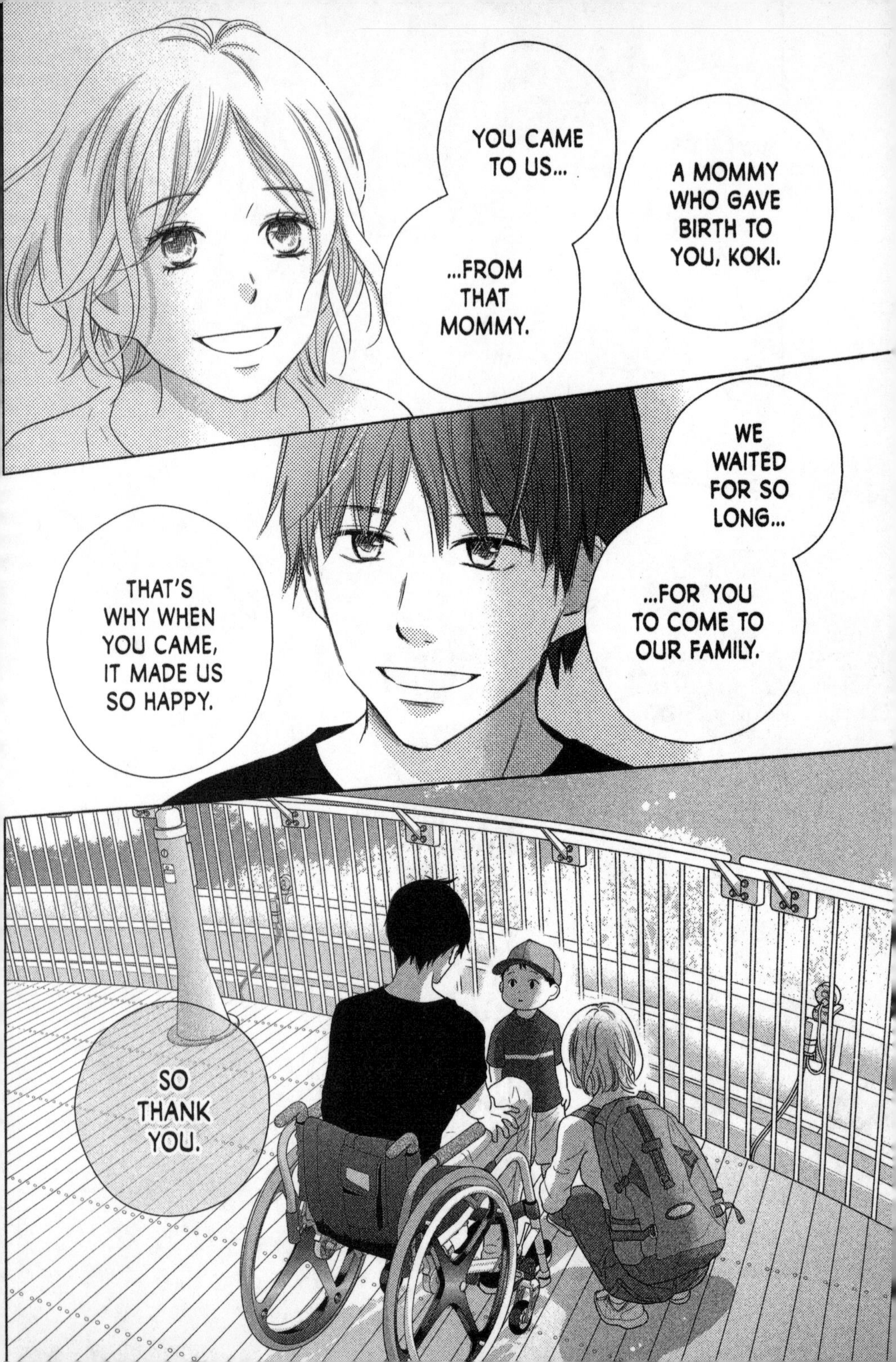
A MOMMY WHO GAVE BIRTH TO YOU, KOKI.
YOU CAME TO US...
...FROM THAT MOMMY.
WE WAITED FOR SO LONG...
...FOR YOU TO COME TO OUR FAMILY.
THAT'S WHY WHEN YOU CAME, IT MADE US SO HAPPY.
SO THANK YOU.

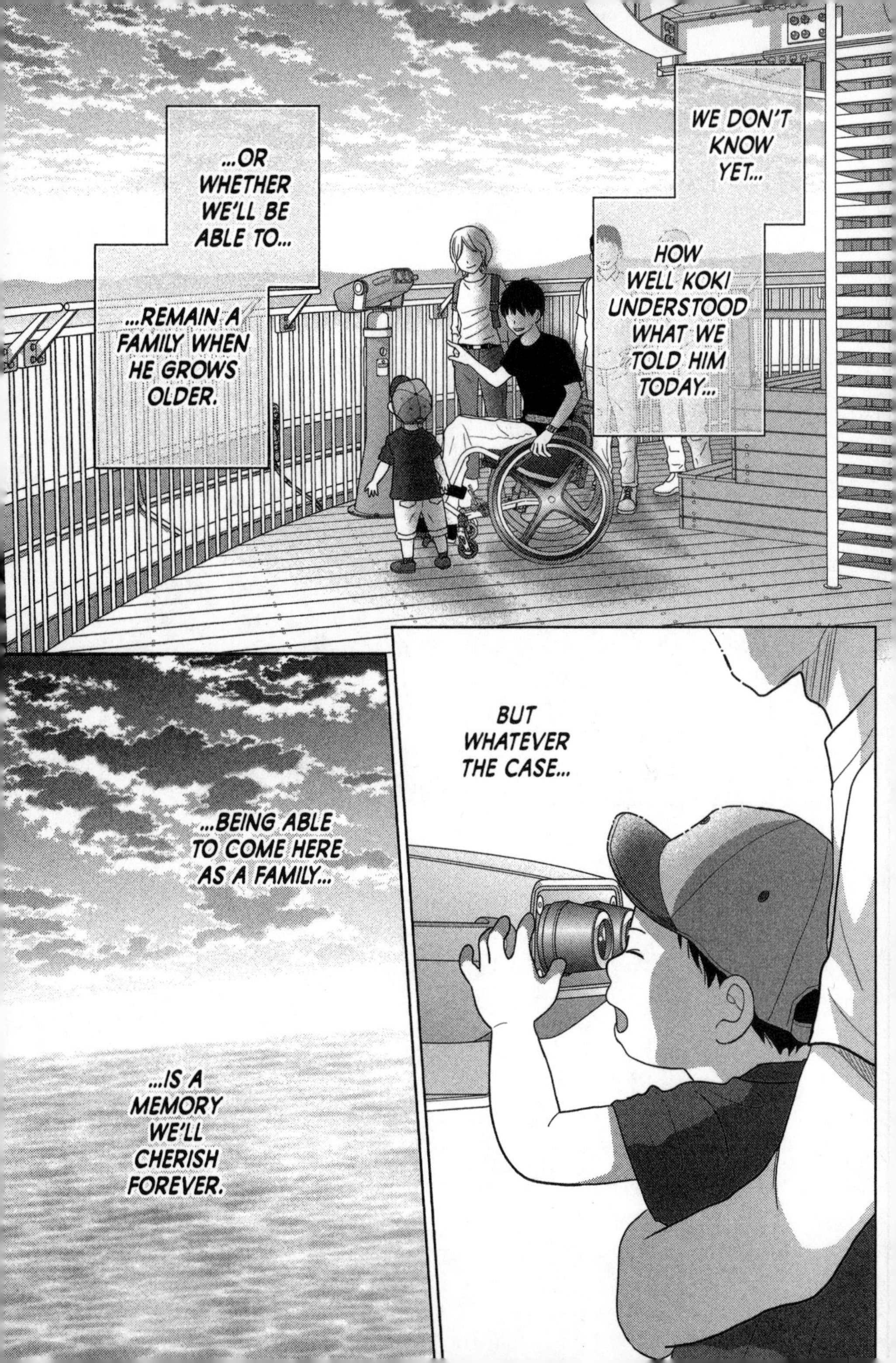
WE DON'T KNOW YET...
HOW WELL KOKI UNDERSTOOD WHAT WE TOLD HIM TODAY...
...OR WHETHER WE'LL BE ABLE TO...
...REMAIN A FAMILY WHEN HE GROWS OLDER.
BUT WHATEVER THE CASE...
...BEING ABLE TO COME HERE AS A FAMILY...
...IS A MEMORY WE'LL CHERISH FOREVER.

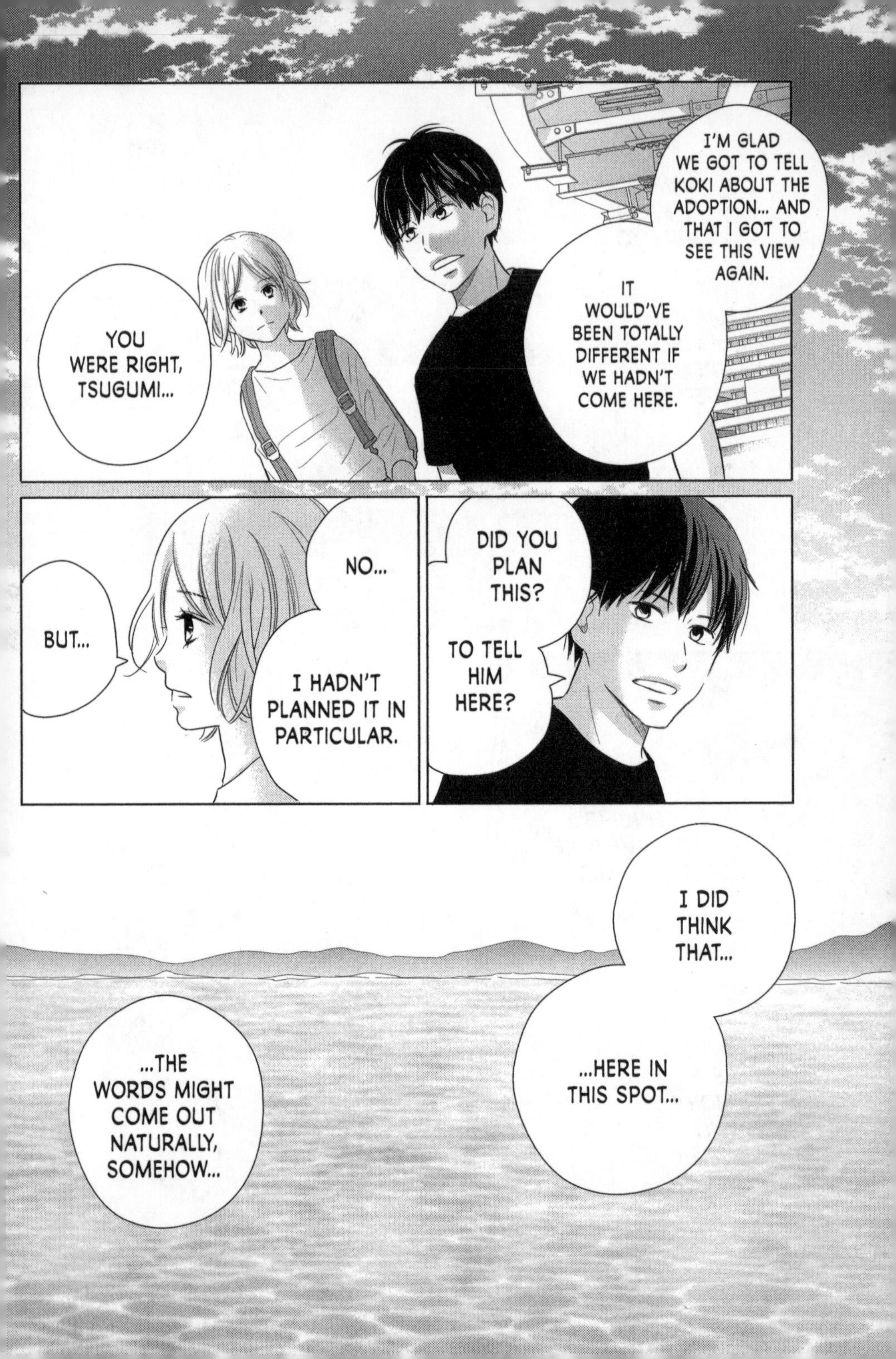
I'M GLAD WE GOT TO TELL KOKI ABOUT THE ADOPTION... AND THAT I GOT TO SEE THIS VIEW AGAIN.
IT WOULD'VE BEEN TOTALLY DIFFERENT IF WE HADN'T COME HERE.
YOU WERE RIGHT, TSUGUMI...
DID YOU PLAN THIS?
TO TELL HIM HERE?
NO...
I HADN'T PLANNED IT IN PARTICULAR.
BUT...
I DID THINK THAT...
...HERE IN THIS SPOT...
...THE WORDS MIGHT COME OUT NATURALLY, SOMEHOW...

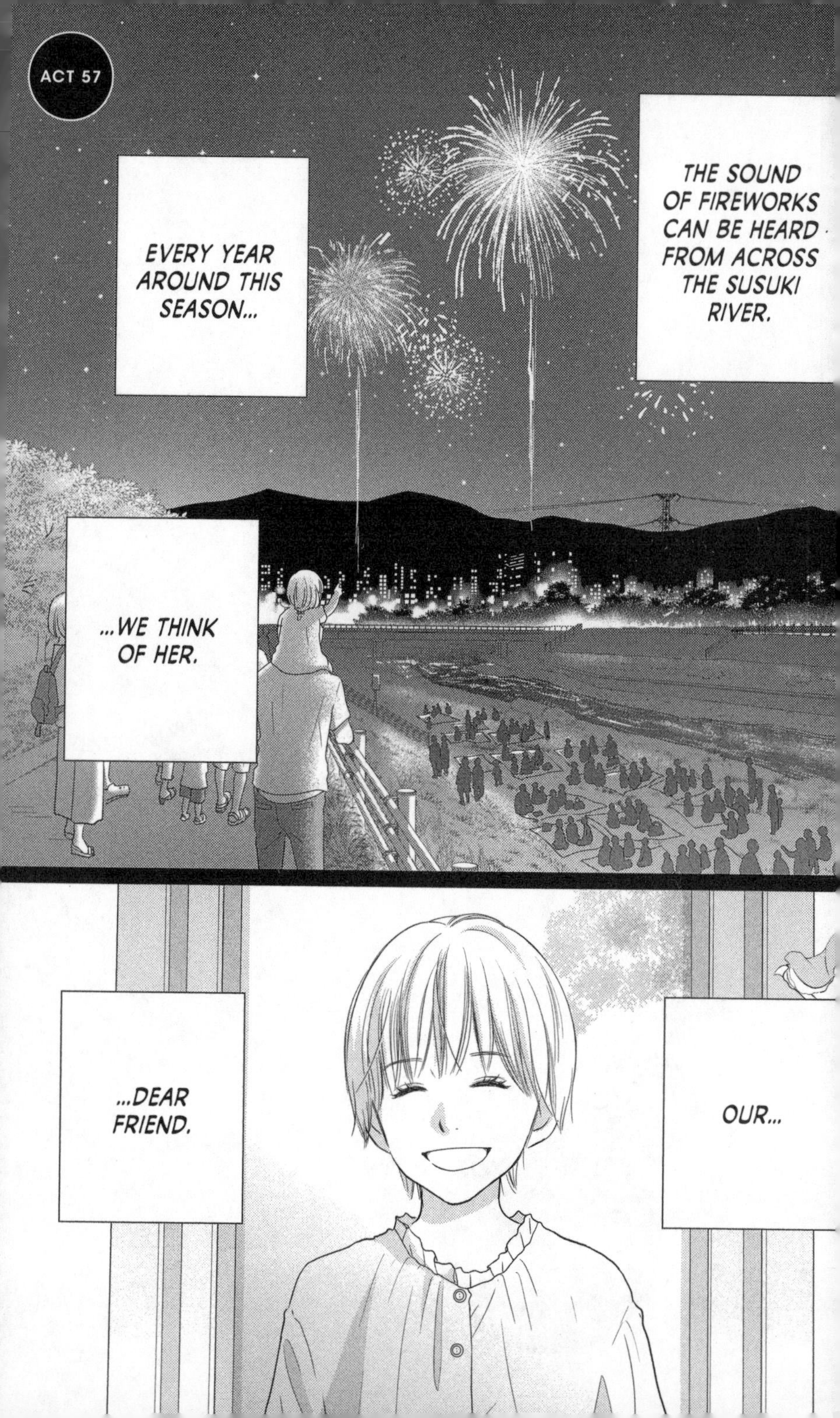
ACT 57
THE SOUND OF FIREWORKS CAN BE HEARD FROM ACROSS THE SUSUKI RIVER.
EVERY YEAR AROUND THIS SEASON...
...WE THINK OF HER.
OUR...
...DEAR FRIEND.

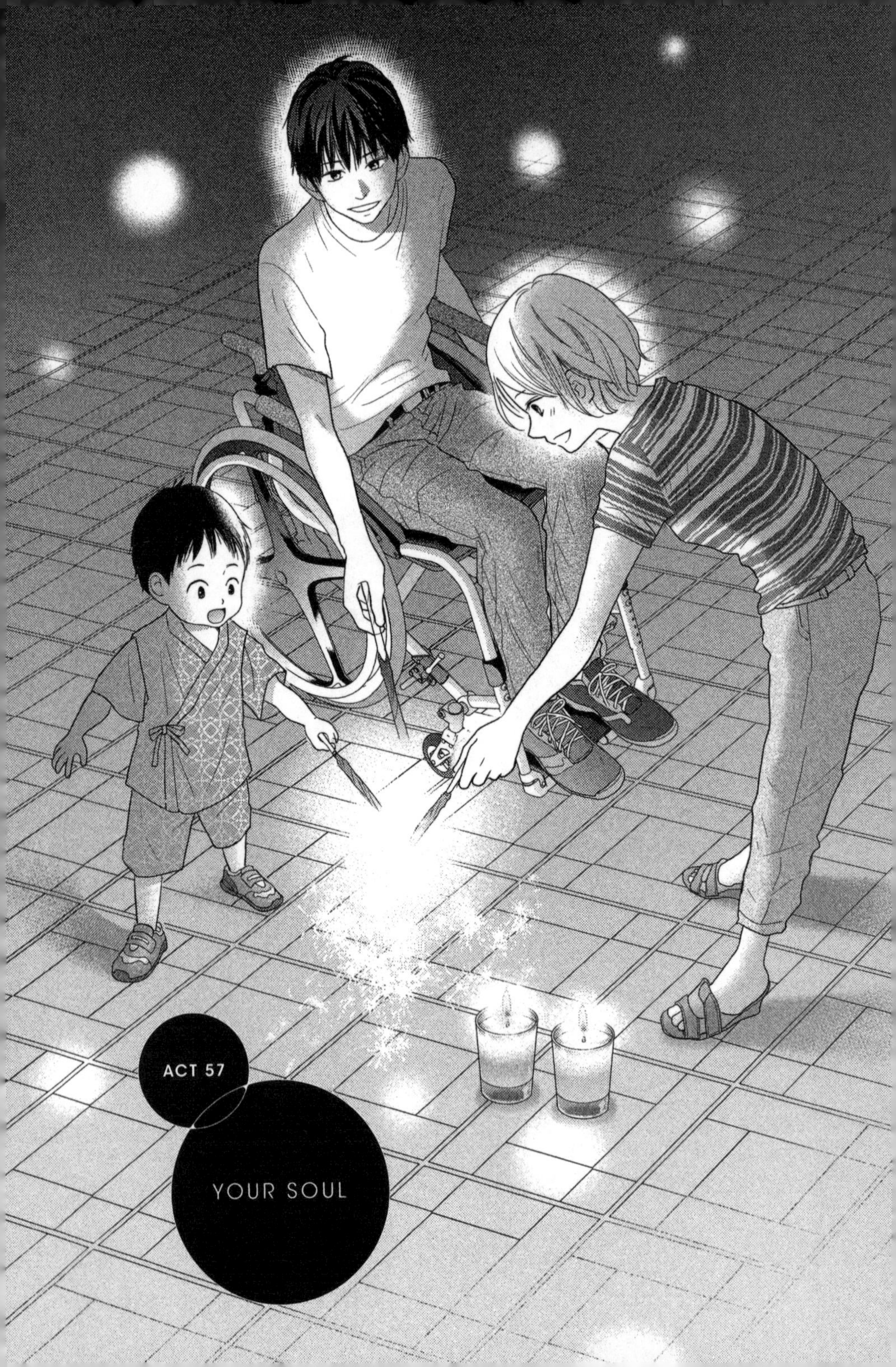
ACT 57
YOUR SOUL

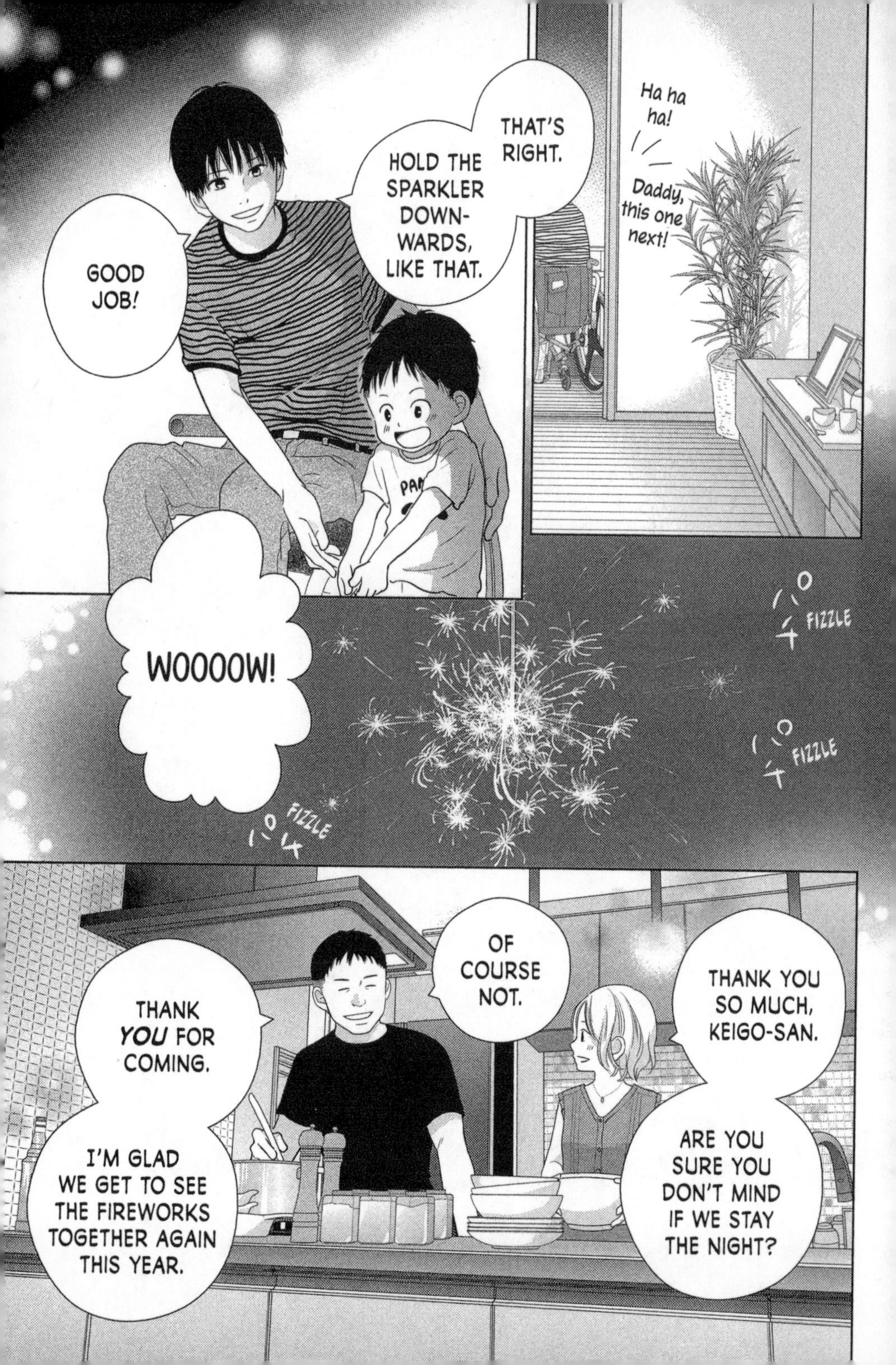
Ha ha ha!
Daddy, this one next!
THAT'S RIGHT.
HOLD THE SPARKLER DOWN-WARDS, LIKE THAT.
GOOD JOB!
FIZZLE
FIZZLE
WOOOOW!
FIZZLE
THANK YOU SO MUCH, KEIGO-SAN.
ARE YOU SURE YOU DON'T MIND IF WE STAY THE NIGHT?
OF COURSE NOT.
THANK *YOU* FOR COMING.
I'M GLAD WE GET TO SEE THE FIREWORKS TOGETHER AGAIN THIS YEAR.

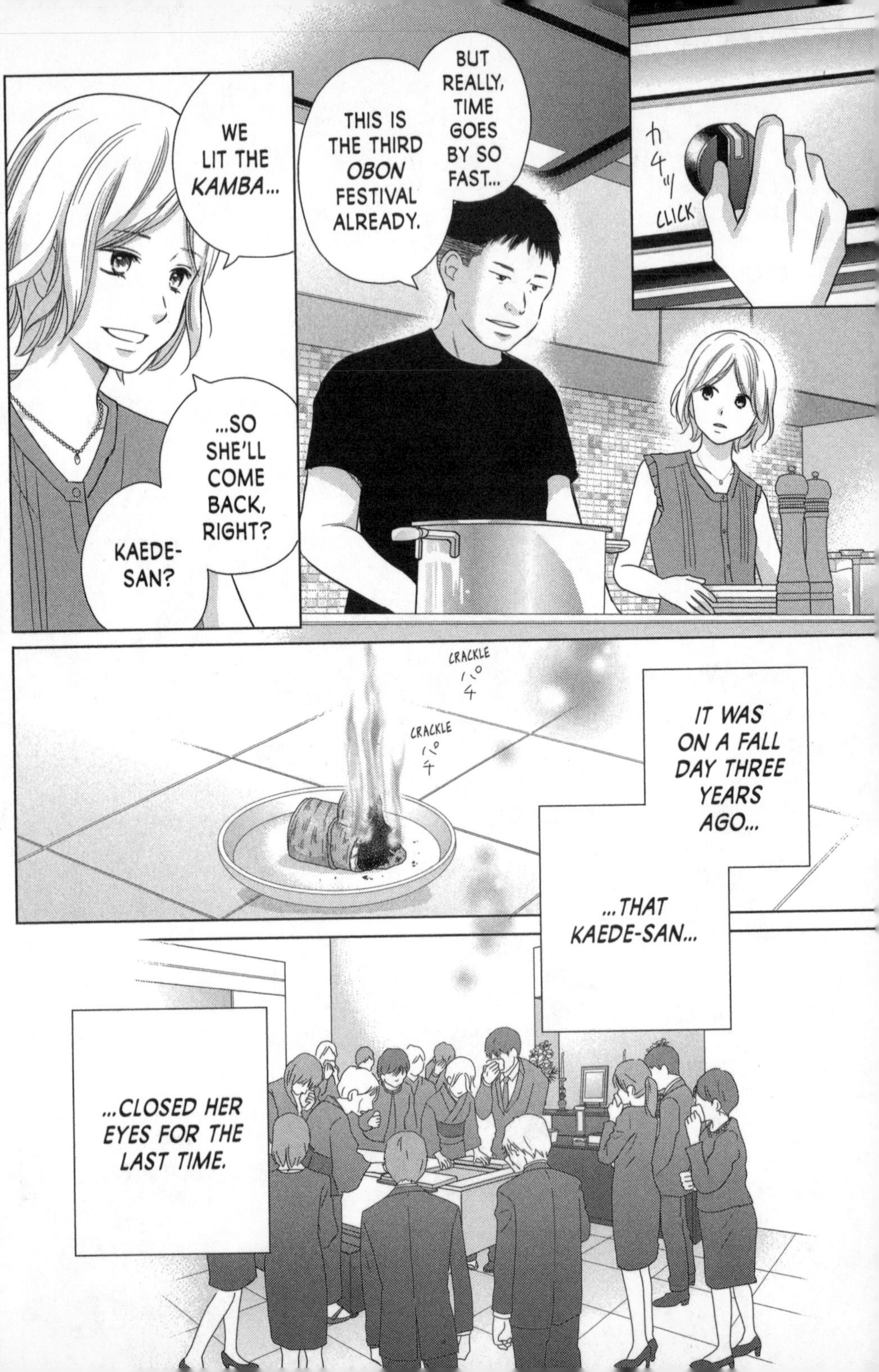
カチッ
CLICK
BUT REALLY, TIME GOES BY SO FAST...
THIS IS THE THIRD *OBON* FESTIVAL ALREADY.
WE LIT THE *KAMBA*...
...SO SHE'LL COME BACK, RIGHT?
KAEDE-SAN?
CRACKLE
パチ
CRACKLE
パチ
IT WAS ON A FALL DAY THREE YEARS AGO...
...THAT KAEDE-SAN...
...CLOSED HER EYES FOR THE LAST TIME.

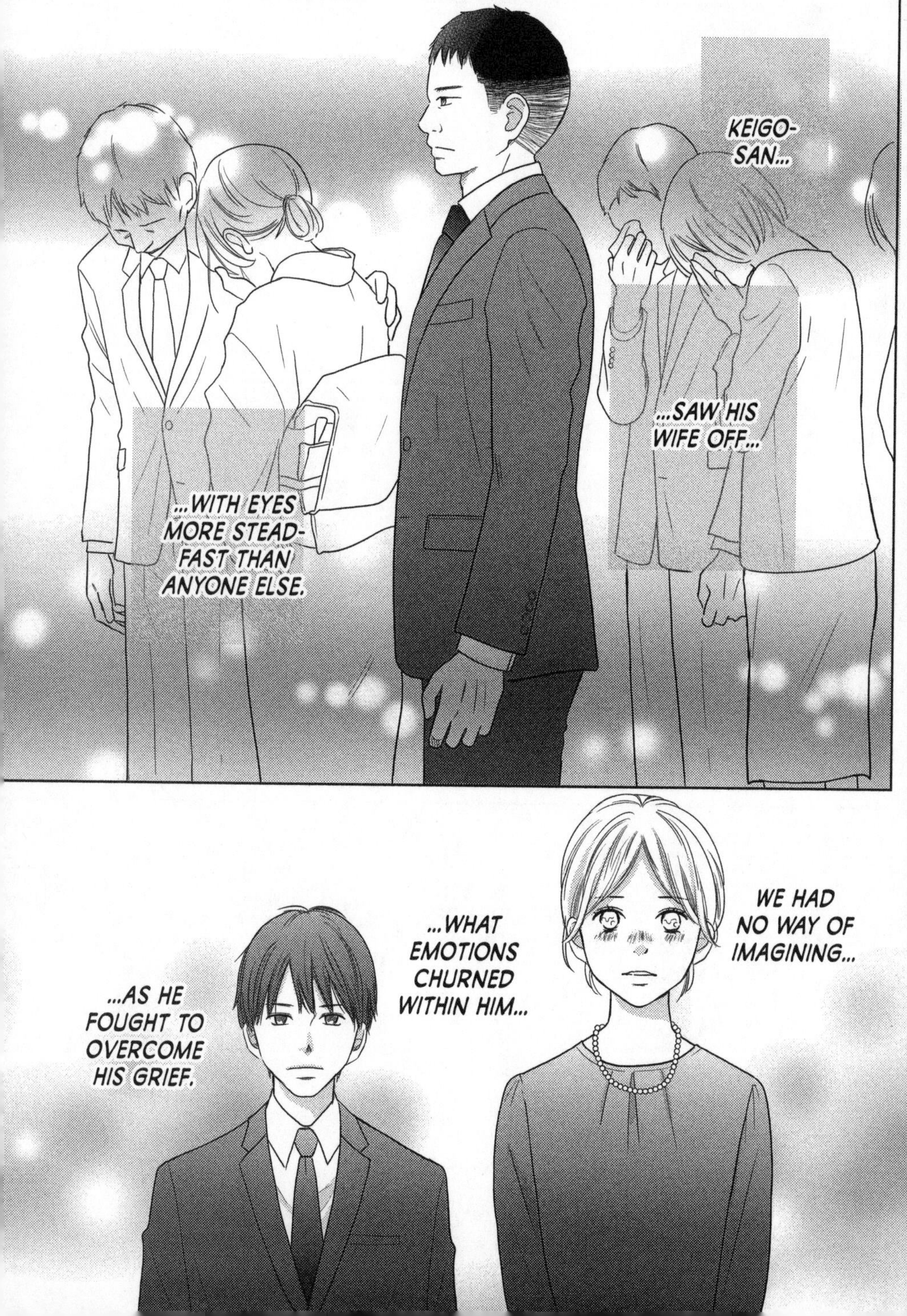
KEIGO-SAN...
...SAW HIS WIFE OFF...
...WITH EYES MORE STEAD-FAST THAN ANYONE ELSE.
WE HAD NO WAY OF IMAGINING...
...WHAT EMOTIONS CHURNED WITHIN HIM...
...AS HE FOUGHT TO OVERCOME HIS GRIEF.

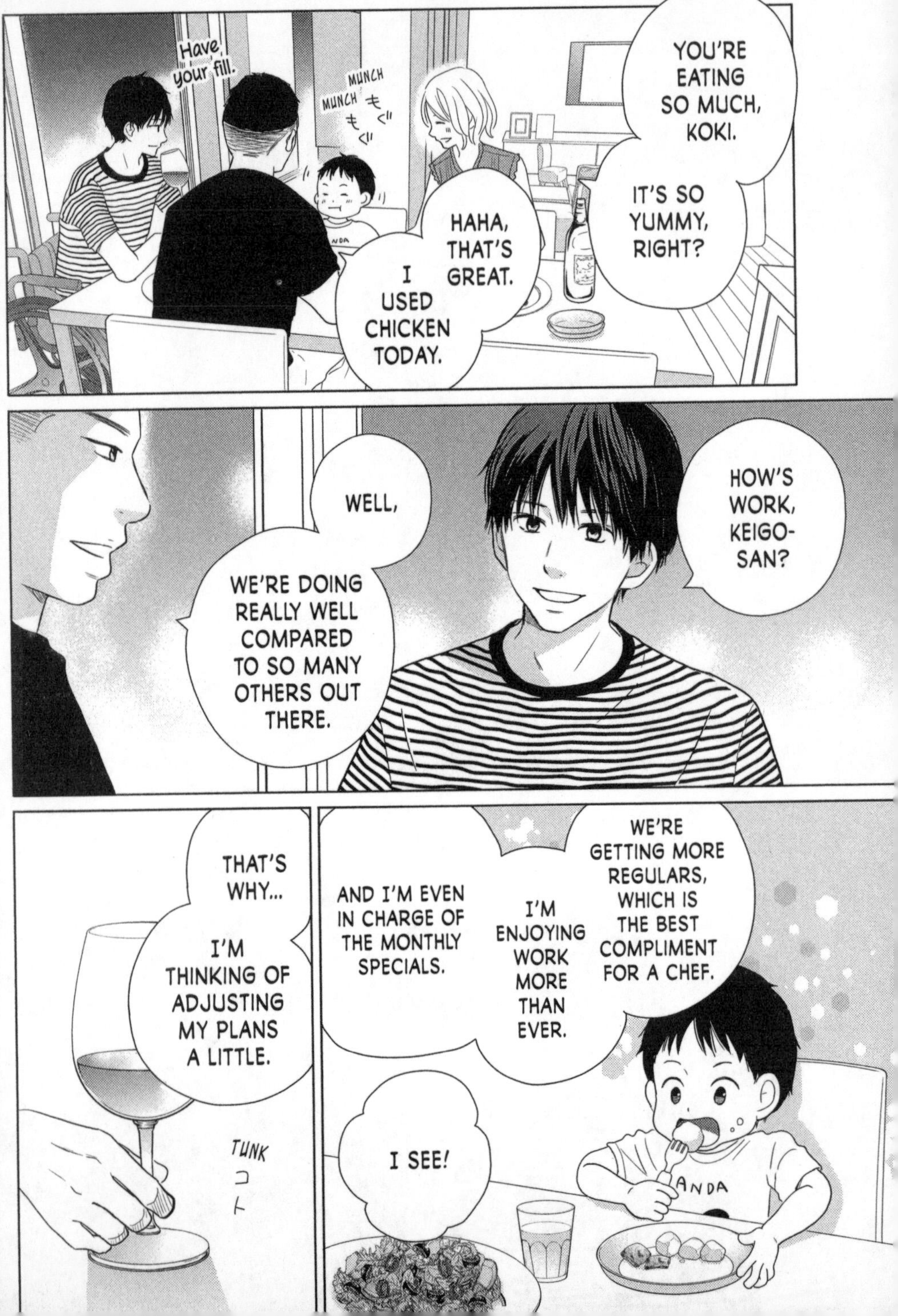
YOU'RE EATING SO MUCH, KOKI.
IT'S SO YUMMY, RIGHT?
HAHA, THAT'S GREAT.
I USED CHICKEN TODAY.
MUNCH MUNCH もぐもぐ
Have your fill.
HOW'S WORK, KEIGO-SAN?
WELL,
WE'RE DOING REALLY WELL COMPARED TO SO MANY OTHERS OUT THERE.
WE'RE GETTING MORE REGULARS, WHICH IS THE BEST COMPLIMENT FOR A CHEF.
I'M ENJOYING WORK MORE THAN EVER.
AND I'M EVEN IN CHARGE OF THE MONTHLY SPECIALS.
I SEE!
ANDA
THAT'S WHY...
I'M THINKING OF ADJUSTING MY PLANS A LITTLE.
TUNK コト

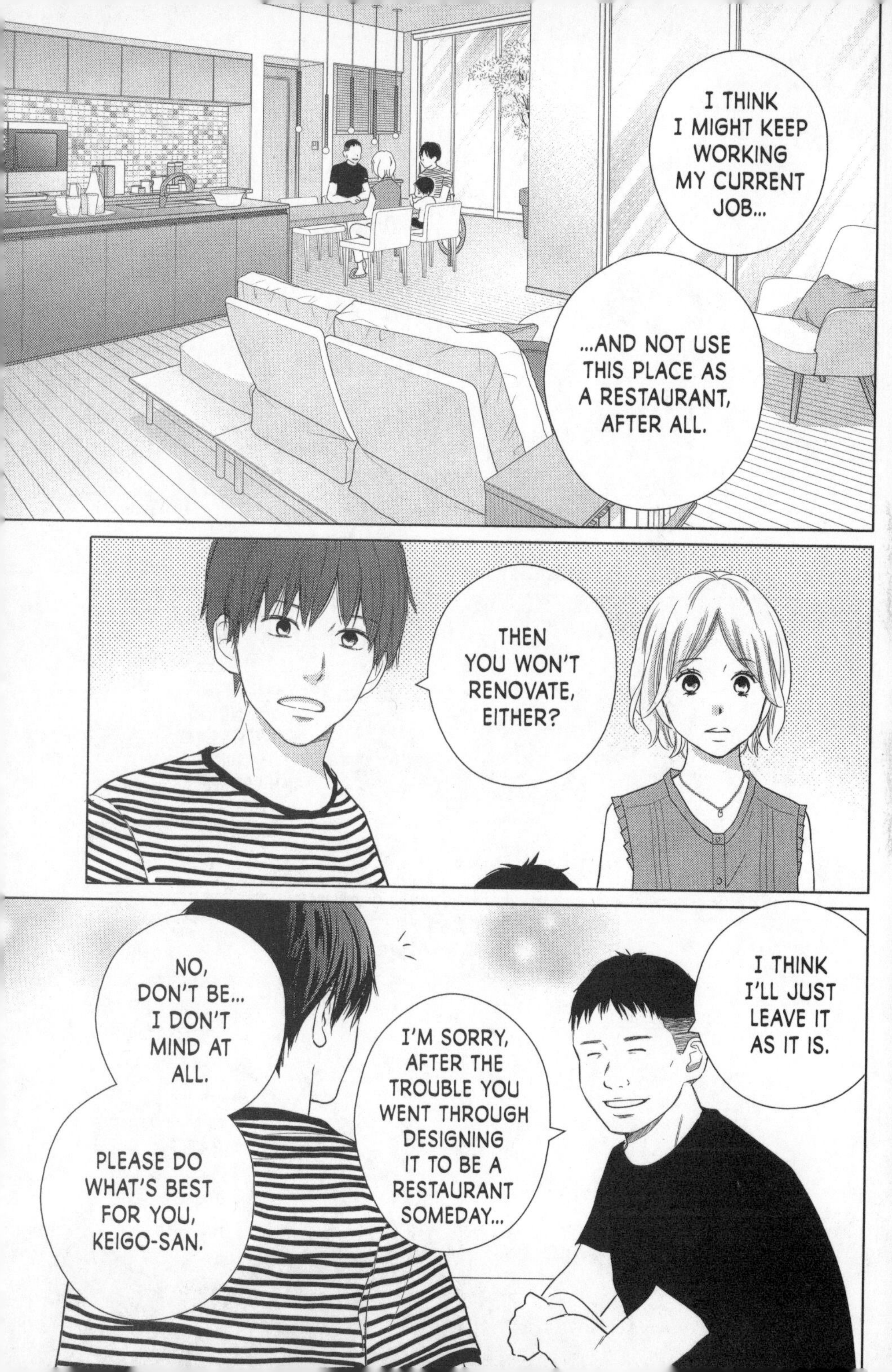
I THINK I MIGHT KEEP WORKING MY CURRENT JOB...
...AND NOT USE THIS PLACE AS A RESTAURANT, AFTER ALL.
THEN YOU WON'T RENOVATE, EITHER?
I THINK I'LL JUST LEAVE IT AS IT IS.
I'M SORRY, AFTER THE TROUBLE YOU WENT THROUGH DESIGNING IT TO BE A RESTAURANT SOMEDAY...
NO, DON'T BE... I DON'T MIND AT ALL.
PLEASE DO WHAT'S BEST FOR YOU, KEIGO-SAN.

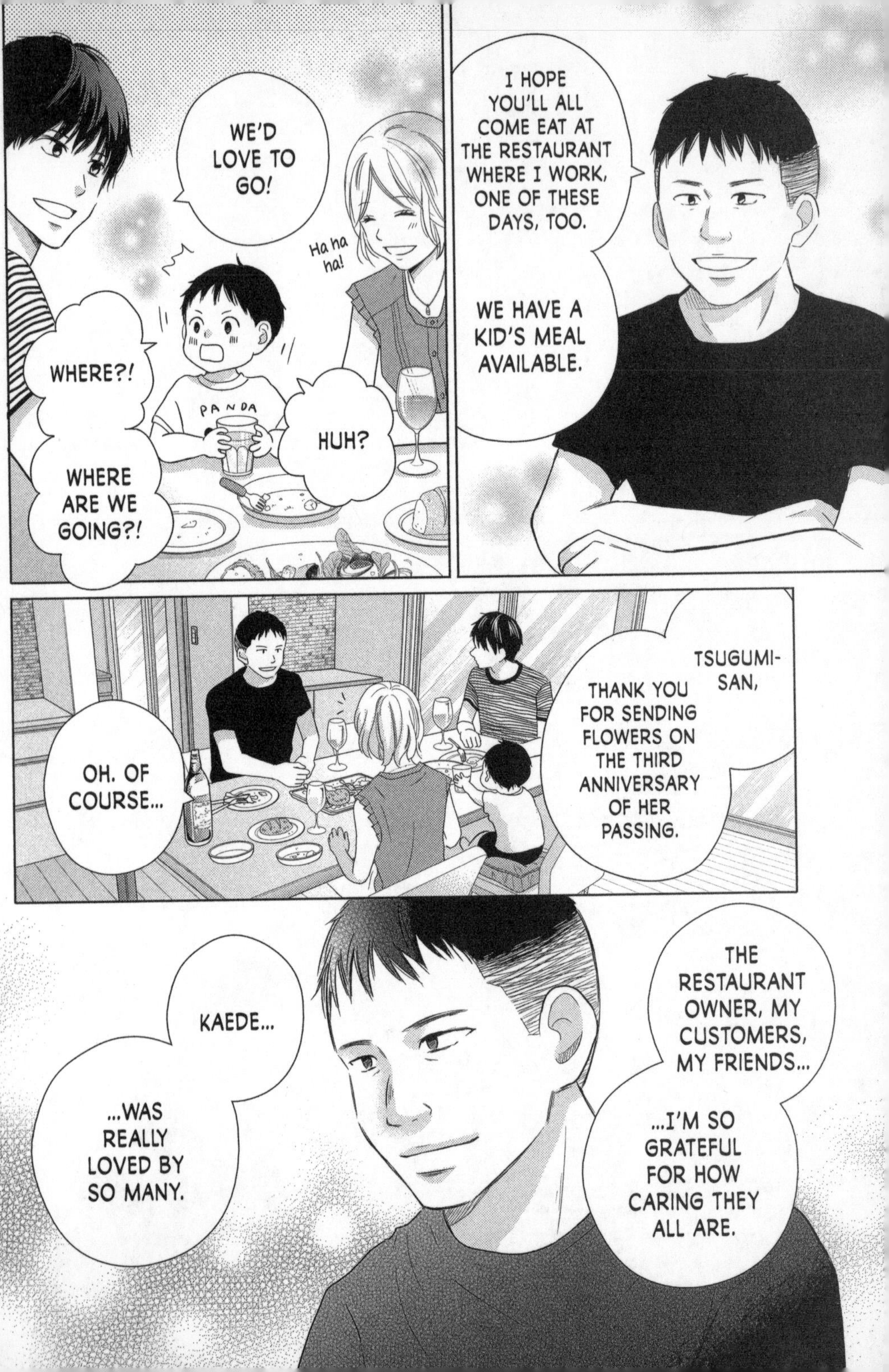
I HOPE YOU'LL ALL COME EAT AT THE RESTAURANT WHERE I WORK, ONE OF THESE DAYS, TOO.
WE HAVE A KID'S MEAL AVAILABLE.
WE'D LOVE TO GO!
Ha ha ha!
HUH?
WHERE?!
PANDA
WHERE ARE WE GOING?!
TSUGUMI-SAN,
THANK YOU FOR SENDING FLOWERS ON THE THIRD ANNIVERSARY OF HER PASSING.
OH. OF COURSE...
THE RESTAURANT OWNER, MY CUSTOMERS, MY FRIENDS...
...I'M SO GRATEFUL FOR HOW CARING THEY ALL ARE.
KAEDE...
...WAS REALLY LOVED BY SO MANY.

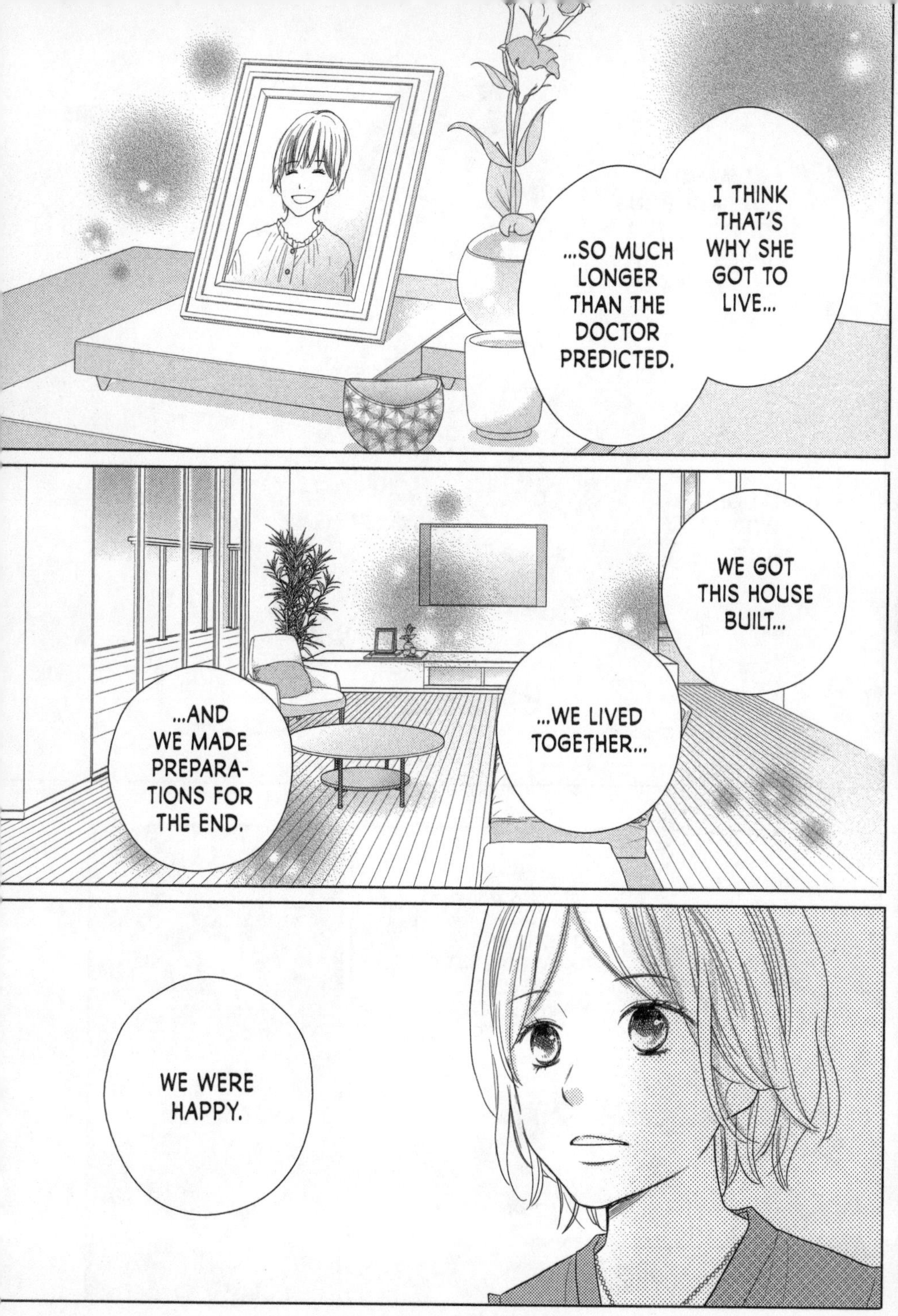
I THINK THAT'S WHY SHE GOT TO LIVE...
...SO MUCH LONGER THAN THE DOCTOR PREDICTED.
WE GOT THIS HOUSE BUILT...
...WE LIVED TOGETHER...
...AND WE MADE PREPARATIONS FOR THE END.
WE WERE HAPPY.

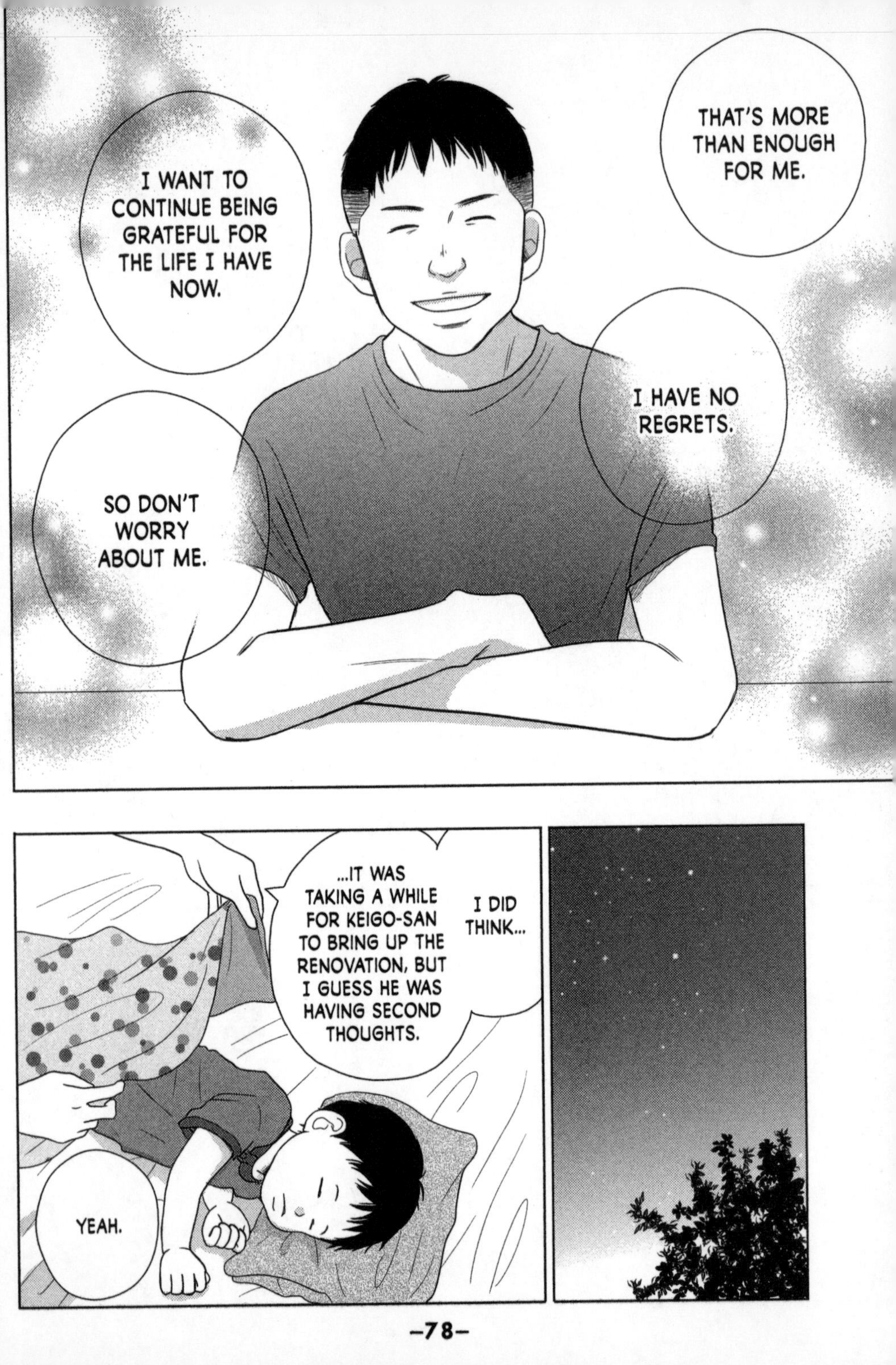
THAT'S MORE THAN ENOUGH FOR ME.
I WANT TO CONTINUE BEING GRATEFUL FOR THE LIFE I HAVE NOW.
I HAVE NO REGRETS.
SO DON'T WORRY ABOUT ME.
I DID THINK...
...IT WAS TAKING A WHILE FOR KEIGO-SAN TO BRING UP THE RENOVATION, BUT I GUESS HE WAS HAVING SECOND THOUGHTS.
YEAH.

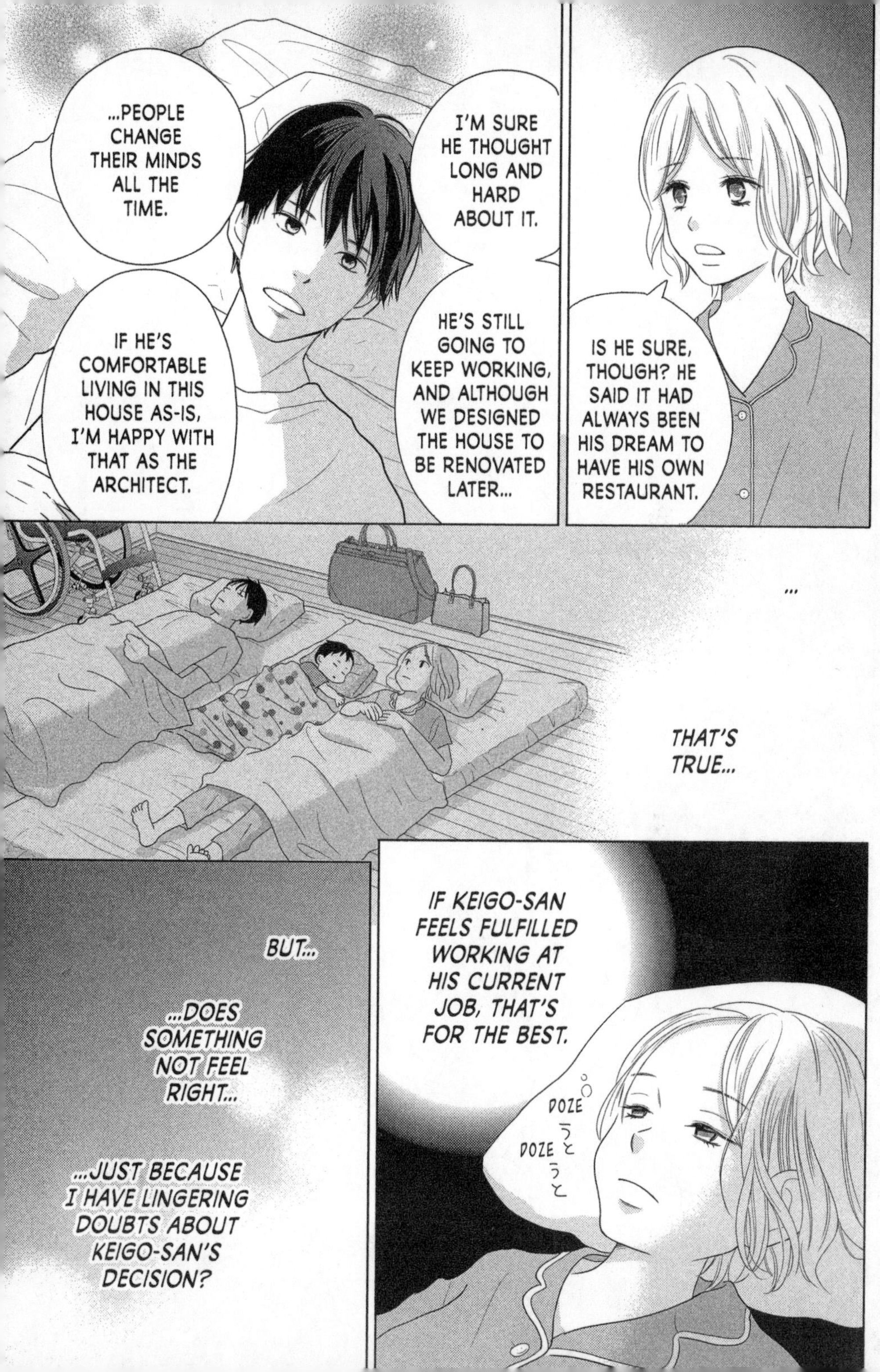
IS HE SURE, THOUGH? HE SAID IT HAD ALWAYS BEEN HIS DREAM TO HAVE HIS OWN RESTAURANT.
I'M SURE HE THOUGHT LONG AND HARD ABOUT IT.
...PEOPLE CHANGE THEIR MINDS ALL THE TIME.
HE'S STILL GOING TO KEEP WORKING, AND ALTHOUGH WE DESIGNED THE HOUSE TO BE RENOVATED LATER...
IF HE'S COMFORTABLE LIVING IN THIS HOUSE AS-IS, I'M HAPPY WITH THAT AS THE ARCHITECT.
...
THAT'S TRUE...
IF KEIGO-SAN FEELS FULFILLED WORKING AT HIS CURRENT JOB, THAT'S FOR THE BEST.
DOZE うと
DOZE うと
BUT...
...DOES SOMETHING NOT FEEL RIGHT...
...JUST BECAUSE I HAVE LINGERING DOUBTS ABOUT KEIGO-SAN'S DECISION?

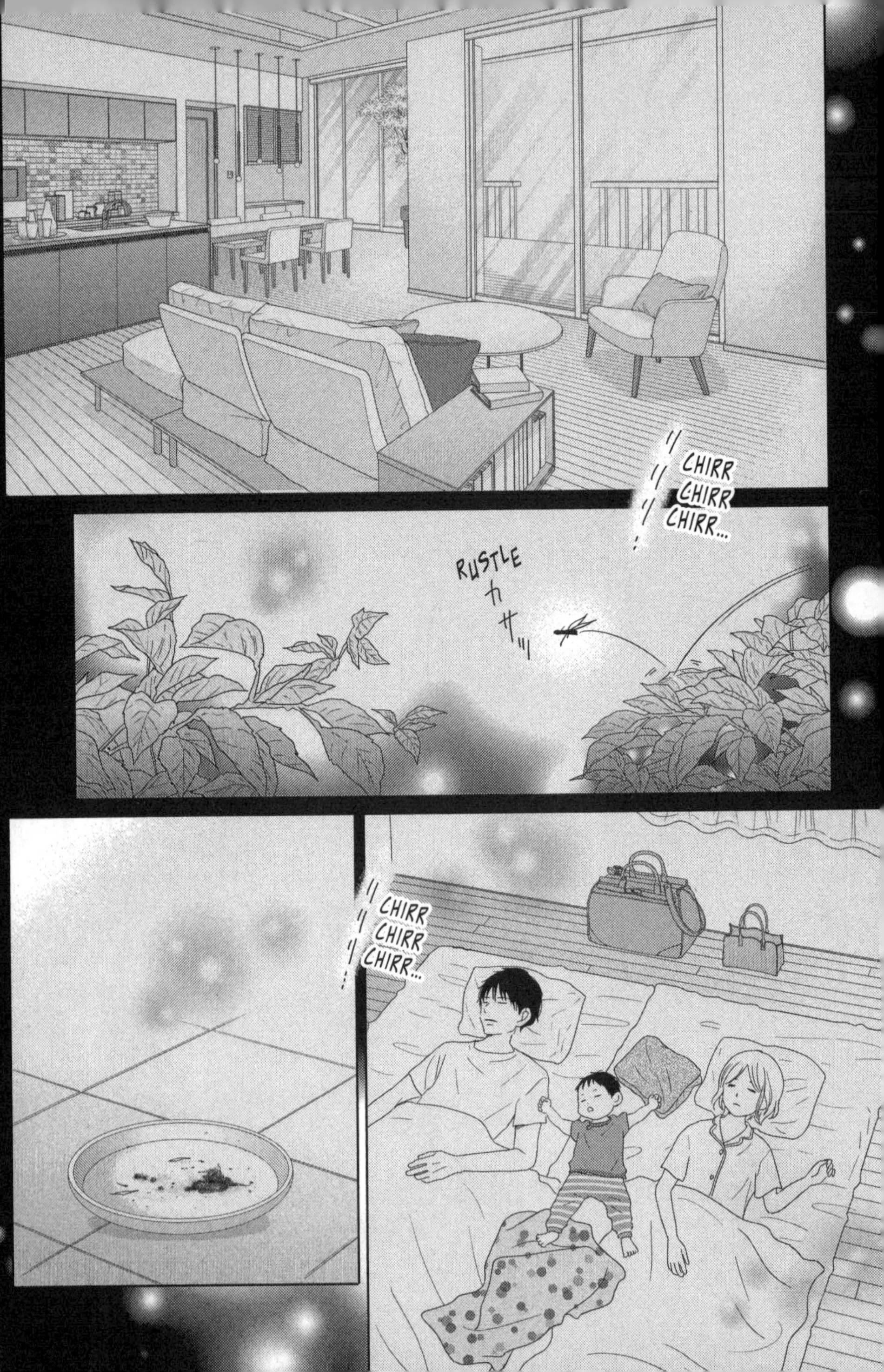
CHIRR
CHIRR
CHIRR...
RUSTLE
カサッ
CHIRR
CHIRR
CHIRR...

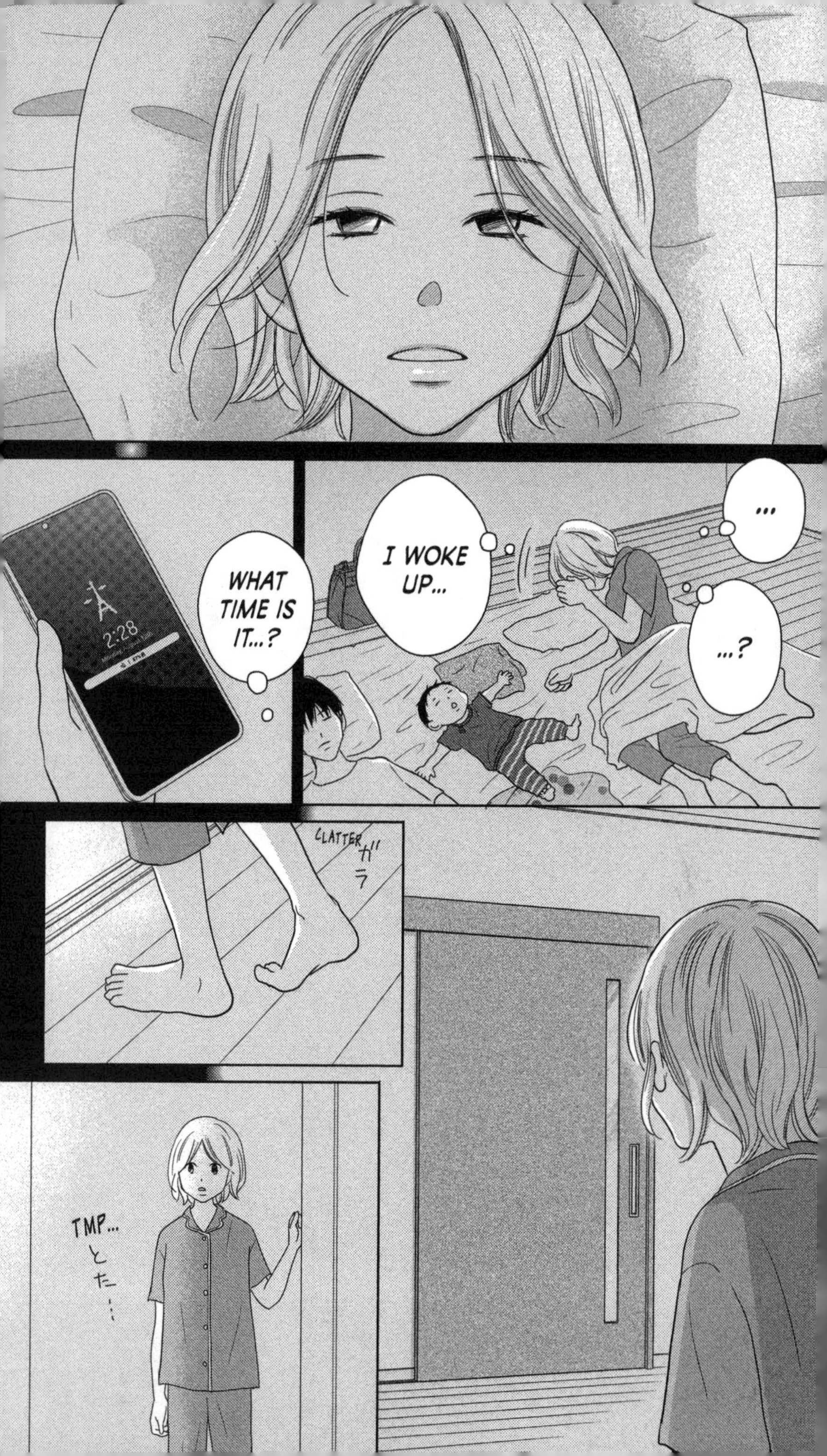
...
I WOKE UP...
...?
2:28
WHAT TIME IS IT...?
CLATTER ガラ
TMP... とた...

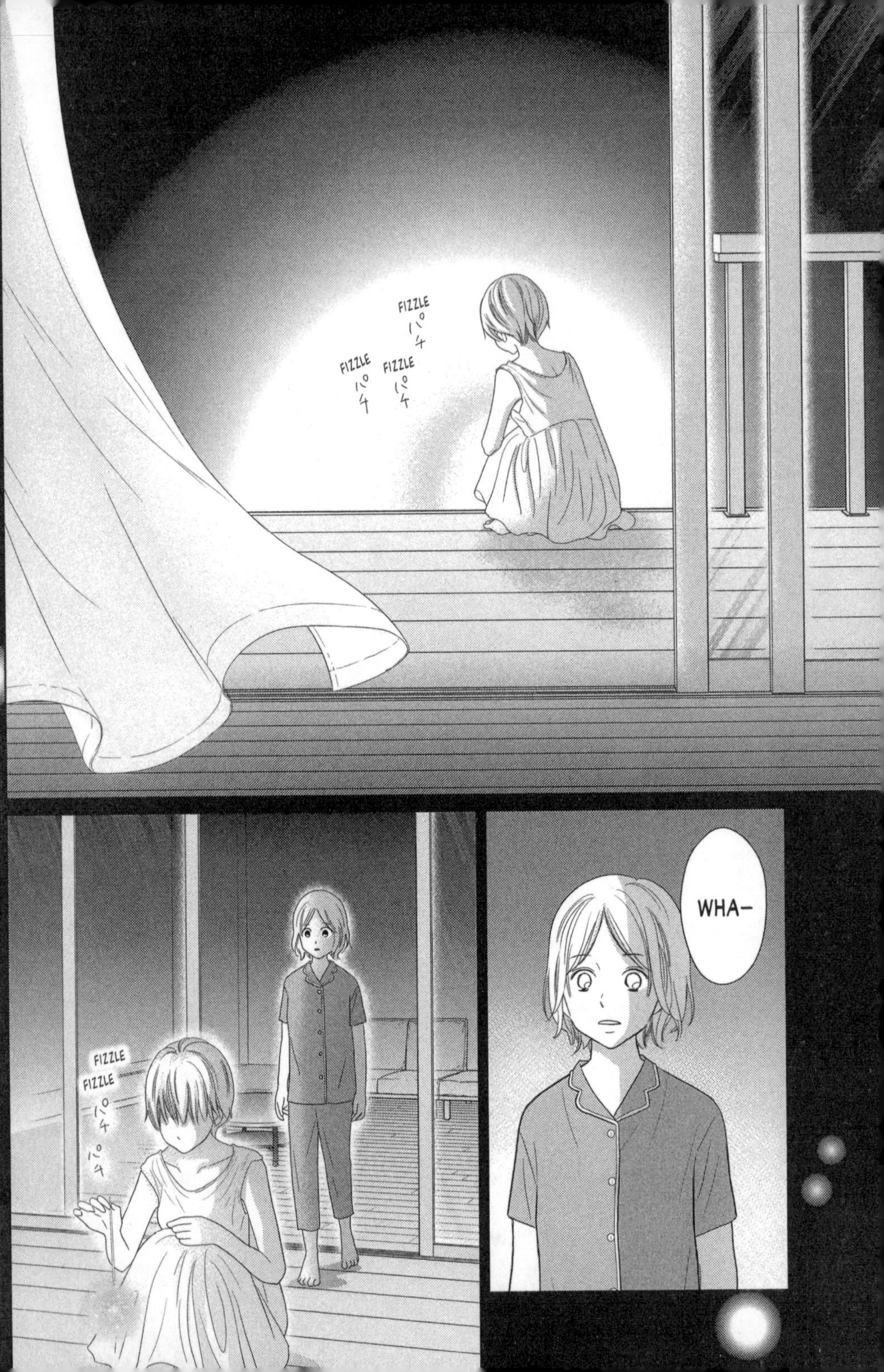
FIZZLE
パチ
FIZZLE
パチ
FIZZLE
パチ
WHA–
FIZZLE
FIZZLE
パチ
パチ

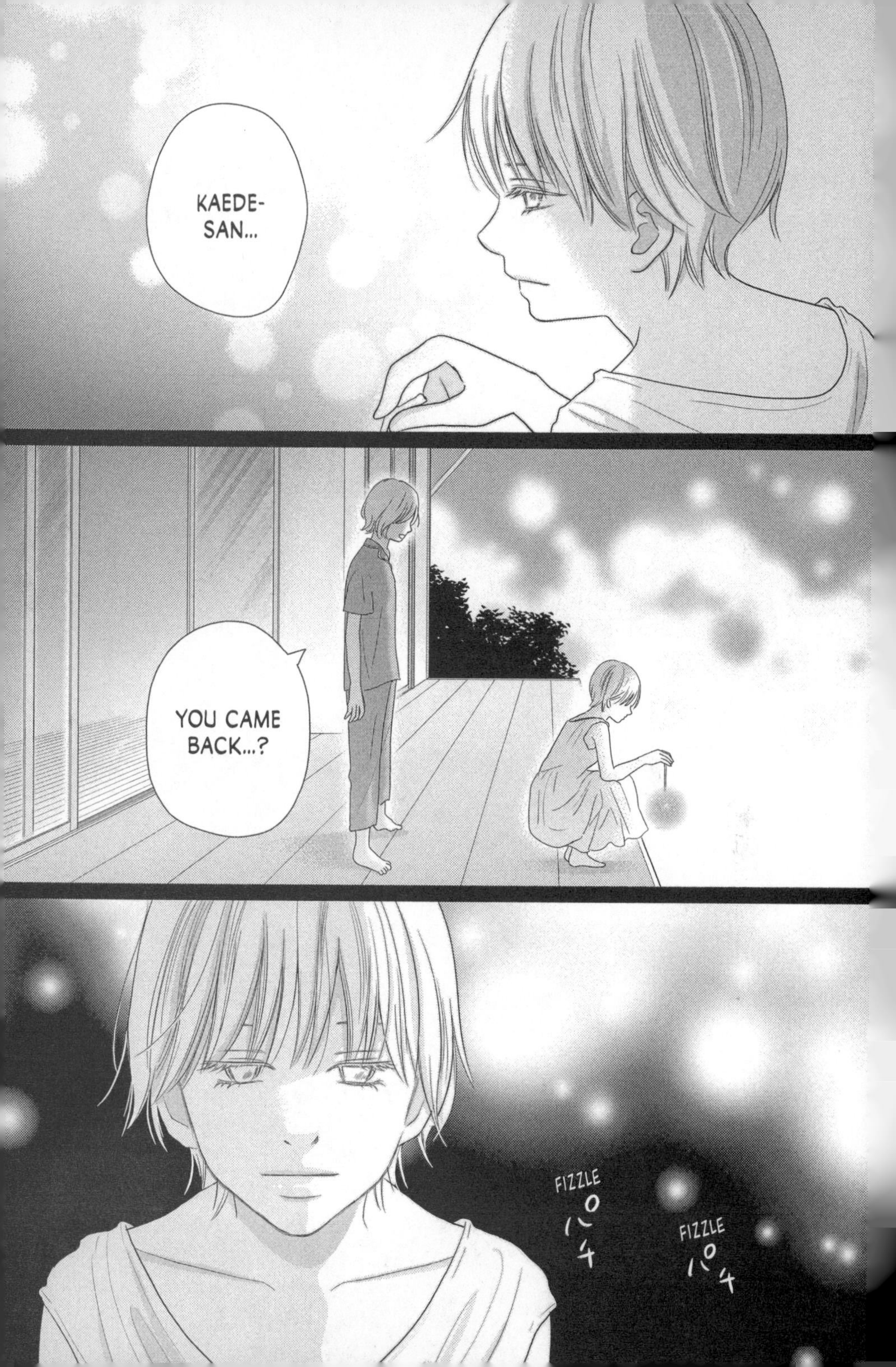
KAEDE-SAN...
YOU CAME BACK...?
FIZZLE パチ
FIZZLE パチ

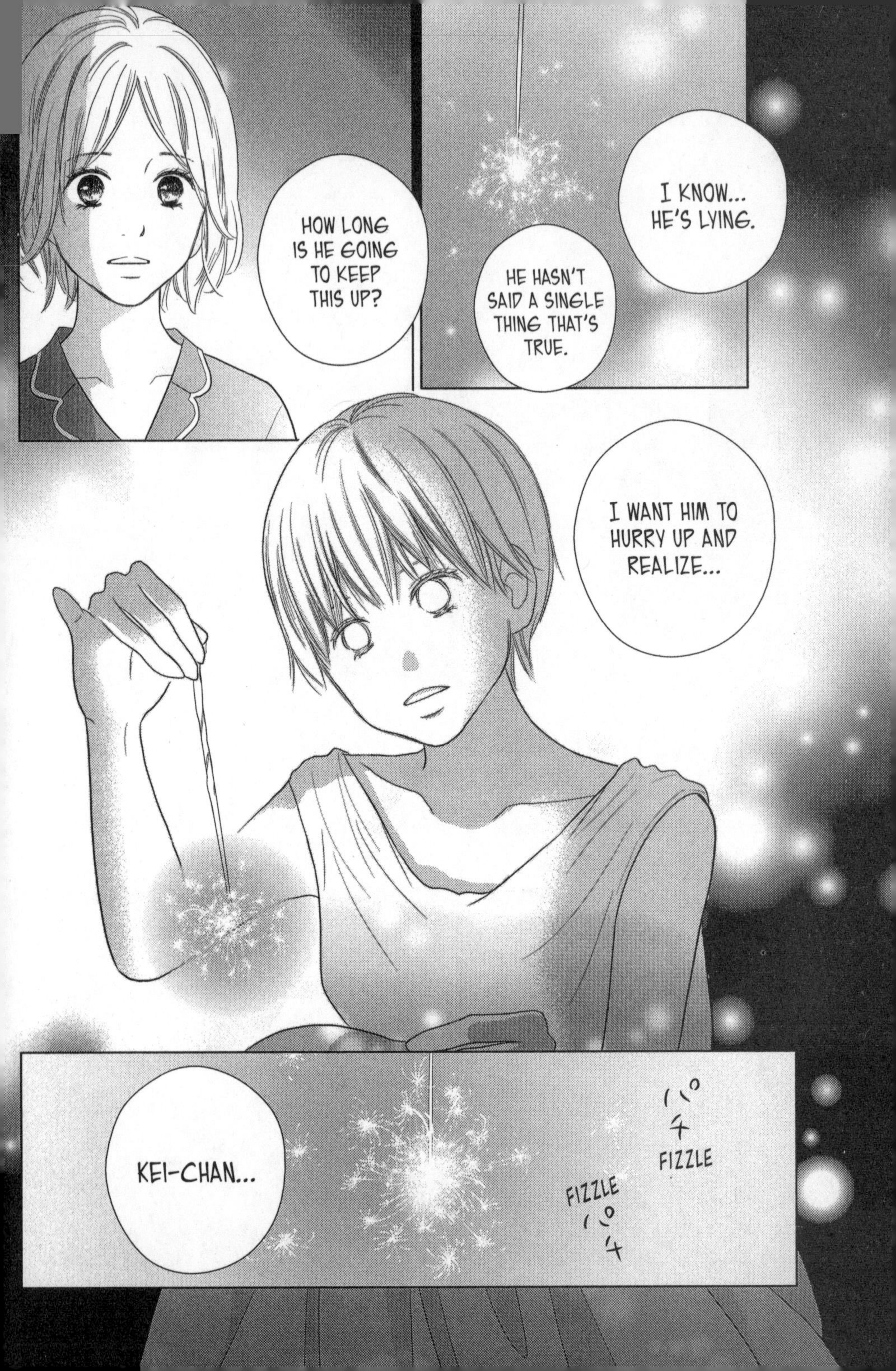
I KNOW... HE'S LYING.
HE HASN'T SAID A SINGLE THING THAT'S TRUE.
HOW LONG IS HE GOING TO KEEP THIS UP?
I WANT HIM TO HURRY UP AND REALIZE...
パチ
FIZZLE
FIZZLE
パチ
KEI-CHAN...

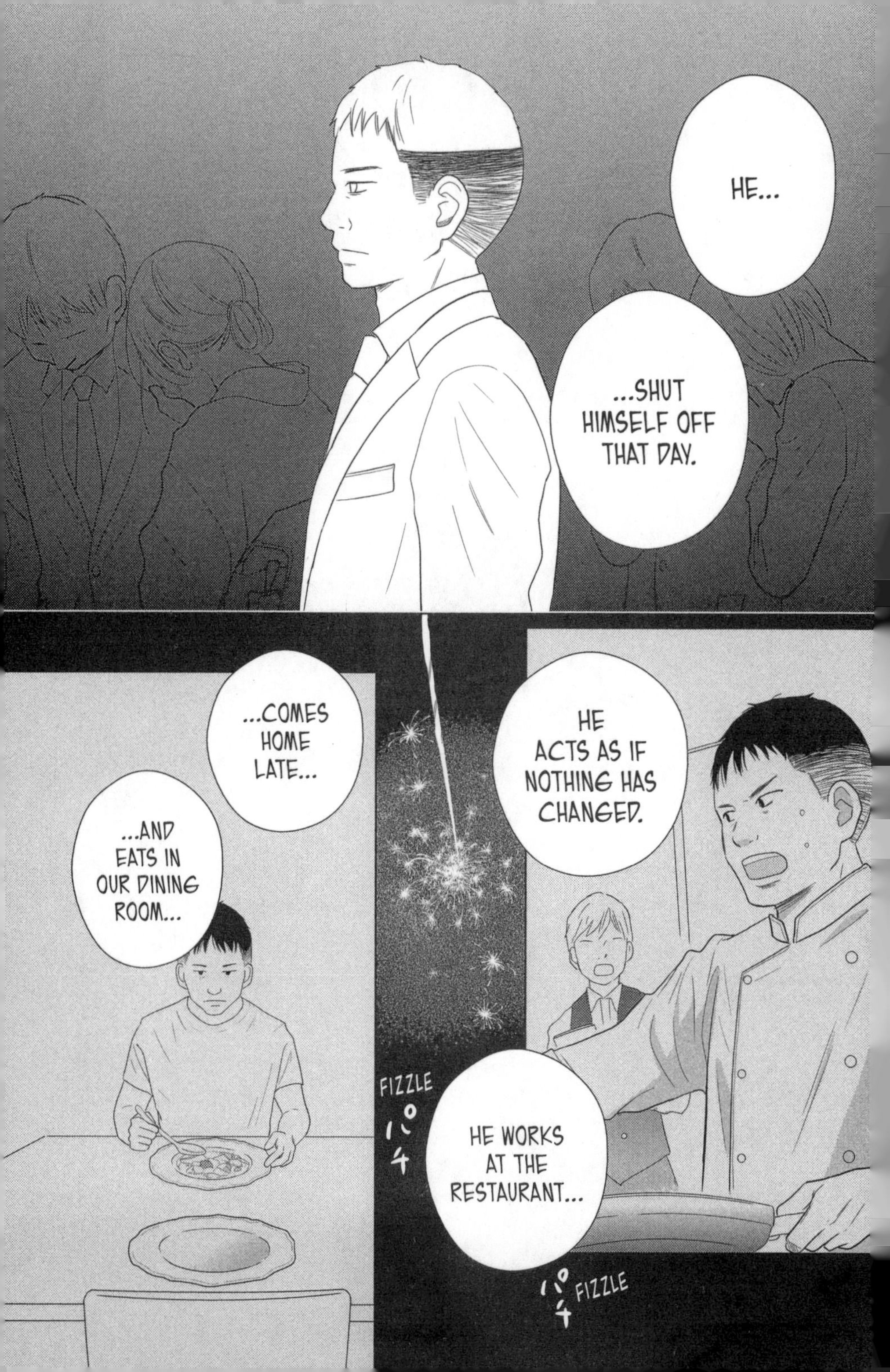
HE...
...SHUT HIMSELF OFF THAT DAY.
HE ACTS AS IF NOTHING HAS CHANGED.
HE WORKS AT THE RESTAURANT...
パチ FIZZLE
FIZZLE パチ
...COMES HOME LATE...
...AND EATS IN OUR DINING ROOM...

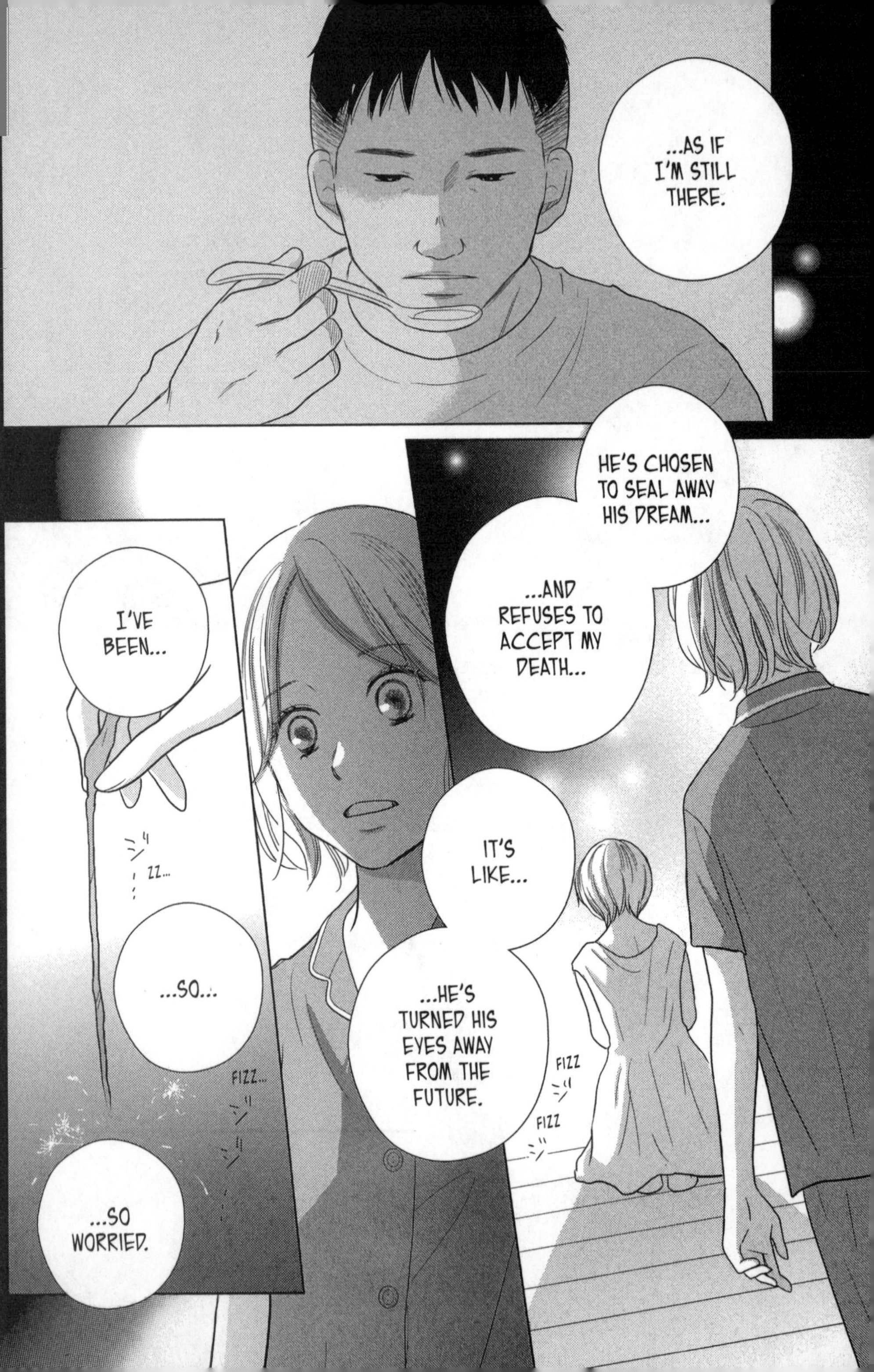
...AS IF I'M STILL THERE.
HE'S CHOSEN TO SEAL AWAY HIS DREAM...
...AND REFUSES TO ACCEPT MY DEATH...
IT'S LIKE...
...HE'S TURNED HIS EYES AWAY FROM THE FUTURE.
FIZZ
FIZZ
I'VE BEEN...
ZZ...
...SO...
FIZZ...
...SO WORRIED.

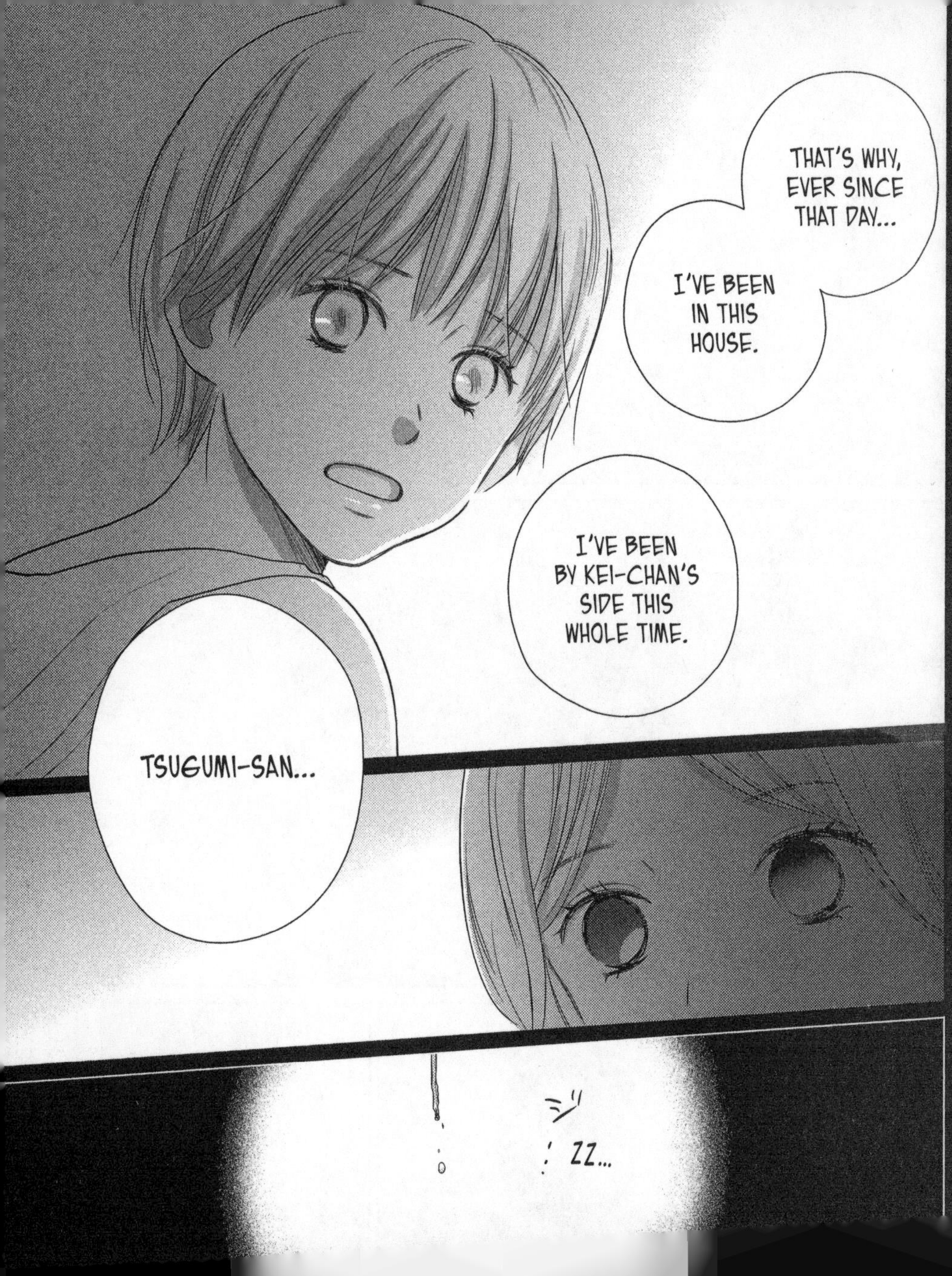
THAT'S WHY, EVER SINCE THAT DAY...
I'VE BEEN IN THIS HOUSE.
I'VE BEEN BY KEI-CHAN'S SIDE THIS WHOLE TIME.
TSUGUMI-SAN...
ZZ...

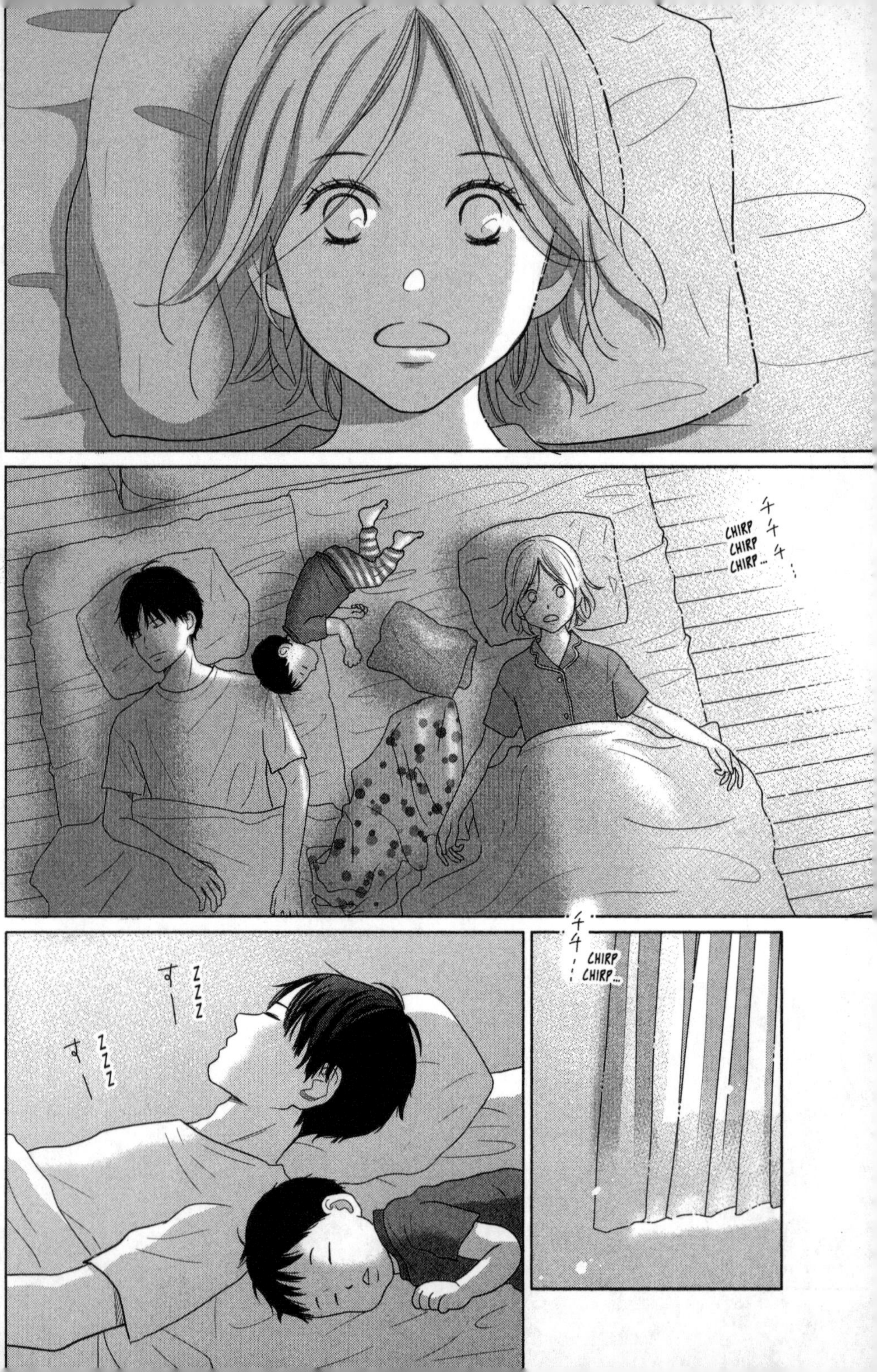
チチチ…
CHIRP CHIRP CHIRP...
チチ…
CHIRP CHIRP...
すー
ZZZ
すー
ZZZ

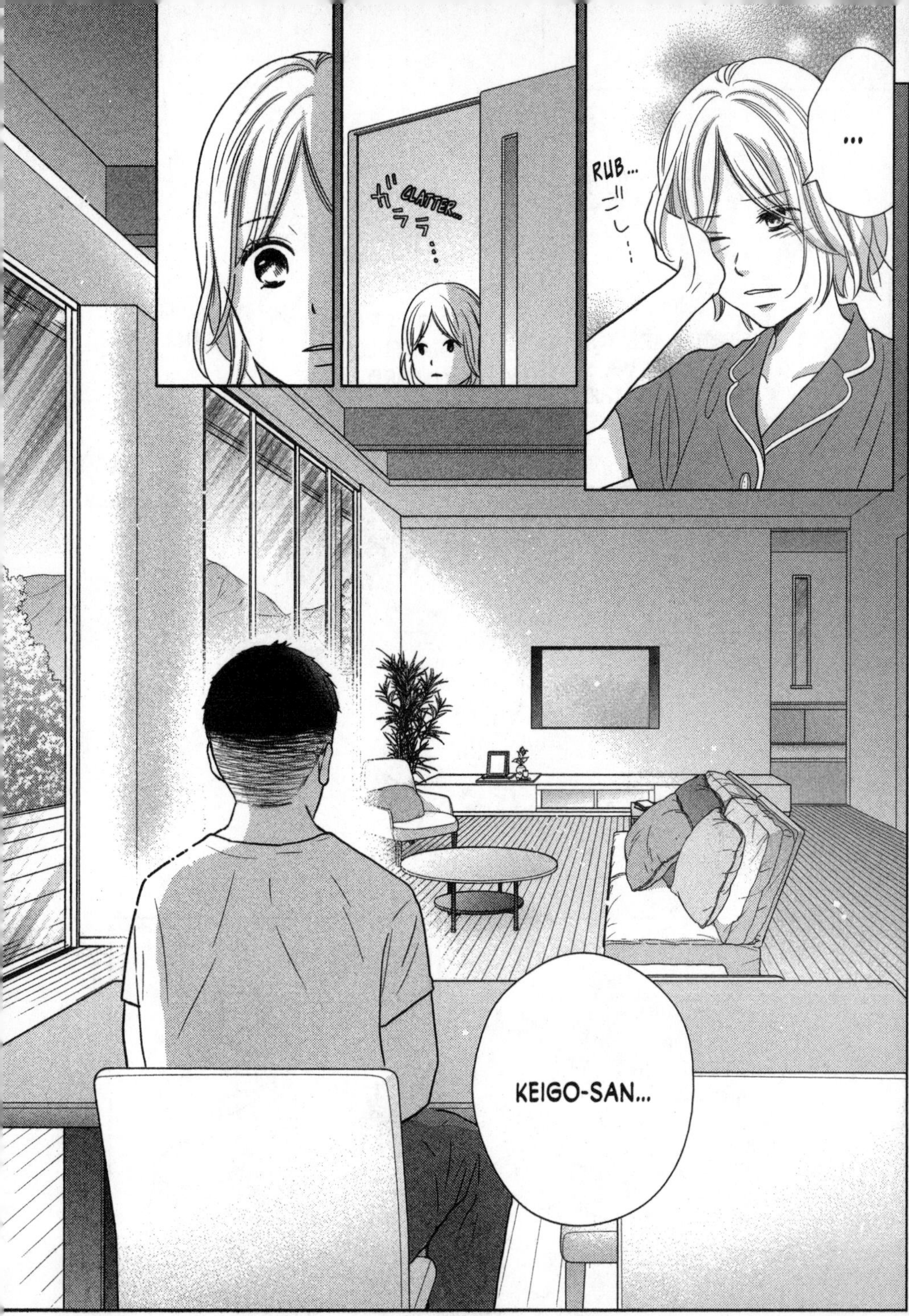
...
RUB...
CLATTER...
KEIGO-SAN...

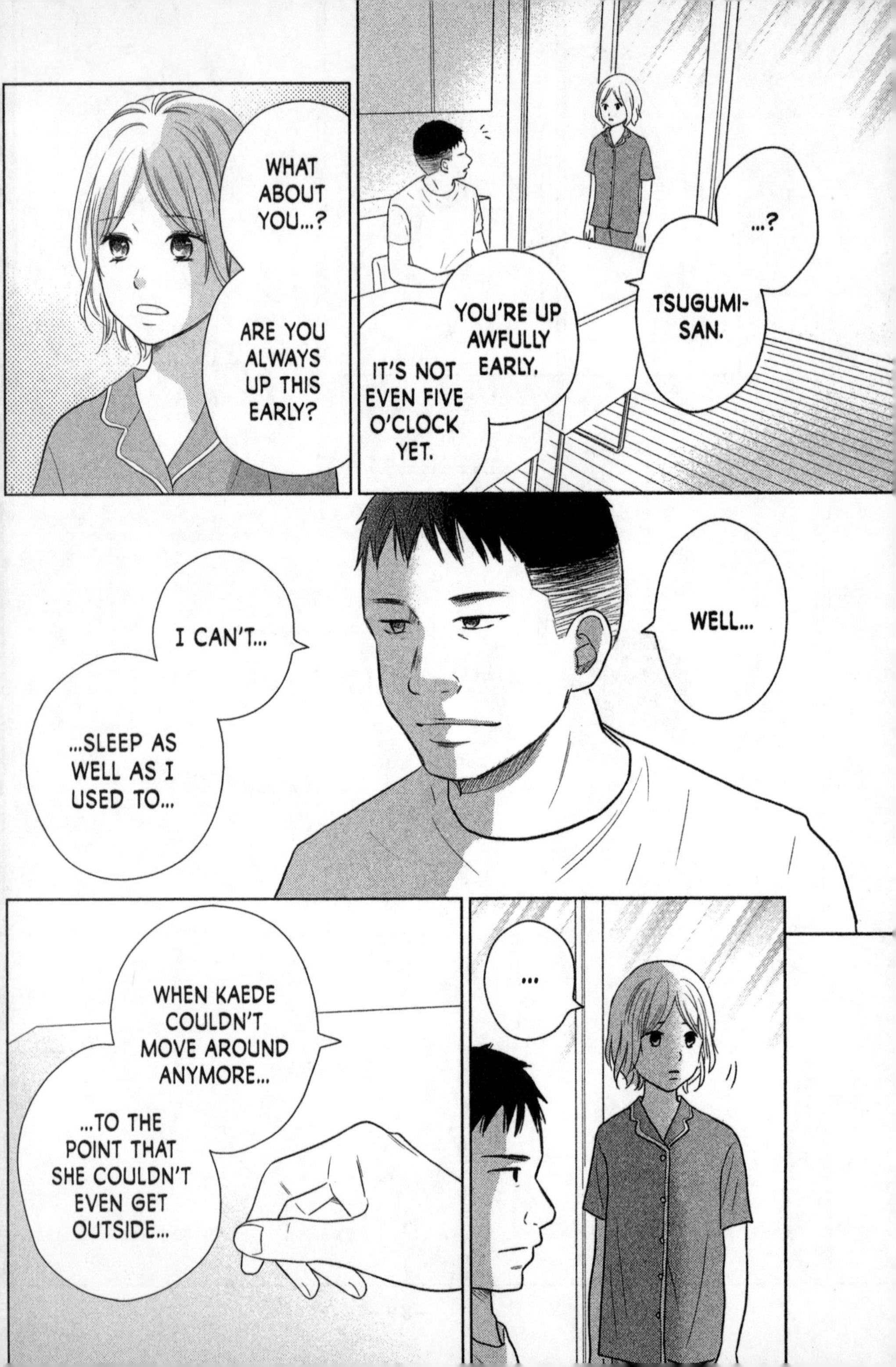
...?
TSUGUMI-SAN.
YOU'RE UP AWFULLY EARLY.
IT'S NOT EVEN FIVE O'CLOCK YET.
WHAT ABOUT YOU...?
ARE YOU ALWAYS UP THIS EARLY?
WELL...
I CAN'T...
...SLEEP AS WELL AS I USED TO...
...
WHEN KAEDE COULDN'T MOVE AROUND ANYMORE...
...TO THE POINT THAT SHE COULDN'T EVEN GET OUTSIDE...

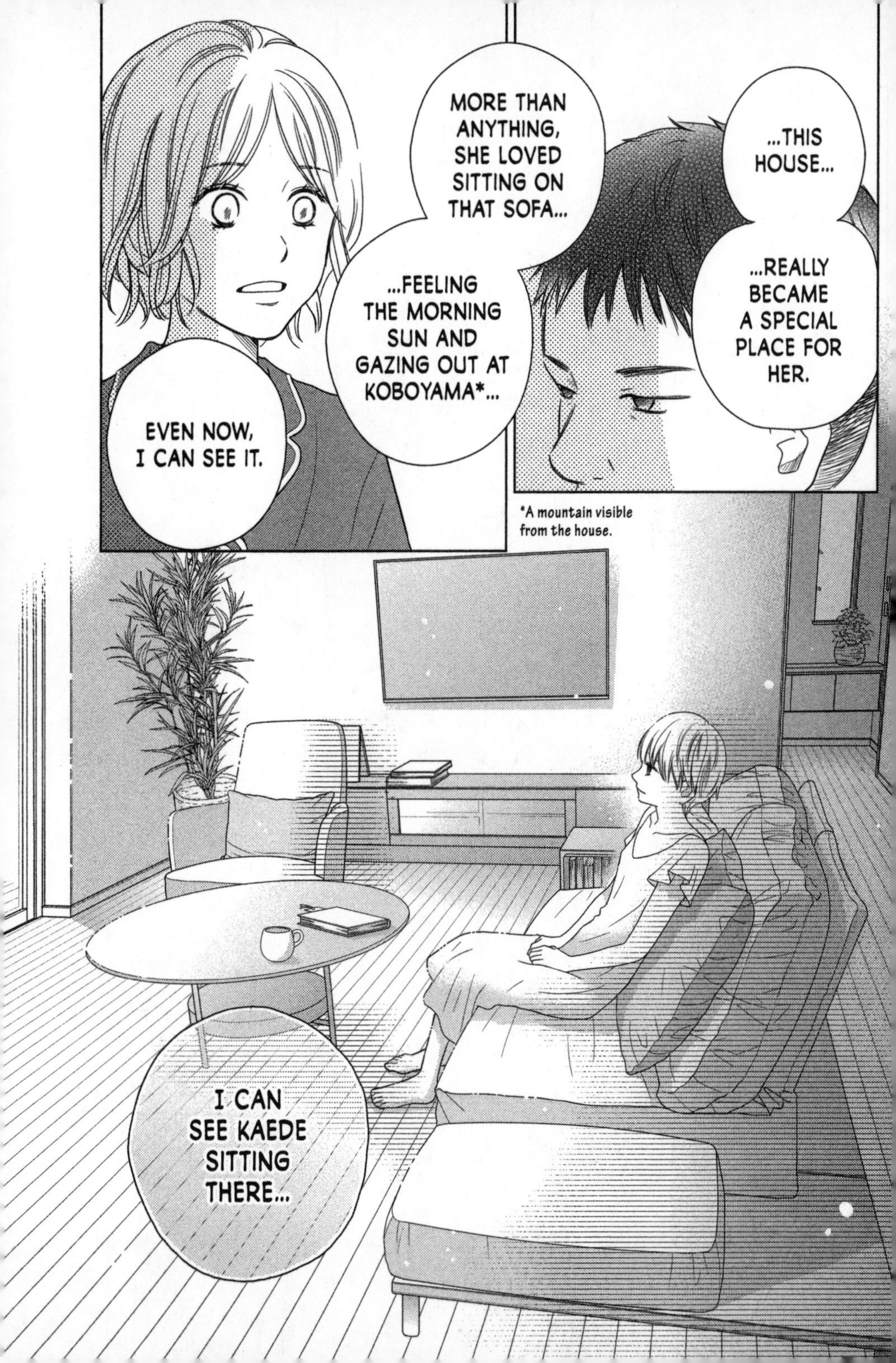
...THIS HOUSE...
...REALLY BECAME A SPECIAL PLACE FOR HER.
MORE THAN ANYTHING, SHE LOVED SITTING ON THAT SOFA...
...FEELING THE MORNING SUN AND GAZING OUT AT KOBOYAMA*...
EVEN NOW, I CAN SEE IT.
*A mountain visible from the house.
I CAN SEE KAEDE SITTING THERE...

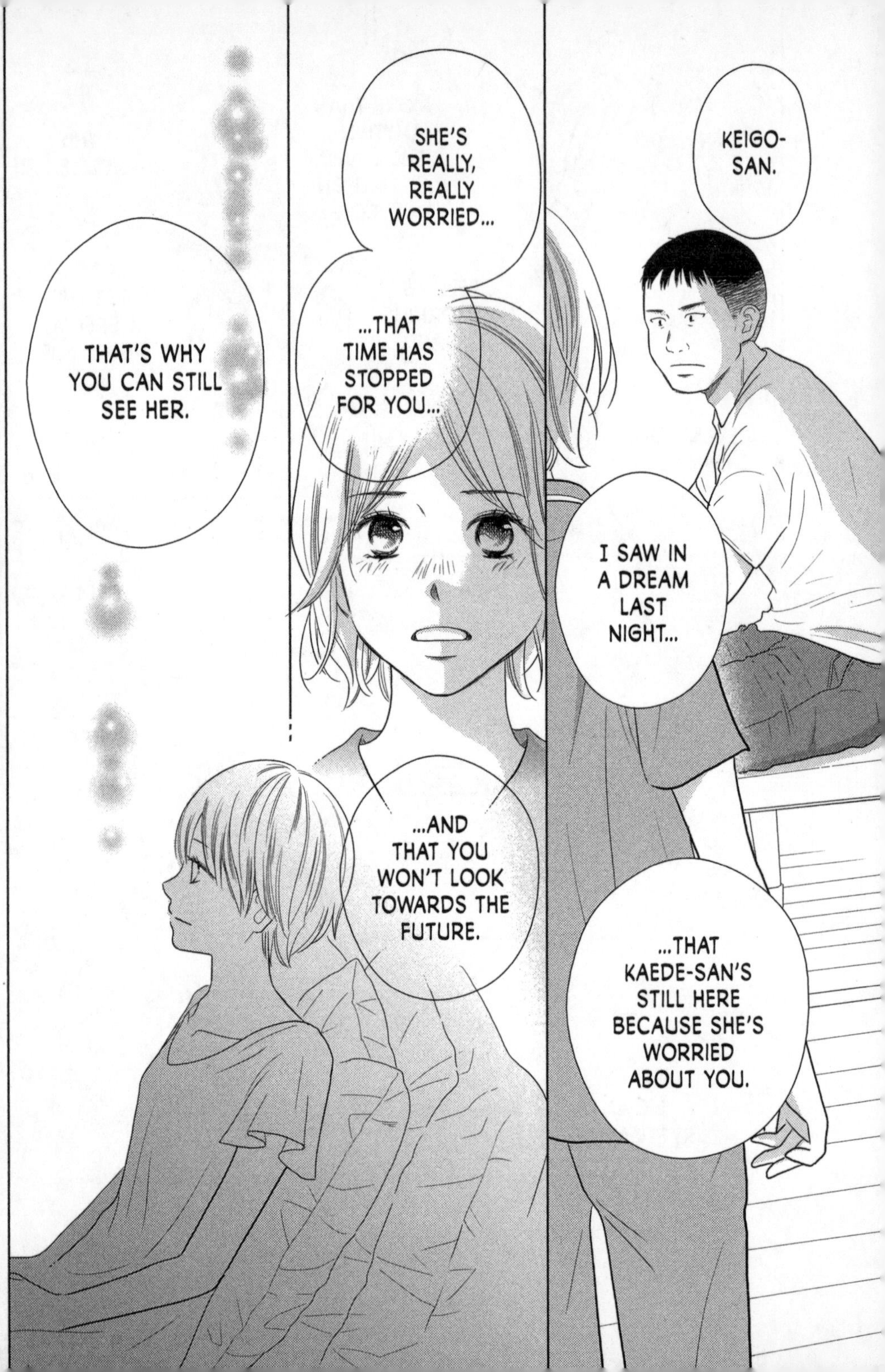
KEIGO-SAN.
I SAW IN A DREAM LAST NIGHT...
...THAT KAEDE-SAN'S STILL HERE BECAUSE SHE'S WORRIED ABOUT YOU.
SHE'S REALLY, REALLY WORRIED...
...THAT TIME HAS STOPPED FOR YOU...
...AND THAT YOU WON'T LOOK TOWARDS THE FUTURE.
THAT'S WHY YOU CAN STILL SEE HER.

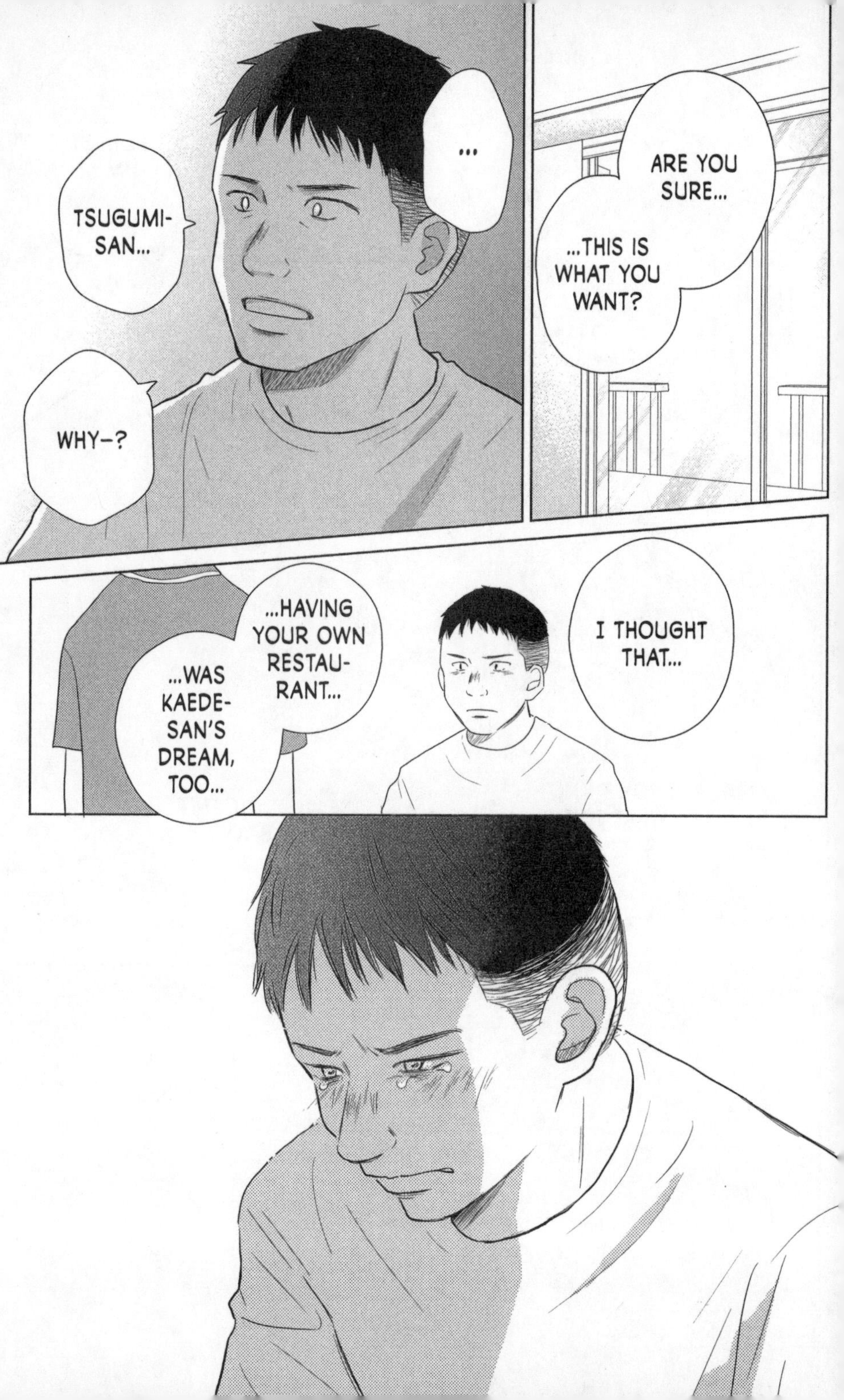
ARE YOU SURE...
...THIS IS WHAT YOU WANT?
...
TSUGUMI-SAN...
WHY–?
I THOUGHT THAT...
...HAVING YOUR OWN RESTAURANT...
...WAS KAEDE-SAN'S DREAM, TOO...

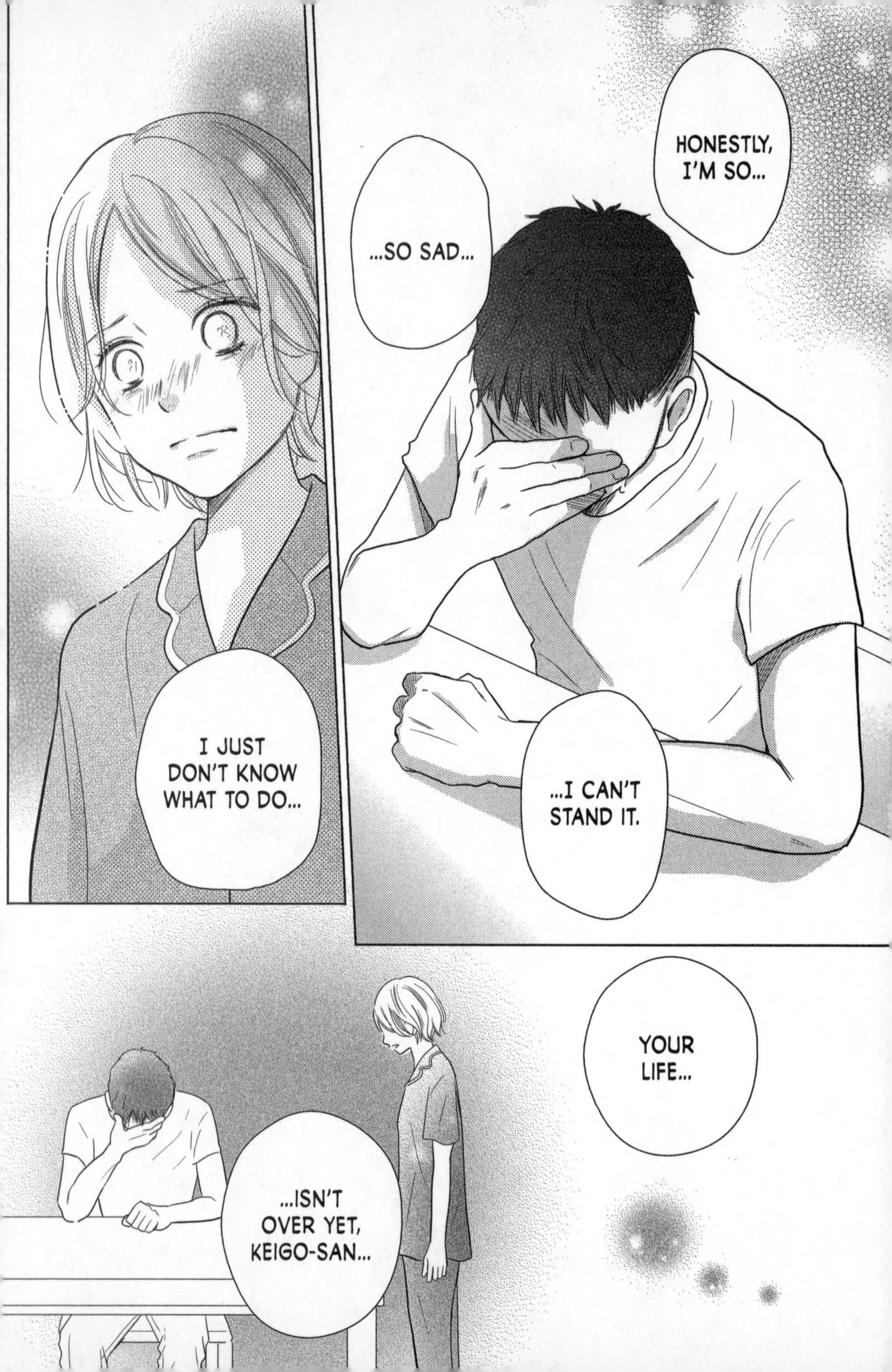
HONESTLY, I'M SO...
...SO SAD...
...I CAN'T STAND IT.
I JUST DON'T KNOW WHAT TO DO...
YOUR LIFE...
...ISN'T OVER YET, KEIGO-SAN...

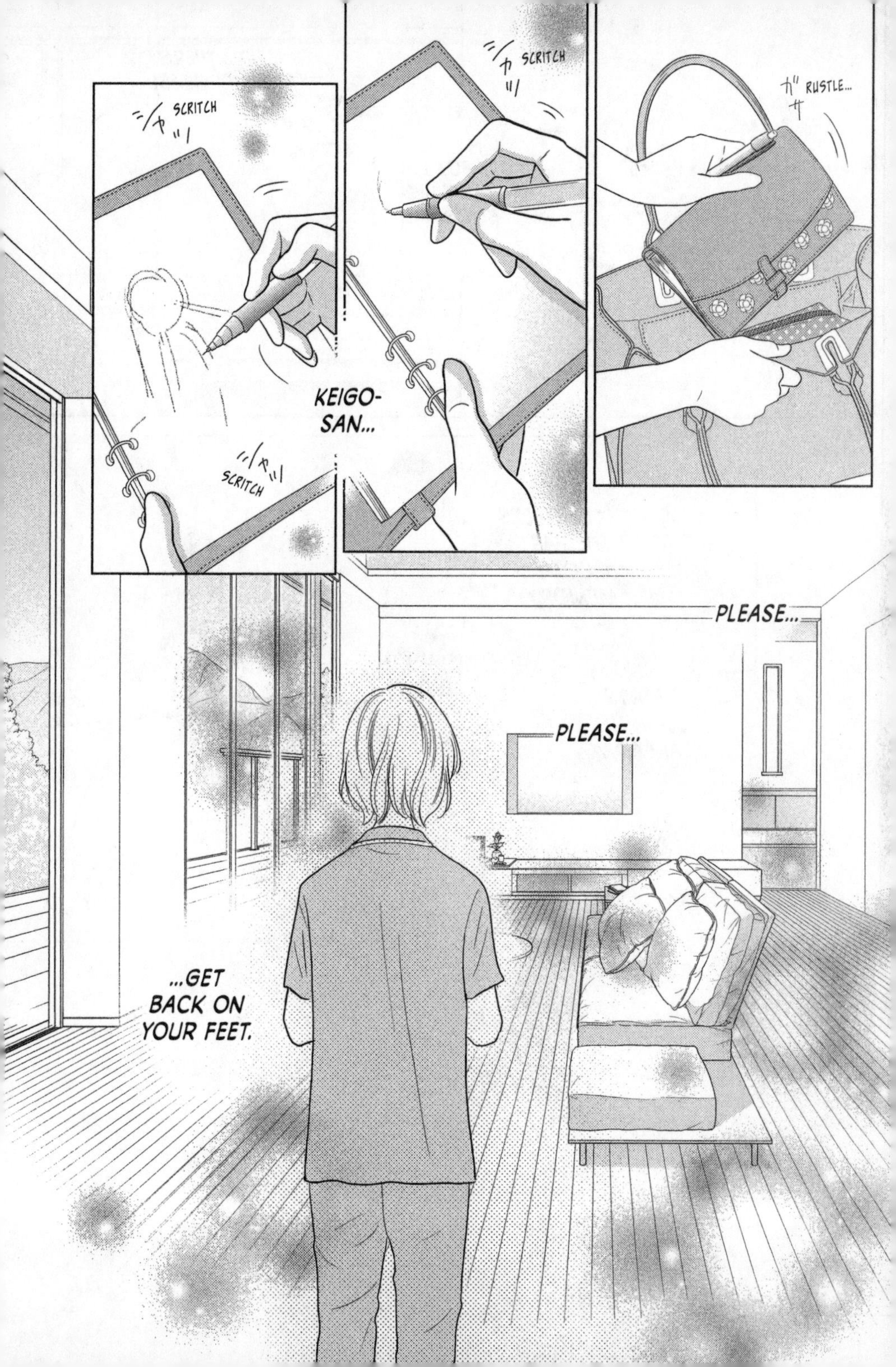
RUSTLE...
SCRITCH
SCRITCH
KEIGO-SAN...
SCRITCH
PLEASE...
PLEASE...
...GET BACK ON YOUR FEET.

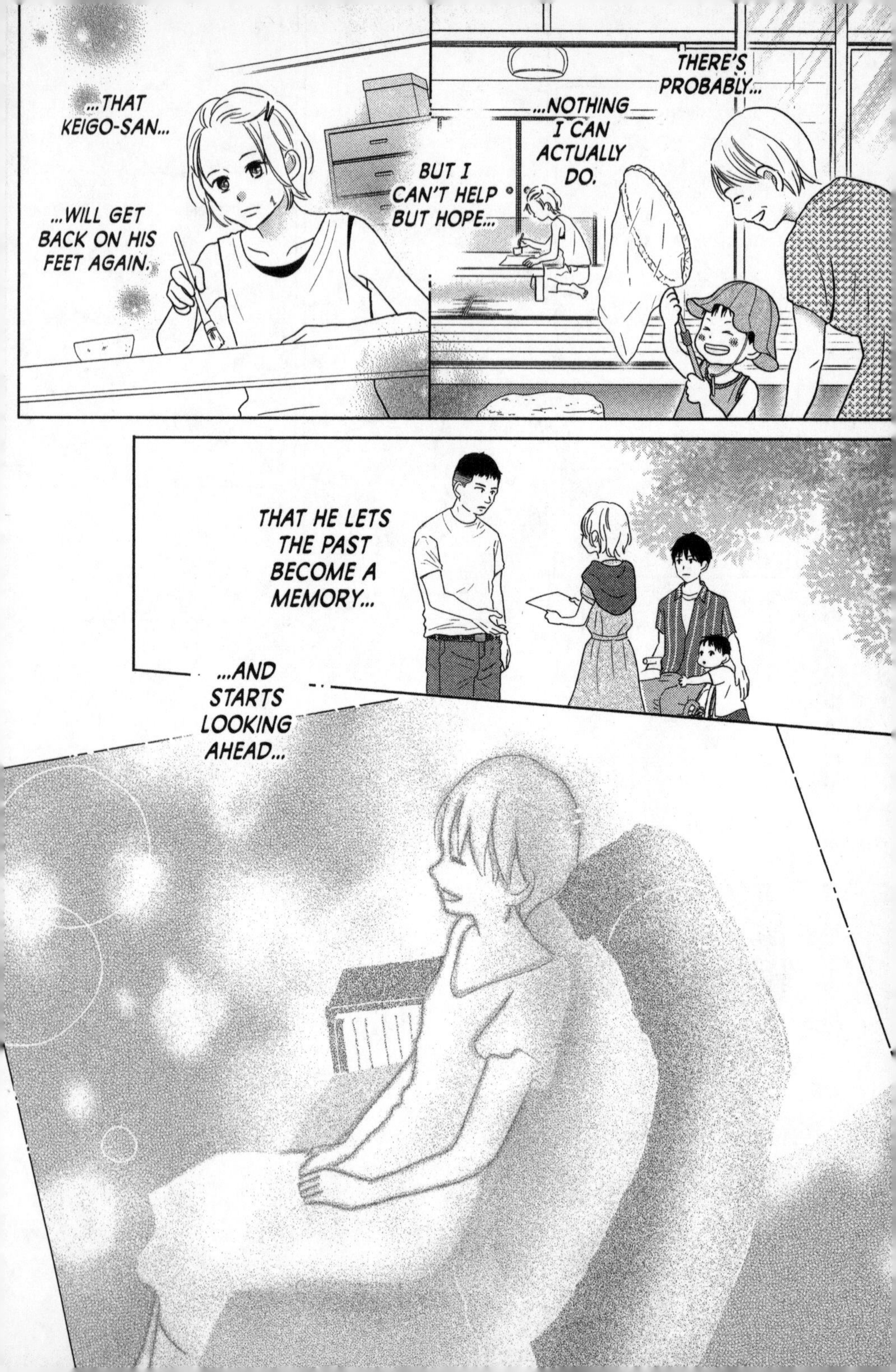
THERE'S PROBABLY...
...NOTHING I CAN ACTUALLY DO.
BUT I CAN'T HELP BUT HOPE...
...THAT KEIGO-SAN...
...WILL GET BACK ON HIS FEET AGAIN.
THAT HE LETS THE PAST BECOME A MEMORY...
...AND STARTS LOOKING AHEAD...

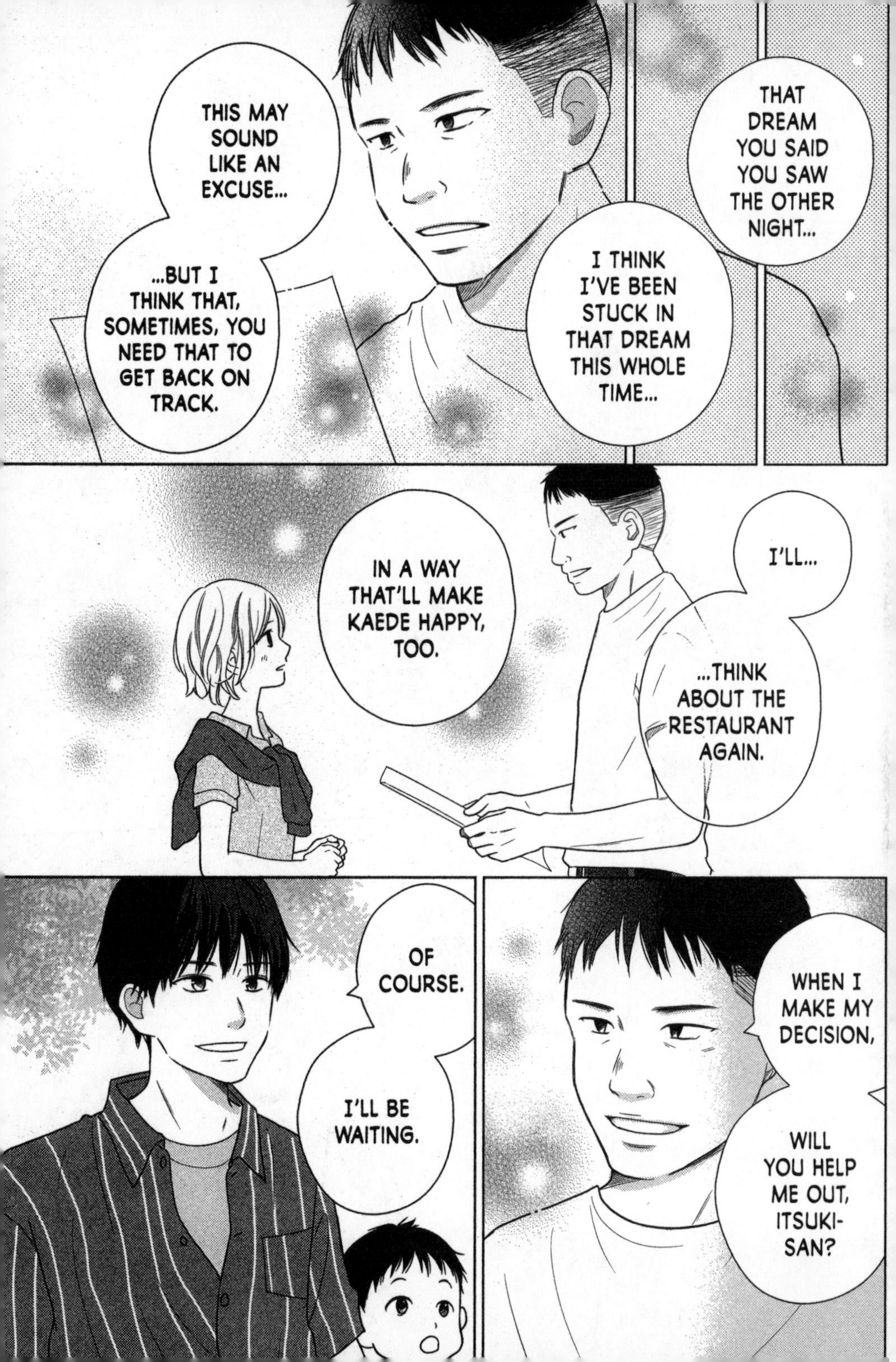
THAT DREAM YOU SAID YOU SAW THE OTHER NIGHT...
I THINK I'VE BEEN STUCK IN THAT DREAM THIS WHOLE TIME...
THIS MAY SOUND LIKE AN EXCUSE...
...BUT I THINK THAT, SOMETIMES, YOU NEED THAT TO GET BACK ON TRACK.
I'LL...
...THINK ABOUT THE RESTAURANT AGAIN.
IN A WAY THAT'LL MAKE KAEDE HAPPY, TOO.
WHEN I MAKE MY DECISION,
WILL YOU HELP ME OUT, ITSUKI-SAN?
OF COURSE.
I'LL BE WAITING.

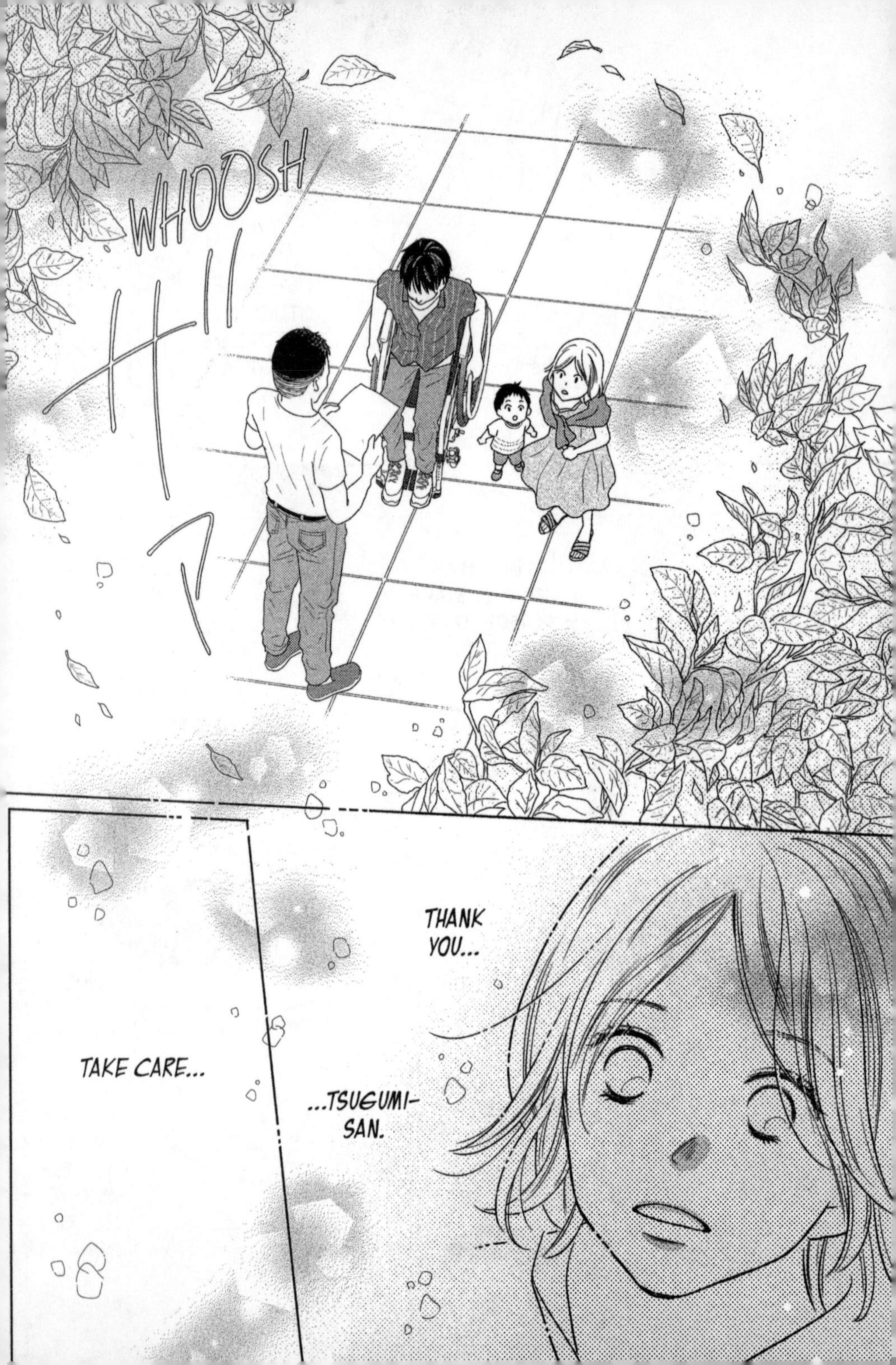
WHOOSH
THANK YOU...
...TSUGUMI-SAN.
TAKE CARE...

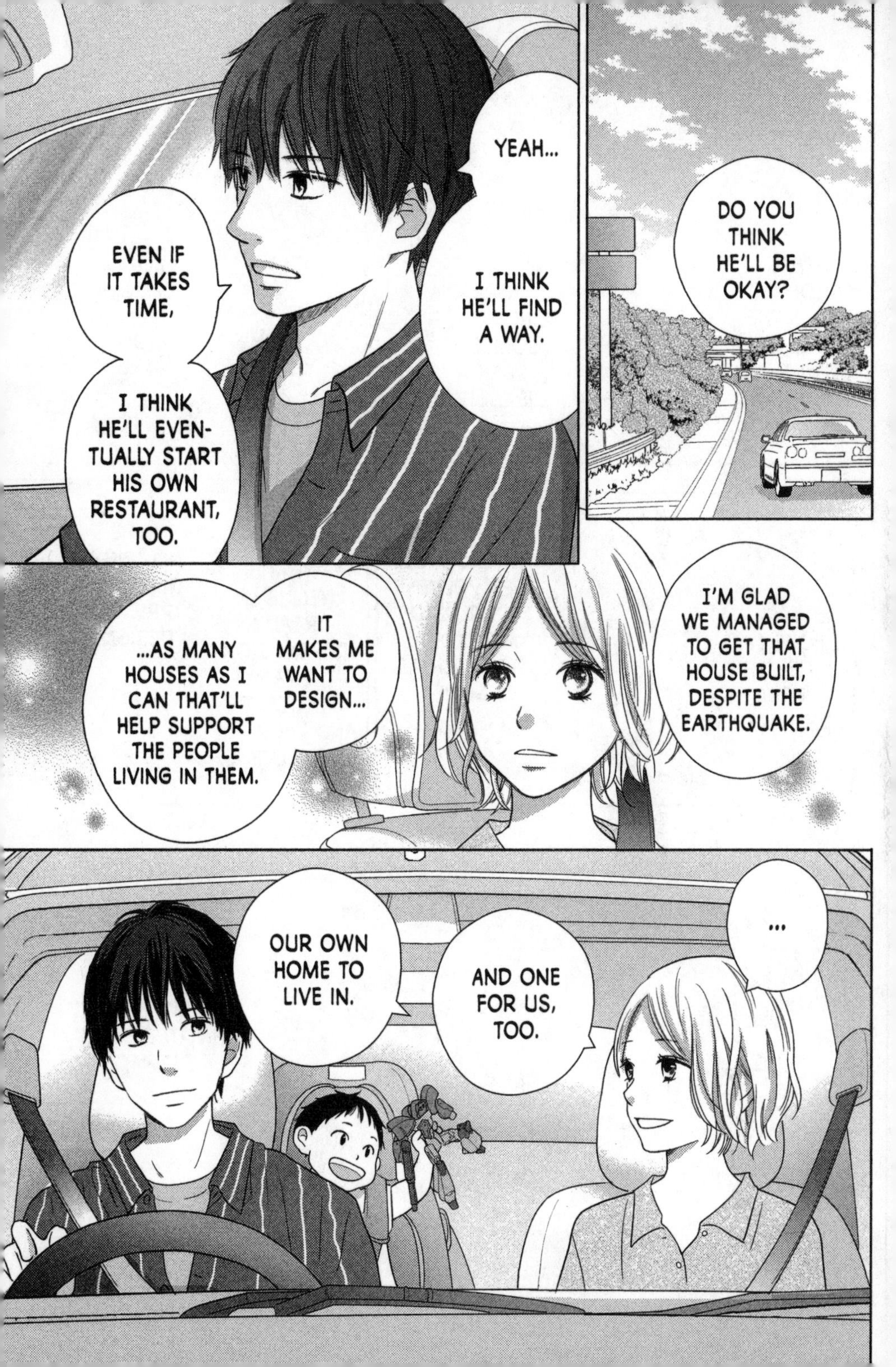
DO YOU THINK HE'LL BE OKAY?
YEAH...
I THINK HE'LL FIND A WAY.
EVEN IF IT TAKES TIME,
I THINK HE'LL EVENTUALLY START HIS OWN RESTAURANT, TOO.
I'M GLAD WE MANAGED TO GET THAT HOUSE BUILT, DESPITE THE EARTHQUAKE.
IT MAKES ME WANT TO DESIGN...
...AS MANY HOUSES AS I CAN THAT'LL HELP SUPPORT THE PEOPLE LIVING IN THEM.
...
AND ONE FOR US, TOO.
OUR OWN HOME TO LIVE IN.

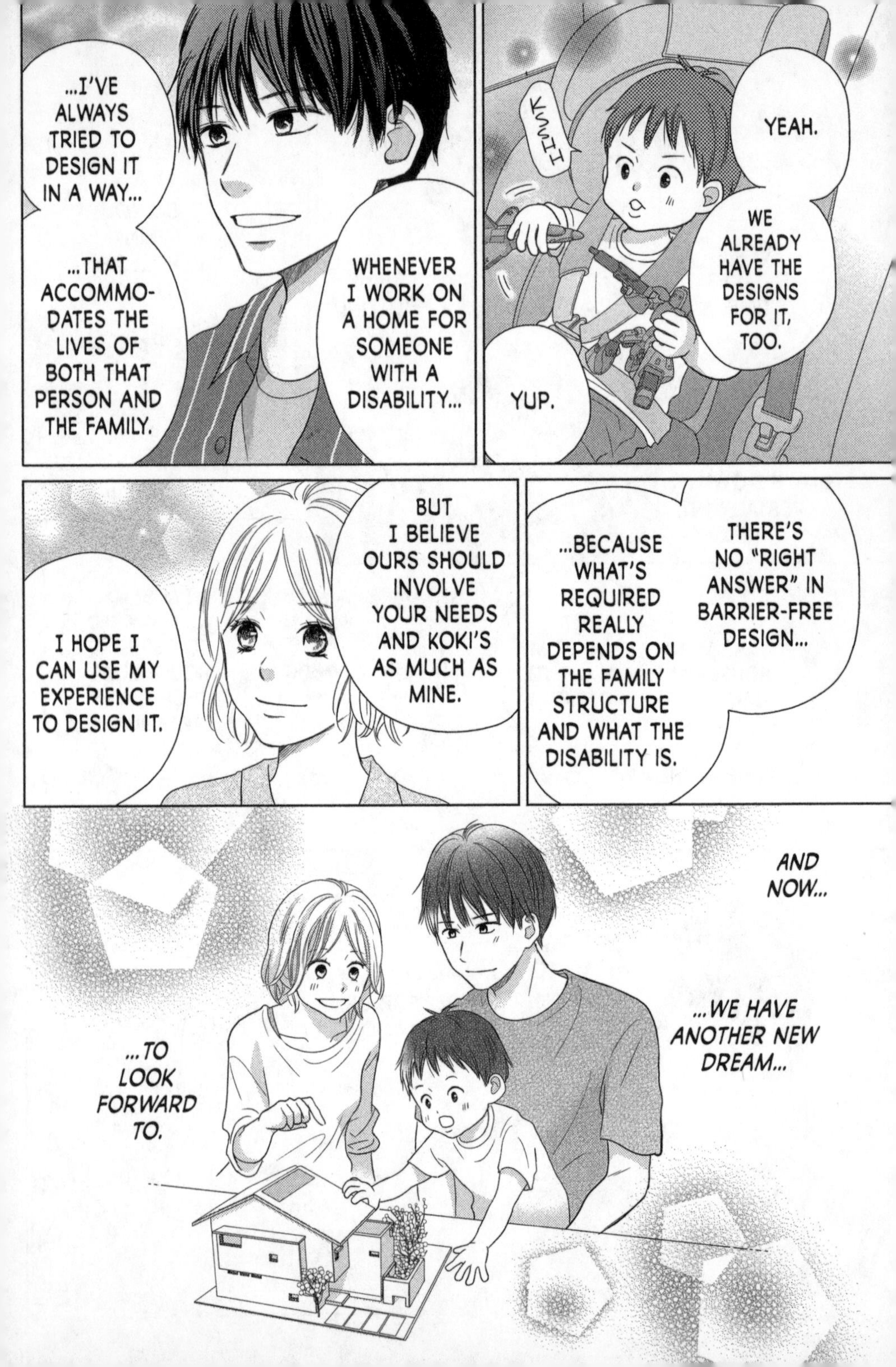
YEAH.
WE ALREADY HAVE THE DESIGNS FOR IT, TOO.
YUP.
...I'VE ALWAYS TRIED TO DESIGN IT IN A WAY...
WHENEVER I WORK ON A HOME FOR SOMEONE WITH A DISABILITY...
...THAT ACCOMMODATES THE LIVES OF BOTH THAT PERSON AND THE FAMILY.
THERE'S NO "RIGHT ANSWER" IN BARRIER-FREE DESIGN...
...BECAUSE WHAT'S REQUIRED REALLY DEPENDS ON THE FAMILY STRUCTURE AND WHAT THE DISABILITY IS.
BUT I BELIEVE OURS SHOULD INVOLVE YOUR NEEDS AND KOKI'S AS MUCH AS MINE.
I HOPE I CAN USE MY EXPERIENCE TO DESIGN IT.
AND NOW...
...WE HAVE ANOTHER NEW DREAM...
...TO LOOK FORWARD TO.

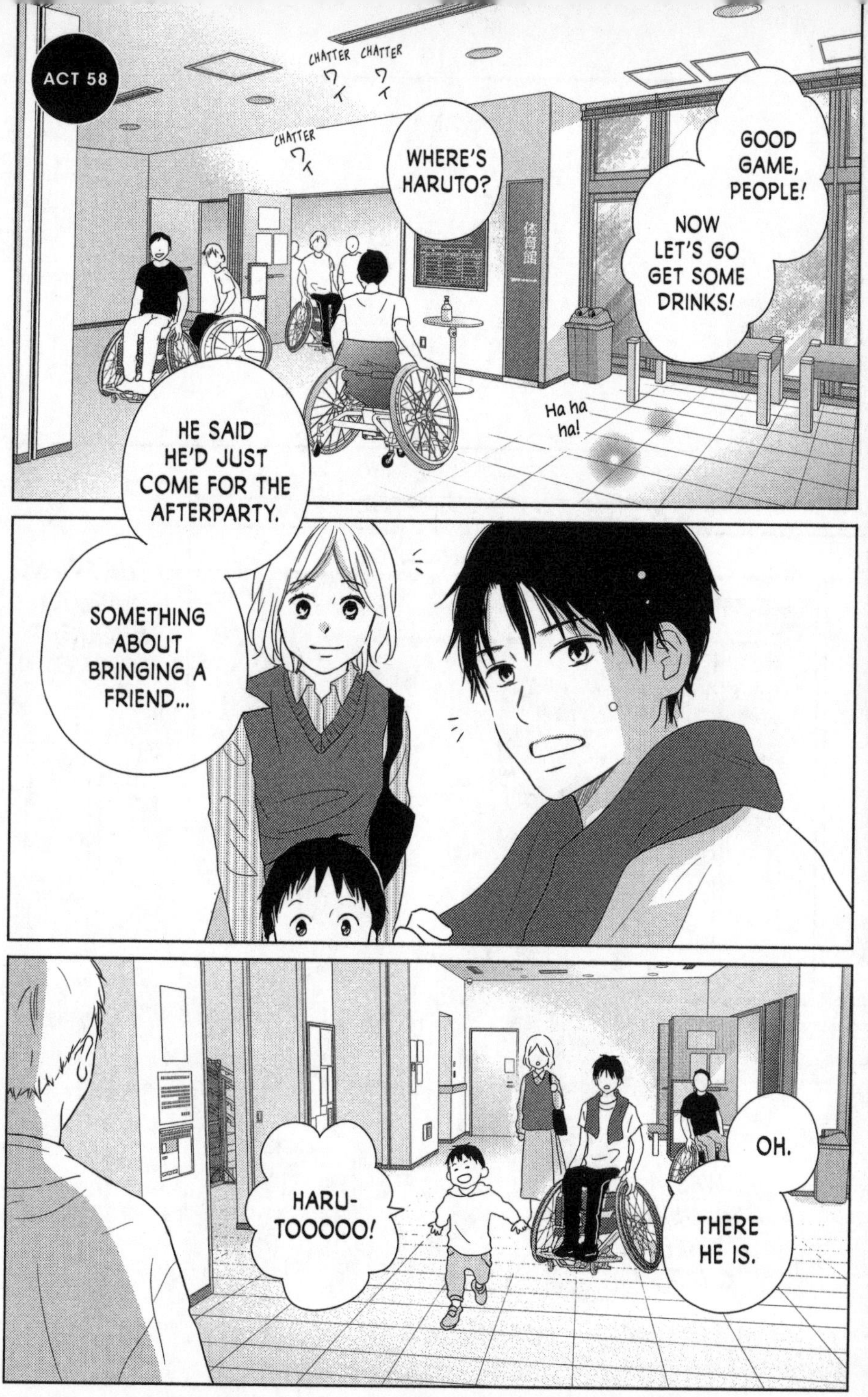
ACT 58
GOOD GAME, PEOPLE!
NOW LET'S GO GET SOME DRINKS!
CHATTER CHATTER
ワイワイ
WHERE'S HARUTO?
CHATTER
ワイ
Ha ha ha!
HE SAID HE'D JUST COME FOR THE AFTERPARTY.
SOMETHING ABOUT BRINGING A FRIEND...
OH.
THERE HE IS.
HARU-TOOOOO!

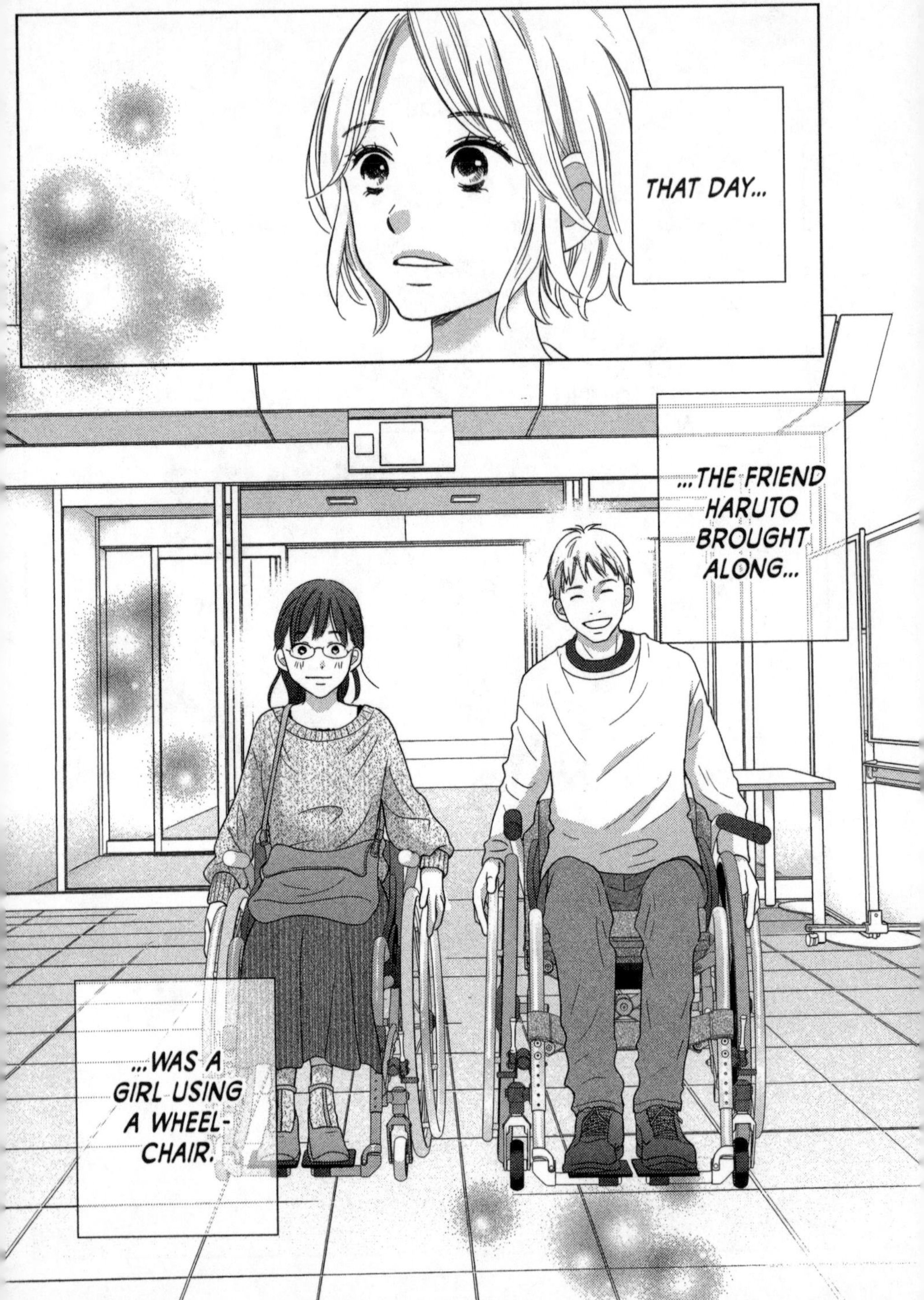
THAT DAY...
...THE FRIEND HARUTO BROUGHT ALONG...
...WAS A GIRL USING A WHEEL-CHAIR.

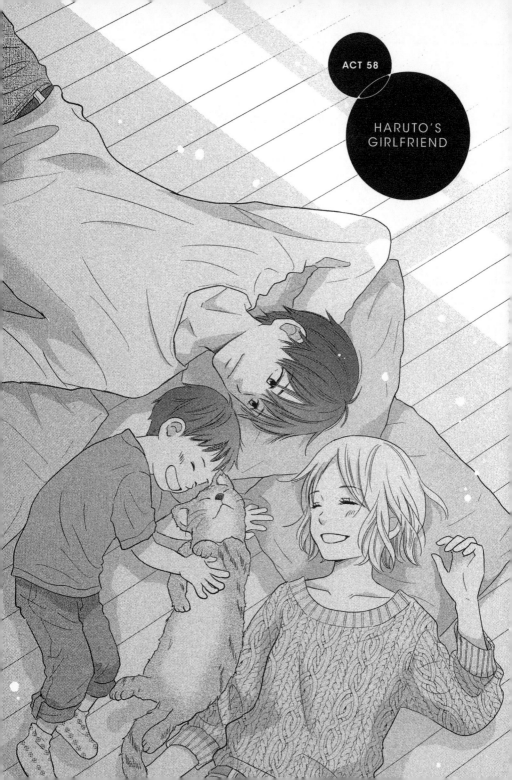

ACT 58

HARUTO'S
GIRLFRIEND

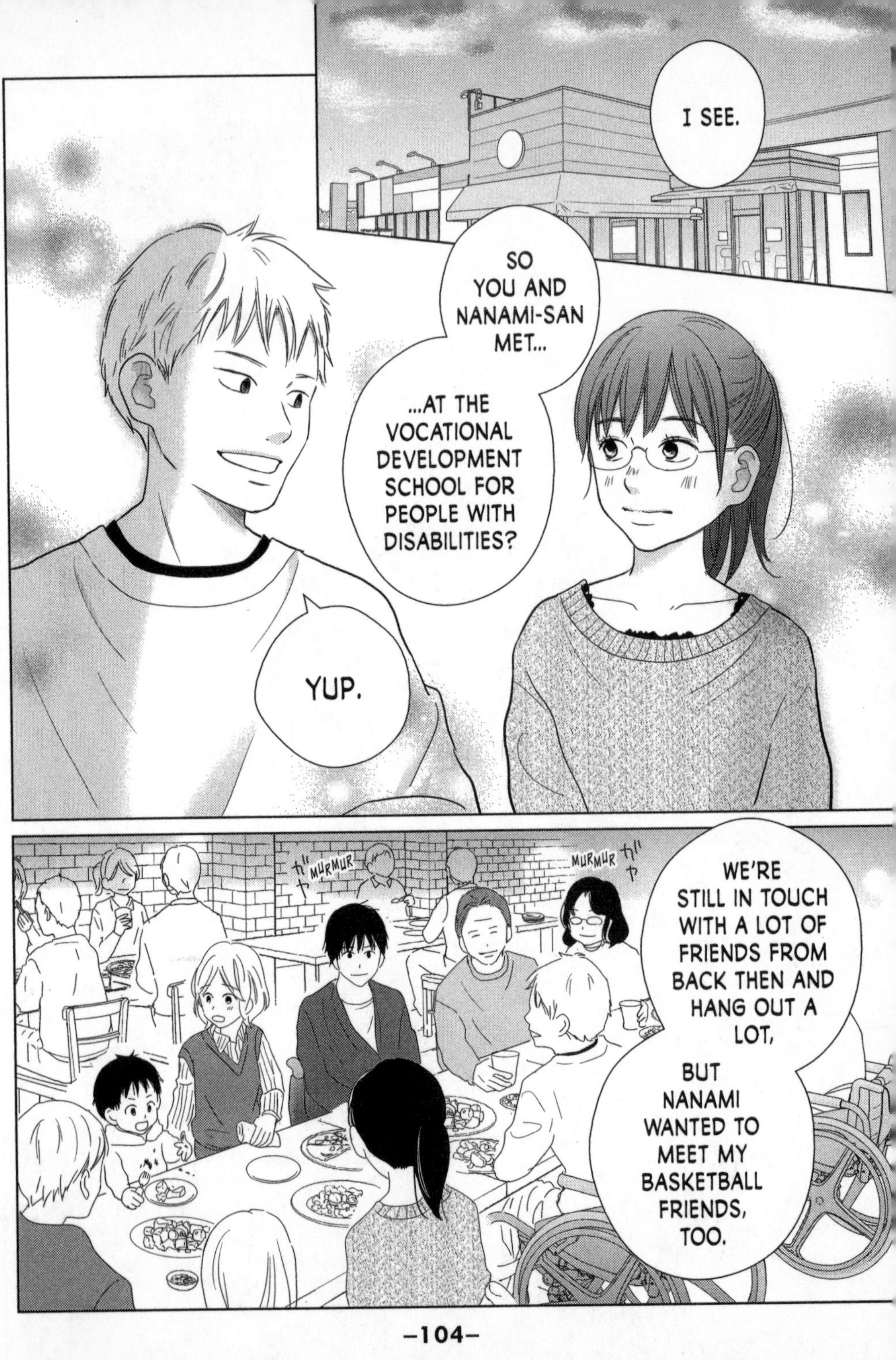
I SEE.
SO YOU AND NANAMI-SAN MET...
...AT THE VOCATIONAL DEVELOPMENT SCHOOL FOR PEOPLE WITH DISABILITIES?
YUP.
ガヤ
MURMUR
ガヤ
MURMUR
WE'RE STILL IN TOUCH WITH A LOT OF FRIENDS FROM BACK THEN AND HANG OUT A LOT,
BUT NANAMI WANTED TO MEET MY BASKETBALL FRIENDS, TOO.

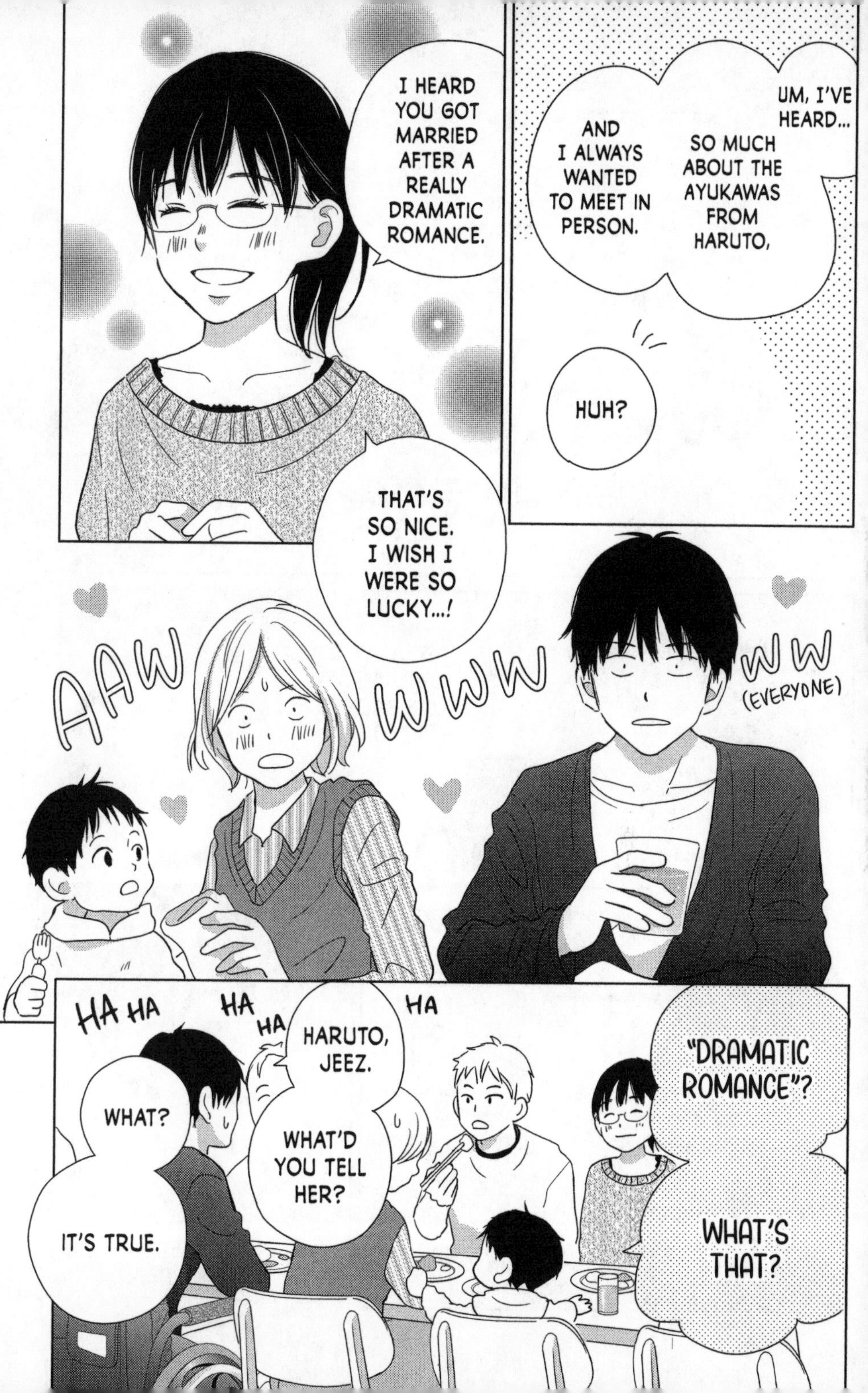
UM, I'VE HEARD...
SO MUCH ABOUT THE AYUKAWAS FROM HARUTO,
AND I ALWAYS WANTED TO MEET IN PERSON.
HUH?
I HEARD YOU GOT MARRIED AFTER A REALLY DRAMATIC ROMANCE.
THAT'S SO NICE. I WISH I WERE SO LUCKY...!
AAWWWWWWW
(EVERYONE)
"DRAMATIC ROMANCE"?
WHAT'S THAT?
HA HA HA HA HA
HARUTO, JEEZ.
WHAT'D YOU TELL HER?
WHAT?
IT'S TRUE.

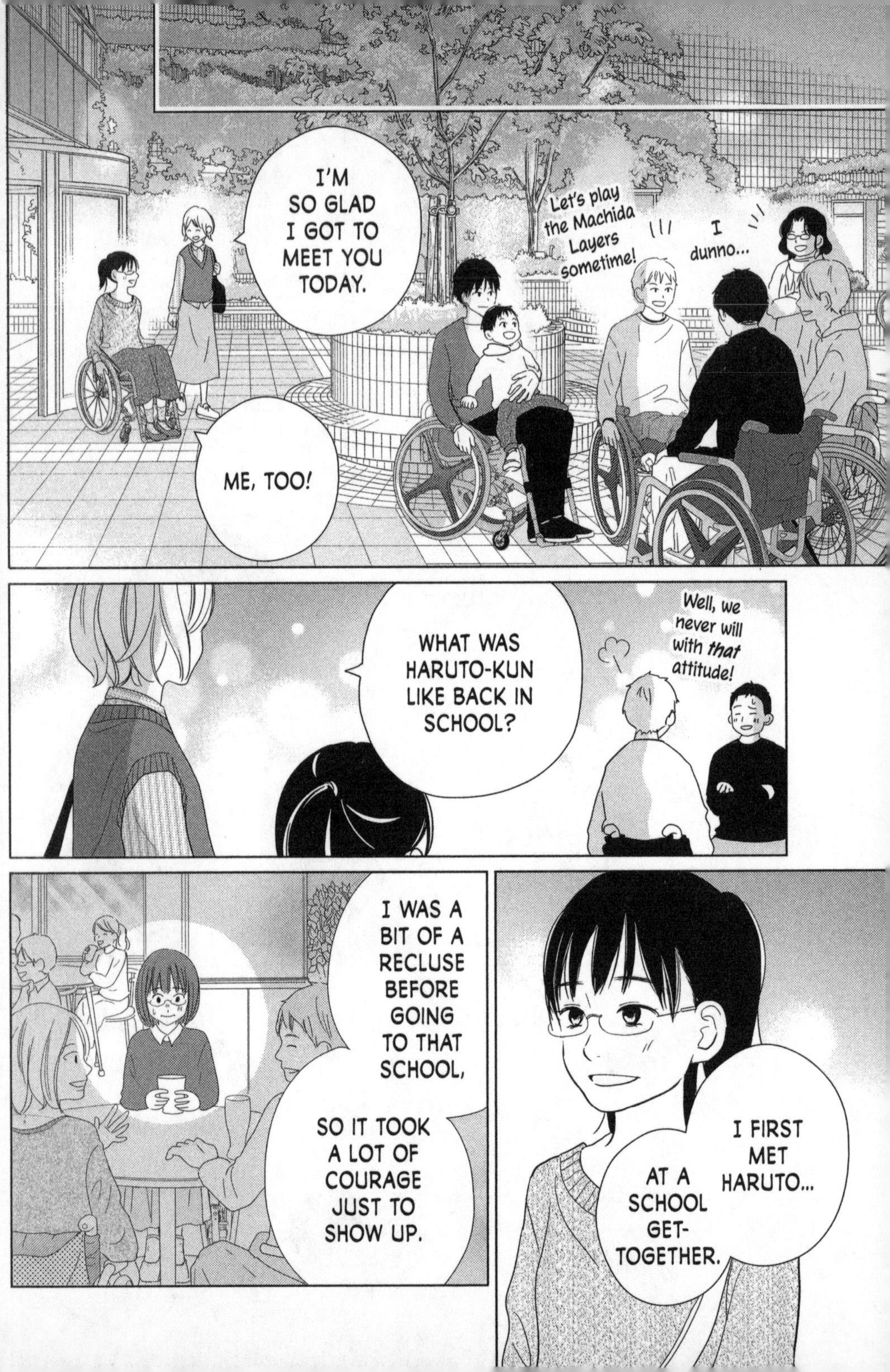

Let's play the Machida Layers sometime!
I dunno...
I'M SO GLAD I GOT TO MEET YOU TODAY.
ME, TOO!
Well, we never will with *that* attitude!
WHAT WAS HARUTO-KUN LIKE BACK IN SCHOOL?
I FIRST MET HARUTO...
AT A SCHOOL GET-TOGETHER.
I WAS A BIT OF A RECLUSE BEFORE GOING TO THAT SCHOOL,
SO IT TOOK A LOT OF COURAGE JUST TO SHOW UP.

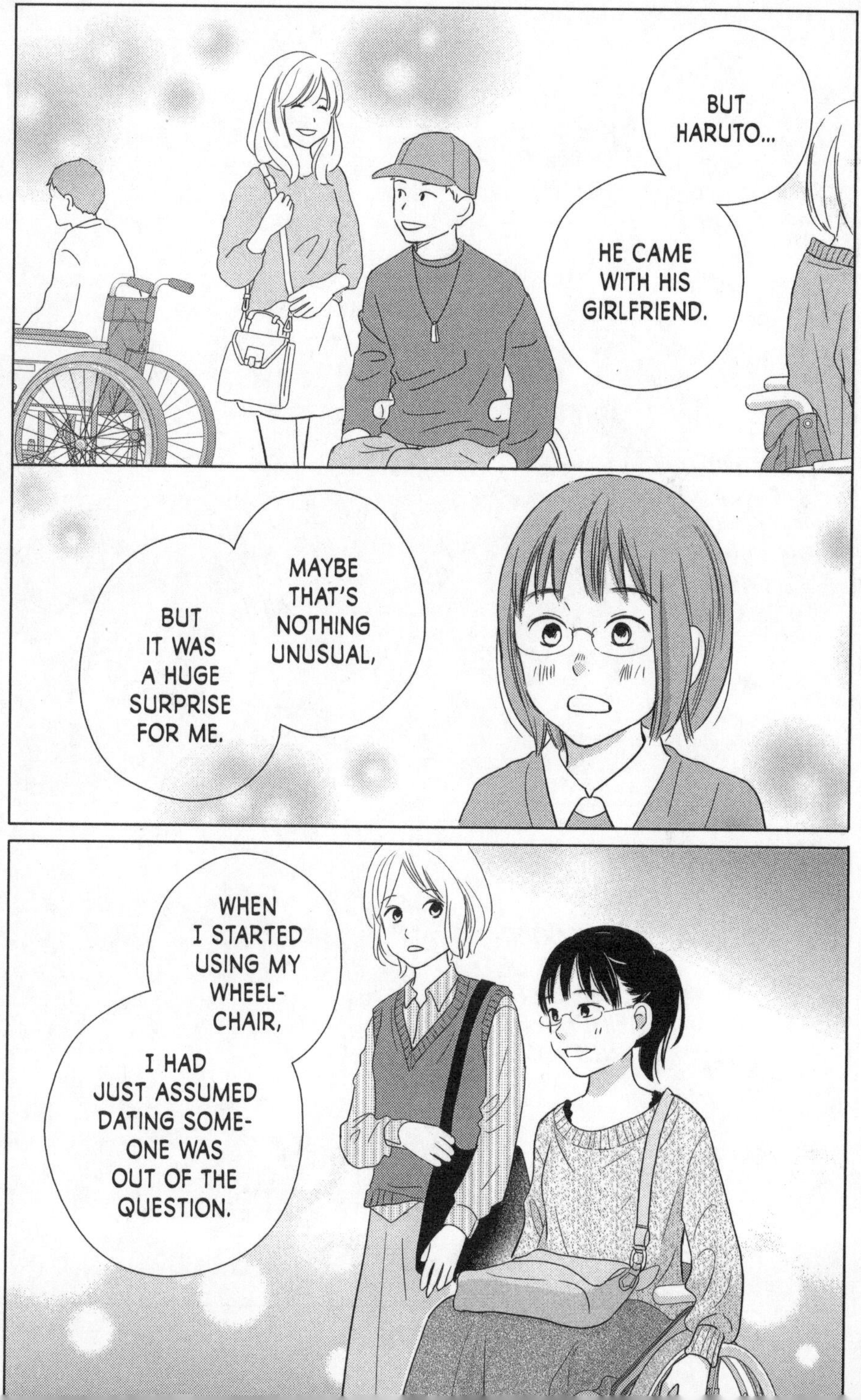
BUT HARUTO...
HE CAME WITH HIS GIRLFRIEND.
MAYBE THAT'S NOTHING UNUSUAL,
BUT IT WAS A HUGE SURPRISE FOR ME.
WHEN I STARTED USING MY WHEEL-CHAIR,
I HAD JUST ASSUMED DATING SOME-ONE WAS OUT OF THE QUESTION.

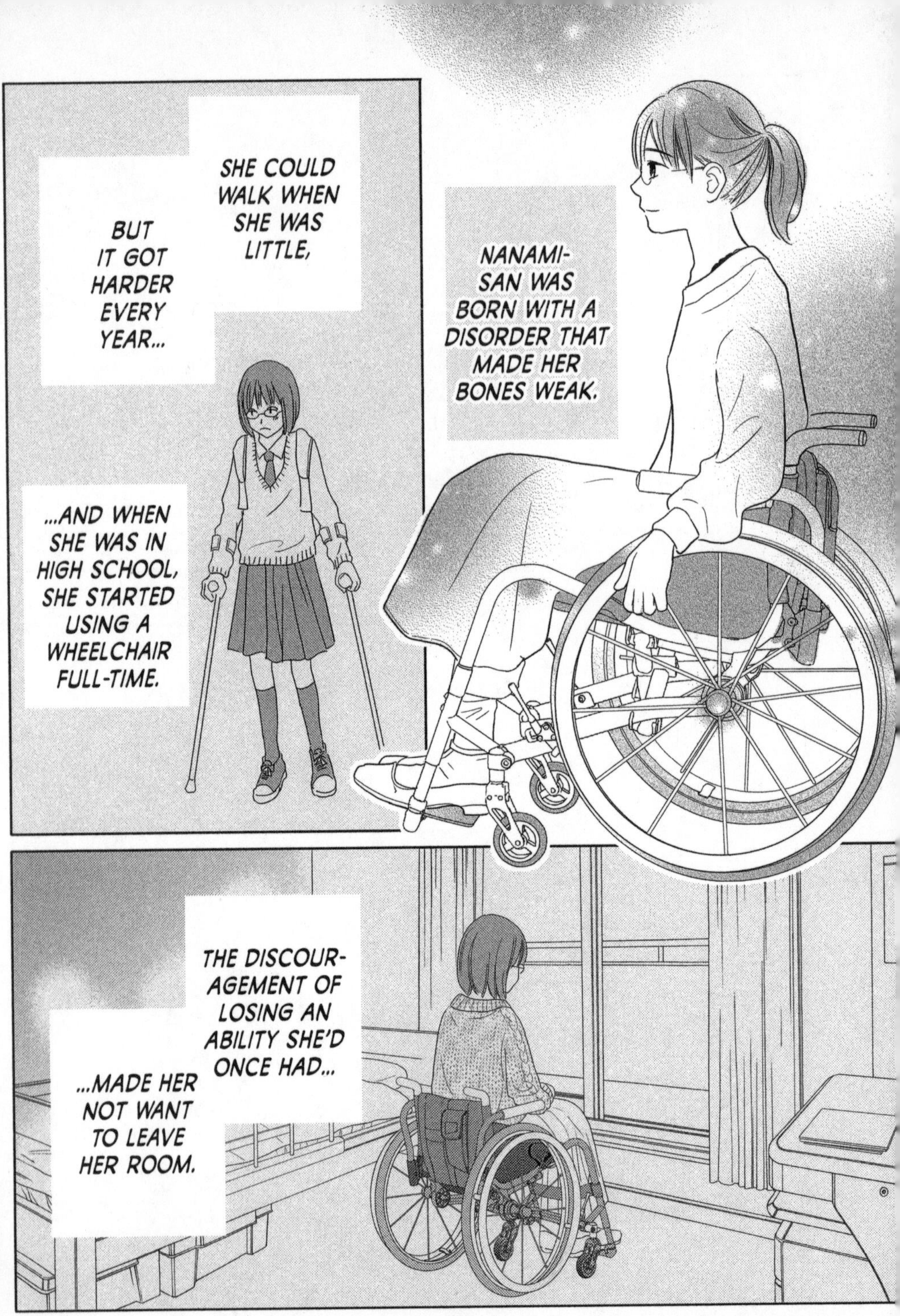
NANAMI-SAN WAS BORN WITH A DISORDER THAT MADE HER BONES WEAK.
SHE COULD WALK WHEN SHE WAS LITTLE,
BUT IT GOT HARDER EVERY YEAR...
...AND WHEN SHE WAS IN HIGH SCHOOL, SHE STARTED USING A WHEELCHAIR FULL-TIME.
THE DISCOUR-AGEMENT OF LOSING AN ABILITY SHE'D ONCE HAD...
...MADE HER NOT WANT TO LEAVE HER ROOM.

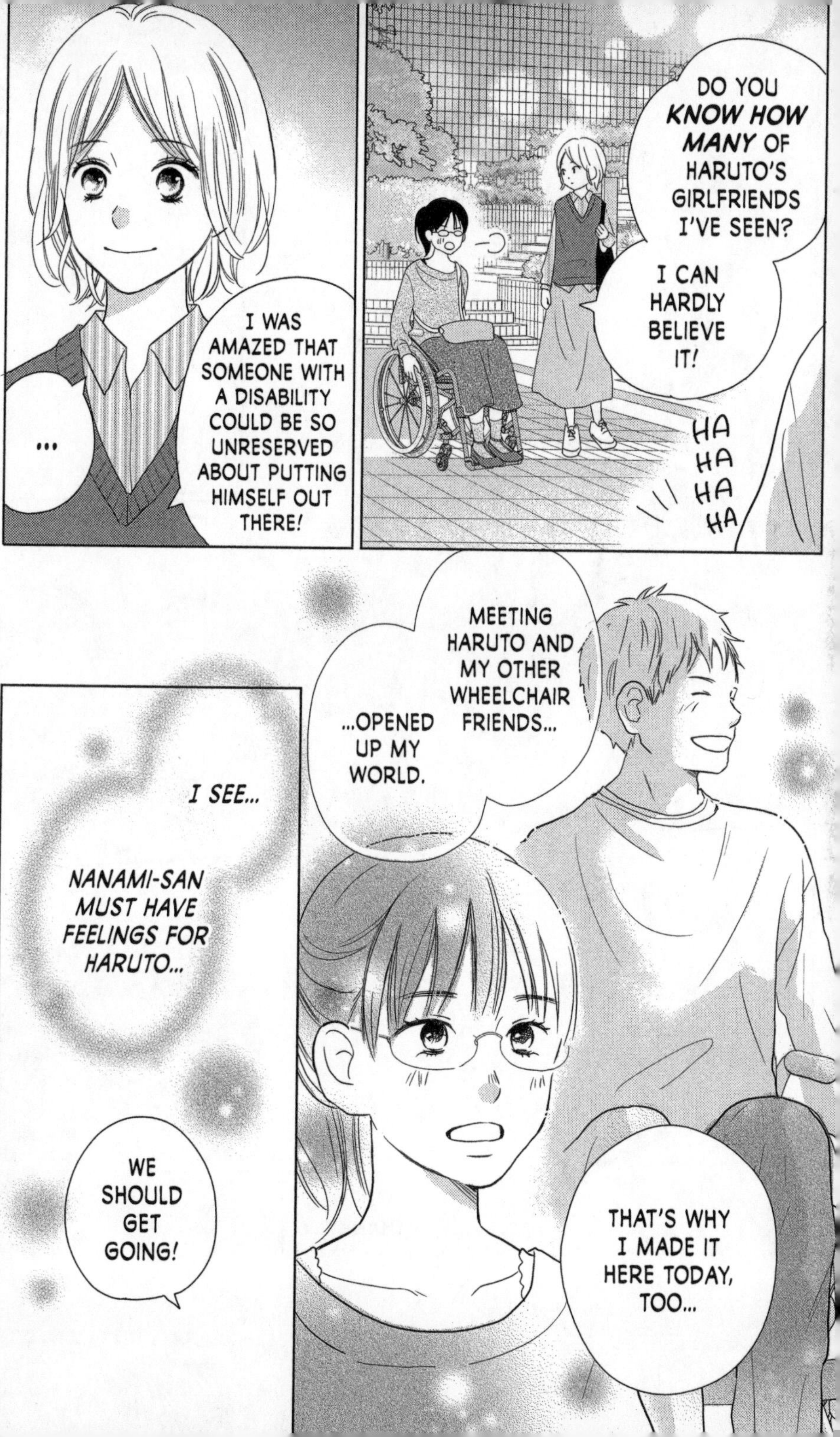
DO YOU *KNOW HOW MANY* OF HARUTO'S GIRLFRIENDS I'VE SEEN?
I CAN HARDLY BELIEVE IT!
HA HA HA HA
I WAS AMAZED THAT SOMEONE WITH A DISABILITY COULD BE SO UNRESERVED ABOUT PUTTING HIMSELF OUT THERE!
...
MEETING HARUTO AND MY OTHER WHEELCHAIR FRIENDS...
...OPENED UP MY WORLD.
THAT'S WHY I MADE IT HERE TODAY, TOO...
I SEE...
NANAMI-SAN MUST HAVE FEELINGS FOR HARUTO...
WE SHOULD GET GOING!

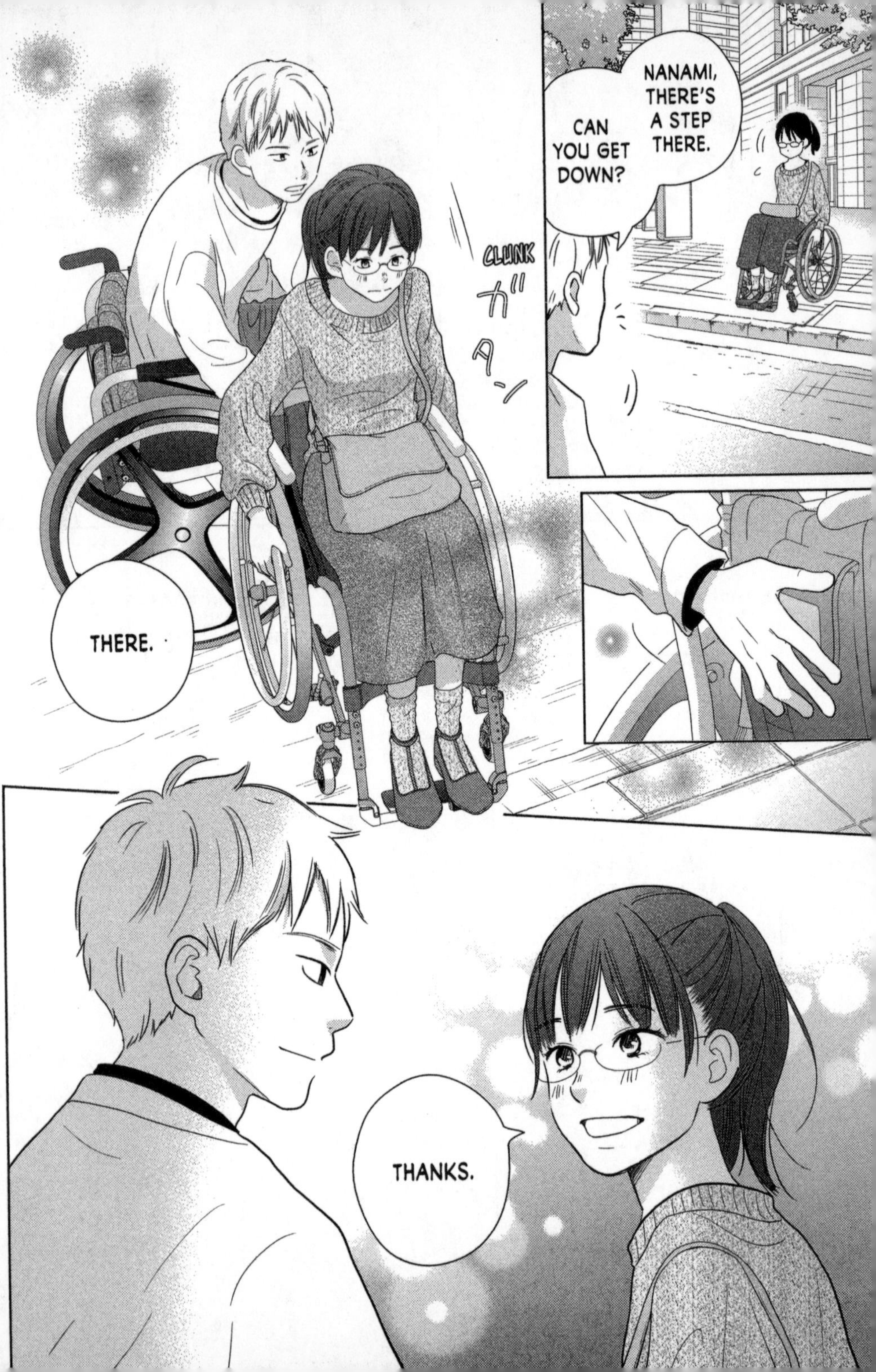
NANAMI, THERE'S A STEP THERE.
CAN YOU GET DOWN?
CLUNK
ガターン
THERE.
THANKS.

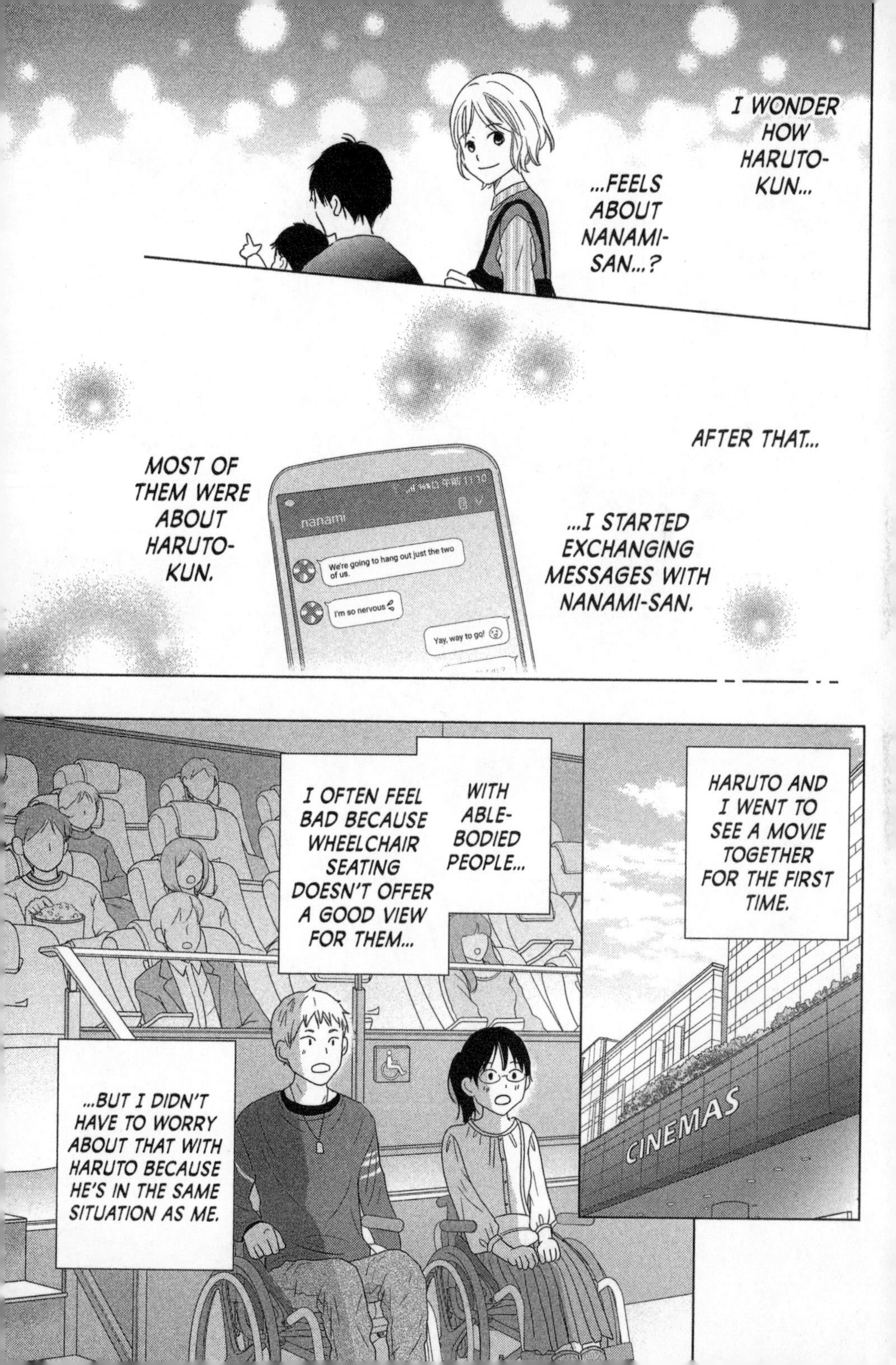
I WONDER HOW HARUTO-KUN...
...FEELS ABOUT NANAMI-SAN...?
AFTER THAT...
...I STARTED EXCHANGING MESSAGES WITH NANAMI-SAN.
nanami
We're going to hang out just the two of us.
I'm so nervous
Yay, way to go!
MOST OF THEM WERE ABOUT HARUTO-KUN.
HARUTO AND I WENT TO SEE A MOVIE TOGETHER FOR THE FIRST TIME.
CINEMAS
WITH ABLE-BODIED PEOPLE...
I OFTEN FEEL BAD BECAUSE WHEELCHAIR SEATING DOESN'T OFFER A GOOD VIEW FOR THEM...
...BUT I DIDN'T HAVE TO WORRY ABOUT THAT WITH HARUTO BECAUSE HE'S IN THE SAME SITUATION AS ME.

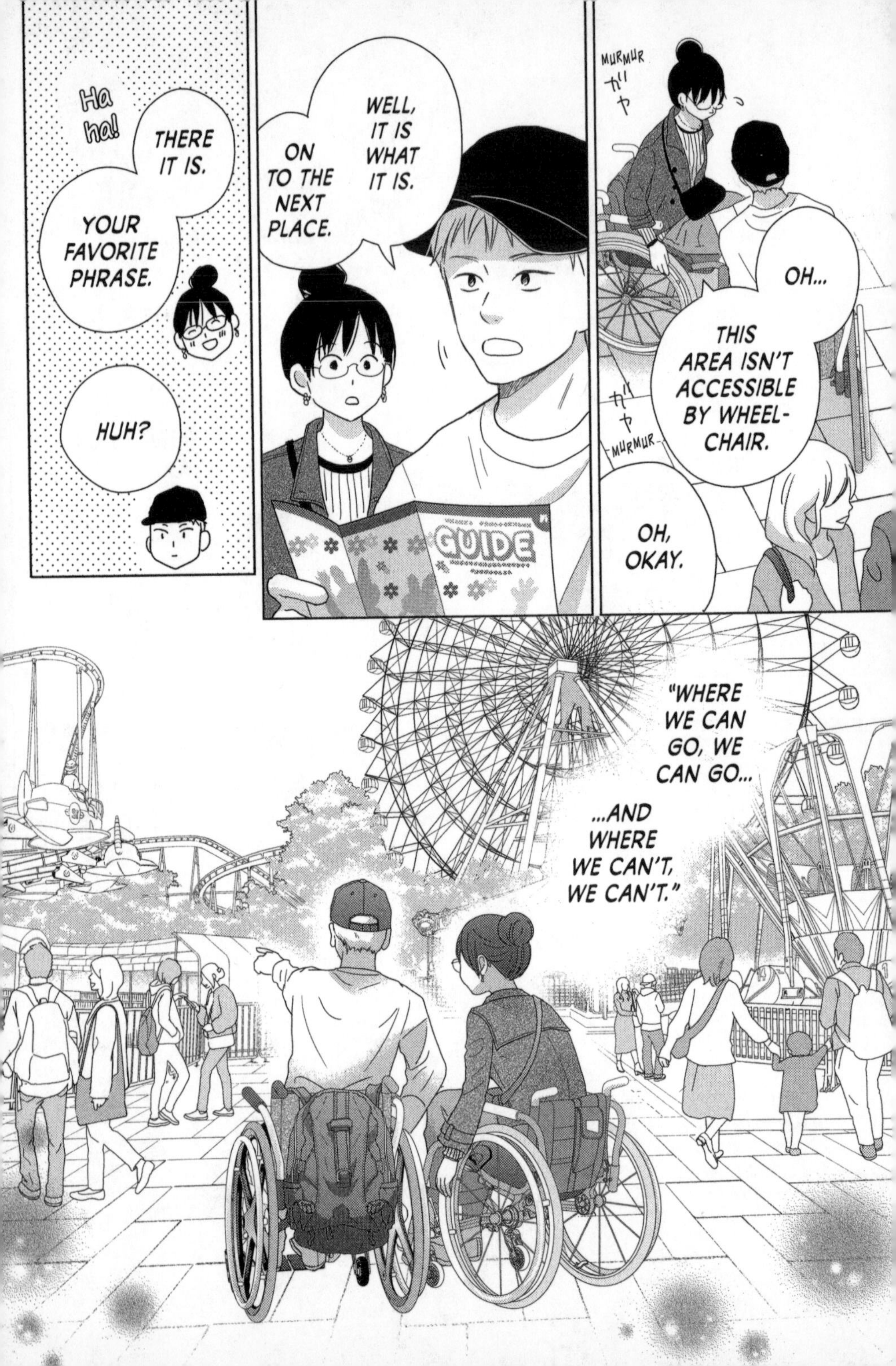
MURMUR ガヤ
OH... THIS AREA ISN'T ACCESSIBLE BY WHEEL-CHAIR.
ガヤ MURMUR
OH, OKAY.
WELL, IT IS WHAT IT IS.
ON TO THE NEXT PLACE.
GUIDE
Ha ha!
THERE IT IS.
YOUR FAVORITE PHRASE.
HUH?
"WHERE WE CAN GO, WE CAN GO...
...AND WHERE WE CAN'T, WE CAN'T."

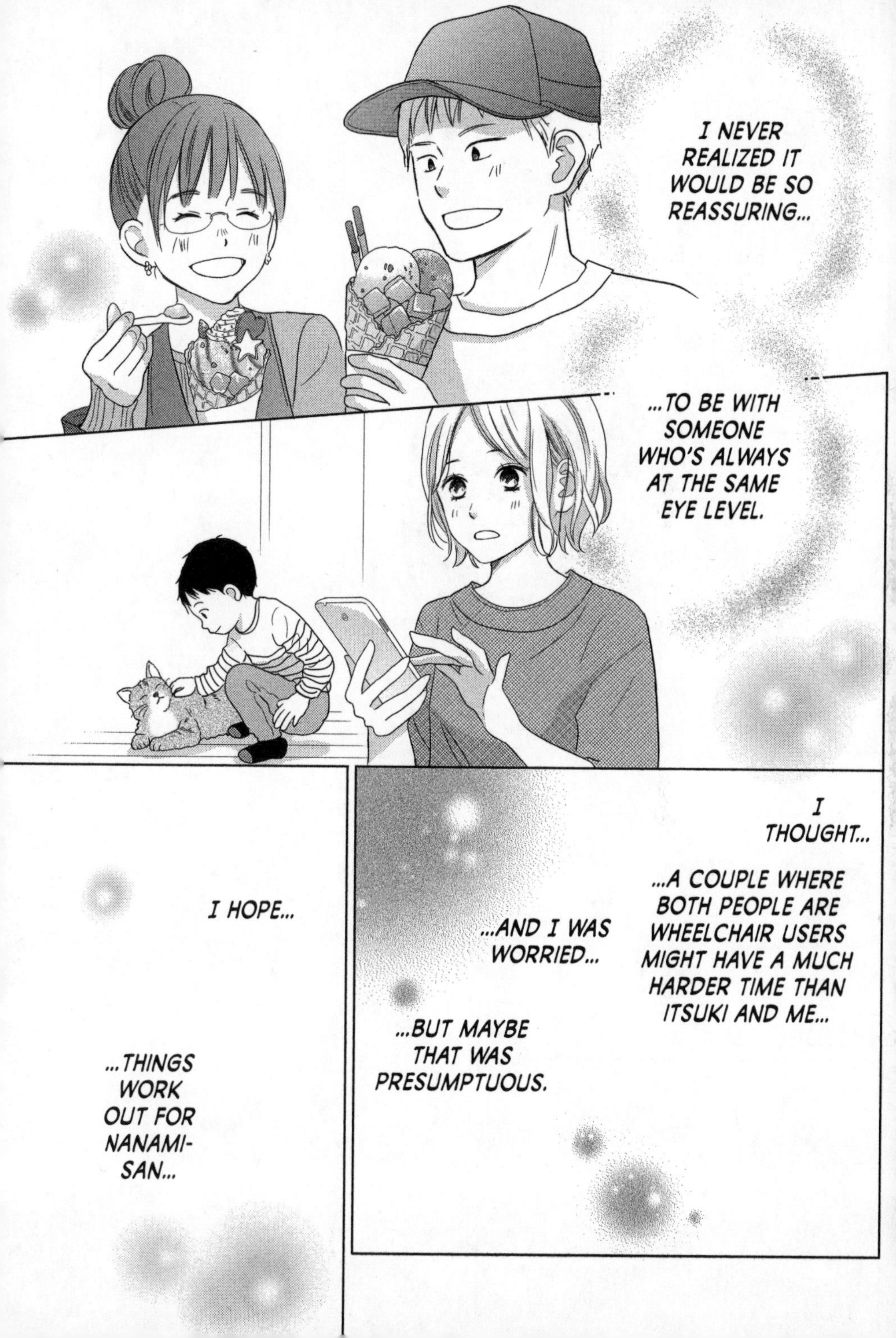
I NEVER REALIZED IT WOULD BE SO REASSURING...
...TO BE WITH SOMEONE WHO'S ALWAYS AT THE SAME EYE LEVEL.
I THOUGHT...
...A COUPLE WHERE BOTH PEOPLE ARE WHEELCHAIR USERS MIGHT HAVE A MUCH HARDER TIME THAN ITSUKI AND ME...
...AND I WAS WORRIED...
...BUT MAYBE THAT WAS PRESUMPTUOUS.
I HOPE...
...THINGS WORK OUT FOR NANAMI-SAN...

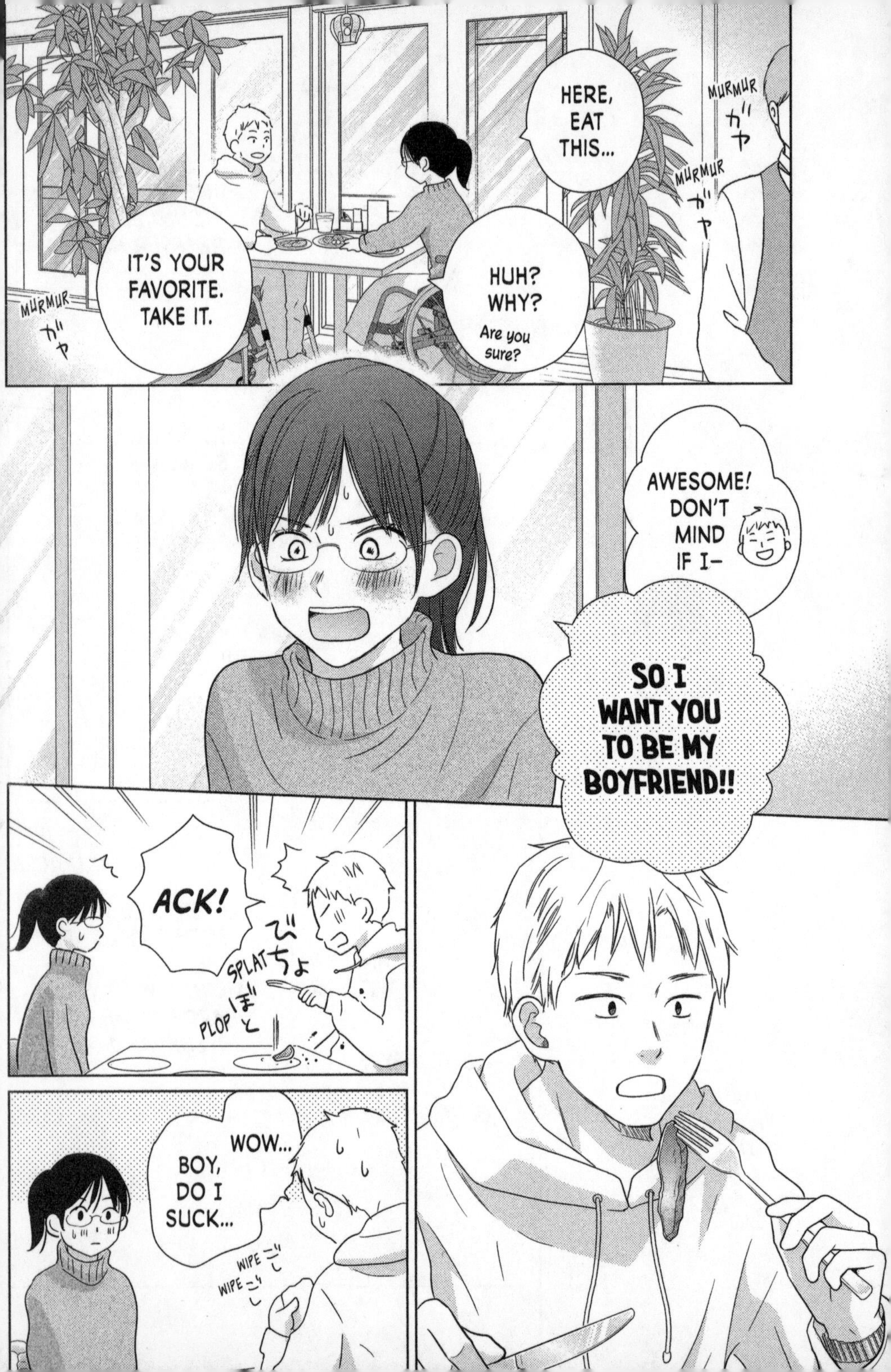
MURMUR
ガヤ
HERE, EAT THIS...
MURMUR
ガヤ
HUH? WHY?
Are you sure?
IT'S YOUR FAVORITE. TAKE IT.
MURMUR
ガヤ
AWESOME! DON'T MIND IF I–
SO I WANT YOU TO BE MY BOYFRIEND!!
ACK!
びちょ
SPLAT
ぼと
PLOP
WOW...
BOY, DO I SUCK...
WIPE
ごし
WIPE
ごし

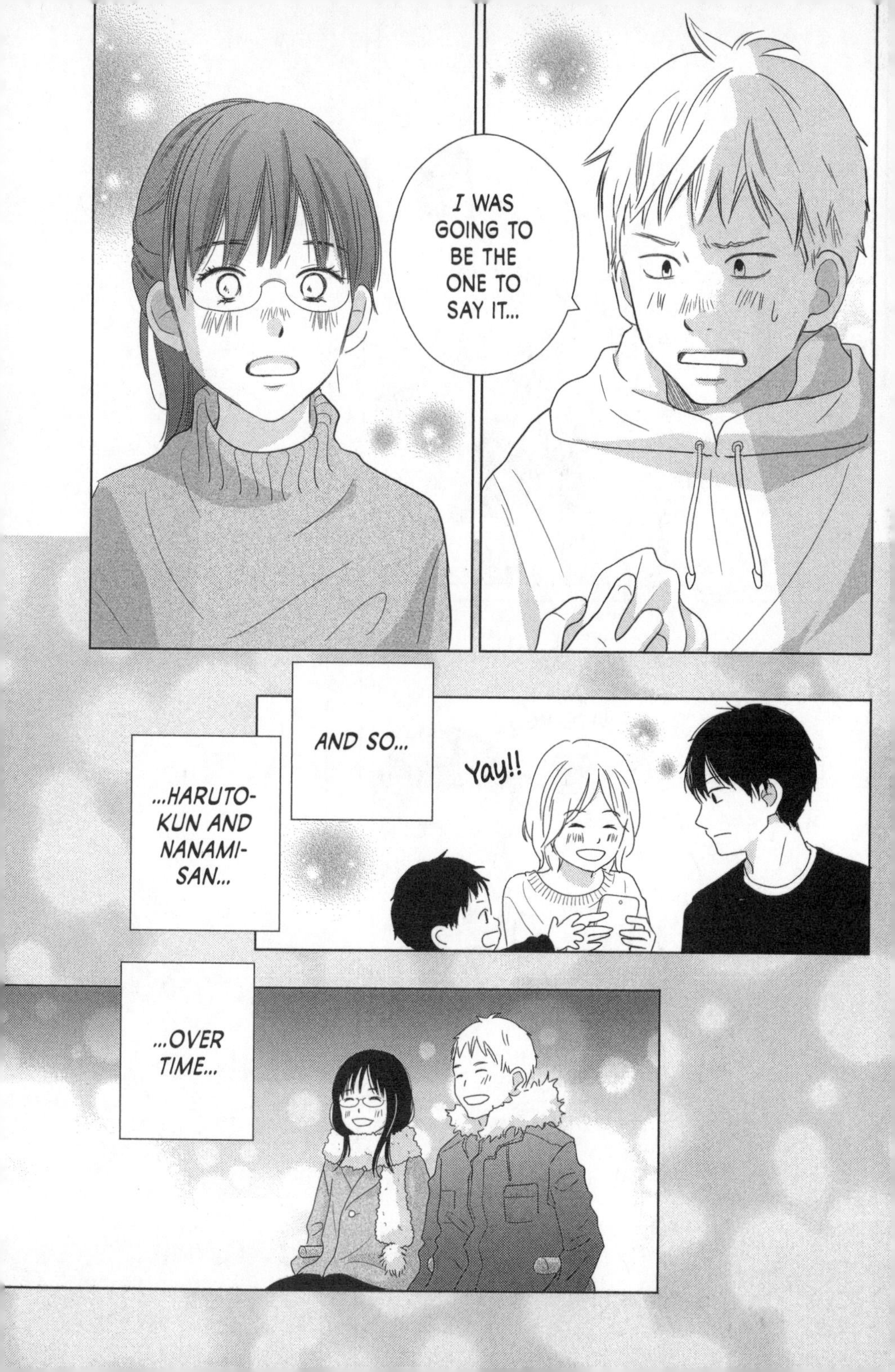
I WAS GOING TO BE THE ONE TO SAY IT...
AND SO...
Yay!!
...HARUTO-KUN AND NANAMI-SAN...
...OVER TIME...

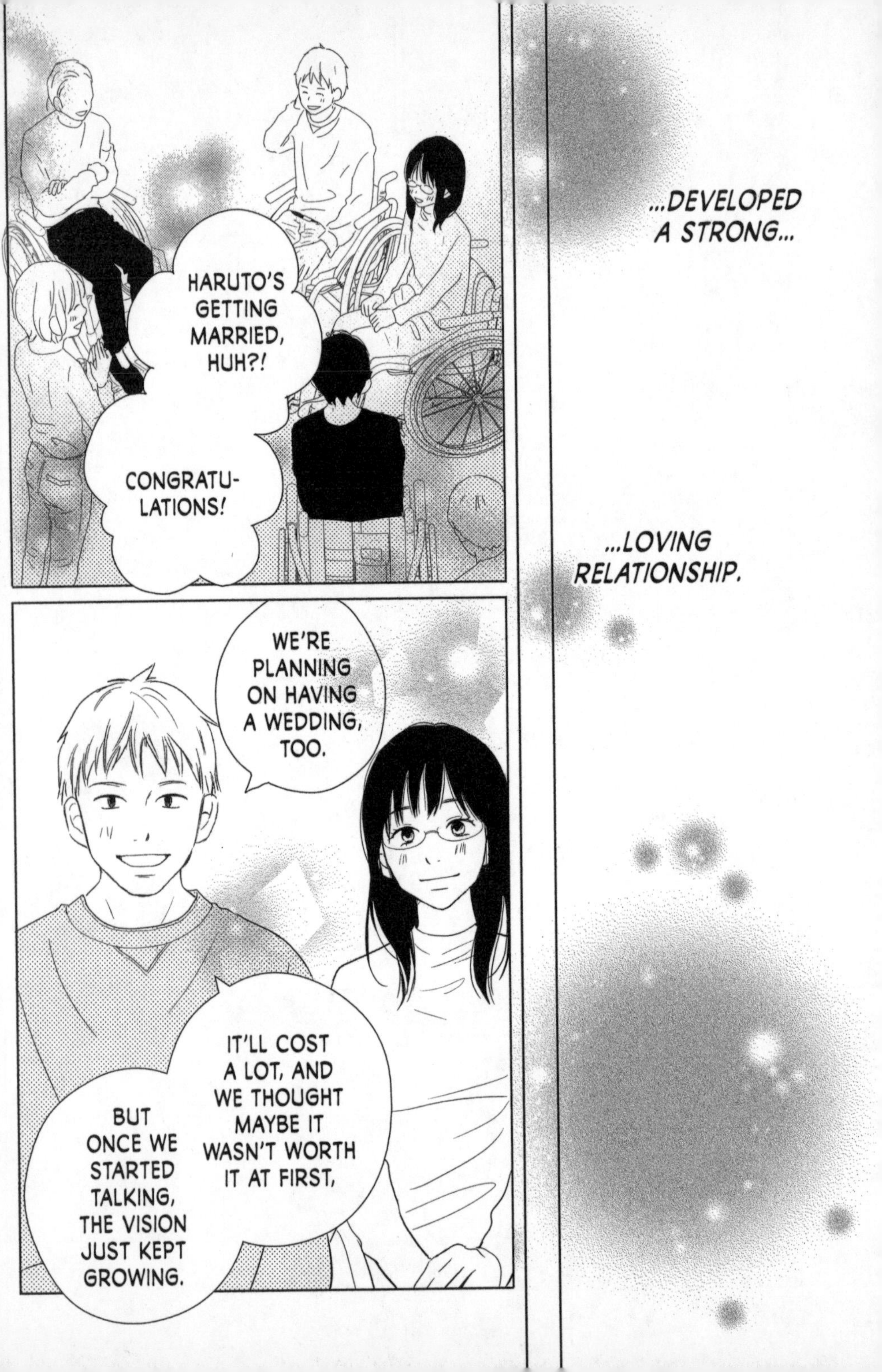
...DEVELOPED A STRONG...
...LOVING RELATIONSHIP.
HARUTO'S GETTING MARRIED, HUH?!
CONGRATU-LATIONS!
WE'RE PLANNING ON HAVING A WEDDING, TOO.
IT'LL COST A LOT, AND WE THOUGHT MAYBE IT WASN'T WORTH IT AT FIRST,
BUT ONCE WE STARTED TALKING, THE VISION JUST KEPT GROWING.

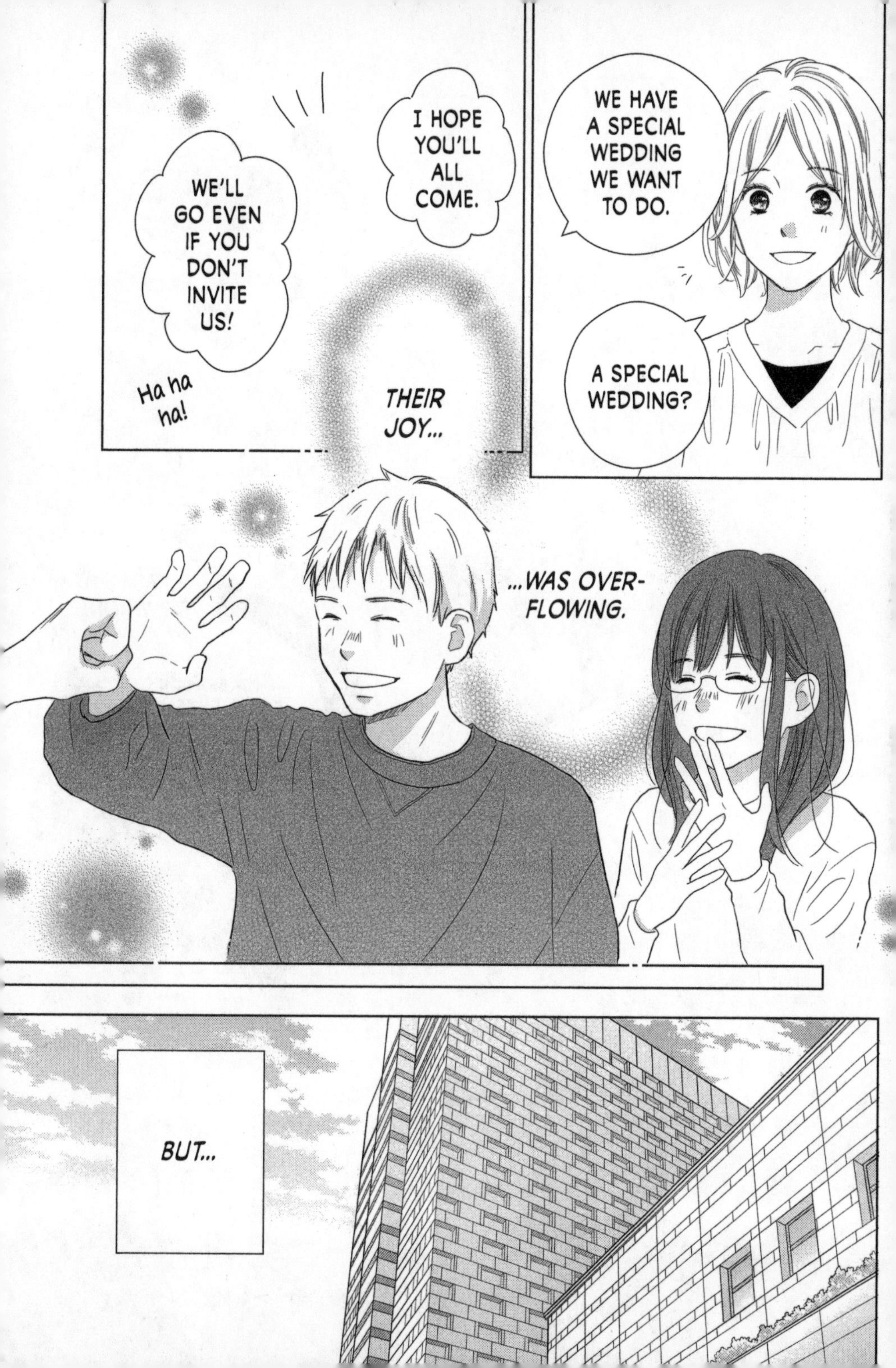
WE HAVE A SPECIAL WEDDING WE WANT TO DO.
A SPECIAL WEDDING?
I HOPE YOU'LL ALL COME.
WE'LL GO EVEN IF YOU DON'T INVITE US!
Ha ha ha!
THEIR JOY...
...WAS OVER-FLOWING.
BUT...

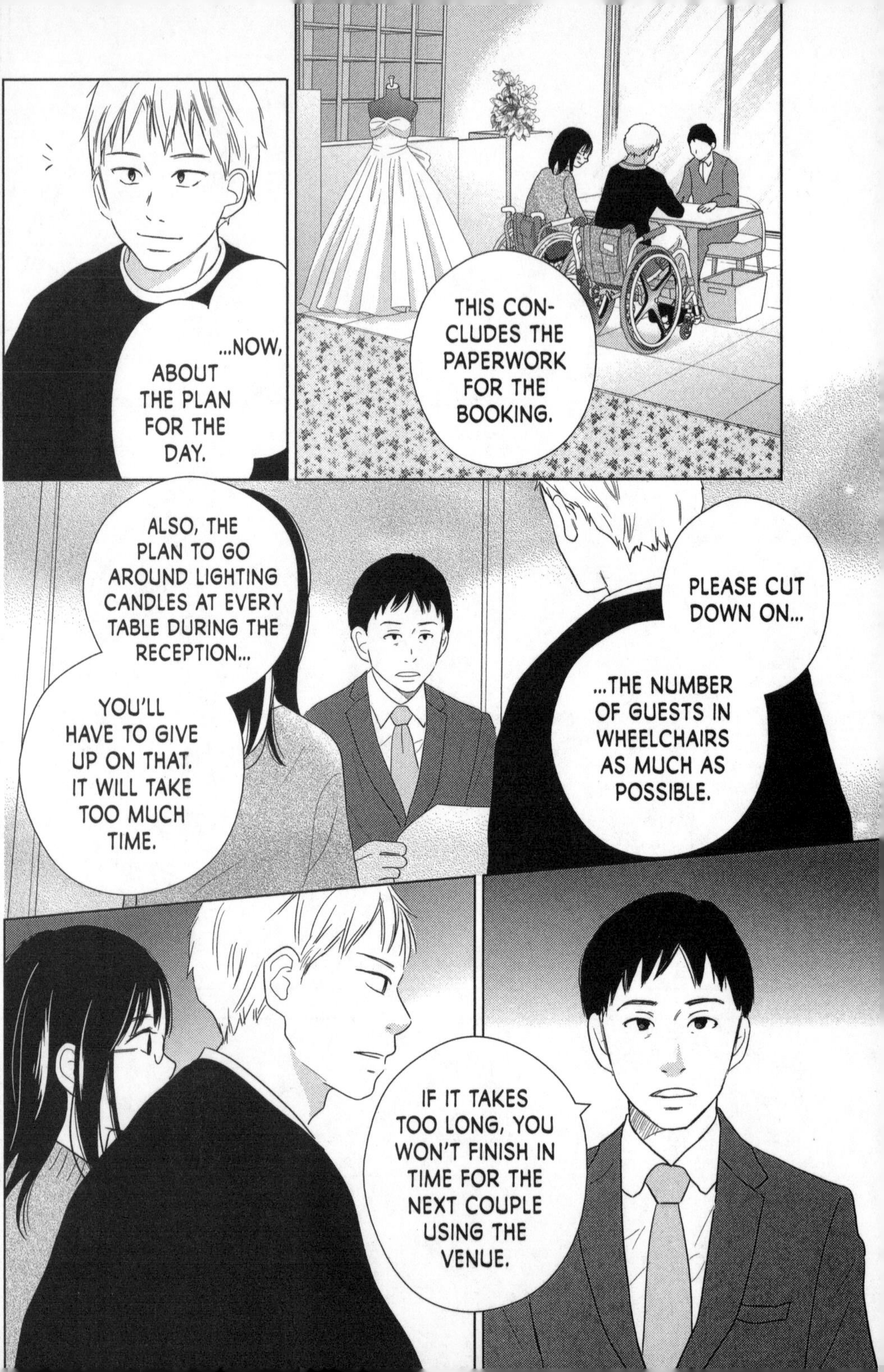
THIS CONCLUDES THE PAPERWORK FOR THE BOOKING.
...NOW, ABOUT THE PLAN FOR THE DAY.
PLEASE CUT DOWN ON...
...THE NUMBER OF GUESTS IN WHEELCHAIRS AS MUCH AS POSSIBLE.
ALSO, THE PLAN TO GO AROUND LIGHTING CANDLES AT EVERY TABLE DURING THE RECEPTION...
YOU'LL HAVE TO GIVE UP ON THAT. IT WILL TAKE TOO MUCH TIME.
IF IT TAKES TOO LONG, YOU WON'T FINISH IN TIME FOR THE NEXT COUPLE USING THE VENUE.

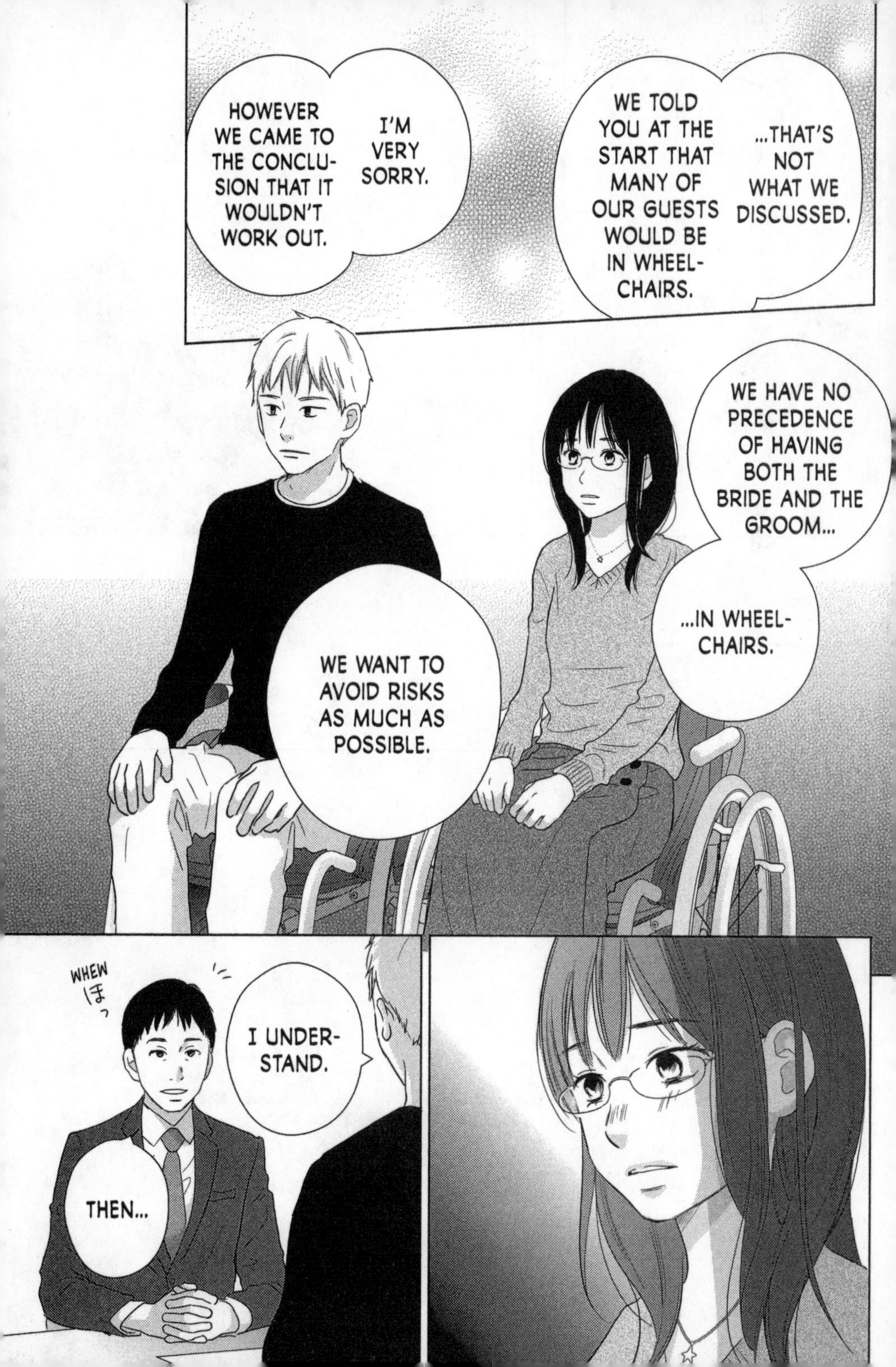
...THAT'S NOT WHAT WE DISCUSSED.
WE TOLD YOU AT THE START THAT MANY OF OUR GUESTS WOULD BE IN WHEELCHAIRS.
I'M VERY SORRY.
HOWEVER WE CAME TO THE CONCLUSION THAT IT WOULDN'T WORK OUT.
WE HAVE NO PRECEDENCE OF HAVING BOTH THE BRIDE AND THE GROOM...
...IN WHEELCHAIRS.
WE WANT TO AVOID RISKS AS MUCH AS POSSIBLE.
I UNDERSTAND.
WHEW ほっ
THEN...

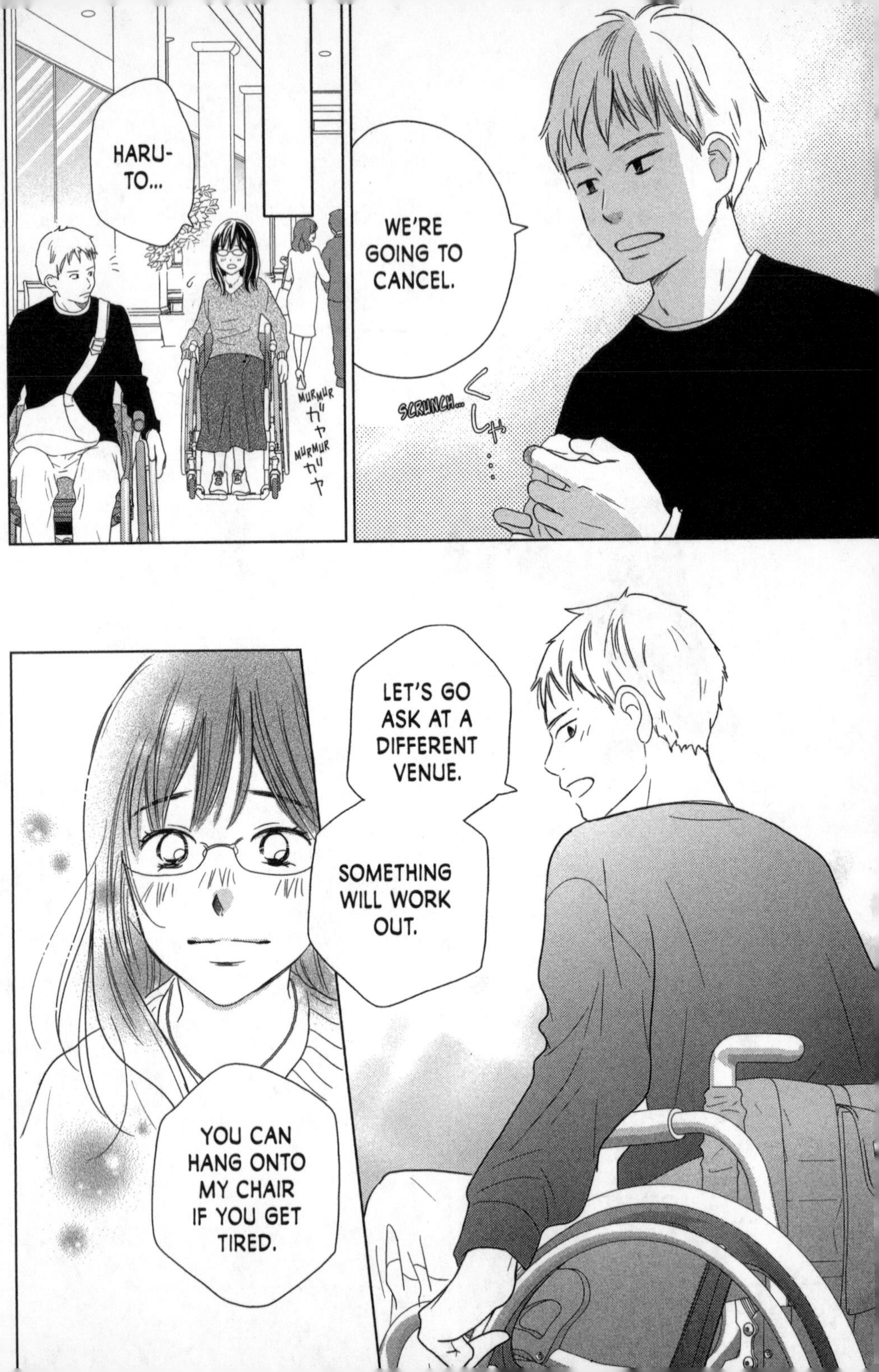
WE'RE GOING TO CANCEL.
SCRUNCH...
くしゃ...
HARU-TO...
MURMUR
ガヤ
MURMUR
ガヤ
LET'S GO ASK AT A DIFFERENT VENUE.
SOMETHING WILL WORK OUT.
YOU CAN HANG ONTO MY CHAIR IF YOU GET TIRED.

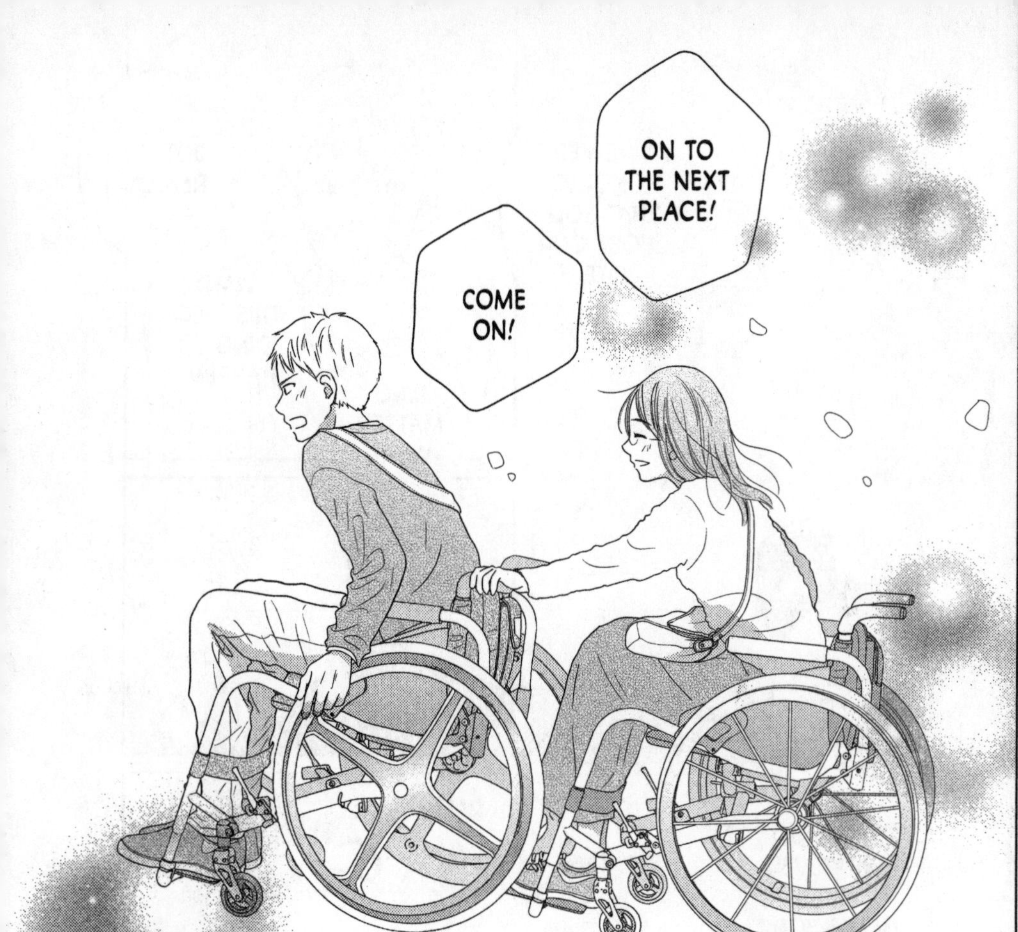
ON TO THE NEXT PLACE!
COME ON!

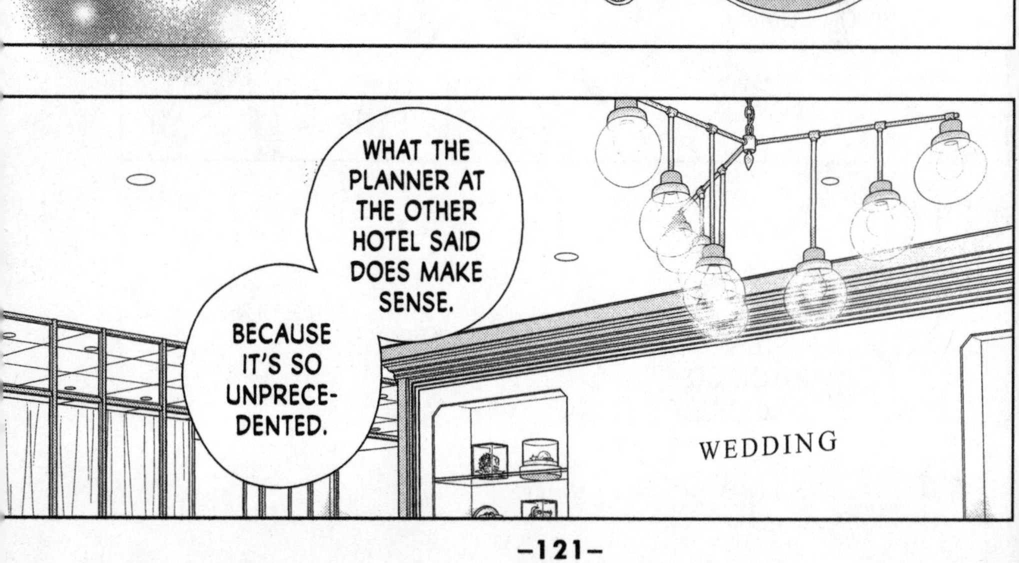
WHAT THE PLANNER AT THE OTHER HOTEL SAID DOES MAKE SENSE.
BECAUSE IT'S SO UNPRECE-DENTED.
WEDDING

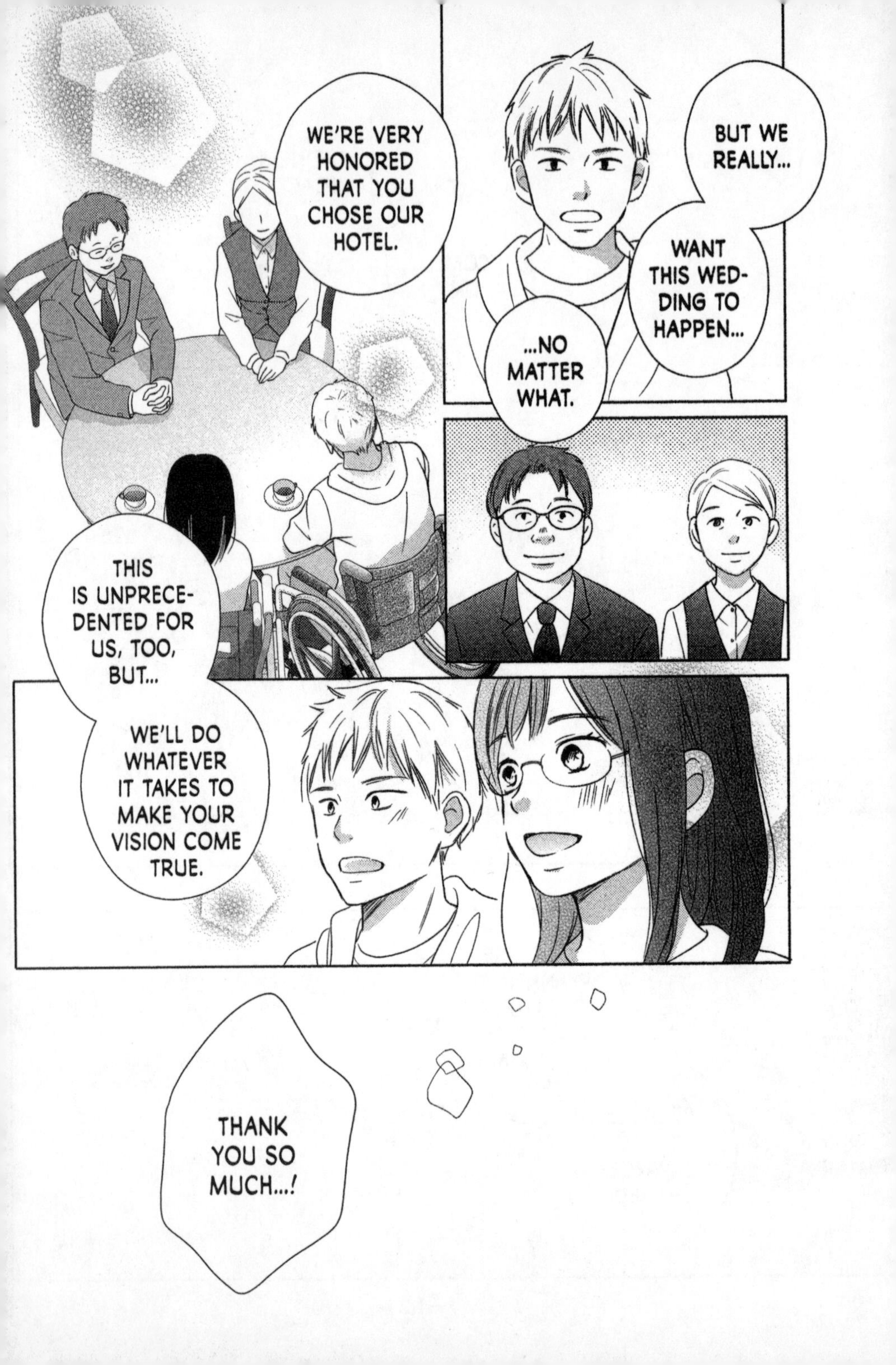
BUT WE REALLY...
WANT THIS WEDDING TO HAPPEN...
...NO MATTER WHAT.
WE'RE VERY HONORED THAT YOU CHOSE OUR HOTEL.
THIS IS UNPRECEDENTED FOR US, TOO, BUT...
WE'LL DO WHATEVER IT TAKES TO MAKE YOUR VISION COME TRUE.
THANK YOU SO MUCH...!

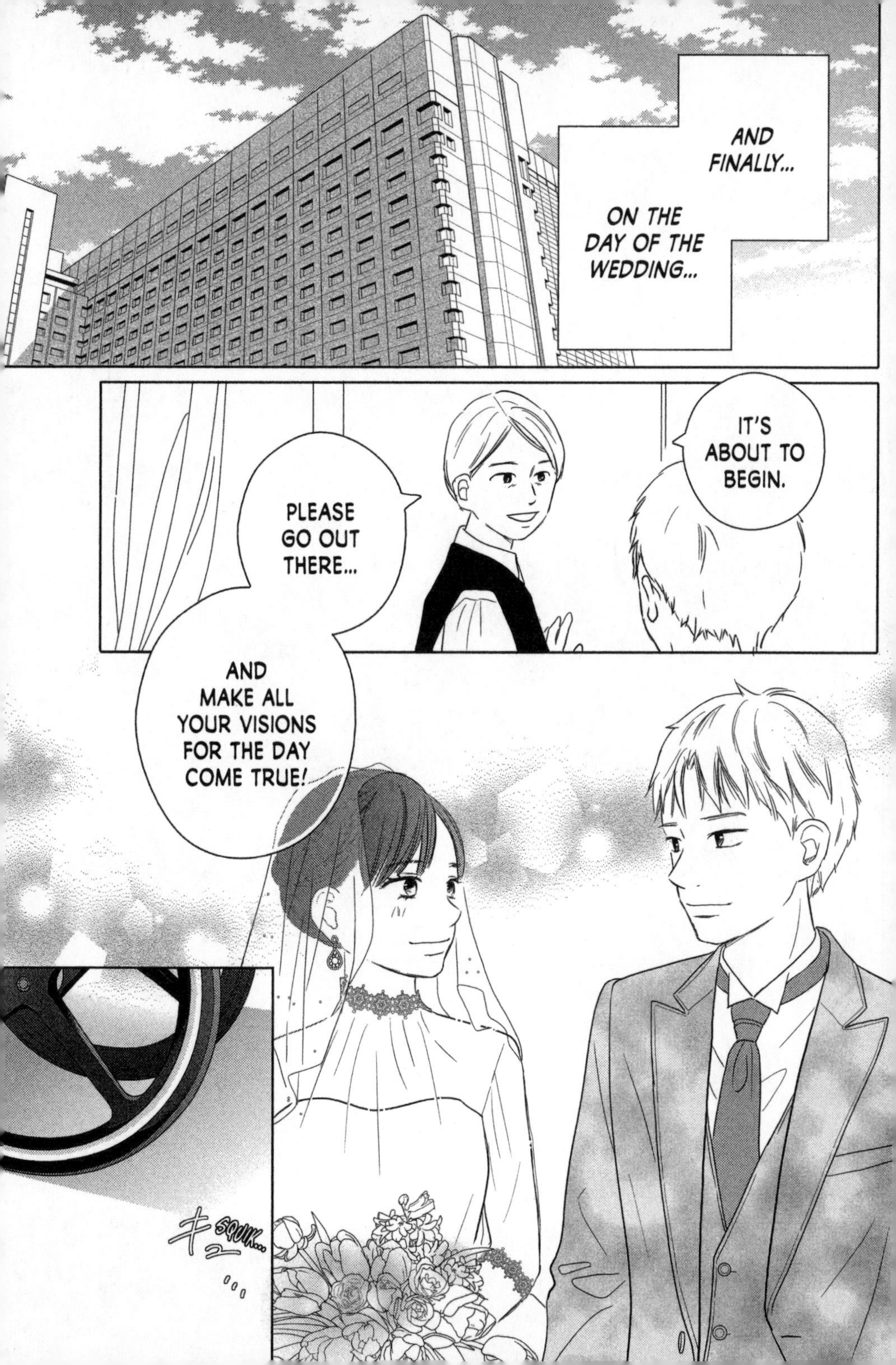
AND FINALLY...
ON THE DAY OF THE WEDDING...
IT'S ABOUT TO BEGIN.
PLEASE GO OUT THERE...
AND MAKE ALL YOUR VISIONS FOR THE DAY COME TRUE!
SQUIK...

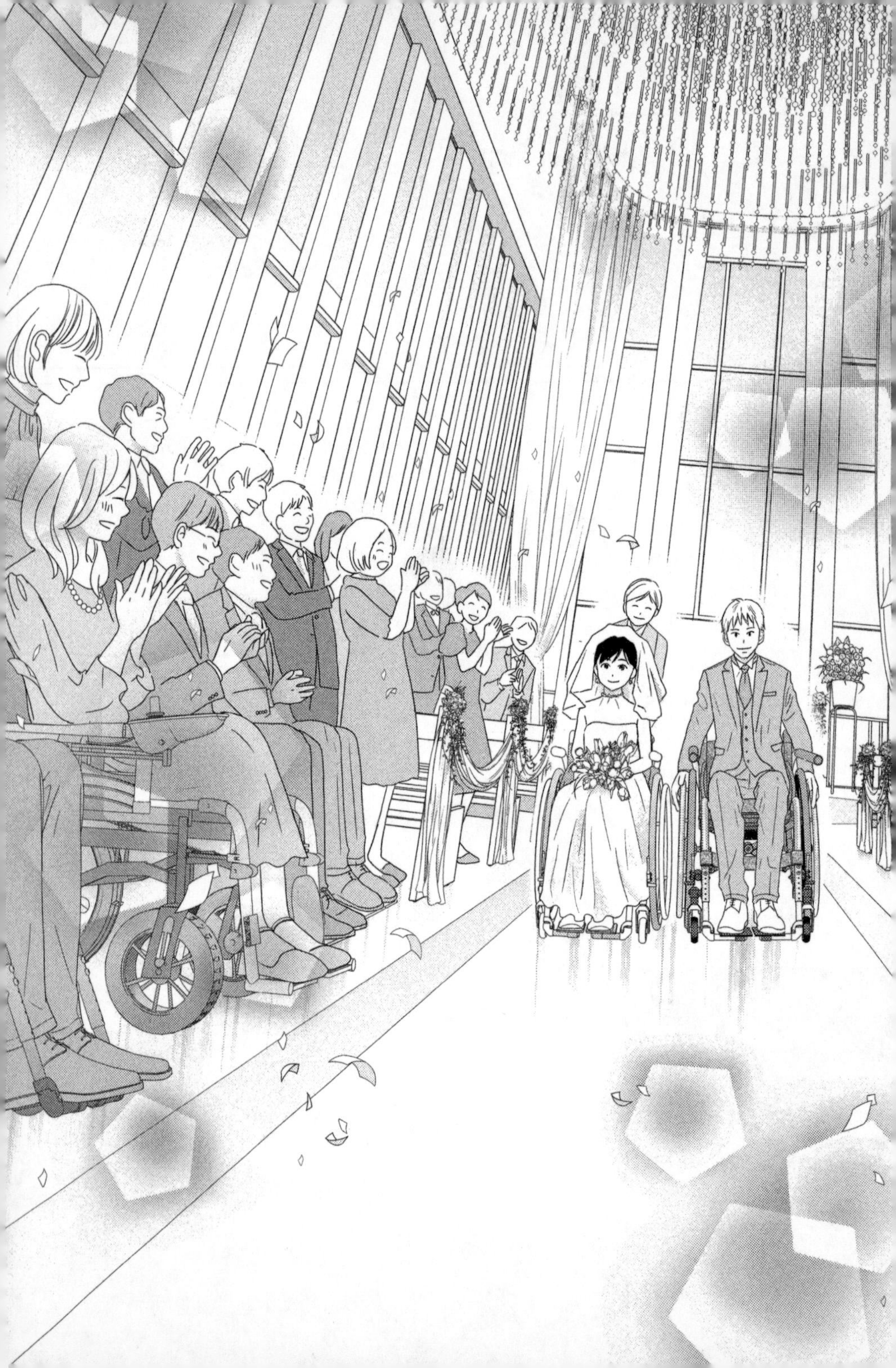

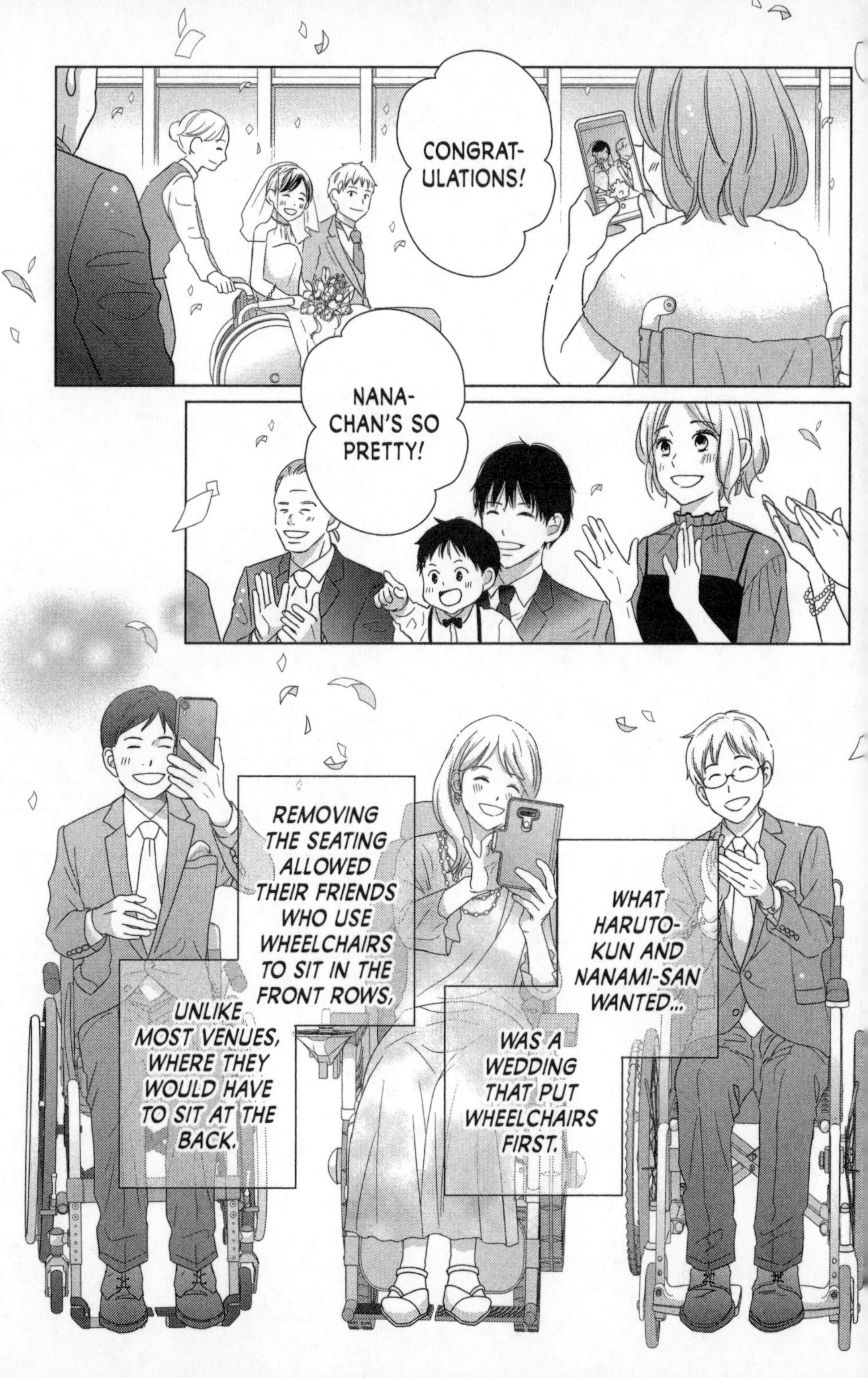
CONGRAT-ULATIONS!
NANA-CHAN'S SO PRETTY!
WHAT HARUTO-KUN AND NANAMI-SAN WANTED...
WAS A WEDDING THAT PUT WHEELCHAIRS FIRST.
REMOVING THE SEATING ALLOWED THEIR FRIENDS WHO USE WHEELCHAIRS TO SIT IN THE FRONT ROWS,
UNLIKE MOST VENUES, WHERE THEY WOULD HAVE TO SIT AT THE BACK.

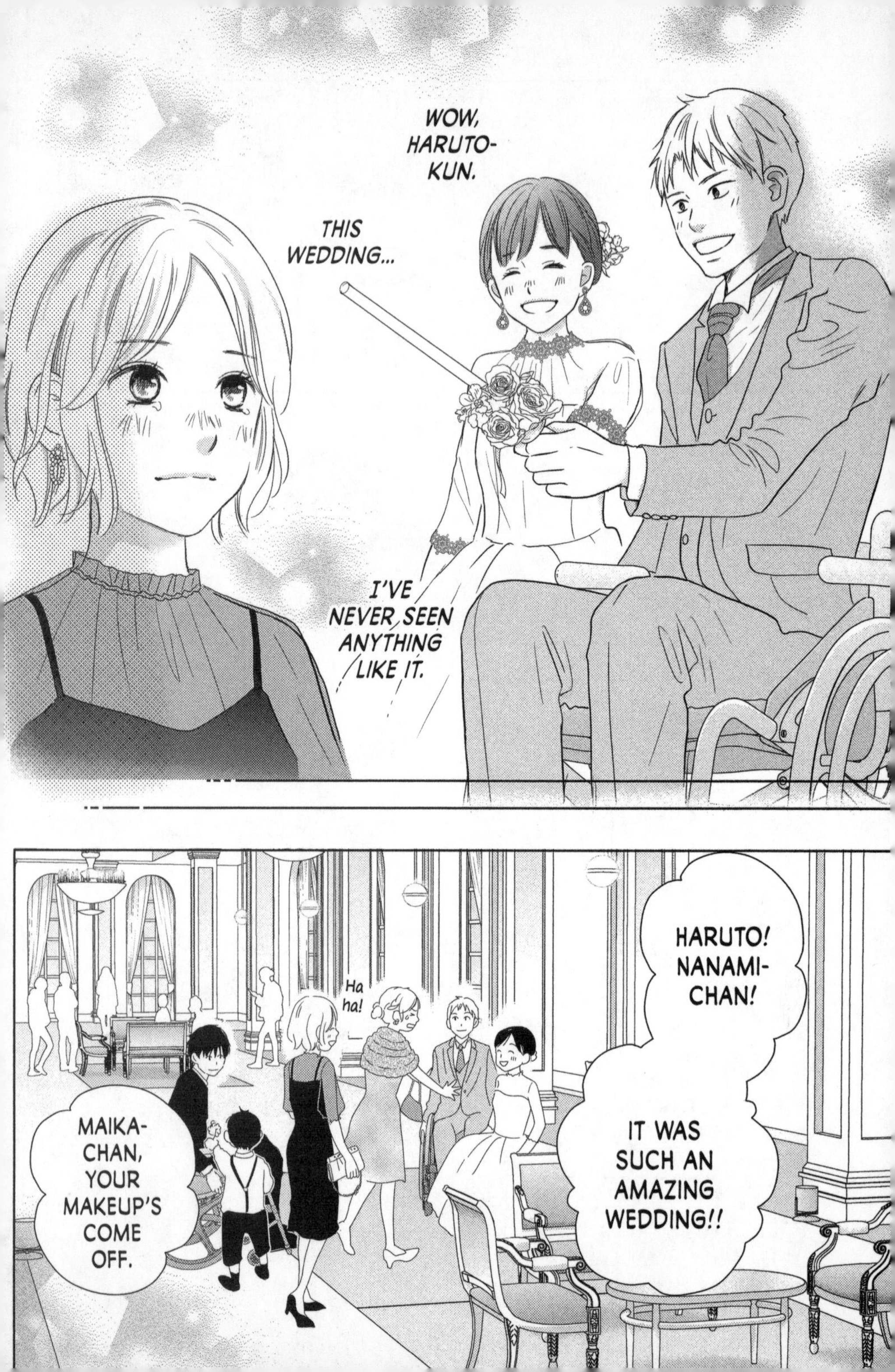
WOW, HARUTO-KUN.
THIS WEDDING...
I'VE NEVER SEEN ANYTHING LIKE IT.
HARUTO! NANAMI-CHAN!
IT WAS SUCH AN AMAZING WEDDING!!
Ha ha!
MAIKA-CHAN, YOUR MAKEUP'S COME OFF.

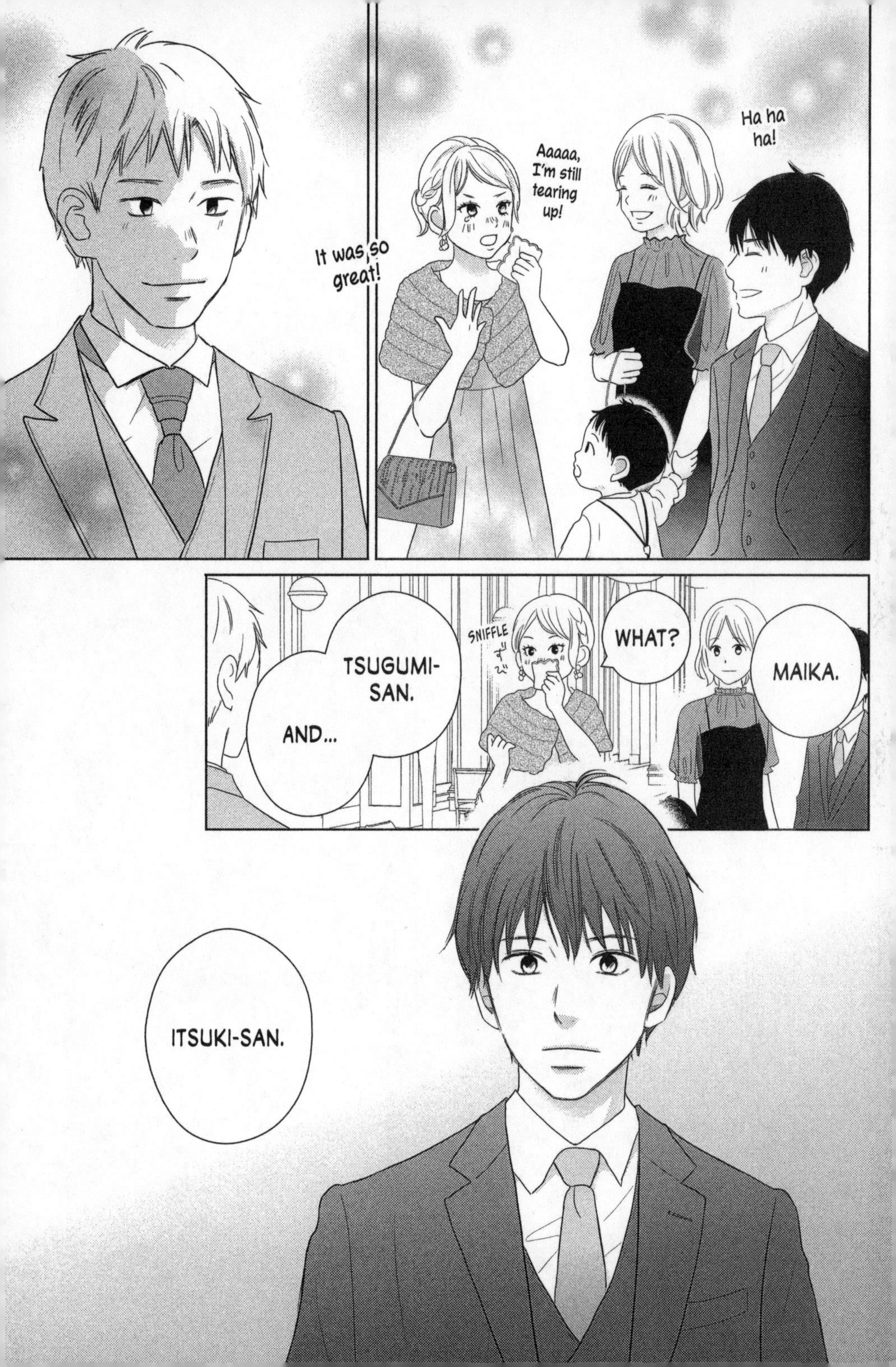
Ha ha ha!
Aaaaa, I'm still tearing up!
It was so great!
MAIKA.
WHAT?
SNIFFLE
TSUGUMI-SAN.
AND...
ITSUKI-SAN.

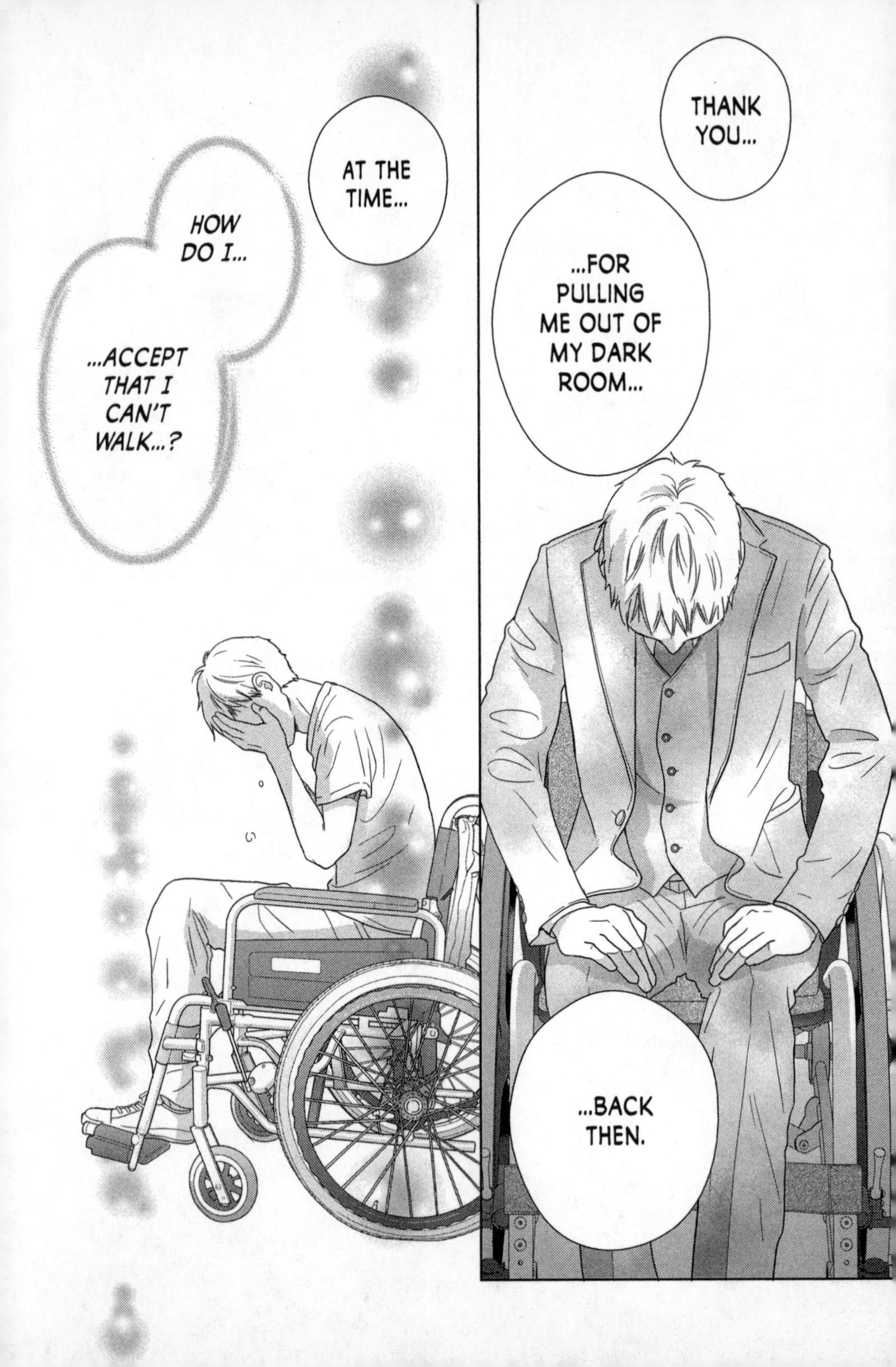
THANK YOU...
...FOR PULLING ME OUT OF MY DARK ROOM...
...BACK THEN.
AT THE TIME...
HOW DO I...
...ACCEPT THAT I CAN'T WALK...?

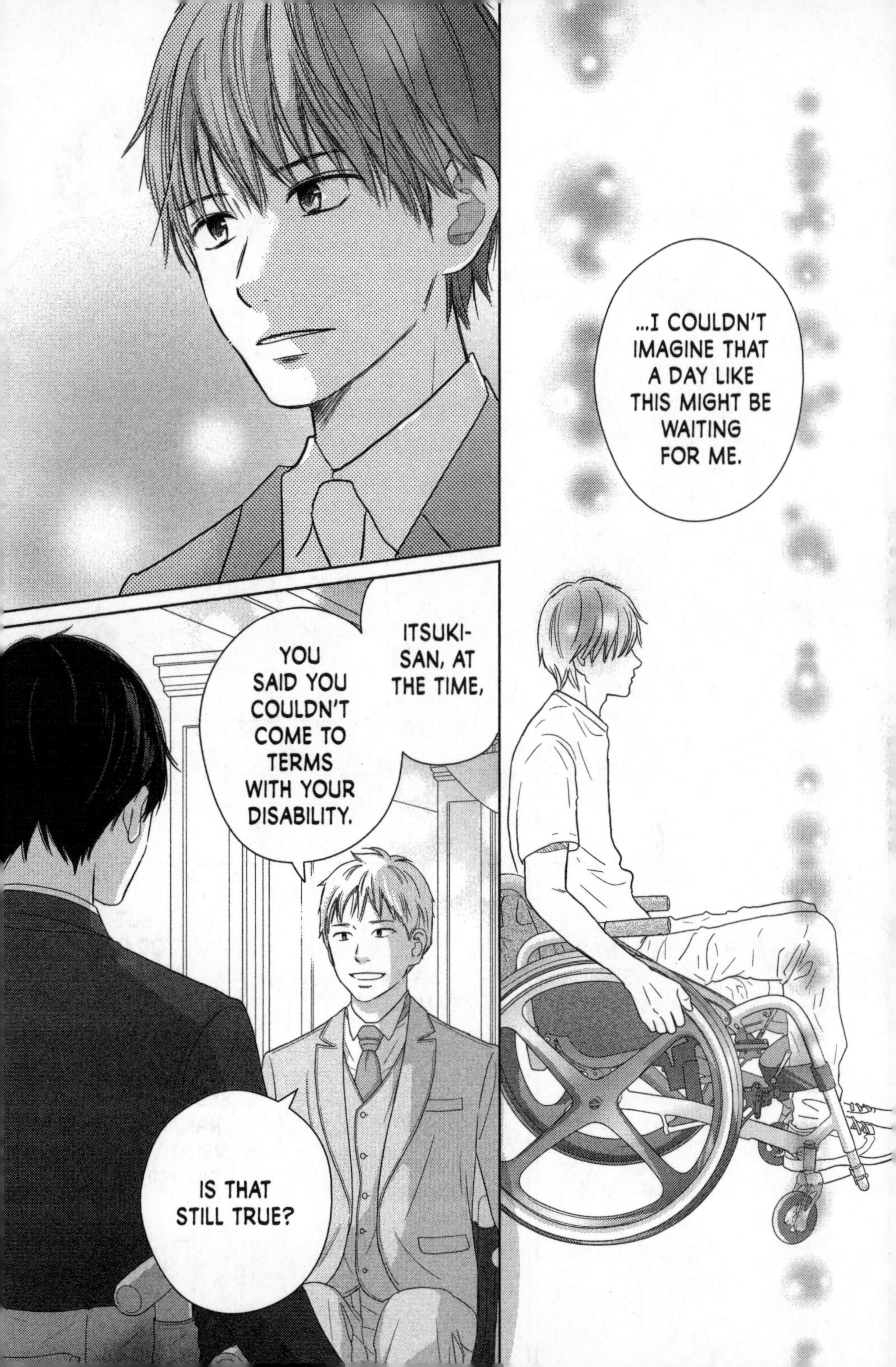
...I COULDN'T IMAGINE THAT A DAY LIKE THIS MIGHT BE WAITING FOR ME.
ITSUKI-SAN, AT THE TIME,
YOU SAID YOU COULDN'T COME TO TERMS WITH YOUR DISABILITY.
IS THAT STILL TRUE?

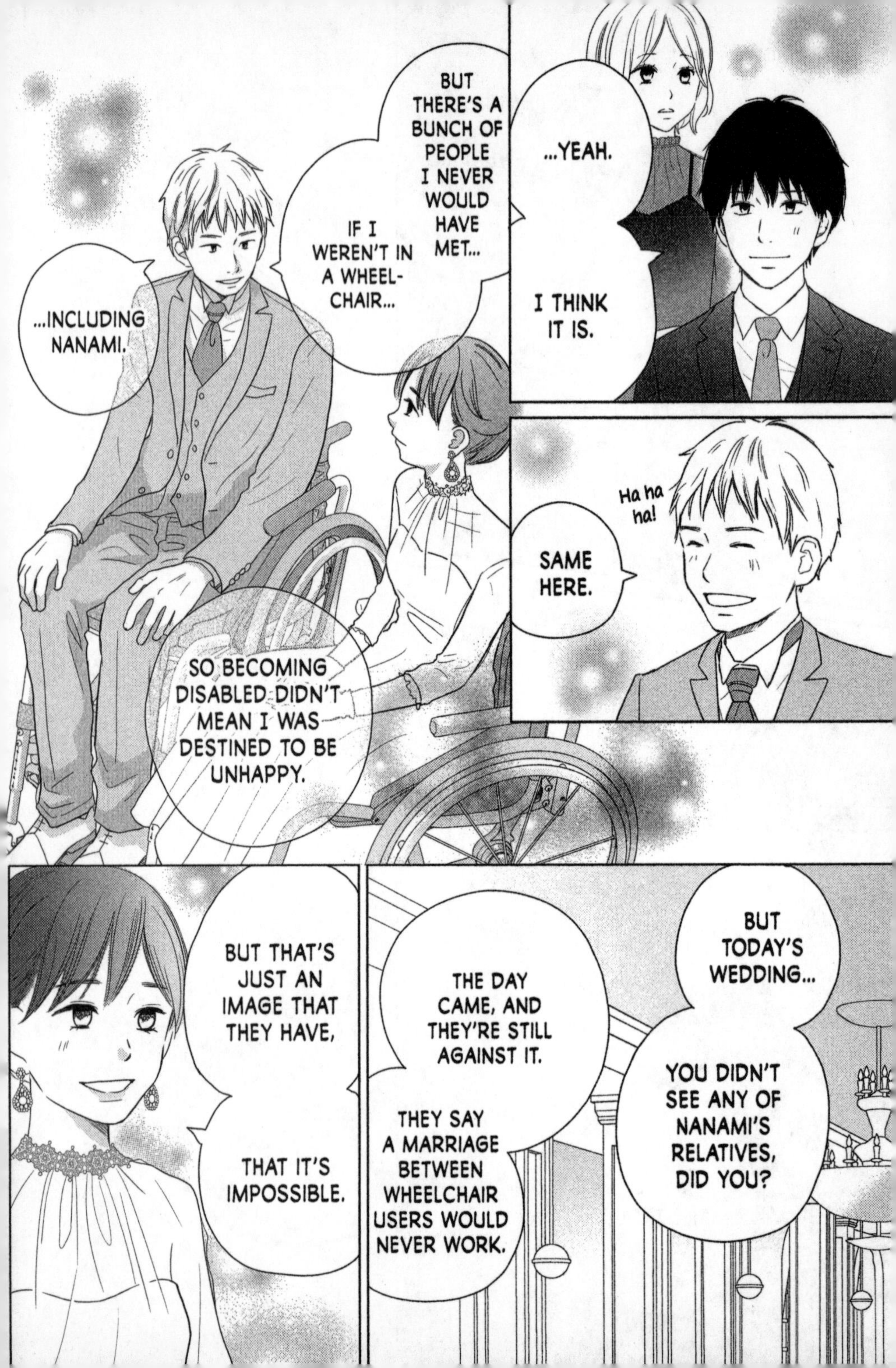
...YEAH.
I THINK IT IS.
Ha ha ha!
SAME HERE.
BUT THERE'S A BUNCH OF PEOPLE I NEVER WOULD HAVE MET...
IF I WEREN'T IN A WHEELCHAIR...
...INCLUDING NANAMI.
SO BECOMING DISABLED DIDN'T MEAN I WAS DESTINED TO BE UNHAPPY.
BUT TODAY'S WEDDING...
YOU DIDN'T SEE ANY OF NANAMI'S RELATIVES, DID YOU?
THE DAY CAME, AND THEY'RE STILL AGAINST IT.
THEY SAY A MARRIAGE BETWEEN WHEELCHAIR USERS WOULD NEVER WORK.
BUT THAT'S JUST AN IMAGE THAT THEY HAVE,
THAT IT'S IMPOSSIBLE.

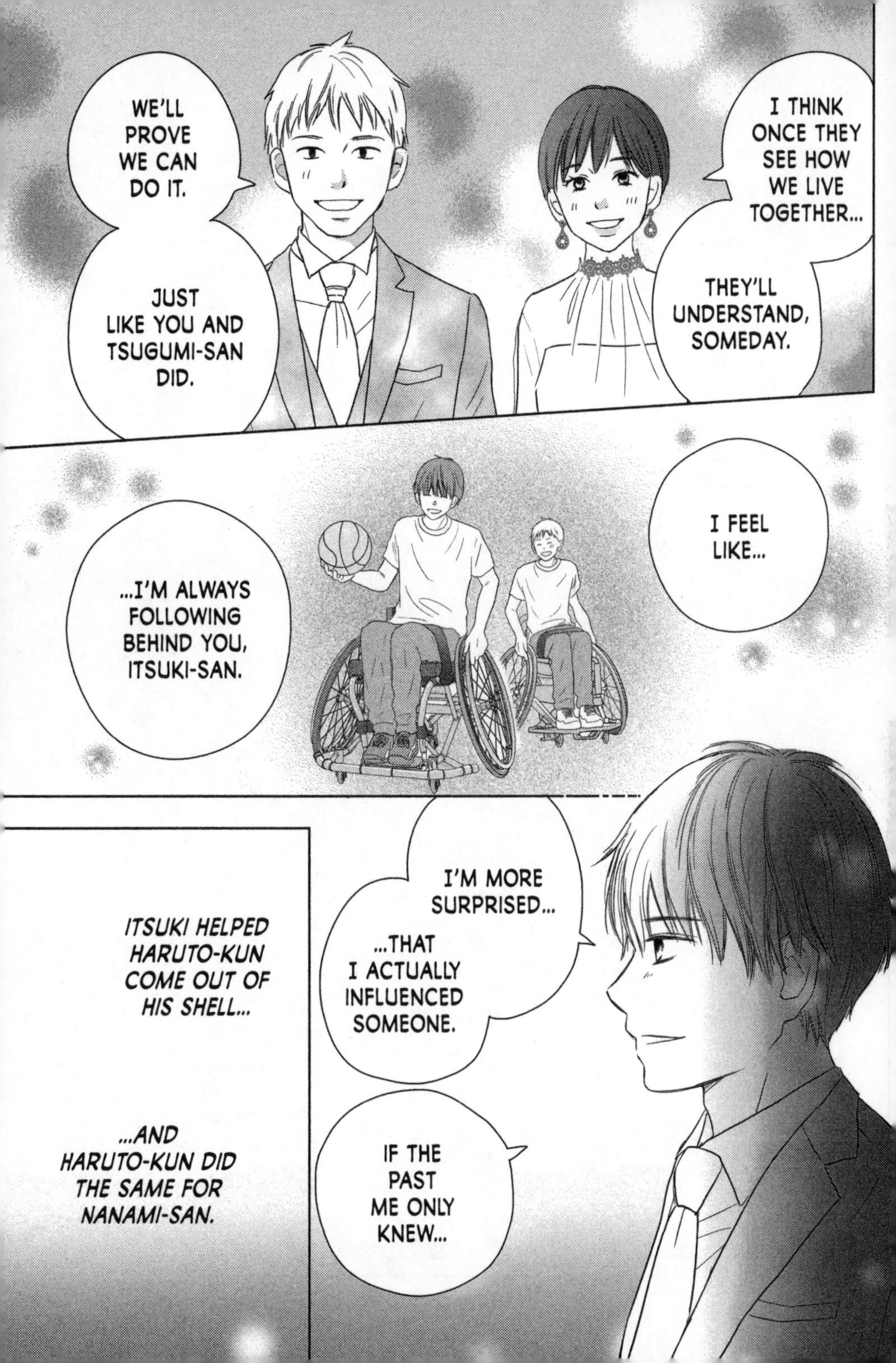
I THINK ONCE THEY SEE HOW WE LIVE TOGETHER...
THEY'LL UNDERSTAND, SOMEDAY.
WE'LL PROVE WE CAN DO IT.
JUST LIKE YOU AND TSUGUMI-SAN DID.
I FEEL LIKE...
...I'M ALWAYS FOLLOWING BEHIND YOU, ITSUKI-SAN.
I'M MORE SURPRISED...
...THAT I ACTUALLY INFLUENCED SOMEONE.
IF THE PAST ME ONLY KNEW...
ITSUKI HELPED HARUTO-KUN COME OUT OF HIS SHELL...
...AND HARUTO-KUN DID THE SAME FOR NANAMI-SAN.

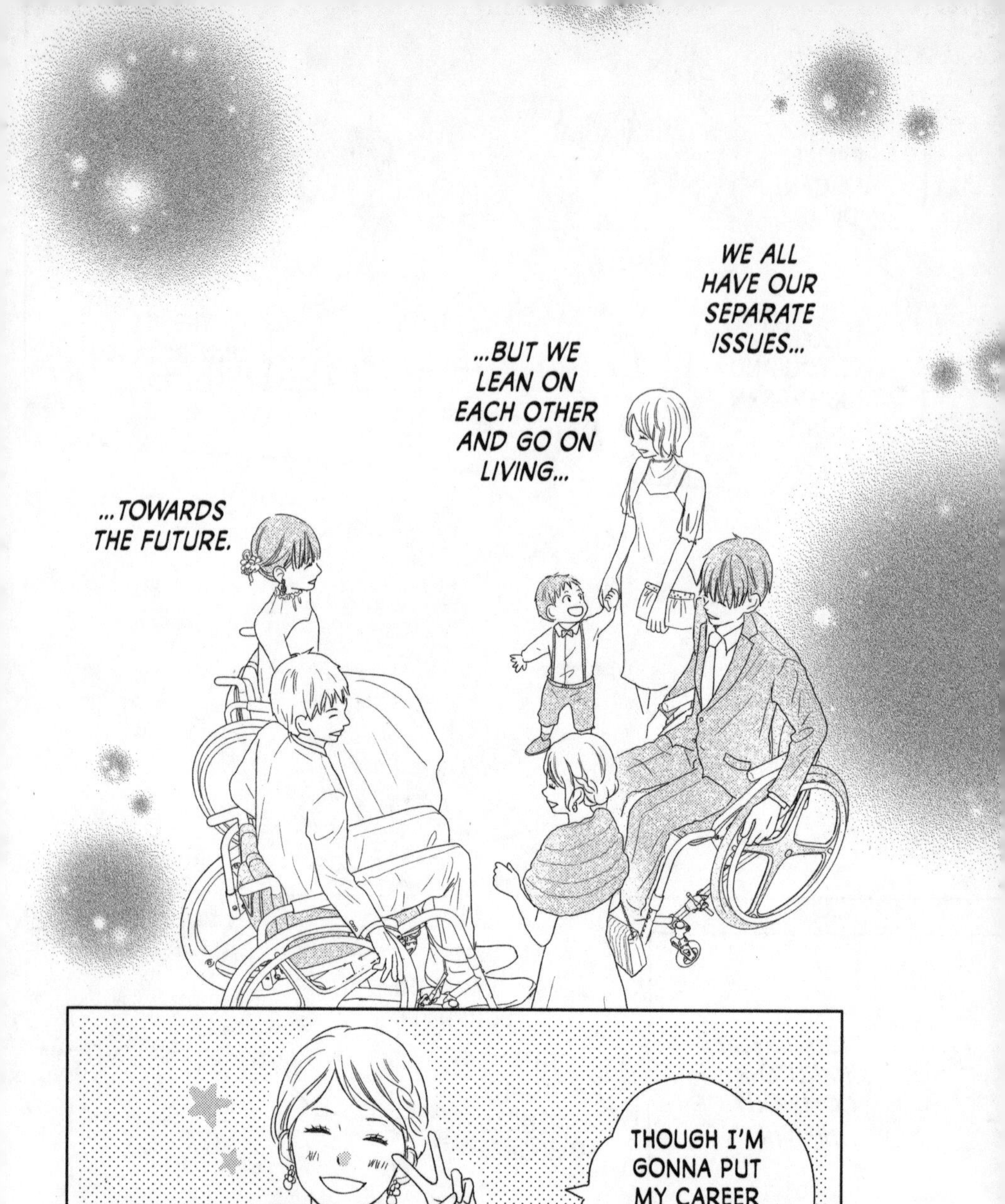
WE ALL HAVE OUR SEPARATE ISSUES...
...BUT WE LEAN ON EACH OTHER AND GO ON LIVING...
...TOWARDS THE FUTURE.

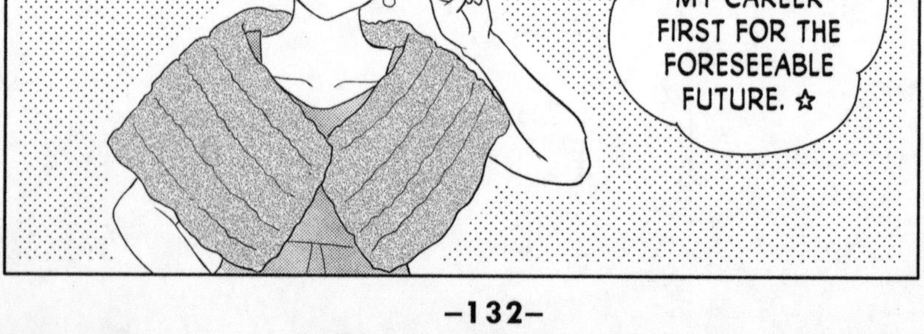
THOUGH I'M GONNA PUT MY CAREER FIRST FOR THE FORESEEABLE FUTURE. ☆

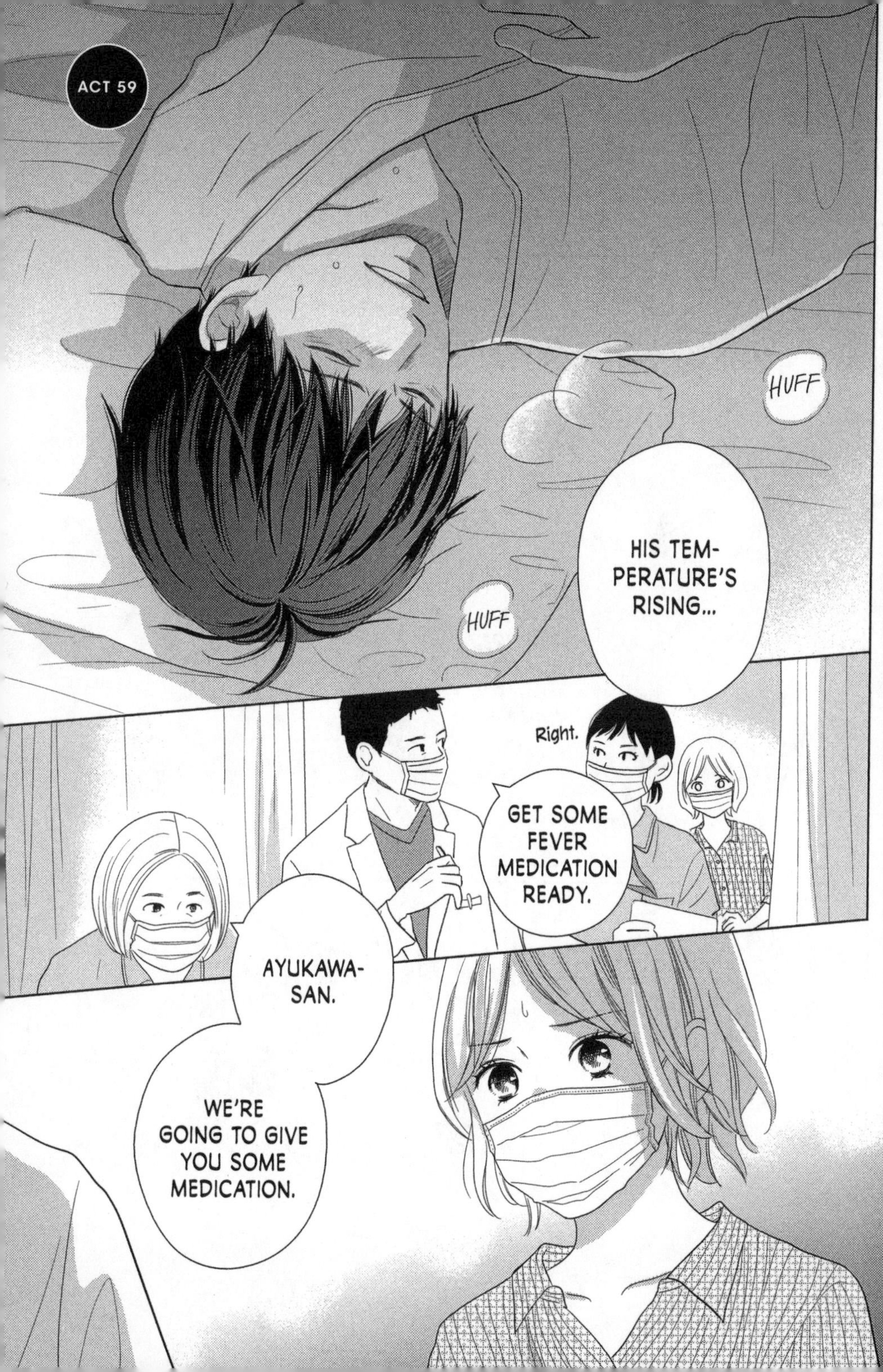
ACT 59
HUFF
HIS TEMPERATURE'S RISING...
HUFF
Right.
GET SOME FEVER MEDICATION READY.
AYUKAWA-SAN.
WE'RE GOING TO GIVE YOU SOME MEDICATION.

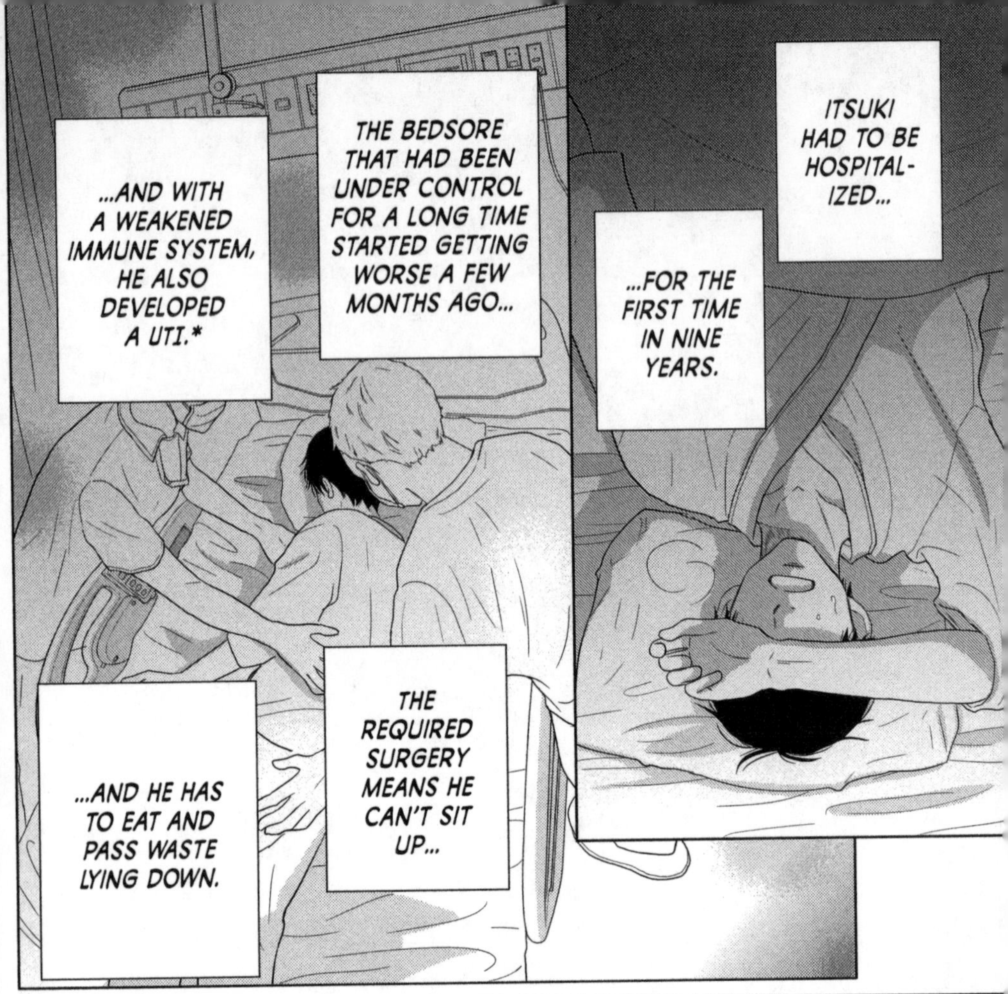
ITSUKI HAD TO BE HOSPITAL-IZED...
...FOR THE FIRST TIME IN NINE YEARS.
THE BEDSORE THAT HAD BEEN UNDER CONTROL FOR A LONG TIME STARTED GETTING WORSE A FEW MONTHS AGO...
...AND WITH A WEAKENED IMMUNE SYSTEM, HE ALSO DEVELOPED A UTI.*
THE REQUIRED SURGERY MEANS HE CAN'T SIT UP...
...AND HE HAS TO EAT AND PASS WASTE LYING DOWN.

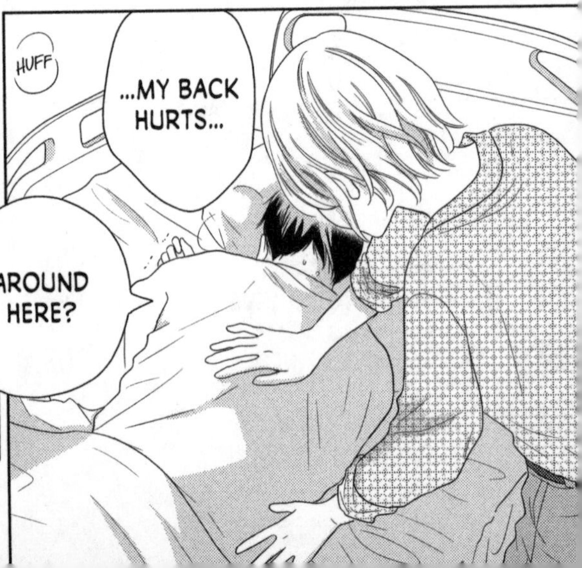
HUFF
...MY BACK HURTS...
AROUND HERE?

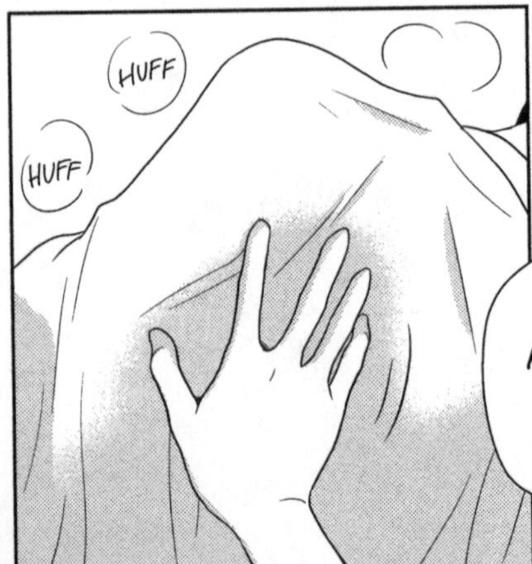
HUFF
HUFF

*Urinary tract infection

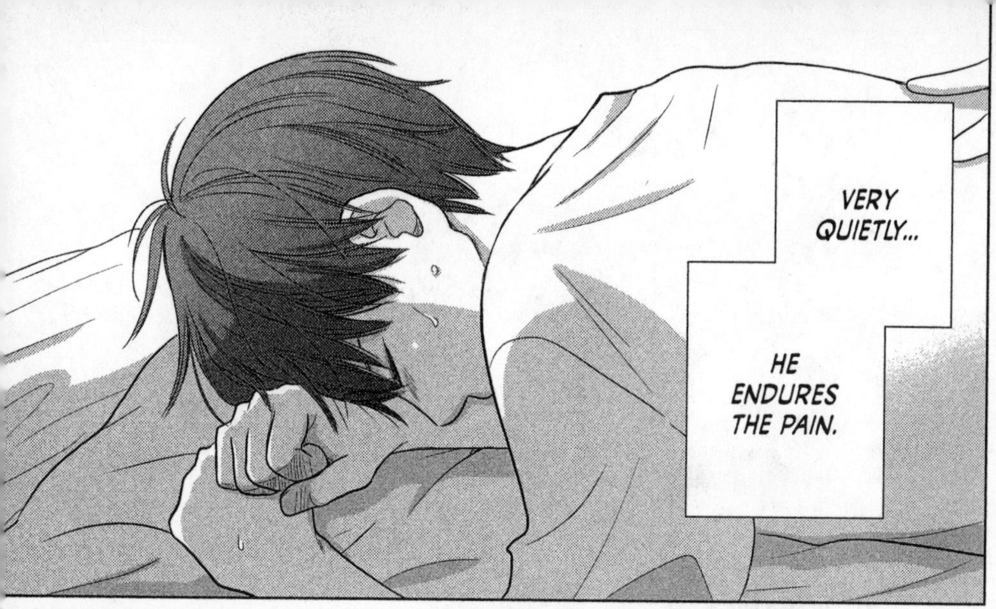
VERY QUIETLY...
HE ENDURES THE PAIN.

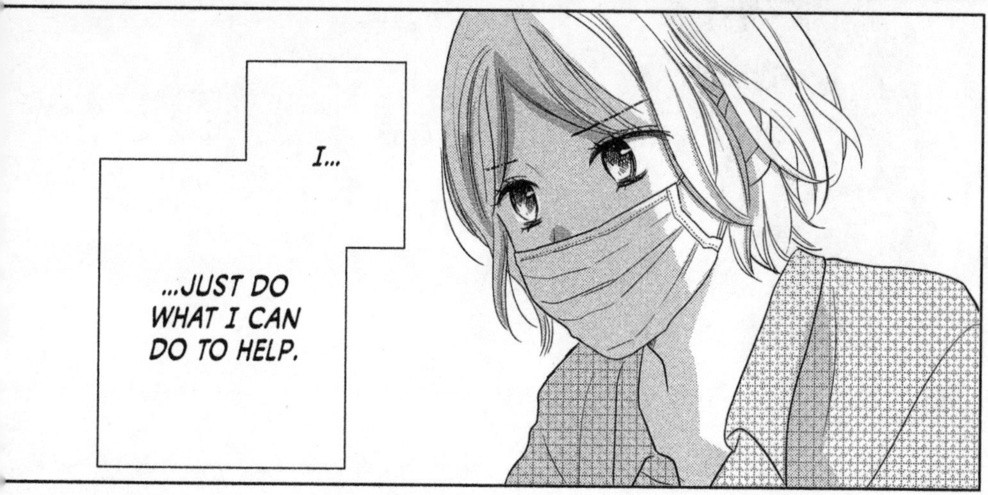
I...
...JUST DO WHAT I CAN DO TO HELP.

THIS IS AN ORDINARY PART...

...OF OUR EVERYDAY LIFE.

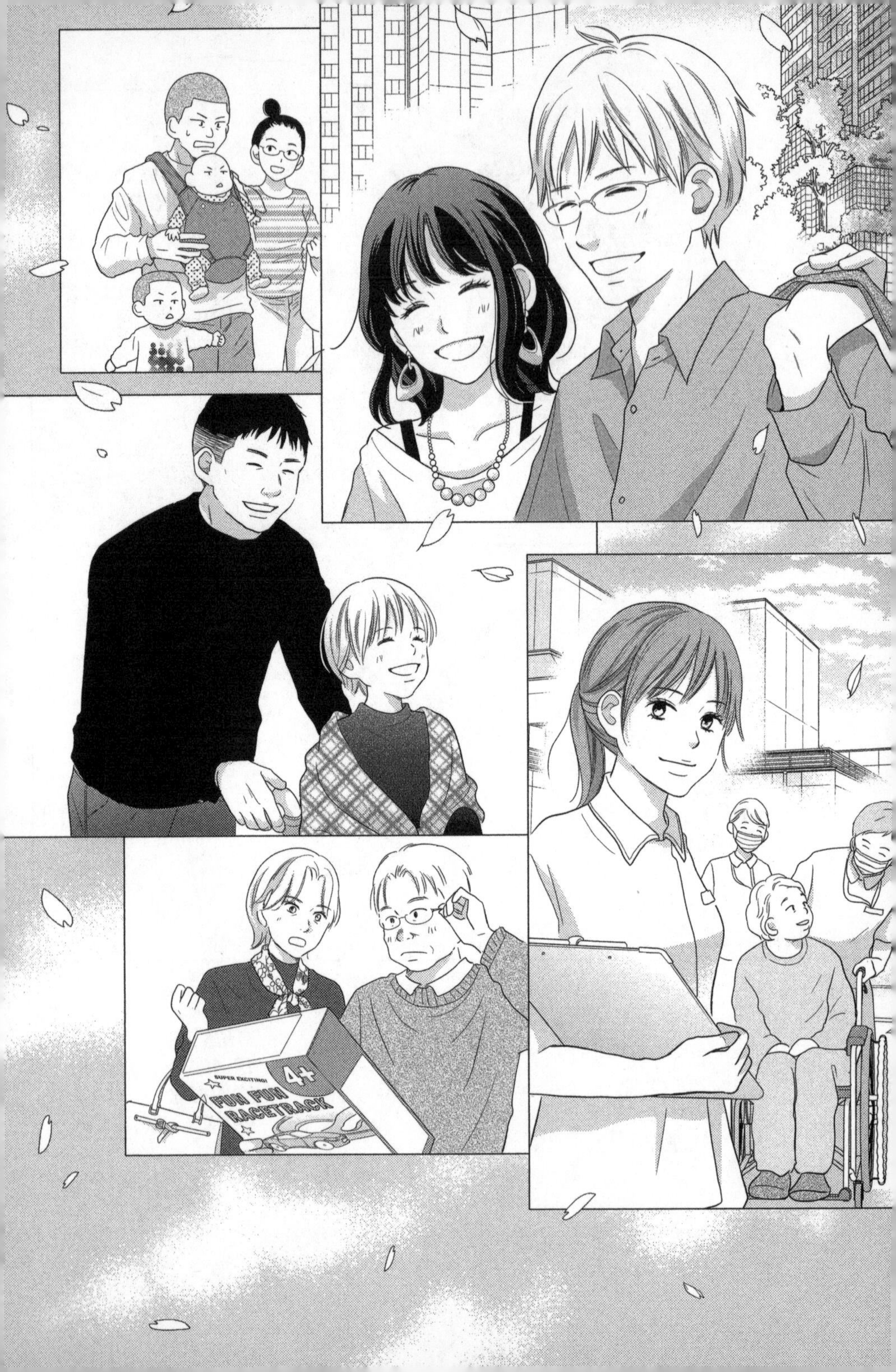
SUPER EXCITING!
4+
FUN FUN RACETRACK

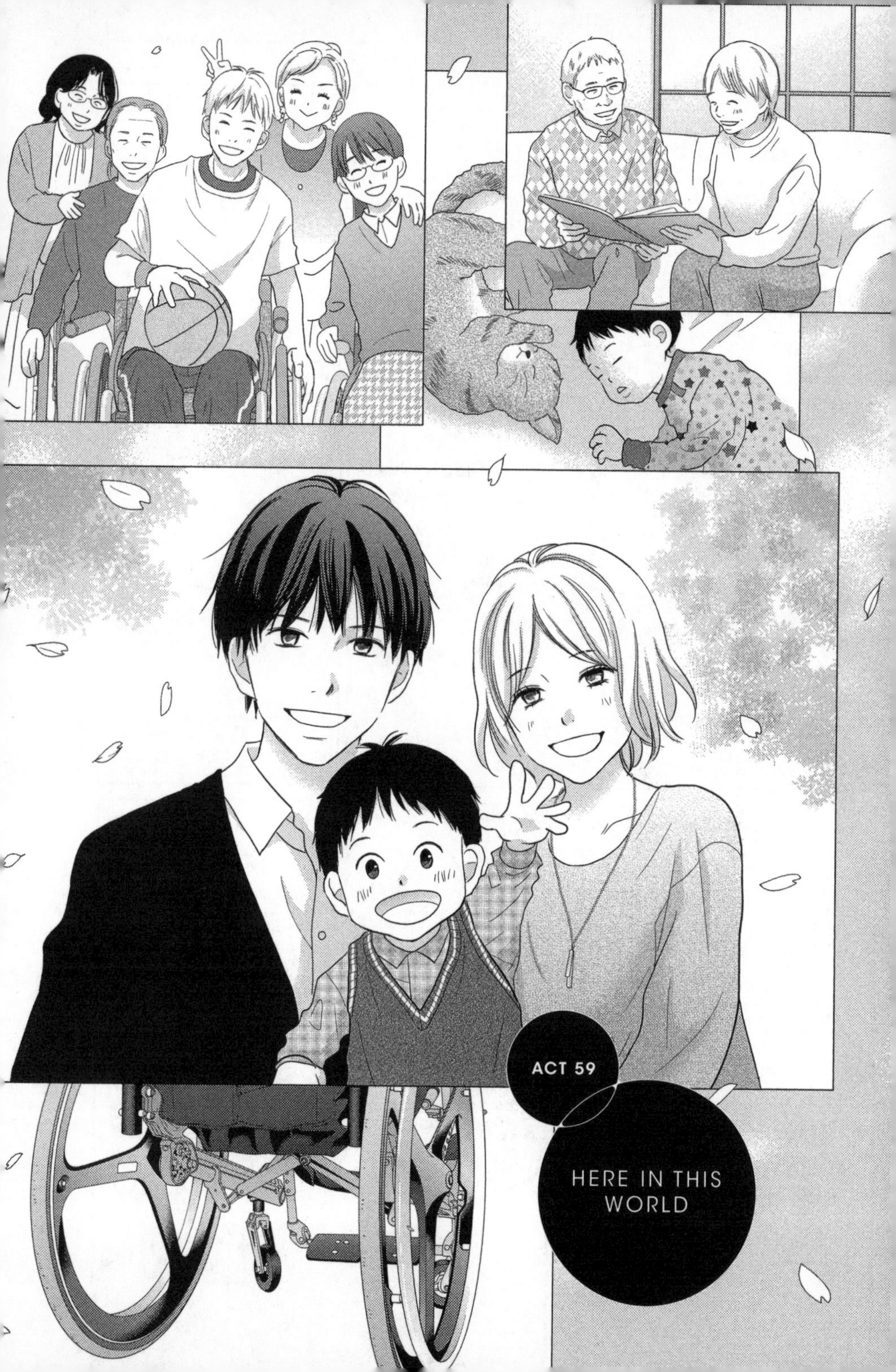
ACT 59
HERE IN THIS WORLD

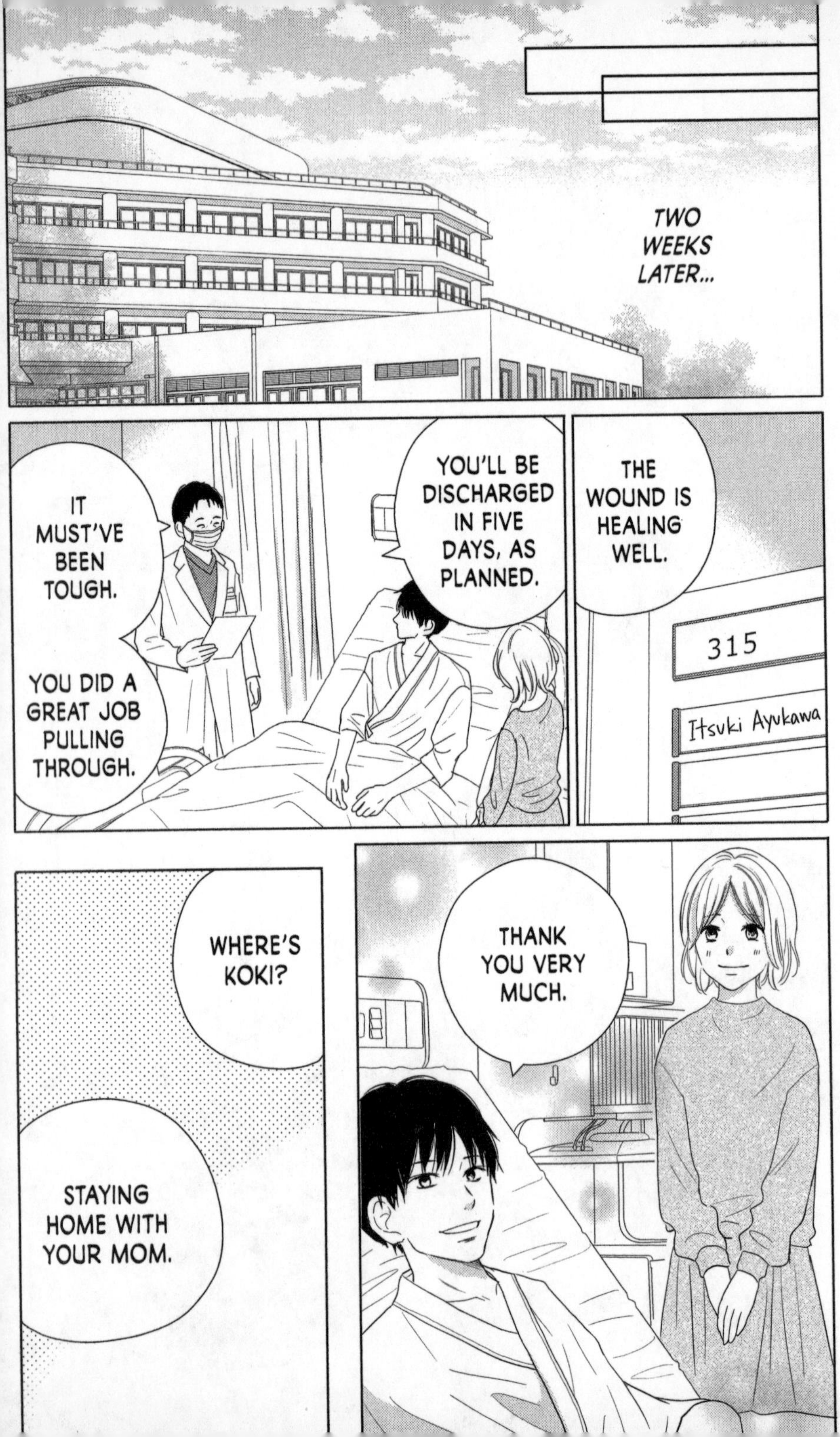
TWO WEEKS LATER...
THE WOUND IS HEALING WELL.
315
Itsuki Ayukawa
YOU'LL BE DISCHARGED IN FIVE DAYS, AS PLANNED.
IT MUST'VE BEEN TOUGH.
YOU DID A GREAT JOB PULLING THROUGH.
THANK YOU VERY MUCH.
WHERE'S KOKI?
STAYING HOME WITH YOUR MOM.

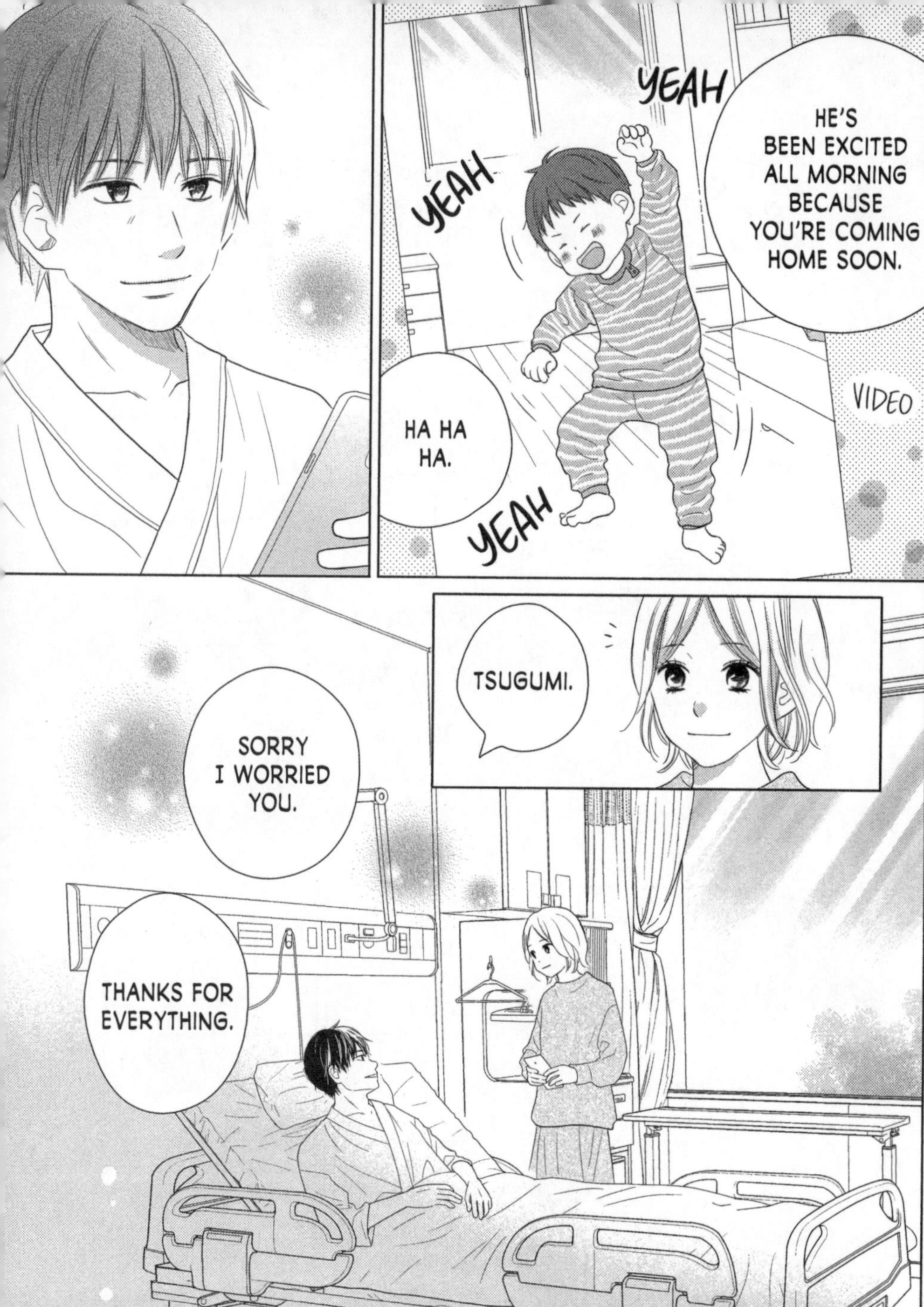
YEAH
HE'S BEEN EXCITED ALL MORNING BECAUSE YOU'RE COMING HOME SOON.
YEAH
VIDEO
HA HA HA.
YEAH
TSUGUMI.
SORRY I WORRIED YOU.
THANKS FOR EVERYTHING.

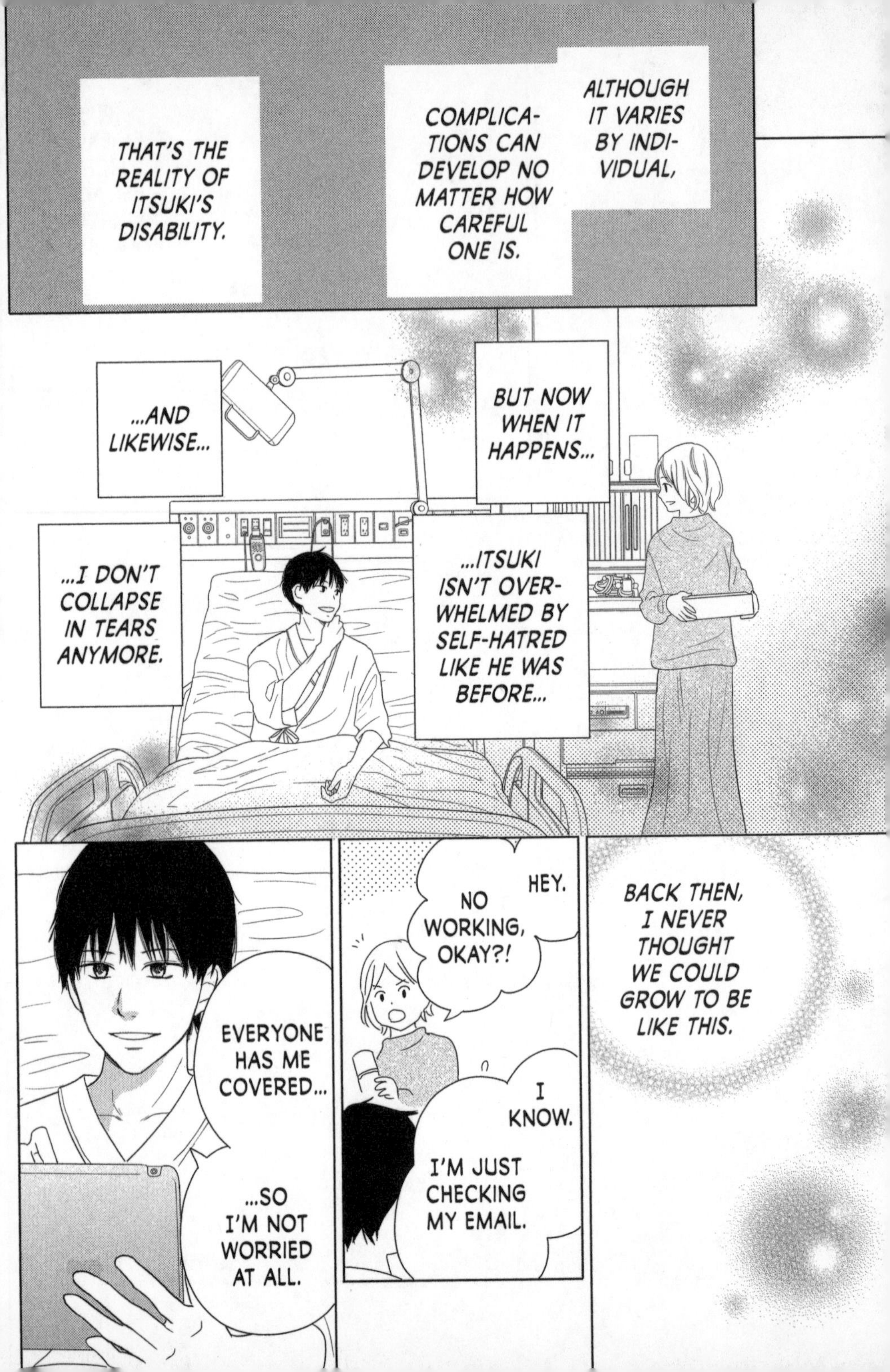

ALTHOUGH IT VARIES BY INDIVIDUAL,
COMPLICATIONS CAN DEVELOP NO MATTER HOW CAREFUL ONE IS.
THAT'S THE REALITY OF ITSUKI'S DISABILITY.
BUT NOW WHEN IT HAPPENS...
...ITSUKI ISN'T OVERWHELMED BY SELF-HATRED LIKE HE WAS BEFORE...
...AND LIKEWISE...
...I DON'T COLLAPSE IN TEARS ANYMORE.
BACK THEN, I NEVER THOUGHT WE COULD GROW TO BE LIKE THIS.
HEY.
NO WORKING, OKAY?!
I KNOW.
I'M JUST CHECKING MY EMAIL.
EVERYONE HAS ME COVERED...
...SO I'M NOT WORRIED AT ALL.

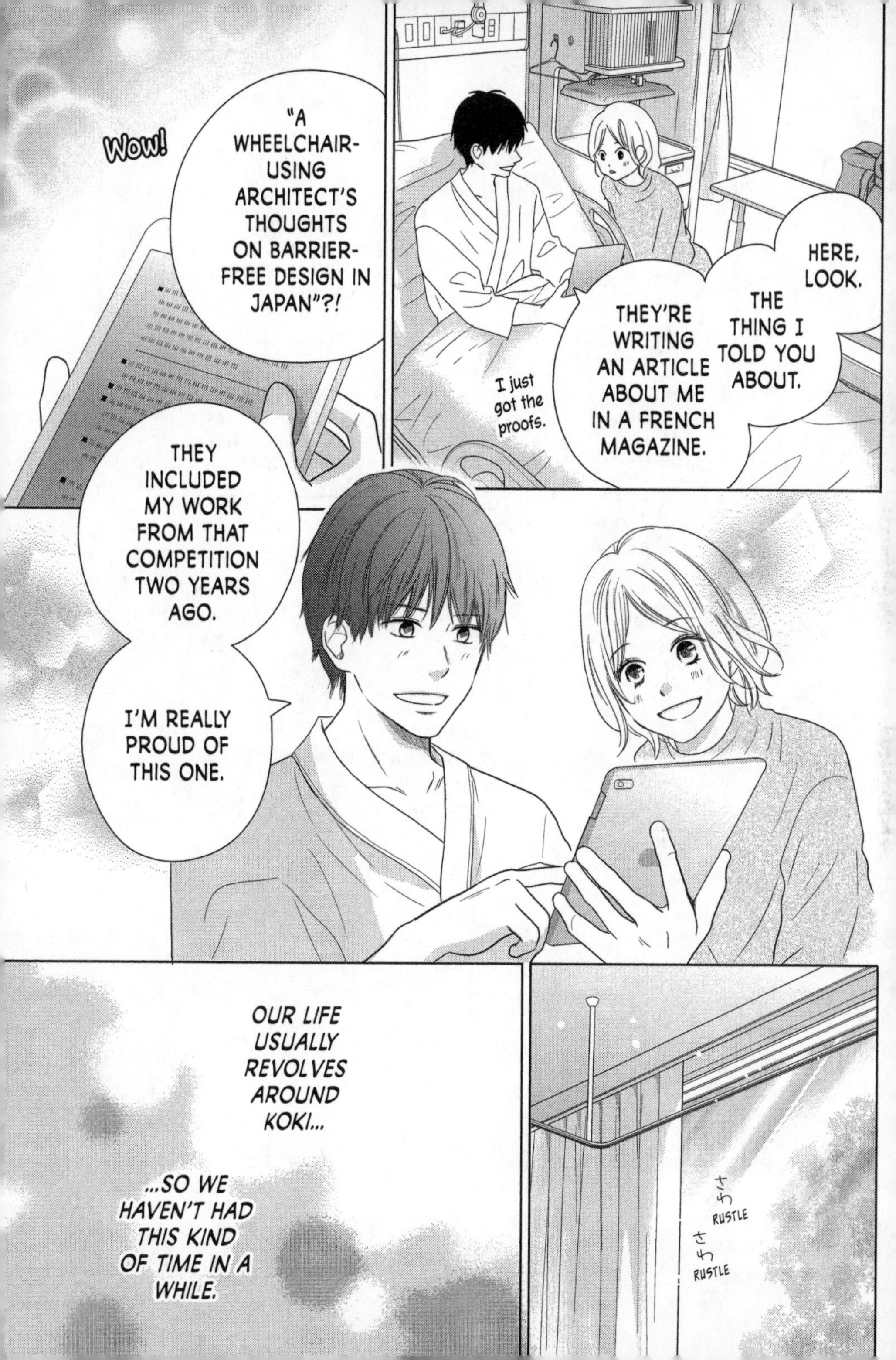
HERE, LOOK.
THE THING I TOLD YOU ABOUT.
THEY'RE WRITING AN ARTICLE ABOUT ME IN A FRENCH MAGAZINE.
I just got the proofs.
Wow!
"A WHEELCHAIR-USING ARCHITECT'S THOUGHTS ON BARRIER-FREE DESIGN IN JAPAN"?!
THEY INCLUDED MY WORK FROM THAT COMPETITION TWO YEARS AGO.
I'M REALLY PROUD OF THIS ONE.
RUSTLE
RUSTLE
OUR LIFE USUALLY REVOLVES AROUND KOKI...
...SO WE HAVEN'T HAD THIS KIND OF TIME IN A WHILE.

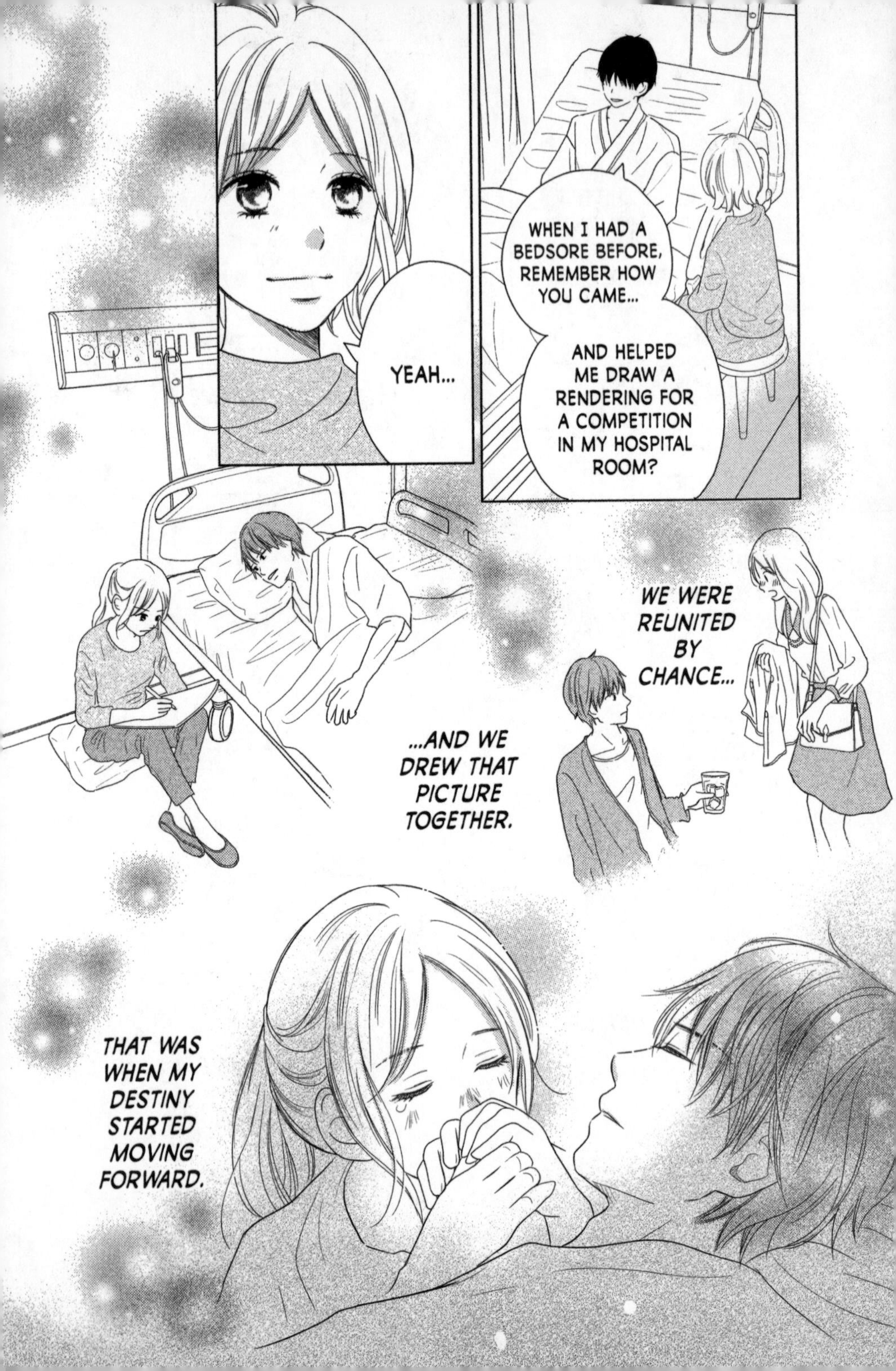
WHEN I HAD A BEDSORE BEFORE, REMEMBER HOW YOU CAME...
AND HELPED ME DRAW A RENDERING FOR A COMPETITION IN MY HOSPITAL ROOM?
YEAH...
WE WERE REUNITED BY CHANCE...
...AND WE DREW THAT PICTURE TOGETHER.
THAT WAS WHEN MY DESTINY STARTED MOVING FORWARD.

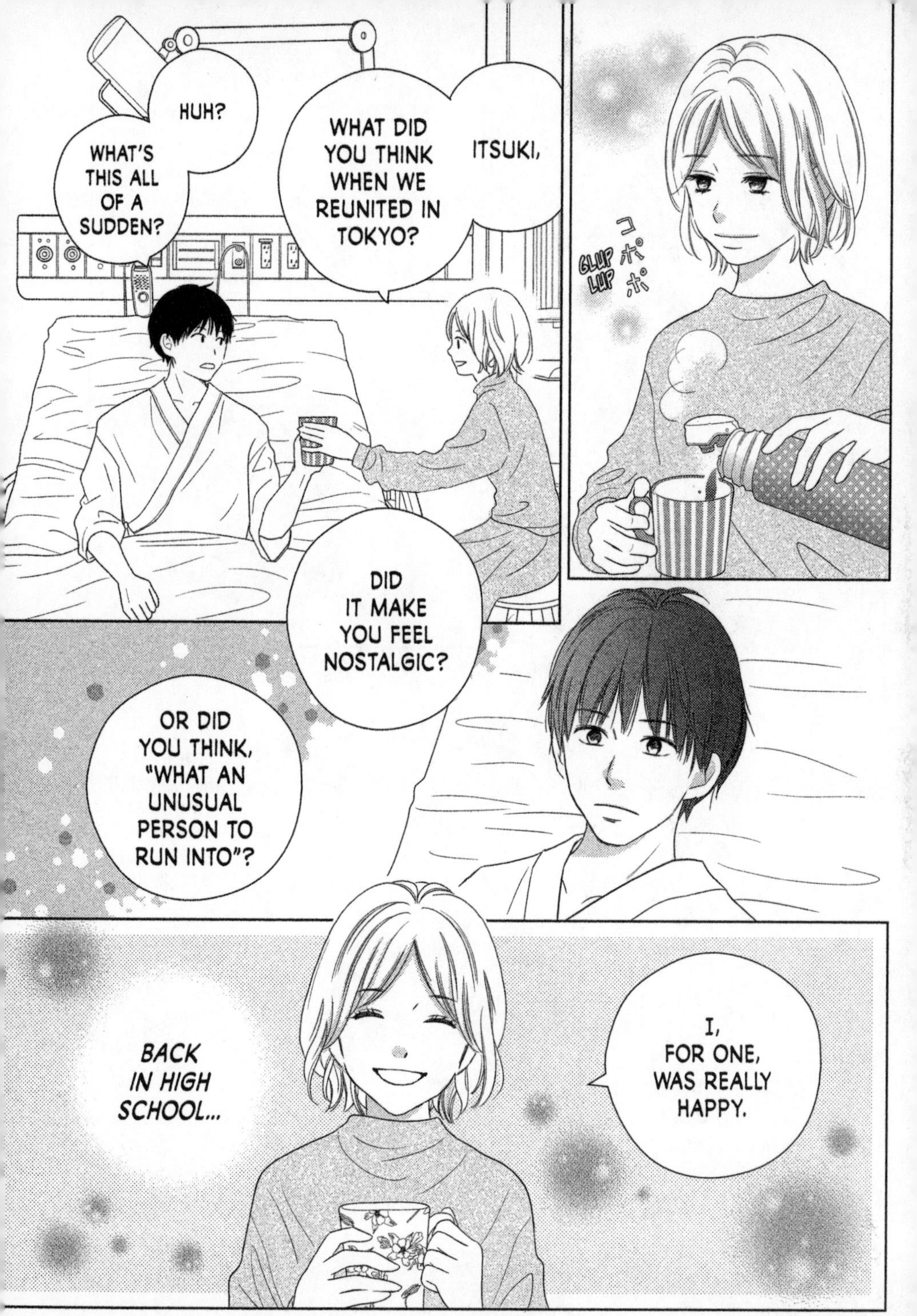
GLUP LUP
コポポ
ITSUKI,
WHAT DID YOU THINK WHEN WE REUNITED IN TOKYO?
HUH?
WHAT'S THIS ALL OF A SUDDEN?
DID IT MAKE YOU FEEL NOSTALGIC?
OR DID YOU THINK, "WHAT AN UNUSUAL PERSON TO RUN INTO"?
I, FOR ONE, WAS REALLY HAPPY.
BACK IN HIGH SCHOOL...

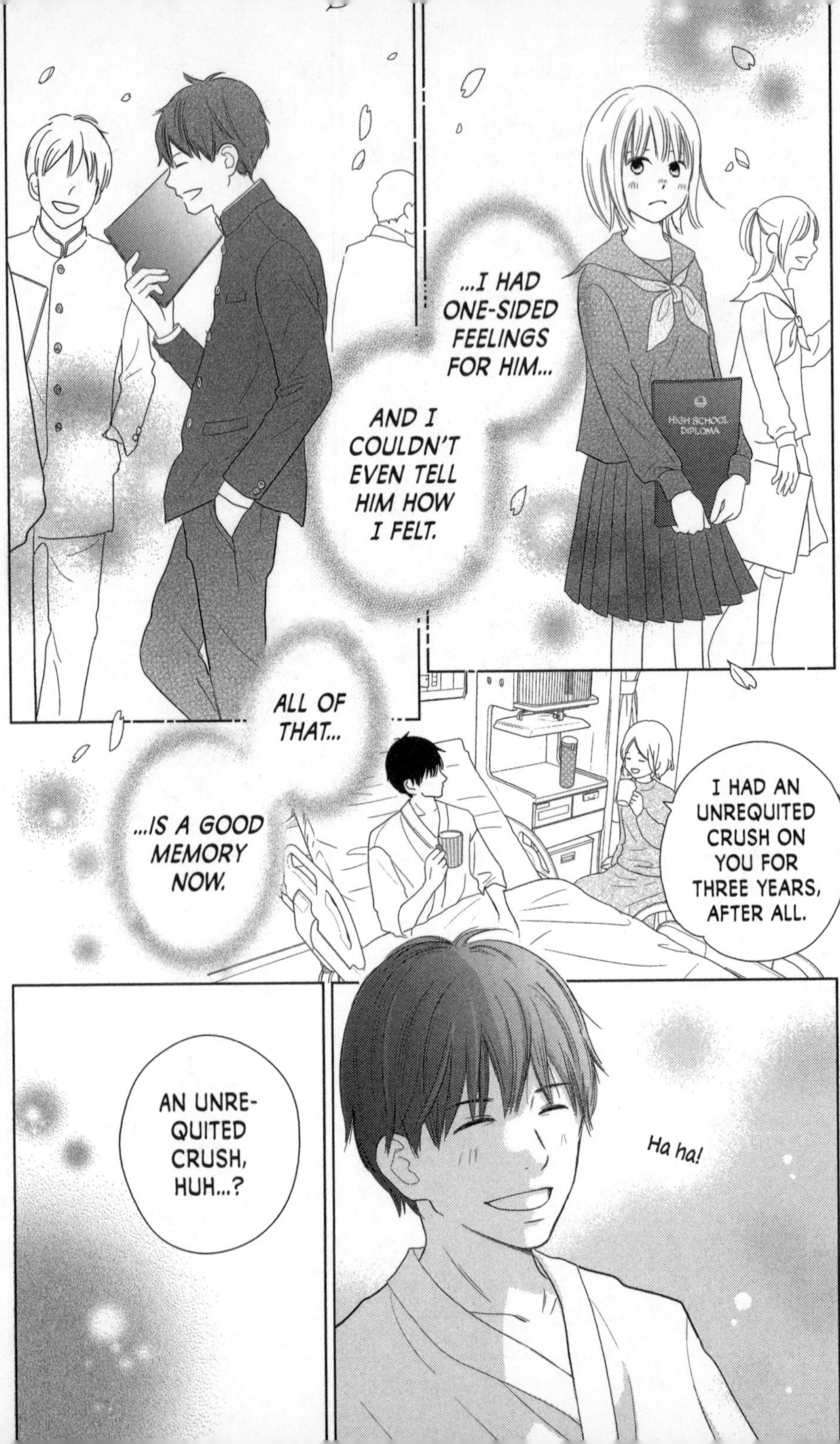
...I HAD ONE-SIDED FEELINGS FOR HIM...
AND I COULDN'T EVEN TELL HIM HOW I FELT.
HIGH SCHOOL DIPLOMA
ALL OF THAT...
...IS A GOOD MEMORY NOW.
I HAD AN UNREQUITED CRUSH ON YOU FOR THREE YEARS, AFTER ALL.
Ha ha!
AN UNRE-QUITED CRUSH, HUH...?

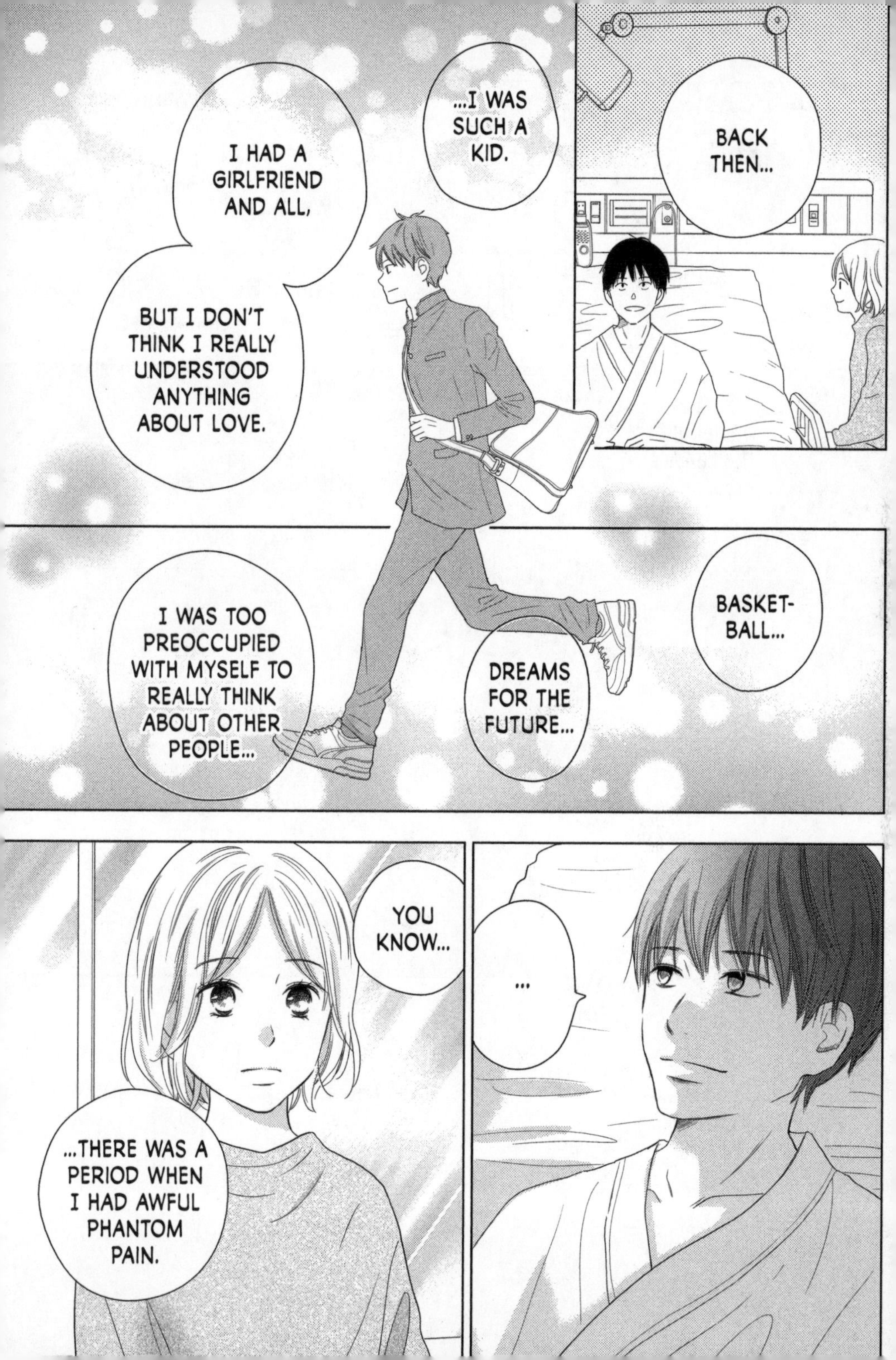
BACK THEN...
...I WAS SUCH A KID.
I HAD A GIRLFRIEND AND ALL,
BUT I DON'T THINK I REALLY UNDERSTOOD ANYTHING ABOUT LOVE.
BASKET-BALL...
DREAMS FOR THE FUTURE...
I WAS TOO PREOCCUPIED WITH MYSELF TO REALLY THINK ABOUT OTHER PEOPLE...
...
YOU KNOW...
...THERE WAS A PERIOD WHEN I HAD AWFUL PHANTOM PAIN.

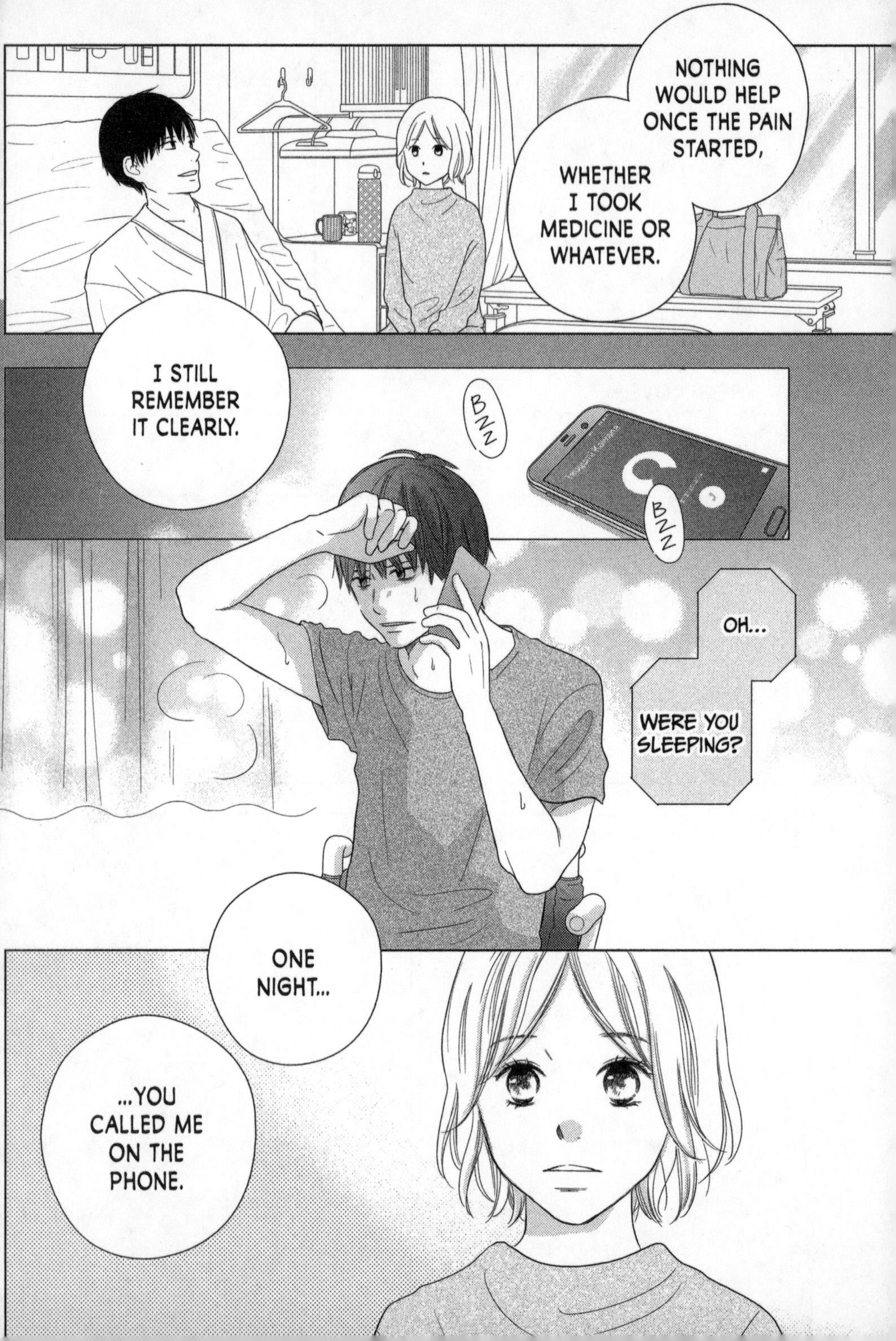
NOTHING WOULD HELP ONCE THE PAIN STARTED,
WHETHER I TOOK MEDICINE OR WHATEVER.
I STILL REMEMBER IT CLEARLY.
BZZ
BZZ
OH...
WERE YOU SLEEPING?
ONE NIGHT...
...YOU CALLED ME ON THE PHONE.

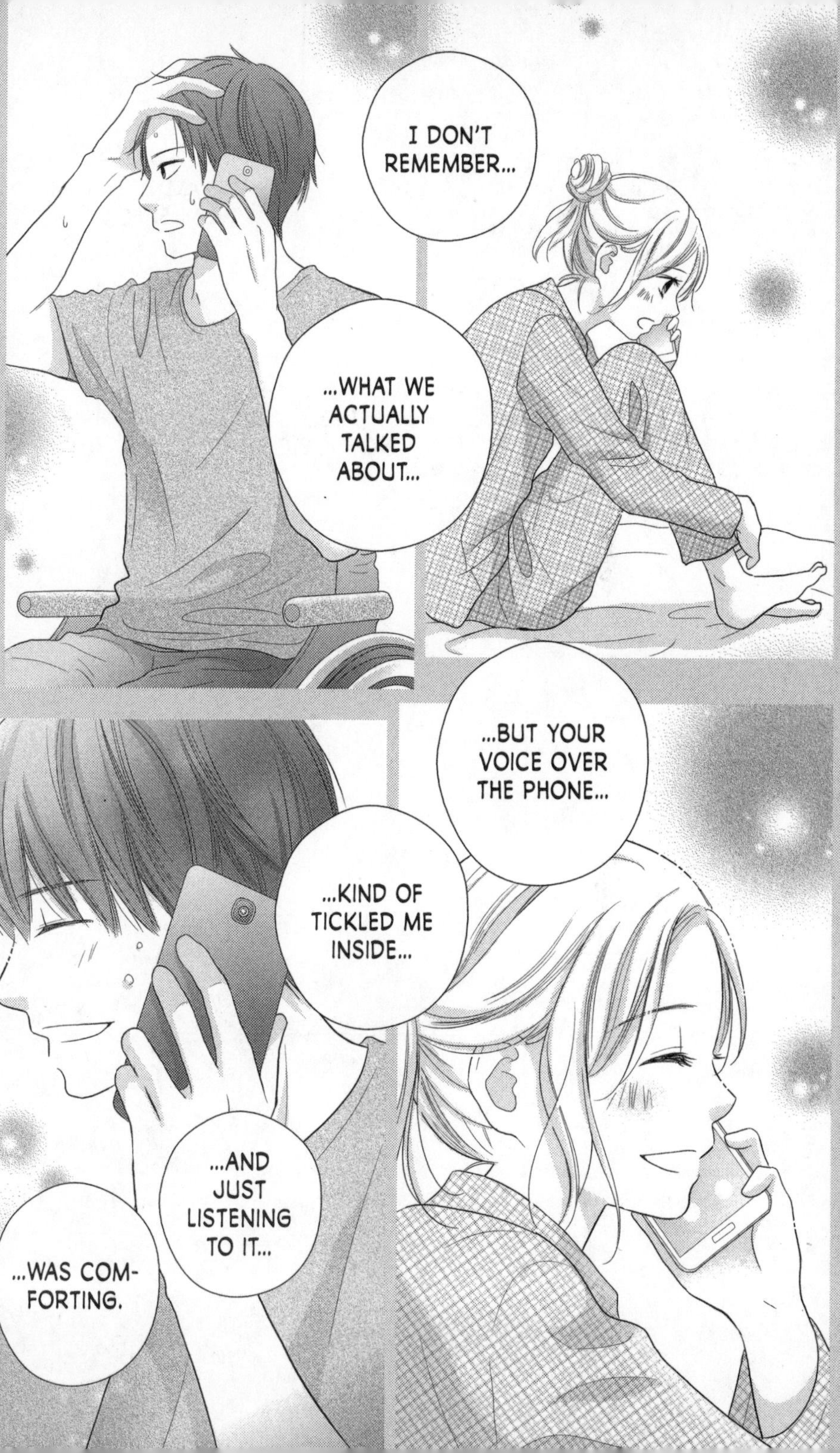
I DON'T REMEMBER...
...WHAT WE ACTUALLY TALKED ABOUT...
...BUT YOUR VOICE OVER THE PHONE...
...KIND OF TICKLED ME INSIDE...
...AND JUST LISTENING TO IT...
...WAS COM-FORTING.

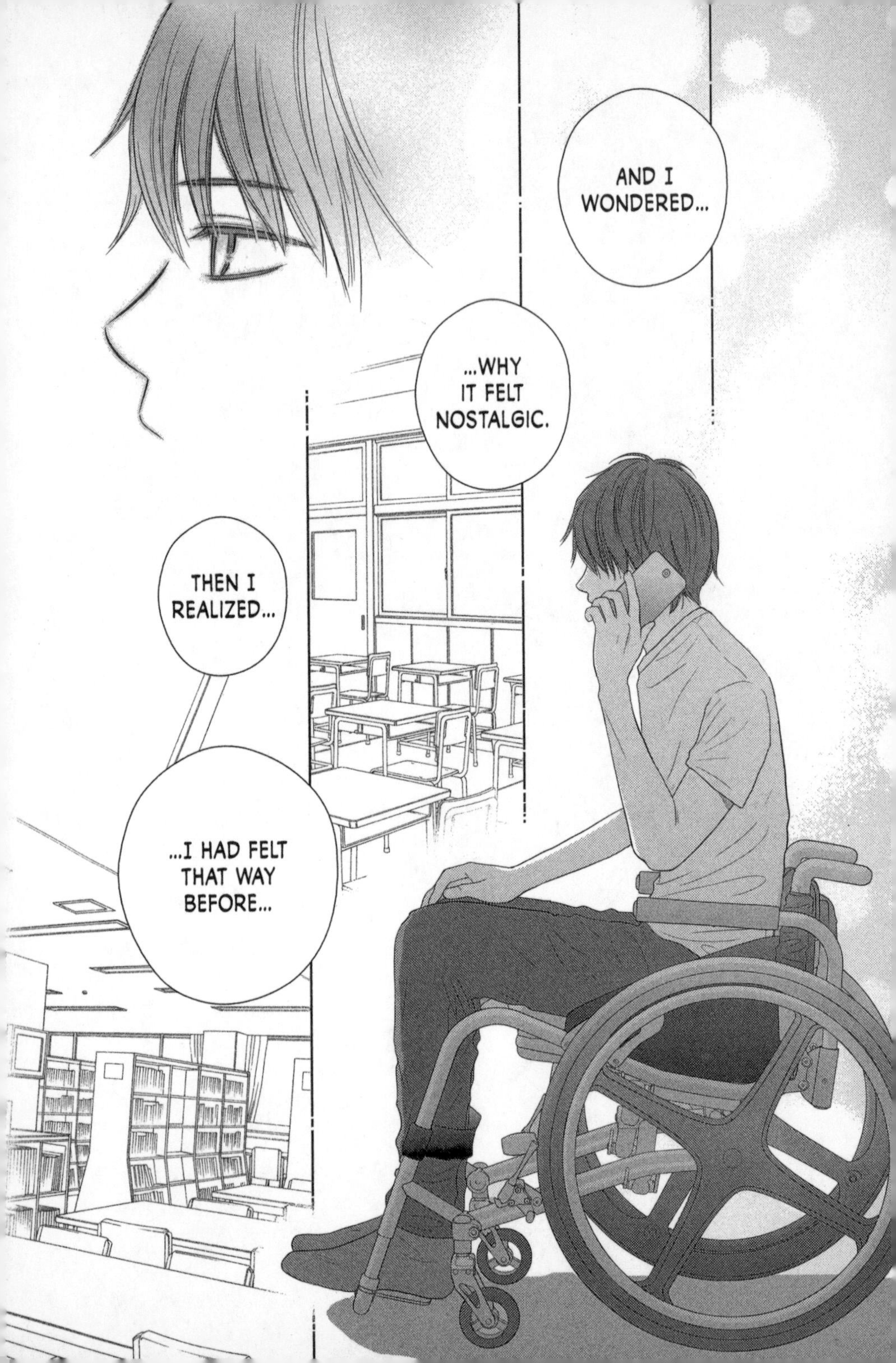
AND I WONDERED...
...WHY IT FELT NOSTALGIC.
THEN I REALIZED...
...I HAD FELT THAT WAY BEFORE...

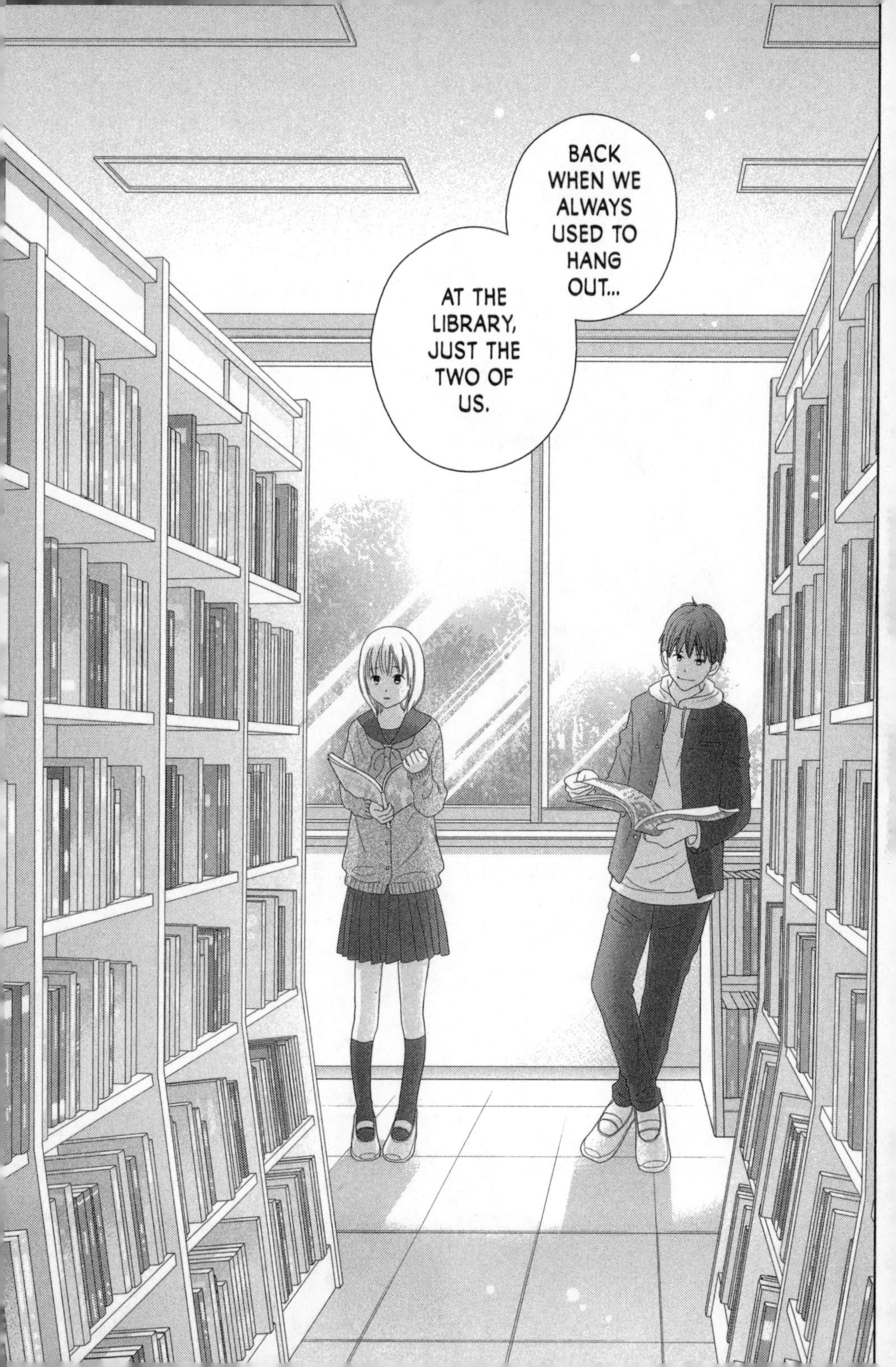
BACK WHEN WE ALWAYS USED TO HANG OUT...
AT THE LIBRARY, JUST THE TWO OF US.

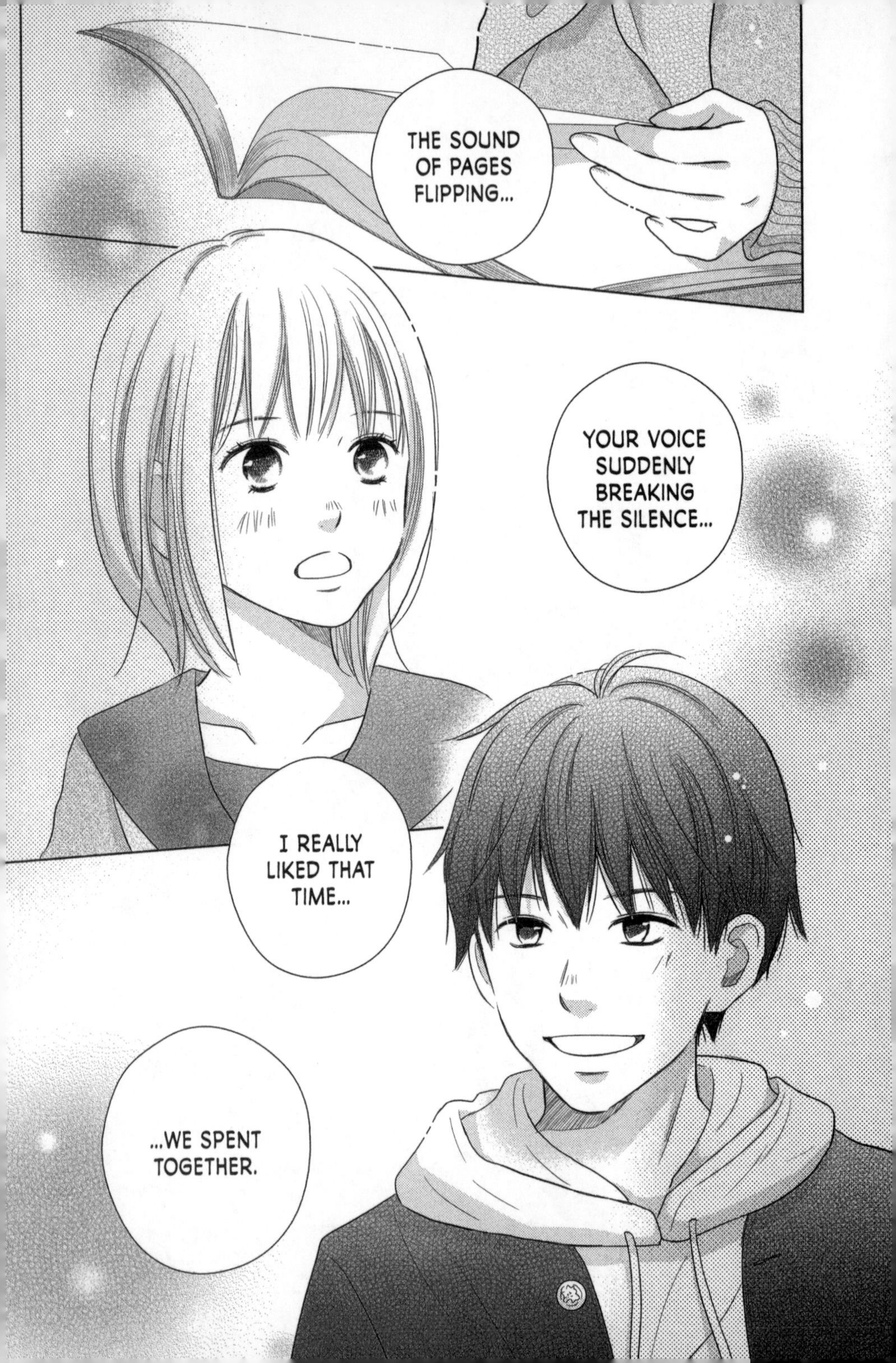
THE SOUND OF PAGES FLIPPING...
YOUR VOICE SUDDENLY BREAKING THE SILENCE...
I REALLY LIKED THAT TIME...
...WE SPENT TOGETHER.

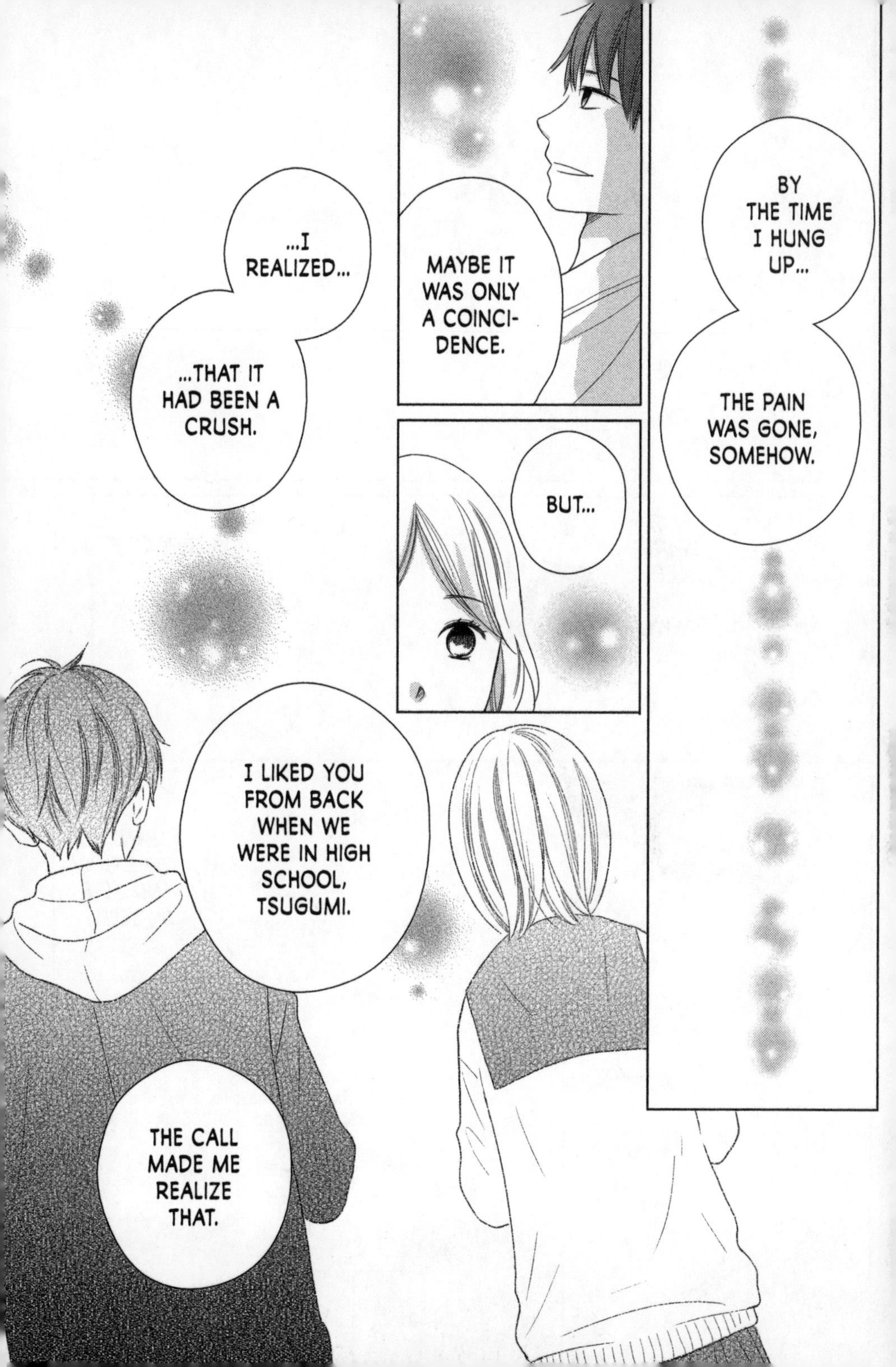
BY THE TIME I HUNG UP...
THE PAIN WAS GONE, SOMEHOW.
MAYBE IT WAS ONLY A COINCIDENCE.
BUT...
...I REALIZED...
...THAT IT HAD BEEN A CRUSH.
I LIKED YOU FROM BACK WHEN WE WERE IN HIGH SCHOOL, TSUGUMI.
THE CALL MADE ME REALIZE THAT.

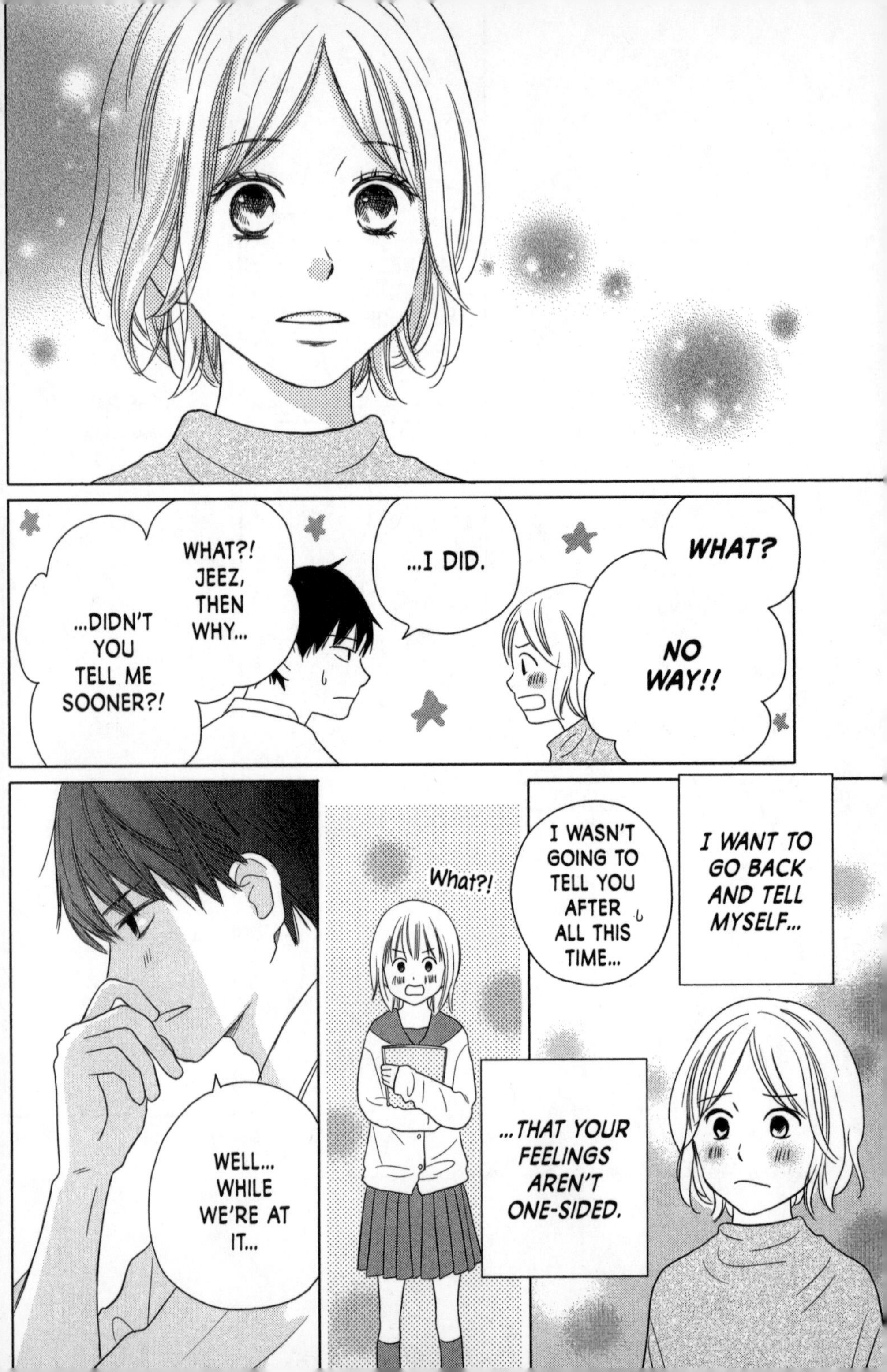
WHAT? NO WAY!!
...I DID.
WHAT?! JEEZ, THEN WHY...
...DIDN'T YOU TELL ME SOONER?!
I WANT TO GO BACK AND TELL MYSELF...
I WASN'T GOING TO TELL YOU AFTER ALL THIS TIME...
...THAT YOUR FEELINGS AREN'T ONE-SIDED.
What?!
WELL... WHILE WE'RE AT IT...

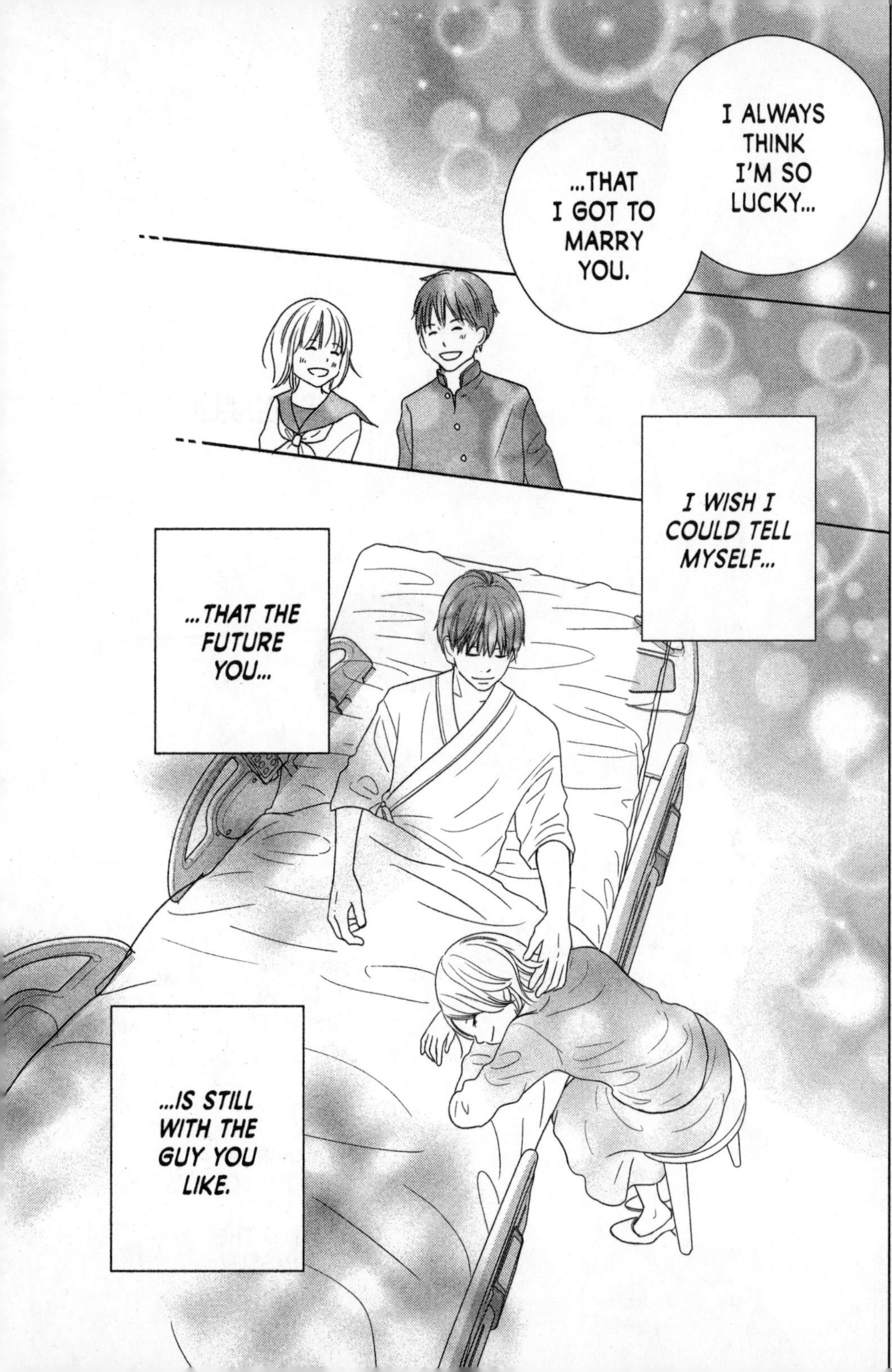
I ALWAYS THINK I'M SO LUCKY...
...THAT I GOT TO MARRY YOU.
I WISH I COULD TELL MYSELF...
...THAT THE FUTURE YOU...
...IS STILL WITH THE GUY YOU LIKE.

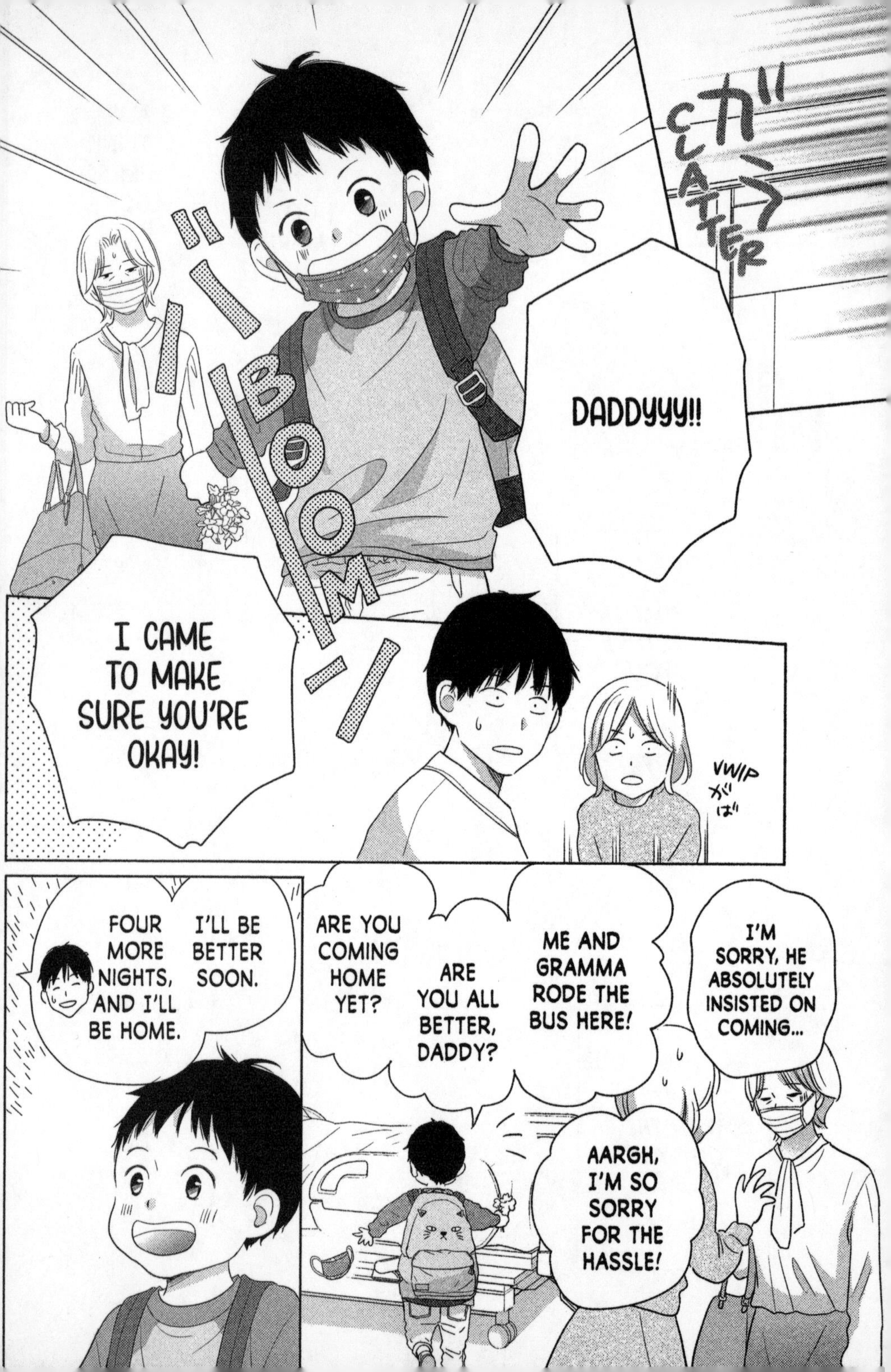
CLATTER
DADDYYY!!
BOOOM
I CAME TO MAKE SURE YOU'RE OKAY!
VWIP
がば
I'M SORRY, HE ABSOLUTELY INSISTED ON COMING...
ME AND GRAMMA RODE THE BUS HERE!
ARE YOU ALL BETTER, DADDY?
ARE YOU COMING HOME YET?
AARGH, I'M SO SORRY FOR THE HASSLE!
I'LL BE BETTER SOON.
FOUR MORE NIGHTS, AND I'LL BE HOME.

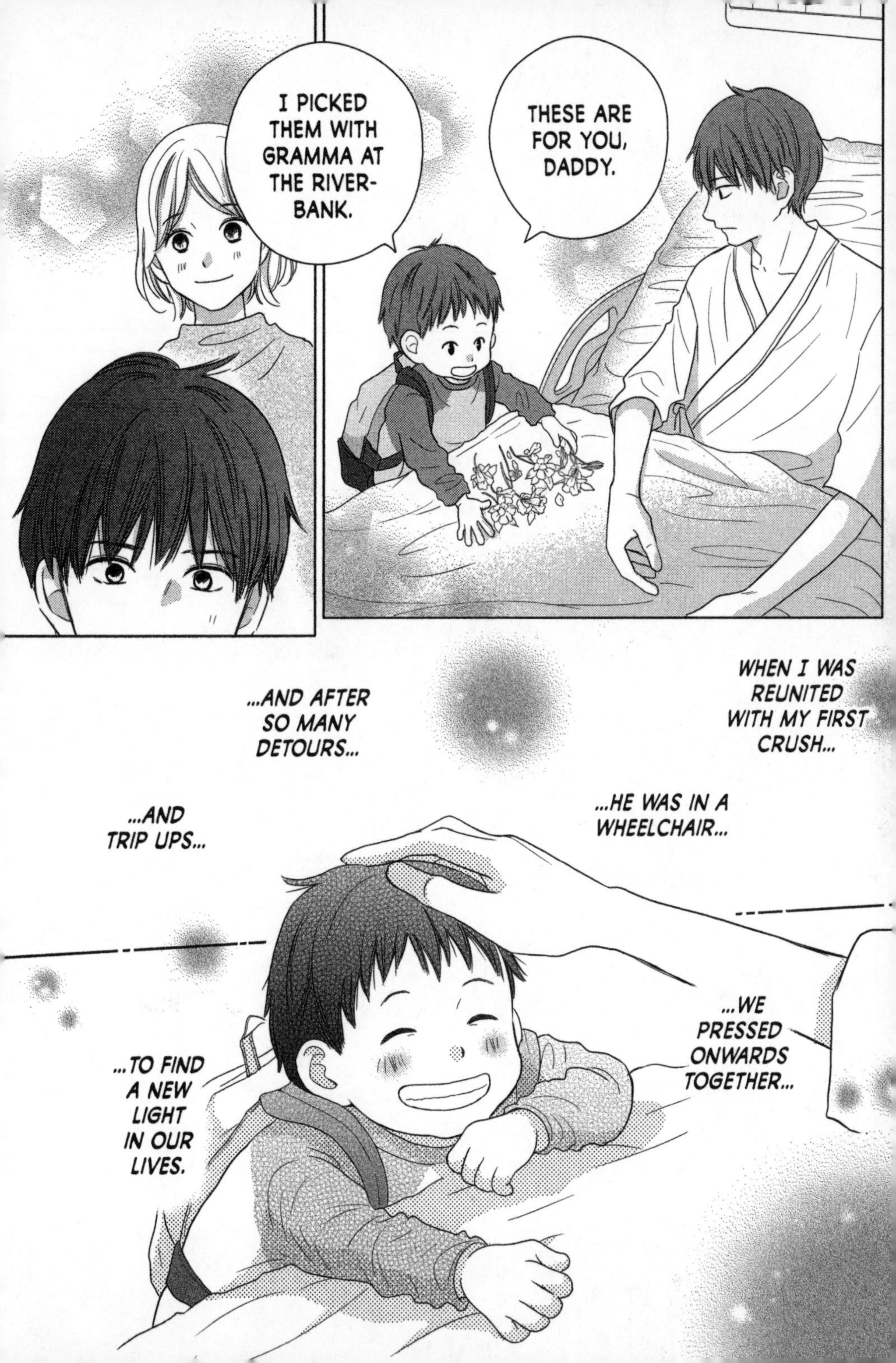
THESE ARE FOR YOU, DADDY.
I PICKED THEM WITH GRAMMA AT THE RIVER-BANK.
WHEN I WAS REUNITED WITH MY FIRST CRUSH...
...HE WAS IN A WHEELCHAIR...
...AND AFTER SO MANY DETOURS...
...AND TRIP UPS...
...WE PRESSED ONWARDS TOGETHER...
...TO FIND A NEW LIGHT IN OUR LIVES.

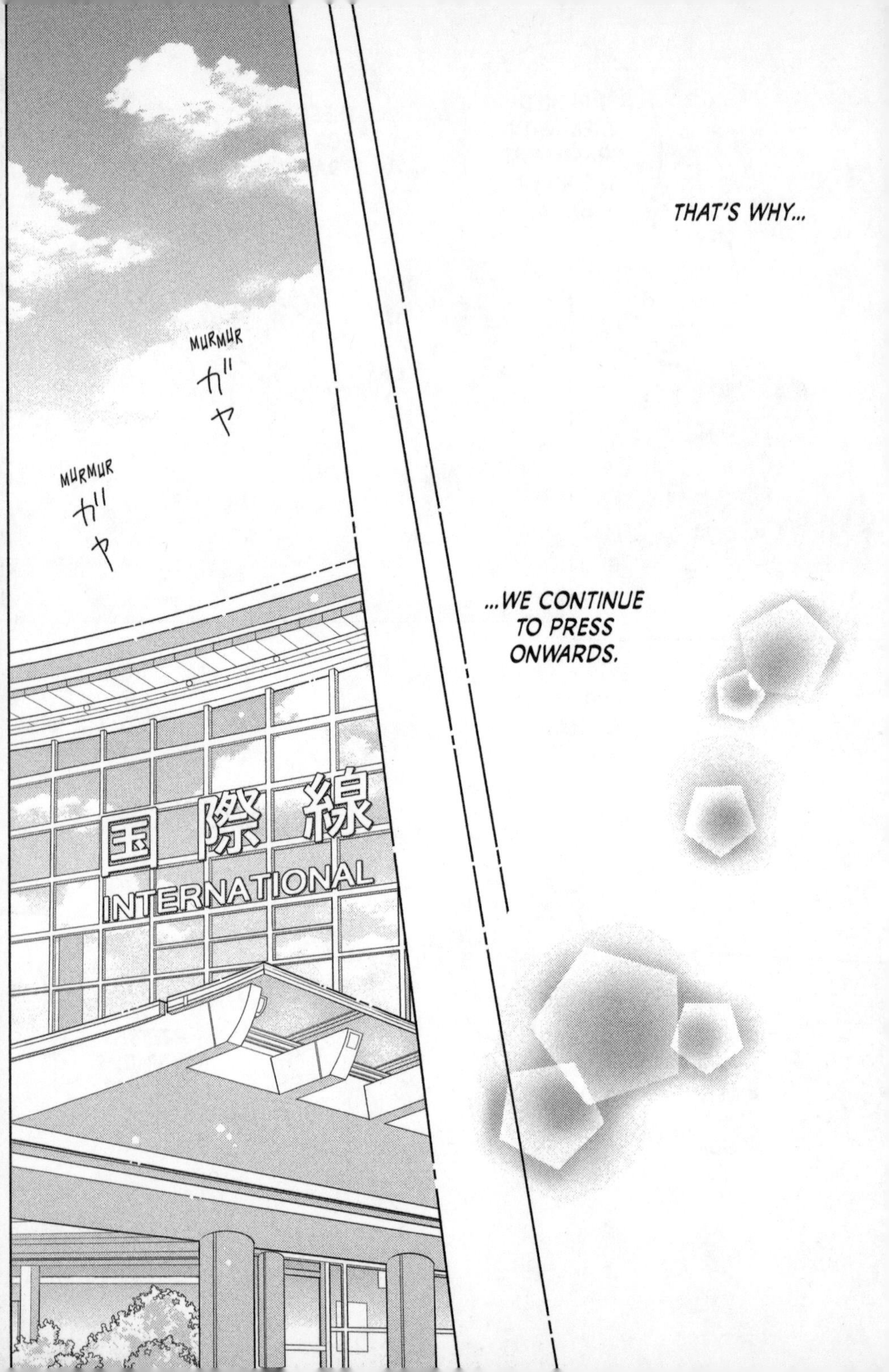
THAT'S WHY...
...WE CONTINUE TO PRESS ONWARDS.
MURMUR
ガヤ
MURMUR
ガヤ
国際線
INTERNATIONAL

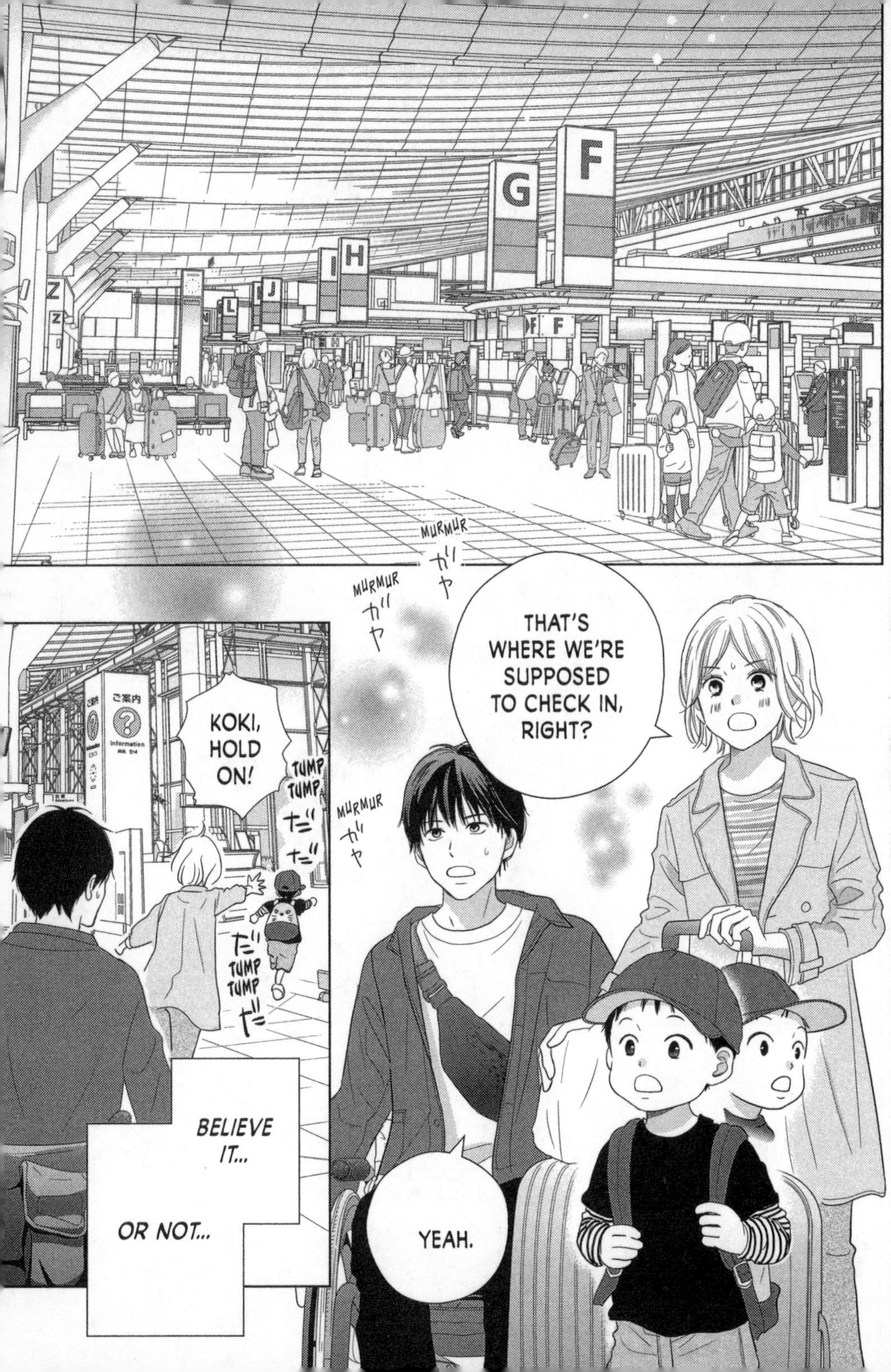
MURMUR
ガヤ
MURMUR
ガヤ
THAT'S WHERE WE'RE SUPPOSED TO CHECK IN, RIGHT?
MURMUR
ガヤ
YEAH.
KOKI, HOLD ON!
TUMP TUMP
TUMP TUMP
BELIEVE IT...
OR NOT...

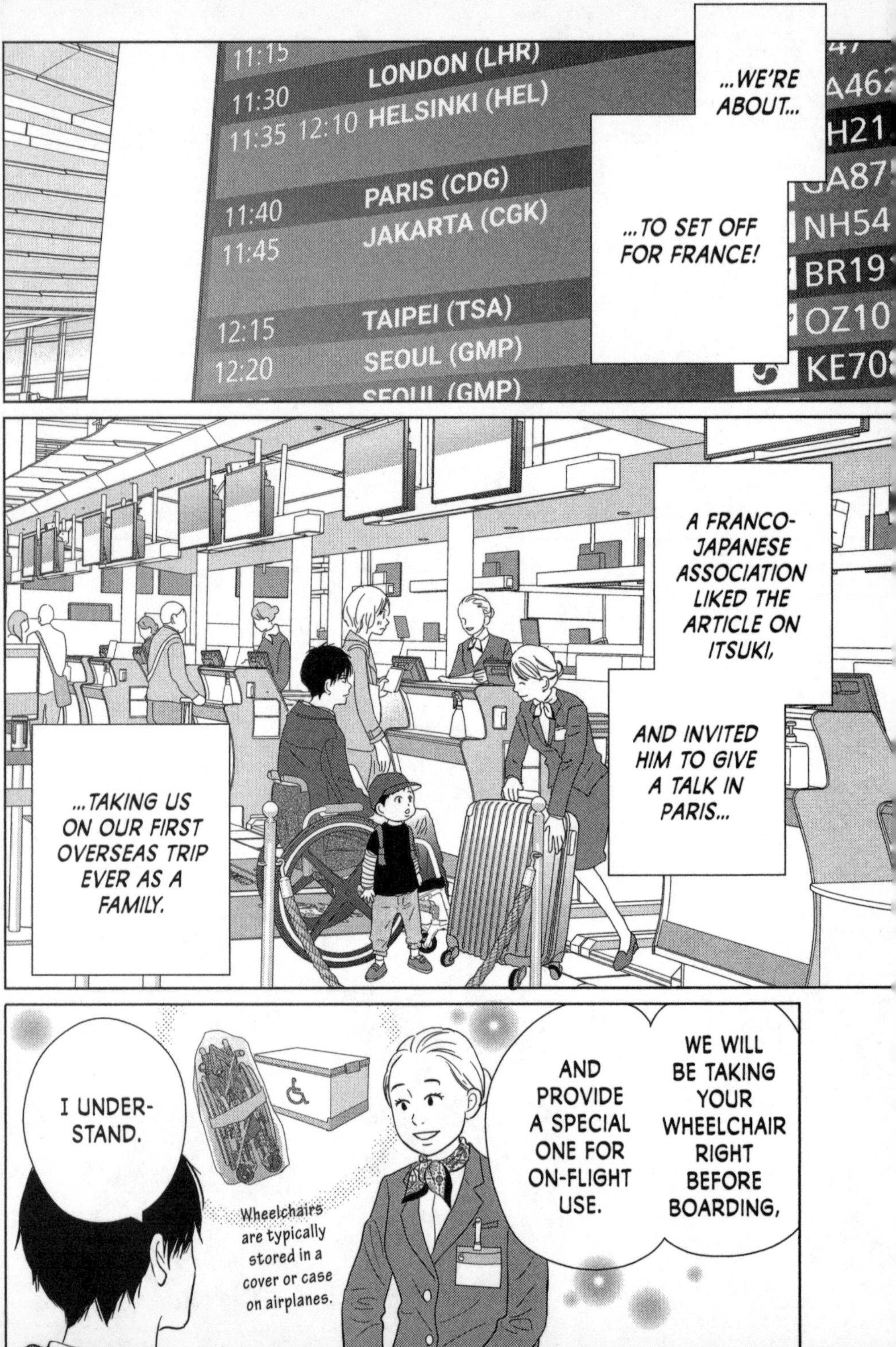
...WE'RE ABOUT...
...TO SET OFF FOR FRANCE!
11:15 LONDON (LHR)
11:30 HELSINKI (HEL)
11:35 12:10
PARIS (CDG)
11:40 JAKARTA (CGK)
11:45
TAIPEI (TSA)
12:15 SEOUL (GMP)
12:20
A FRANCO-JAPANESE ASSOCIATION LIKED THE ARTICLE ON ITSUKI,
AND INVITED HIM TO GIVE A TALK IN PARIS...
...TAKING US ON OUR FIRST OVERSEAS TRIP EVER AS A FAMILY.
WE WILL BE TAKING YOUR WHEELCHAIR RIGHT BEFORE BOARDING,
AND PROVIDE A SPECIAL ONE FOR ON-FLIGHT USE.
Wheelchairs are typically stored in a cover or case on airplanes.
I UNDER-STAND.

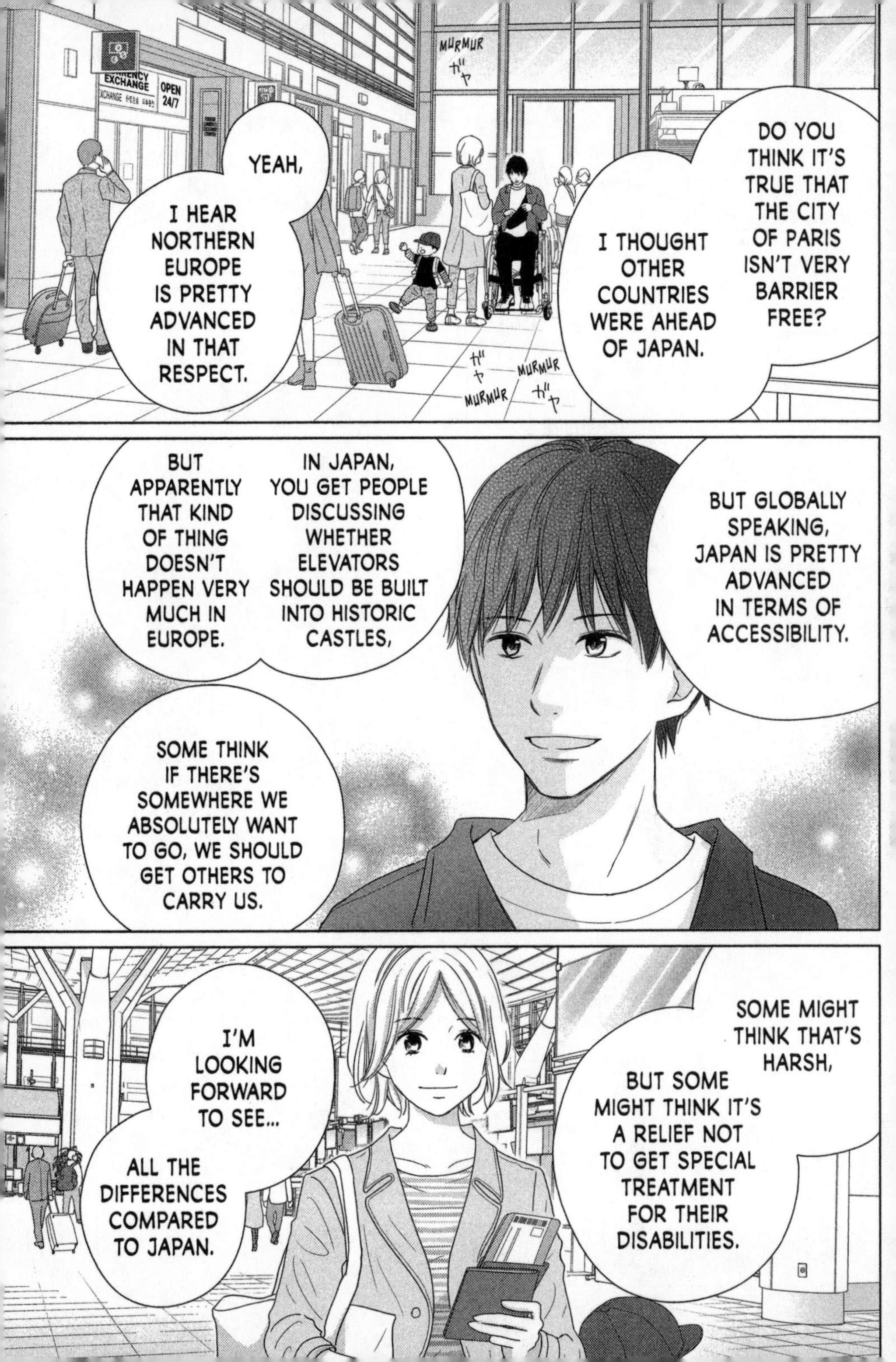

CURRENCY EXCHANGE
OPEN 24/7
MURMUR
ガヤ
DO YOU THINK IT'S TRUE THAT THE CITY OF PARIS ISN'T VERY BARRIER FREE?
I THOUGHT OTHER COUNTRIES WERE AHEAD OF JAPAN.
MURMUR
ガヤ
MURMUR
ガヤ
YEAH,
I HEAR NORTHERN EUROPE IS PRETTY ADVANCED IN THAT RESPECT.
BUT GLOBALLY SPEAKING, JAPAN IS PRETTY ADVANCED IN TERMS OF ACCESSIBILITY.
IN JAPAN, YOU GET PEOPLE DISCUSSING WHETHER ELEVATORS SHOULD BE BUILT INTO HISTORIC CASTLES,
BUT APPARENTLY THAT KIND OF THING DOESN'T HAPPEN VERY MUCH IN EUROPE.
SOME THINK IF THERE'S SOMEWHERE WE ABSOLUTELY WANT TO GO, WE SHOULD GET OTHERS TO CARRY US.
SOME MIGHT THINK THAT'S HARSH,
BUT SOME MIGHT THINK IT'S A RELIEF NOT TO GET SPECIAL TREATMENT FOR THEIR DISABILITIES.
I'M LOOKING FORWARD TO SEE...
ALL THE DIFFERENCES COMPARED TO JAPAN.

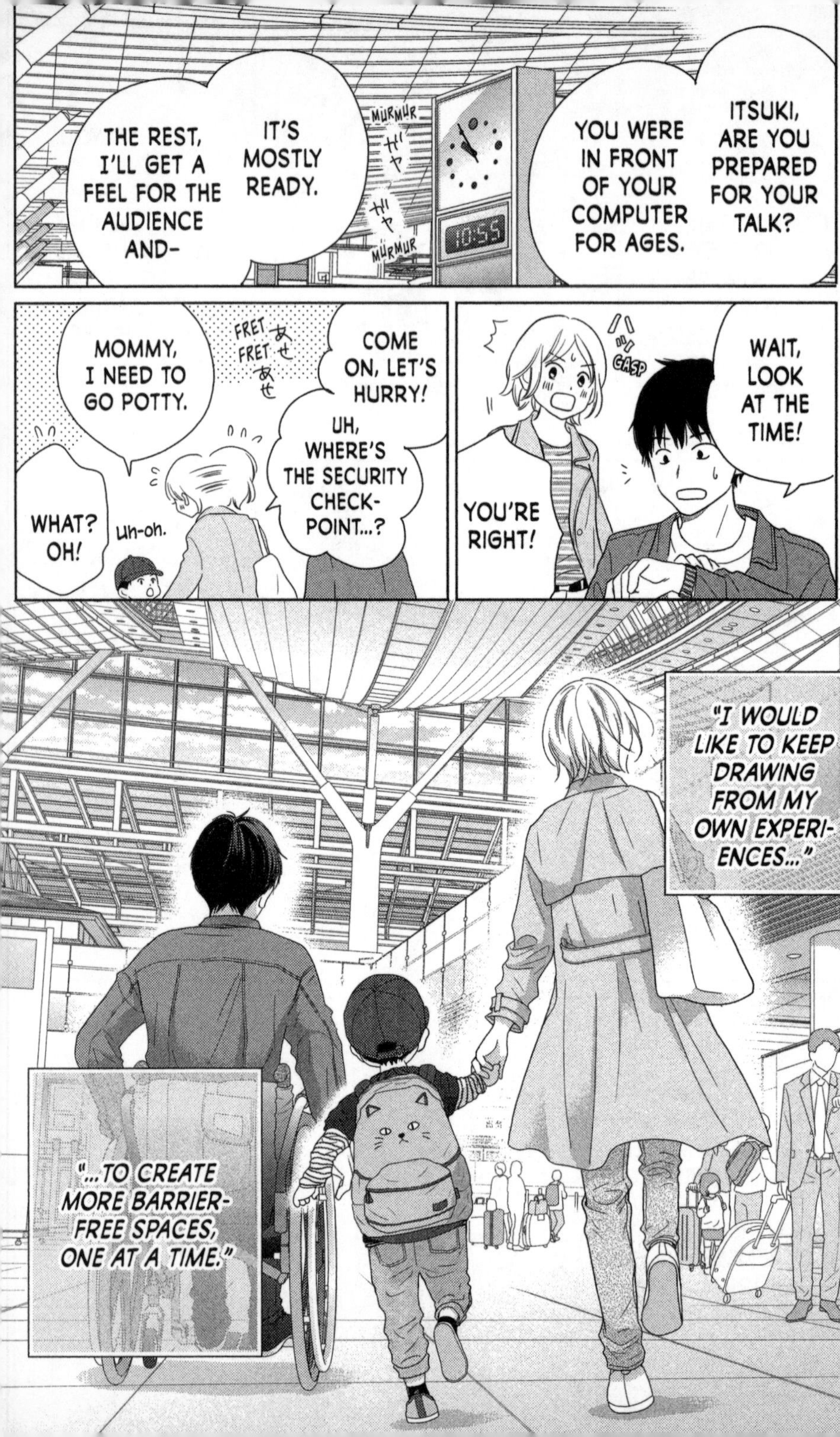
ITSUKI, ARE YOU PREPARED FOR YOUR TALK?
YOU WERE IN FRONT OF YOUR COMPUTER FOR AGES.
MURMUR ガヤ
ガヤ MURMUR
10:55
IT'S MOSTLY READY.
THE REST, I'LL GET A FEEL FOR THE AUDIENCE AND–
WAIT, LOOK AT THE TIME!
GASP
YOU'RE RIGHT!
COME ON, LET'S HURRY!
UH, WHERE'S THE SECURITY CHECKPOINT...?
FRET FRET あせ あせ
MOMMY, I NEED TO GO POTTY.
WHAT? OH!
Uh-oh.
"I WOULD LIKE TO KEEP DRAWING FROM MY OWN EXPERIENCES..."
"...TO CREATE MORE BARRIER-FREE SPACES, ONE AT A TIME."

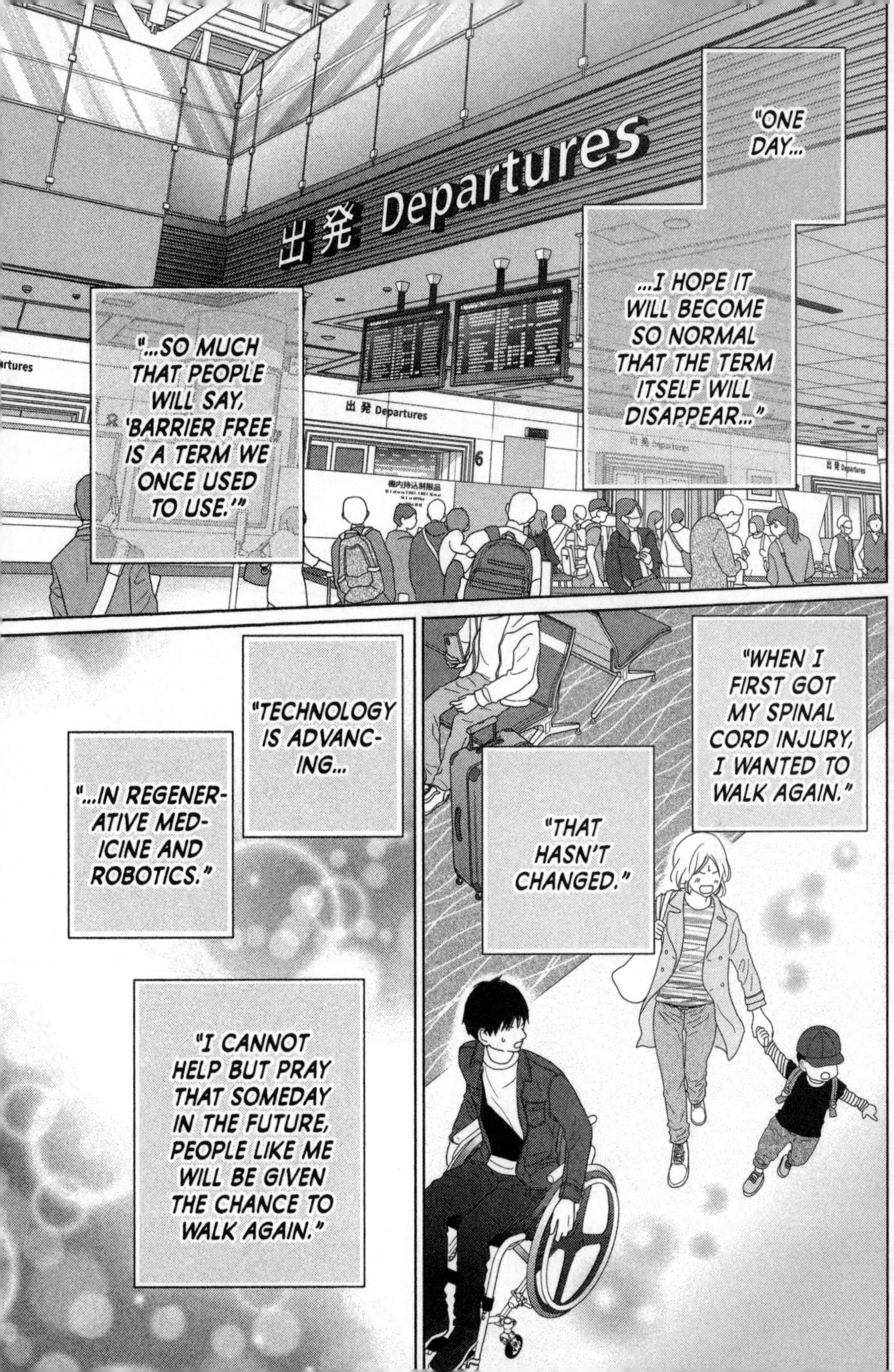
出発 Departures
"ONE DAY...
...I HOPE IT WILL BECOME SO NORMAL THAT THE TERM ITSELF WILL DISAPPEAR..."
"...SO MUCH THAT PEOPLE WILL SAY, 'BARRIER FREE IS A TERM WE ONCE USED TO USE.'"
"WHEN I FIRST GOT MY SPINAL CORD INJURY, I WANTED TO WALK AGAIN."
"THAT HASN'T CHANGED."
"TECHNOLOGY IS ADVANCING...
"...IN REGENERATIVE MEDICINE AND ROBOTICS."
"I CANNOT HELP BUT PRAY THAT SOMEDAY IN THE FUTURE, PEOPLE LIKE ME WILL BE GIVEN THE CHANCE TO WALK AGAIN."

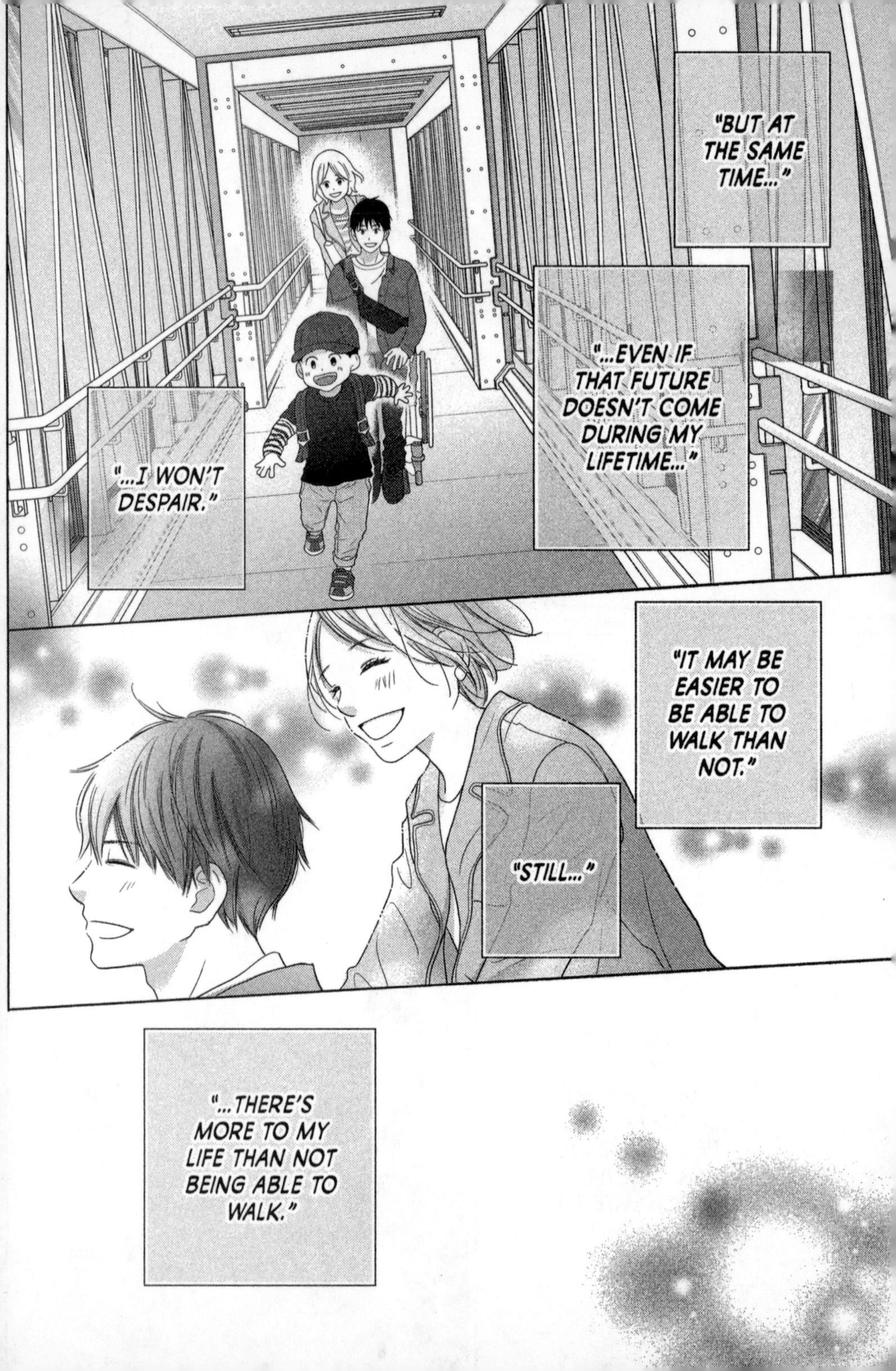
"BUT AT THE SAME TIME..."
"...EVEN IF THAT FUTURE DOESN'T COME DURING MY LIFETIME..."
"...I WON'T DESPAIR."
"IT MAY BE EASIER TO BE ABLE TO WALK THAN NOT."
"STILL..."
"...THERE'S MORE TO MY LIFE THAN NOT BEING ABLE TO WALK."

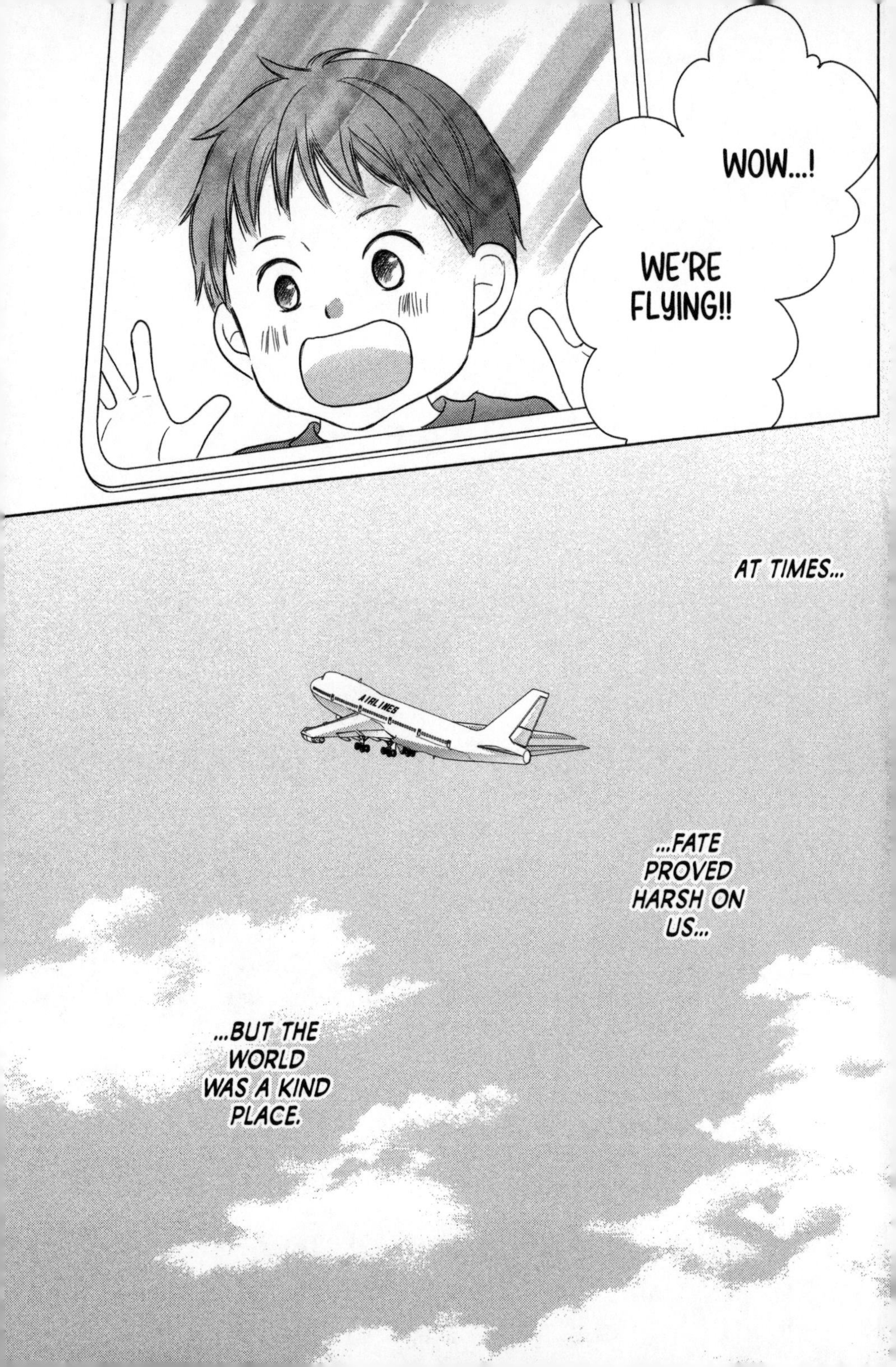
WOW...!
WE'RE FLYING!!
AT TIMES...
...FATE PROVED HARSH ON US...
...BUT THE WORLD WAS A KIND PLACE.

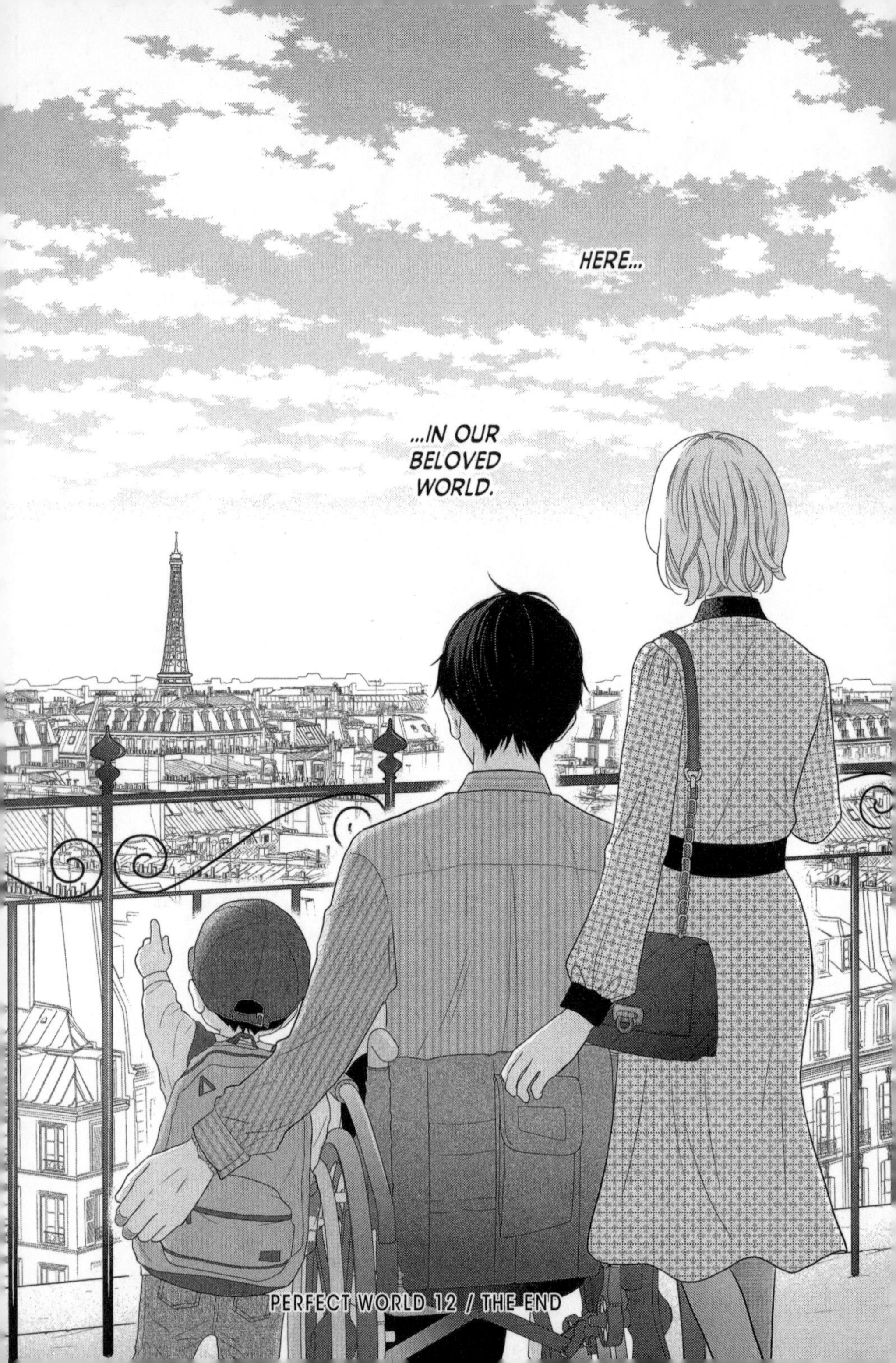
HERE...
...IN OUR BELOVED WORLD.
PERFECT WORLD 12 / THE END

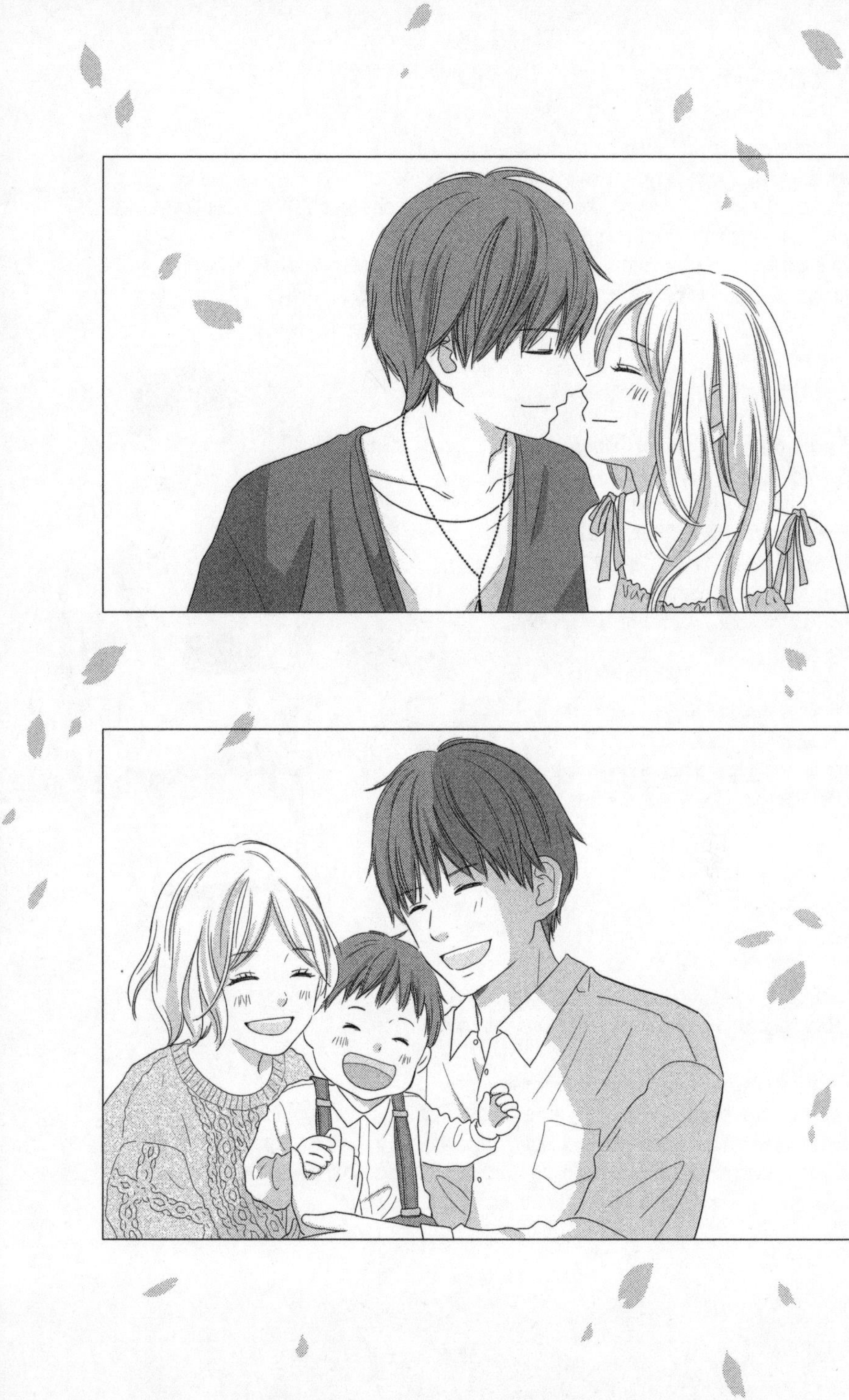

~Afterword~

This concludes *Perfect World*.
Thank you to everyone for your support throughout the series.
I'm sure it left a lot to be desired (like my drawing style, which keeps shifting...), but I put my heart and soul into it for these past seven years.
What encouraged me more than anything was the presence of my readers. Knowing that there were people out there reading it gave me the energy to keep going.

I enjoyed working on the final volume more than any of the others. Although I struggle drawing children, which I hadn't had much experience with, drawing Koki was more fun than I expected. At the very end, it left me wanting more, and I wish I could have drawn more daily life episodes about this wheelchair family.

I'm very sad that I won't get to draw Itsuki and Tsugumi anymore, but I know that they'll continue to laugh, and occasionally fight, and live life together.

Koki playing with Daddy's wheelchair (he's good at moving it)

Haruto's story was based on an interview with an actual wheelchair couple who got married. I also enjoyed that very much, and the interview went by in a flash.

This is something the wife said in that interview:
"I love *Perfect World*, but there's one thing about it that I can't relate to. Itsuki-kun said that he 'never once felt glad to be disabled,' but *I'm* glad that I'm in this body, from the bottom of my heart. If it weren't for this, there are so many things I never would have known, and so many people I never would have met. I think my life is pretty great."

Her words were very striking.

Ever since I started working on this series, I had the chance to travel east and west to visit so many different people and listen to so many valuable stories. Not all of them were positive or touching or dramatic. Some were fun, some were sad, some full of regret, and some were laugh-out-loud funny. They were about the day-to-day of the people I met—about their lives.
Each one is a treasure and an inspiration. Thank you so much for your cooperation. I never would have been able to create this series on my own.

Finally, I would like to thank all of my readers who are reading this right now one last time. I sincerely hope for your happiness.

Hopefully, we can meet again sometime, somewhere...

· Kazuo Abe-sama from Abe Kensetsu Inc.

· Yaguchi-sama   · Sato-sama   · Yamada-sama   · Kamata-sama   · Tomomi-sama   · K-sama
· Hirose-sama   · Nakamura-sama   · Kimura-sama   · Itabe-sama   · Ito-sama   · Ouchi-sama
· Wheelchair Family   · Nakamura-sama   · Nakajima-sama   · Yuko-sama

· Chibaminato Rehabilitation Hospital
· Kamakura Rehabilitation St. Therese Hospital
· AJU Center for Independent Living   · Social Welfare Corporation Fureai Nagoya
· Certified NPO Florence   · OX Kanto Vivit

· Those involved in the *Perfect World* film
· Those involved in the *Perfect World* TV drama adaptation
· Those involved in the *Perfect World* motion comic

· My editor, Ito-sama
· Everyone from editorial at Kiss   · Kiss magazine title page art designer, Omura-sama
· The Rights Division   · The International Rights Department
· The printing house   · The designer, Kusume-sama   · My assistants, Matsuzaki-sama, Tanaka-sama, and Hori-sama

· All the overseas publishers involved
· Bookstore staff all over Japan   · E-book sites

· My family and friends
· Everyone involved in publishing this series

Thank you, from the bottom of my heart.

Rie Aruga

TRANSLATION NOTES

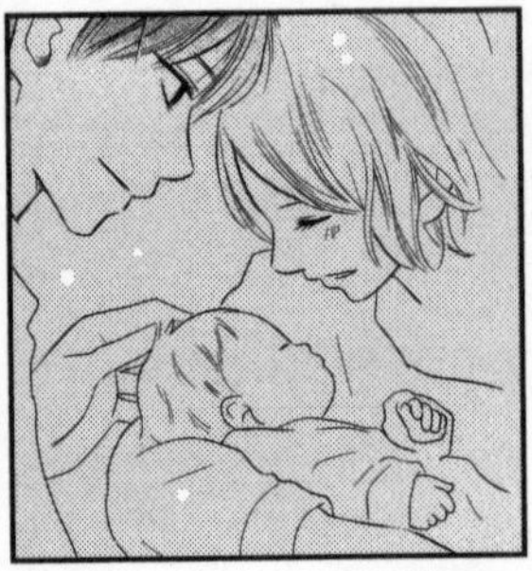

SPECIAL ADOPTION, PAGE 9

THE SPECIAL ADOPTION SYSTEM IN JAPAN WAS INTRODUCED IN 1988 IN LINE WITH MORE INTERNATIONAL CONCEPTS OF ADOPTION. SPECIAL ADOPTION SEVERS LEGAL TIES WITH THE ADOPTEE'S BIOLOGICAL PARENTS SO THAT THE ADOPTIVE PARENTS TRULY BECOME THE SOLE PARENTS OF THE CHILD, WHO HAS TO BE UNDER SIX YEARS OLD. THE CONCEPT OF SPECIAL ADOPTION IS STILL FAIRLY UNCOMMON.

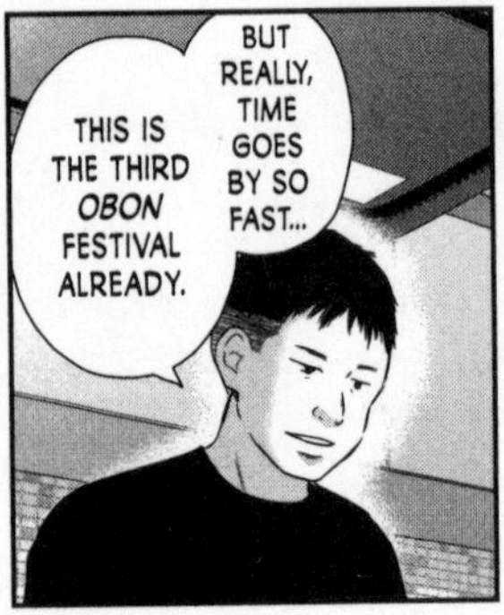
BUT REALLY, TIME GOES BY SO FAST...
THIS IS THE THIRD *OBON* FESTIVAL ALREADY.

OBON FESTIVAL, KAMBA, PAGE 72

THE OBON FESTIVAL HELD DURING THE SUMMER IS A THREE-DAY PERIOD WHEN FAMILIES GET TOGETHER TO WELCOME THE SPIRITS OF THEIR ANCESTORS, WHO SUPPOSEDLY RETURN TO THE HUMAN WORLD FOR A TEMPORARY VISIT TO THEIR HOUSEHOLD ALTARS. IT'S A JOYOUS OCCASION OFTEN ACCOMPANIED BY FIREWORKS, DANCING, PARADES, FOOD STALLS, AND GENERAL FESTIVITIES. NOWADAYS, SOME PEOPLE SIMPLY ENJOY THE FESTIVITIES WITHOUT OBSERVING THE RELIGIOUS ASPECTS. DIFFERENT REGIONS HAVE SPECIFIC RITUALS, AND IN NAGANO, WHERE TSUGUMI AND ITSUKI'S HOMETOWN IS, THEY LIGHT WHITE BIRCH BARK, OR *KAMBA*, OUTSIDE THE FRONT DOOR TO MAKE SURE THE SPIRITS FIND THEIR WAY HOME AND TO SEE THEM OFF WHEN THE FESTIVAL IS OVER.

PERFECT WORLD

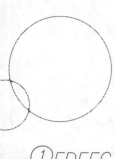

Young characters and steampunk setting, like *Howl's Moving Castle* and *Battle Angel Alita*

Beyond the Clouds © 2018 Nicke / Ki-oon

A boy with a talent for machines and a mysterious girl whose wings he's fixed will take you beyond the clouds! In the tradition of the high-flying, resonant adventure stories of Studio Ghibli comes a gorgeous tale about the longing of young hearts for adventure and friendship!

A SMART, NEW ROMANTIC COMEDY FOR FANS OF *SHORTCAKE CAKE* AND *TERRACE HOUSE*!

A romance manga starring high school girl Meeko, who learns to live on her own in a boarding house whose living room is home to the odd (but handsome) Matsunaga-san. She begins to adjust to her new life away from her parents, but Meeko soon learns that no matter how far away from home she is, she's still a young girl at heart — especially when she finds herself falling for Matsunaga-san.

The boys are back, in 400-page hardcovers that are as pretty and badass as they are!

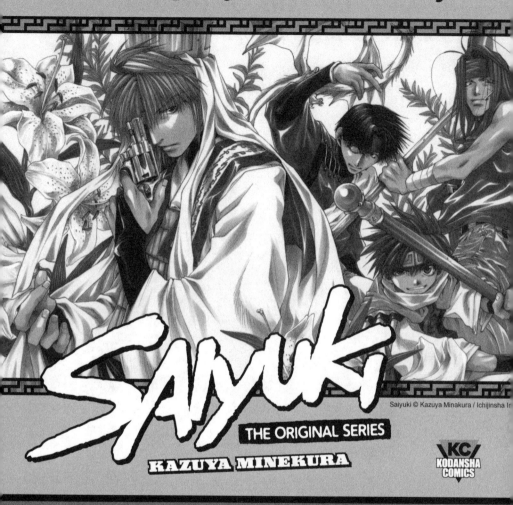

Saiyuki © Kazuya Minakura / Ichijinsha In

SAIYUKI
THE ORIGINAL SERIES
KAZUYA MINEKURA

KC/ KODANSHA COMICS

THE SWEET SCENT OF LOVE IS IN THE AIR! FOR FANS OF OFFBEAT ROMANCES LIKE *WOTAKOI*

Sweat and Soap © Kintetsu Yamada / Kodansha Ltd.

In an office romance, there's a fine line between sexy and awkward... and that line is where Asako — a woman who sweats copiously — meets Koutarou — a perfume developer who can't get enough of Asako's, er, scent. Don't miss a romcom manga like no other!

SAINT ☆ YOUNG MEN

A LONG AWAITED ARRIVAL IN PREMIUM 2-IN-1 HARDCOVER

After centuries of hard work, Jesus and Buddha take a break from their heavenly duties to relax among the people of Japan, and their adventures in this lighthearted buddy comedy are sure to bring mirth and merriment to all!

"Brilliant…the physical comedy and facial expressions will make you literally LOL."

—Sam Humphries (host of *DC Daily*; writer, *Green Lanterns, Legendary Star-Lord*)

Saint Young Men © Hikaru Nakamura/Kodansha Ltd.

The adorable new odd-couple cat comedy manga from the creator of the beloved *Chi's Sweet Home*, in full color!

Praise for Chi's Sweet Home

"Nearly impossible to turn away... a true all-ages title that anyone, young or old, cat lover or not, will enjoy. The stories will bring a smile to your face and warm your heart."

—School Library Journal

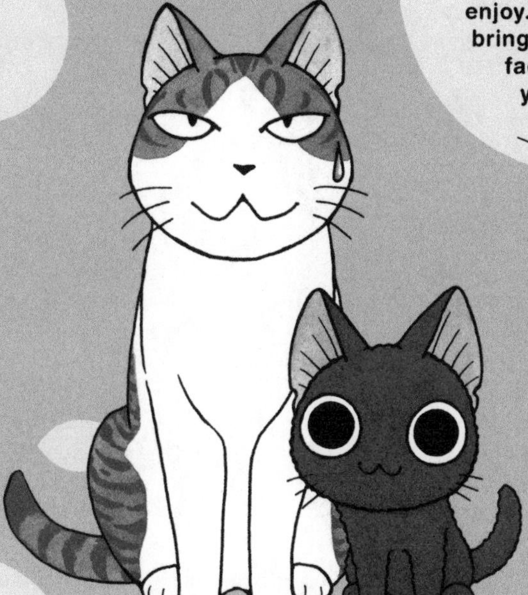

Sue & Tai-chan

Konami Kanata

Sue is an aging housecat who's looking forward to living out her life in peace... but her plans change when the mischievous black tomcat Tai-chan enters the picture! Hey! Sue never signed up to be a catsitter! *Sue & Tai-chan* is the latest from the reigning meow-narch of cute kitty comics, Konami Kanata.

KC KODANSHA COMICS

The beloved characters from *Cardcaptor Sakura* return in a brand new, reimagined fantasy adventure!

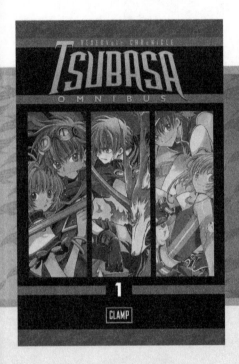

"[*Tsubasa*] takes readers on a fantastic ride that only gets more exhilarating with each successive chapter." —Anime News Network

In the Kingdom of Clow, an archaeological dig unleashes an incredible power, causing Princess Sakura to lose her memories. To save her, her childhood friend Syaoran must follow the orders of the Dimension Witch and travel alongside Kurogane, an unrivaled warrior; Fai, a powerful magician; and Mokona, a curiously strange creature, to retrieve Sakura's dispersed memories!

xxxHOLiC
OMNIBUS 1
CLAMP

xxxHOLiC © CLAMP ShigatsuTsuitachi CO.,LTD./Kodansha Ltd.
xxxHOLiC Rei © CLAMP ShigatsuTsuitachi CO.,LTD./Kodansha Ltd.

Kimihiro Watanuki is haunted by visions of ghosts and spirits. He seeks help from a mysterious woman named Yuko, who claims she can help. However, Watanuki must work for Yuko in order to pay for her aid. Soon Watanuki finds himself employed in Yuko's shop, where he sees things and meets customers that are stranger than anything he could have ever imagined.

KC
KODANSHA
COMICS

A Kodansha Comics Trade Paperback Original
Perfect World 12 copyright © 2021 Rie Aruga
English translation copyright © 2022 Rie Aruga

Published in the United States by Kodansha Comics, an imprint of Kodansha USA Publishing, LLC, New York.

Publication rights for this English edition arranged through Kodansha Ltd., Tokyo.

First published in Japan in 2021 by Kodansha Ltd., Tokyo as *Perfect World*, volume 12.

ISBN 978-1-64651-404-5

Printed in the United States of America.

www.kodansha.us

9 8 7 6 5 4 3 2 1
Translation: Sawa Matsueda Savage
Lettering: Sara Linsley
Editing: Maggie Le
Kodansha Comics edition cover design by Phil Balsman

Publisher: Kiichiro Sugawara

Director of publishing services: Ben Applegate
Director of publishing operations: Dave Barrett
Associate director of publishing operations: Stephen Pakula
Publishing services managing editors: Alanna Ruse, Madison Salters
Production managers: Emi Lotto, Angela Zurlo